Property of
FAMILY OF FAITH
LIBRARY

To Celebrate

Reshaping Holidays and Rites of Passage

Family of Faith Library

To Celebrate

Reshaping Holidays and Rites of Passage

Alternatives
Ellenwood, Georgia

To Grace Walker Winn
Our friend and colleague
Who, by the way she lives,
Teaches us how to celebrate.

Copyright © 1987 by Alternatives
2nd printing, 1988
P.O. Box 429, Ellenwood, GA 30049
Permission to Reprint: This book is for your use. If you wish to reprint
parts of the book on a not-for-profit basis, we are happy for you to do so.
Please limit reprints to no more than six pages and use the following credit
line: This material is from *To Celebrate: Reshaping Holidays and Rites of
Passage* published by Alternatives, P.O. Box 429, Ellenwood, Georgia 30049.
Please notify us that you are using our material or send us a copy of the
publication in which it is printed.

Library of Congress Cataloging-in-Publication Data

To celebrate

   1. Holidays. 2. Rites and ceremonies. 3. Life style.
I. Alternatives (Firm)
GT3932.T6   1987   394.2   87-18697
ISBN: 0-914966-05-7

Table of Contents

Who We Are,   9

Introduction,   11

Part I: Holidays and Holy Days,   15
1. Sabbath and Sunday,   17
The Sabbath: Prototype Celebration
Sunday: The Christian Sabbath
Walter Brueggemann: Interpreting the Sabbath
Sabbath, Holy Communion and World Hunger

2. Advent, Christmas and Epiphany,   27
Christmas in History: Mingling Cultural Traditions
"St. Nicholas," A Puppet Play
Las Posadas
How to Organize an Alternative Christmas Community Festival
"Whose Birthday Is It, Anyway?"

3. Giving and Receiving Gifts,   49
Gift-Giving in the Consumer Society
Double Your Gift of Love
Toys ARE Us! A Parent's Perspective
Best and Worst Christmas Gift Contest

4. Food and Celebrations,   71
Share Responsibility
Keep it Festive and Simple
Help with Change
   Suggested Cookbooks
   Recipes and Menus

5. January and February,   87
New Year's Day: Endings and Beginnings

Emancipation Day: Hope for Slaves
Martin Luther King, Jr.'s Birthday: The Dream Lives On
Valentine's Day: Sweethearts and Prisoners
Day of Remembrance: Painful Memory for Japanese Americans
Presidents' Days: Celebrating Political Leadership
Purim: Celebrating Survival
Chinese New Year

6. March and April,   97
Lent: Preparing for Discipleship
Easter: Celebrating the Resurrection
Passover: Freedom from Slavery
Ramadan: Fast for Muslims
International Women's Day
St. Patrick's Day
Spring: Life After Winter
Central America Week
National Farmer Worker Week

7. May and June,   115
May Day
Pentecost: Descent of the Spirit
Shavuot: First Fruits and the Torah
Mother's and Father's Days: Honoring Parents
Memorial Day: That Others May Not Die
Summer: Long Days and Vacations

8. July and August,   133
Dominion Day: Celebrating a New Canada
Independence Day: Remembering National Ideals
Hiroshima Day: Remembering the Past for the Sake of Peace
Women's Equality Day: Victory for Women's Suffrage

9. September and October,   143
Labor Day
Rosh Hashana
Yom Kippur: Day of Atonement
Sukkot: Festival of Booths
Columbus Day: "Day of the Race"
World Food Day
United Nations Day: Hopes for World Order
Halloween: All Saints' Eve
Reformation Sunday

10. November and December,   155
Thanksgiving
Hanukkah: Feast of Dedication
Festival of the Virgin of Guadalupe
Kwanza: An Afro-American Festival

Part Two: Rites of Passage,   169

11. Birth and Death,   173

Birth
  Naming Ceremony Celebration
  The Passage of Pregnancy Loss
Death: The Last Passage
  Memorial Societies: What They Are and How They Work
  Hospice Care: Dying With Dignity
  The Dead Help the Living: Anatomical Gifts

12. Marriage and Divorce,   191

Marriage: Equality and Commitment
Divorce: When Marriage Doesn't Work
Celebrating in Single-Parent or Blended Families

13. Other Passages,   207

Birthdays
Early Passages
Bar/Bat Mitzvah and Confirmation
Graduations
Retirement

Appendix,   219

Self-Help Craft Groups
Advertisers

'Tis a gift to be simple,
'Tis a gift to be free,
'Tis a gift to come round
where we want to be,
And when we find ourselves
in the place just right
We will be in the valley of
love and delight.

Old Shaker Hymn

Who We Are

Alternatives is a nonprofit organization providing resources for responsible living and celebrating. Started in 1973 as a protest against the commercialization of Christmas, our focus is to encourage celebrations that reflect conscientious ways of living.

We used to talk about simple lifestyles. By that we meant avoiding consumption for consumption's sake; being aware of the individual's role in protecting the environment; recognizing the reality of our relatedness to one another; and being intentional about working toward social, economic and political justice. However, there is nothing simple about trying to live out these ideals, and undertaking such an agenda is more a life's work than a life's style.

It is important to restore moderation and perspective to celebrations that are too often self-indulgent. Change in the ways we celebrate is an important factor in changing the ways we live. Distributing resources designed to help families and groups look at celebrations in more responsible ways is a major part of our work.

Publications like *To Celebrate: Reshaping Holidays and Rites of Passage*; *Have Yourself A Merry Little Christmas* filmstrip, *Christmas* and *Easter packets* challenge the commercialization of our holy days and provide study materials, worship aids, ideas and resources for more joyful, appropriate celebrations.

Our *Bulletin Insert Service* is available for all major holidays, in addition to Christmas and Easter, and offers alternative perspectives on celebrating.

The *Bookstore*, a 16-page tabloid, lists more than 120 publications that support, nourish, inform and enable our constituency to live out their intentions.

The *Alternatives Newsletter*, a 28-page quarterly magazine, makes critical links between how we live and celebrate and global justice issues that challenge people of conscience.

Representatives from about a dozen religious denominations work with us to develop and distribute our resources. Our financial support comes from sale of our materials, grants from denominations and from contributions.

As a *Resource Center*, we would like to assist you in finding materials to organize workshops, seminars or retreats on alternative celebrations or more responsible lifestyles. We encourage you to call or to write telling us how we can serve you better. And come to visit us when you are near Atlanta. We look forward to hearing from you and meeting you.

Photo by Everett Gill.

Left to right: Milo Thornberry, Grace Winn, Kathie Klein, Ondina González, Janie Howell, Rachel Gill, Joe Hayes.

To Celebrate is the result of a collective effort by the Alternatives staff. While all staff members contributed original material, Milo Thornberry was the primary writer for the introductory content. Rachel Gill was general editor and compiled contributed materials. Kathie Klein was responsible for the art and overall design of the book. Ondina Gonzalez solicited and gathered the ads. Although all the staff read proofs, Janie Howell had special responsibility to do so. Joe Hayes saw that our copy was electronically transmitted to the typesetter. Because our friends Grace Winn and Cherry Clements have expertise in "food and celebrations," we asked them to write Chapter 4. The heart of the project is, of course, the contributions from those who shared their experiences: their creativity, frustrations, sorrows and joys.

Introduction: Reshaping Our Celebrations

This is a book about joy, spontaneity, caring, justice and concern for nature. It is a book about celebrating, a book for those who are not satisfied with the models of celebration offered by a consumer society. This book includes the experiences of people with widely varying backgrounds and perspectives, people whose celebrations give voice to the ideals by which they are trying to live.

There is a tradition in this land which holds that the most rewarding life is one shaped around our highest civic and religious ideals, and that the arena for practicing these ideals is in the routine of daily life. It is, to be sure, a minority tradition and in stark contrast to the traditions of the majority—a life of self-gratification through consumption regardless of the adverse effects on other people, on the environmnent and even on our own spirits.

In her book, *Living More With Less*, Doris Janzen Longacre gave new voice to that old tradition. She proposed five "life standards" as guides for living according to our highest ideals. While neither new nor unique, these simple life standards are an important framework for thinking about what it means to live responsibly today:

• **Do Justice.** From Old Testament prophets to our ancestors in this land, the important ideals of fair play and "the common good" are deeply imbedded in our religious and national traditions. Although injustices in our history, in our society and throughout the world tempt us to be cynical, we are called to be attentive to the way our patterns of living affect other people, especially the poor in our country and in the third world.

• **Learn from the World Community.** The notion that United States is a cultural melting pot, no matter how flawed, carries with it the insight that we are enriched by an infusion of knowledge and spirit of people from all over the world. To continue this learning in daily life is more than enriching. It may be necessary for our survival.

★ Imagine a day of the week for spiritual renewal and rest for tired bodies, instead of endless preoccupation with daily tasks.

★ Imagine gift-giving which enhances creative expressions of love, instead of following Madison Avenue's directives.

★ Imagine celebrations whose results are enlarged resources for justice and peace, instead of enlarged profits for business.

● **Nurture People.** The intrinsic worth of all individuals—the importance of their rights and needs—should be the basis of all human interaction. How do we care for each other in ways that neither manipulate nor exploit, but are fair, loving and humane?

● **Cherish the Natural Order.** Rather than seeing nature as a commodity to be exploited or as an obstacle to be overcome, we must learn to respect our environment as a wonderful but finite gift. We must live in harmony with nature if, in the long run, we are to live at all.

● **Nonconform Freely!** "Do not let the world squeeze you into its mold," St. Paul admonished the Christians at Rome. Many European immigrants viewed America as a land where individuals were not forced into rigid social, economic and religious patterns of behavior. Now, in the era of "mass culture," reclaiming the *ideal* of nonconformity may be more important than ever.

Celebrations: Regaining Perspective

While preoccupation with the details of living makes these ideals seem remote, celebrations are opportunities to regain perspective. Celebrations are ritualized interruptions in daily life that give focus to life's meaning and purpose. Whether in public or private worship or in observing a birthday or a national holiday, celebrations remind us of who we are, where we have been and where we want to go. For people committed to living by ideals, celebrations are indispensable.

The experiences which make up the heart of this book are like a symphony with many moods and tempos: certain themes recur again and again to undergird and give coherence to the whole.

● Celebrations are rooted deeply in what it means to be human. Without celebrations we lose important ways of nourishing the human spirit.

● Celebrations in our culture tend to be commercialized, making them impersonal, over-consumptive and destructive to the environment.

● Celebrations are more than entertainment; they are occasions for nourishing relationships and the human spirit.

● Celebrations are times to forget daily cares in order to remember what is true and abiding. Regaining perspective requires that we "forget" in order to "remember."

● Celebrations are more than personal and family occasions; they are occasions for remembering and celebrating our kinship with the whole human family.

● Celebrations are ways to anticipate the future; they are manageable times in our lives when the future envisioned in our ideals can be practiced in the present.

While these themes recur throughout the many celebration experiences in this book, the readers will not find an "ideal" celebration for each holiday or rite of passage. Our intent is to offer possibilities for breaking the tryanny imposed by society (and family) on celebrations, not to impose new ones. We know how far our celebrations are from our ideals. How we go about breaking free of these restrictions and creating new ways of celebrating are matters for individuals and their celebrating communities to decide.

★ Imagine an Advent when the coming of Jesus, not Santa Claus, is the main event.

★ Imagine a Hanukkah when attention centers on the determination of a people to preserve its identity, rather than accomodation to popular culture.

★ Imagine a Christmas that gives meaning to Christ's birth as "good news to the poor," instead of accentuating the gulf between the affluent and the non-affluent.

Celebrations as Identification

"Let all who are hungry enter and eat," is the way the Jewish Passover Seder begins. It catches that essential element in all genuine celebration: reaffirming our kinship with all humankind. This identification in celebration occurs in three ways:

1. The *content* of the celebration: When we observe Martin Luther King, Jr's birthday, we identify with the struggles of black people in this land. In Advent we experience the fears and hopes of a minority people in the first century. At a funeral we hurt with those who suffer the loss of a loved one. At a wedding we rejoice with two people who publicly declare their joy in a new covenant relationship.

2. The *manner* of the celebration: While celebrations often revolve around family and community, they can be enriched by including those who would otherwise be left without community at times of celebration.

3. The *outcome* of the celebration: To identify with others in our celebrating means more than remembering our ties to the whole of humanity, and more than occasions to practice inclusiveness in our households. Celebrations are also occasions to identify with others by diverting resources of time, energy and money to those who are in need. Although celebrations are symbolic acts, resources diverted from celebrations are concrete ways to identify with others.

★ Imagine a celebration that is kind to the earth by conserving non-renewable resources and by reducing waste.

★ Imagine an Easter when our spirits are renewed, instead of being manipulated to consume and waste at irresponsible levels.

Alternative Celebrations Catalogues

Diverting resources from celebrations to those with greater needs was the idea that called Alternatives into existence in 1973. In the first *Alternate Christmas Catalogue* the founder, Bob Kochtitzky, made the connections:

> In 1965 I'd never heard of ecology or limits to growth. But I knew the material things of the world had been unfairly distributed leaving millions of people in misery and poverty. And I knew that we were a middle-class family who really didn't need all the clothing and appliances and gimmicks which we gave each other. If the celebration of Christmas was showing our love with a gift that the other person *really* needed, then I wouldn't give up gift giving. I'd just change the form of the gift. There was no question what my family needed: a world without war, racism, poverty and oppression.
>
> Well, I couldn't pull that off with $100, but I could divide the money up among organizations which I felt were moving us in the direction of a non-violent, cooperative world. I sent checks to three groups.

The purpose of that first *Alternate Christmas Catalogue* was not only to offer alternative ways to celebrate Christmas and other holidays, but also to provide a listing of groups that merited support in their work for justice, peace and a better environment. By 1986, after four editions and a "best of the previous catalogues" published by Pilgrim Press, more than 125,000 Catalogues were in circulation. Beginning with that first Catalogue, Alternatives touched a nerve in a significant minority of people looking for better ways to celebrate and live.

And Now *To Celebrate*

★ Imagine a death and funeral when respect for the dead and the grieving results in supporting life, not greater burdens for the living.

★ Imagine a wedding when meaning and beauty are not overshadowed by pressures to be extravagant.

★ Imagine a Thanksgiving which is fun and relaxing for all the members of the household, instead of a heavier burden for those who ordinarily manage the household.

This is the first Alternatives Catalogue not to be so titled. Although we are reluctant to give up the name, calling these resources "catalogues" has been the occasion for frequent misunderstandings. People often assume that an *Alternative Celebrations Catalogue* is simply a list of materials for sale, not a book of resources. We, and old friends, will probably still refer to this one as the Sixth Edition, but for the benefit of those who do not yet know us, we have changed the title.

What you will find inside is a new and comprehensive collection of resources for alternative celebrations for all the major holidays and rites of passage in our culture. For the first time we have included a chapter on Sabbath, the prototype holiday. Comparing the roles of rites of passage in earlier societies with their roles in this culture provide the context to consider contemporary alternatives. Also new are resources for personal meditation and corporate worship related to celebrations.

Due to popular demand, the "ads" are back. We have not published a book with ads since 1978 with the Fourth Edition. The nonprofit groups—and some publishers—whose ads you will find in this book are here at our invitation. We have invited only groups that we know something about, and who have been willing to make their annual financial reports available to us. We do not suggest that those whose ads appear here exhaust the list of good organizations worthy of your support. We simply include those who accepted our invitation.

The purpose of the ads is: 1) to inform readers of the work of these important organizations; 2) to encourage people to divert money to these organizations as part of their celebrations; 3) to offer further resources for alternative gifts; 4) to call attention to products and services that are consistent with our goals.

At the end of Chapter 3, "Giving and Receiving Gifts" you will find a page of model gift cards designed for use as you send your own gifts to charitable organizations or to inform friends of gifts made in their name. We invite you to copy our gift card.

And now that we have told you what we think is important for you to know about using this book, it is time for you to see what is here. Browse through it, or find the section dealing with your next celebration. Look at the chapter on gifts. Thumb through the ads. Then, you will be ready to celebrate.

Part One:
Holidays and Holy Days

1.
Sabbath and Sunday

THE SABBATH: PROTOTYPE CELEBRATION

The Sabbath ("day of rest") was in all likelihood the original "holiday." Sabbath falls on Saturday, the seventh day of the Jewish week, and is the only holiday mandated by the Ten Commandments:

> Remember the Sabbath day and keep it holy. For six days you shall labor and do all your work, but the seventh day is a Sabbath for Yahweh your God. On that day you shall not work, neither you nor your son nor your daughter nor your servants, men or women, nor your animals nor the stranger who lives with you. For in six days Yahweh made the heavens and the earth and the sea and all that these hold, but on the seventh day he rested; that is why Yahweh has blessed the Sabbath day and made it sacred. (Exodus 20:8-11)

Sabbath served the two-fold purpose of being a day set apart for the worship of God (Exodus 31:13-17) and a day for rest and recreation. Prohibition against work on the Sabbath was regulated by detailed prescription which varied from period to period. During the Maccabean period when regulations were extraordinarily strict, some pious Jews chose to be killed rather than defend themselves on the Sabbath.

It may be true, as some scholars have suggested, that the Jewish Sabbath has roots either in the ancient Babylonian *sapattu* or in a primitive Canaanite agricultural calendar. But Judaism gave the day its uniqueness and spiritual power. The following is Abraham Heschel's description:

> To set apart one day a week for freedom, a day on which we would not use the instruments which have been so easily turned into weapons of destruction, a day for being with ourselves, a day of detachment from the vulgar, of independence of external obligations, a day on which we stop worshiping the idols of technical civilization, a day on which we use no money, a day of armistice in the economic struggle with our fellow men [people] and the forces of nature—is there any institution that holds out greater hope for [humanity's]

progress than the Sabbath? (Abraham Joshua Heschel, *The Sabbath: Its Meaning for Modern Man.* New York: Farrar, Straus and Young, Inc., 1951. p. 28.)

Jewish Sabbath begins on Friday evening when the sun goes down. Meals for Friday night and Saturday are prepared ahead of time. Families gather around a festive dinner table lighted by two candles for the meal and for the special Sabbath ceremony. This ceremony may take place before or after going to the synagogue. The next morning is spent at the synagogue where families pray and listen to the reading of the Torah. The afternoon is a time to relax, take a nap, go for a walk, or visit friends. Sabbath is over when the first three stars of the evening appear, and there is a ceremony—called Havdalah, or "separation"—to tell it goodbye. This ceremony separates Sabbath from the work days of the week. At its beginning on Friday night people greet each other with the wish, "A good Shabbos," or the Hebrew "Shabbat Shalom." On Saturday night they extend to one another the hopeful salutation in the ancient Yiddish, "A good Woch," "a good week." Finally, the candles are extinguished and Sabbath ends.

Sunday: the Christian Sabbath

Early Christians, who were also Jews, observed the Sabbath as a day of worship and rest. But even in New Testament times Sunday began to replace the Jewish Sabbath. That change was due in part to the biblical tradition that light was created upon the first day and Jesus, the light of the world, rose from the dead on Sunday.

A more important factor in choosing Sunday as the Christian Sabbath, however, was the apostle Paul's wish not to impose the Jewish calendar on gentile Christians. He had seen abuses of the Sabbath, when one day of the week was regarded as sacred and dedicated to the service of God, while the other six days were considered secular. Because of this disparity, the apostle Paul thought it a sign of strength to regard all days the same, and a sign of weakness in the faith to distinguish between different days. (Romans 14:5, Col. 2:1623; Gal. 4:9-11) In this case, a practical consideration overcame the apostle's theological problems with Sabbath. Christians felt a real need for a regular time to worship in community. That decided the issue. By making that special day Sunday, and not observing other Jewish festivals, the church emphasized its independence from Judaism.

When Christianity became the official religion of the Roman Empire in the fourth century, the observance of Sunday as a day of rest and

worship was often regulated both by church and civil authorities. Between the sixth and thirteenth centuries, legislation became more and more strict, not only prohibiting business, but making the failure to attend Mass on Sunday a civil as well as religious offense. Initially, Protestants were reluctant to approve special Sunday legislation, but the carnival-like atmosphere in many villages and towns on Sundays convinced Protestants to support such legislation. In the United States "blue laws," civil statutes prohibiting a wide variety of amusements and businesses on Sundays, were passed in many states. A few states still have such laws.

As true for most holidays, the efforts to find the meaning and intent of Sabbath and Sunday are a large part of the history of these two days. Often preoccupied with legal requirements, Sabbath and Sunday protagonists have forgotten Jesus' fundamental insight: "The Sabbath was made for [people], not [people] for the Sabbath." (Mark 2:27) Because Sabbath and Sunday come once a week, we need to know, more than for any other celebrations, how to observe them in ways that truly nourish the human spirit. Whether you observe Sabbath on Saturday or Sunday,

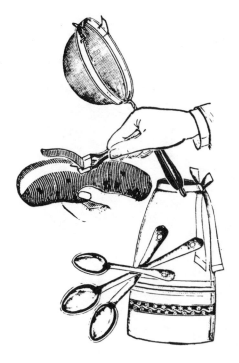

Although Christians generally observe Sunday as a day of worship and rest, it is not as ordered as the Jewish Sabbath. And with the now common pattern of adult household members working outside the home, Sunday is increasingly a day for shopping and housework, activities for which there is little time during the rest of the week.

• Let it be a day of rest. While St. Paul rightly argued that all days are God's, the legalism he had experienced blinded him to the Sabbath's critical contribution to people's need for a respite from the endless cycle of seven-day work weeks. Completely apart from religious considerations, this is a point now recognized by health care authorities, labor and management.

There is also a social dimension to letting Sabbath be a day of rest. The Ten Commandments direct that Sabbath observance should be a day of rest for all on whose labor we depend or for whom we are responsible: women, men, children, servants, strangers, and even animals. It is a prohibition against our resting at others' expense. This means seeing that any in our employ are freed to observe Sabbath. It also means sharing weekend household responsibilities so that all members may rest on that day.

This concern for others raises some questions about Sabbath observance that are not simple to resolve. Always present are those who do not have the luxury of enjoying Sabbath—many because of poverty and others who must work on the Sabbath in order to keep their jobs. To what extent do our consumption patterns on the Sabbath (shopping, eating out, going to movies or ball games, etc.) deprive others of their Sabbaths? In a religiously pluralistic society, should that be of any concern to us? Should we assume that labor laws provide sufficient protection for those who need it?

• Let it be a day of disengagement and reorientation. Sabbath offers an opportunity to break away from the concerns of the week in order to regain perspective. Such an opportunity is no less important today than it was in ancient Israel. We need time for head-clearing and redirection—relief from the relentless pressure of work or school or the constant bombardment of popular culture through the mass media.

19

Worship disengages, reorients and reminds us of a reality that can transcend and replace popular culture's norms and values. A collective remembering of who we are, whose we are and where we have been, worship is also a time to reflect on where we are going. Disengagement of this kind is possible through private prayer, meditation, and even study. It was never intended that corporate and private worship be restricted to the Sabbath, but the discipline of weekly remembering—like the discipline of weekly rest—is a guard against forgetting and procrastination.

WALTER BRUEGGEMANN: INTERPRETING THE SABBATH

The people of Israel, having just fled from the Egyptian empire, were clear on only two things. First, they would no longer submit to the empire's brick production quotas. Second, Yahweh, the Holy God, was the great new fact and force in their life.

In saying, "Let my people go," Yahweh had also said, "...that they may serve me". (Exodus 7:16, 8:1,20; 9:1,13; 10:3) The Exodus was not an offer of unbridled, unqualified, unfocused freedom that had no projection into the future. The Exodus embraced a new bondage, i.e., a new bonding (cf. Leviticus 25:42). The oppressive bonds of Egypt were broken. Israel made its way to Mt. Sinai to be linked in a covenant with Yahweh that replaced its bondage to Pharaoh. Everything was at stake for Israel in this exchange of bondage for bonding.

Yahweh, the God who went with Israel, was not merely an available patron; Yahweh was God for all time. The ten commandments were

20

God's decree for shaping the new bonded relationship. These commands were non-negotiable terms for this alternative to Egypt. They were policies which required interpretation, but they set the character and shape for new life.

I suspect that the most difficult and most important task in trying to come to terms with the commandments is to handle their absoluteness, while at the same time doing the required interpretive work necessary to faithfulness. Biblical faith mandates that the ten commandments are absolute and non-negotiable, taken as God's surest decree. However, the Bible makes it equally clear that Israel and the church maintained and practiced amazing interpretive openness, keeping the commandments pertinent to the on-going ethical burdens of the community's changing circumstances.

Certainly, the Sabbath commandment is part of an on-going interpretive tradition in which we can participate. The commandment can neither be dismissed as unimportant, nor can it be treated as flatly and absolutely obvious. It can and must be interpreted. Among the critical points in that ongoing work of interpretation are the following:

1. The rationale for the Sabbath commandment found in Deuteronomy 5:12-15 differs from that given for the Sinai version in Exodus 20:8-11. The Exodus account prescribes Sabbath as a day of rest in imitation of God's day of rest on the seventh day of creation; while the Deuteronomic Code presents Sabbath as a day for Israel to remember the Exodus. This sacramental reenactment of Exodus as the delivery of Israel from their imperial burden is a more sociologically radical way to deal with Sabbath. This version focuses on community experience, not on the structure of creation.

2. Amos 8:4-8 is a radical prophetic analysis of the commandment. In this passage the Sabbath command functions as a protection for the poor against sharp economic practice and as a cessation from commerce, giving the poor a brief respite from relentless exploitation. The prophet also uses the Sabbath command as grounds for criticizing public practices in Israel that were as abusive as any in ancient Egypt before the Exodus.

3. In exilic and post-exilic thought, Sabbath became a crucial mark, distinguishing this covenant community from those in the empire who had no memory of Exodus. Isaiah 56:2 identifies Sabbath-keeping as characteristic of a blessed person who enjoys the benefits of covenant. In verses 3-7, Sabbath is the qualifying mark admitting foreigners and eunuchs to Israel's worship. That is, the command becomes the not very demanding entrance point through which otherwise unqualified people qualify for the covenant. As such, Sabbath countered extreme legalism which sought to prevent outsiders from becoming a part of the covenant community by dictating stringent entrance requirements.

4. In his ministry Jesus violates the Sabbath for the sake of humaneness. Mark reports that he heals on the Sabbath (3:1-5), and he declares that Sabbath exists for the sake of humanity (2:27-28). In Jesus' day the Sabbath was an oppressive practice of social control. Jesus' response is congruent with and derived from the notion of Exodus bonding; that is, he acts against the commandment for the sake of liberation in the community. The commandment is valid, he seems to say, only in so far as it witnesses to Exodus as a mode for continuing life in covenant. Jesus' ministry becomes dangerous when he rescues

> **"There are few ideas in the world of thought which contain so much spiritual power as the idea of the Sabbath. Aeons hence, when of many of our cherished theories only shreds will remain, that cosmic tapestry will continue to shine."**
>
> Abraham J. Heschel

people from many "houses of bondage," constructions built from following commandments which had lost their Exodus orientation. Commandments which do not serve Exodus stand under harsh criticism.

The purpose of this brief trajectory on the Sabbath commandment is to help us see that, while Israel takes the commandments with great seriousness, it also practices interpretive openness. The most important thing to remember is that this command is a vehicle for God's liberating bonding.

We must criticize laws and commandments which, in fact, enslave those who have been entitled. Thus the prohibition against killing, when read in light of the Exodus, sounds different to oppressed peasants in Latin America. Or the command to honor father or mother is heard differently by children who are abused by their parents. Characteristically, serious evangelical faith understands the commandments as guides for God's liberating activity. When the commandments work against that liberating activity they must be reconsidered, as Jesus does with the Sabbath commandment.

In recent times we have had to work against excessive restrictiveness practiced in the name of Sabbath in a puritanical society. But now we need to be asking what the Sabbath commandment means in a society that reduces humanness to technical transactions. In a society that reduces persons to commodities, the acknowledgement of God's restfulness and the embrace of our own rest may make Sabbath a crucial moral opportunity and an important sacramental protest against the busy profanation of our common life.

Walter Brueggemann
Decatur, Georgia

Never on Sunday: Clergy and the Sabbath

I don't know how it was for the Levites, the ministers of the sanctuary in ancient Israel, but my Sabbath is definitely not on Sunday. Sunday is certainly not a day of rest for me, and sometimes it is not much a day of worship either. There are days when I am so preoccupied with the mechanics of worship that I do not participate in worship. Over the years I have discovered that I need Monday as my day of rest, but I also need it for worship and reflection. About once a month on Monday I get away to a local retreat center to participate in corporate worship and to spend time in reading and reflection.

Unknown contributor

Sabbath and Family

Our favorite way to spend Sabbath is to make it a family day. As children we spent Sundays with grandparents, aunts, uncles and cousins. Now that our family is spread across the country we find it difficult to help our children experience that sense of family.

To make up for our lack of nearby kinfolk, we spend Sunday with several families who are close friends. After mass we sometimes go to one house for coffee and donuts or we might go to a fast food restaurant for a pancake breakfast.

We still try to have family dinner on Sunday. Dinner is served in the dining room with a tablecloth and good china. We sometimes invite others to join us, but usually we have just the immediate family.

22

When our children were younger, we would spend an hour or so on Sunday afternoon walking around the grounds of Ohio State University, where our favorite activity was to climb around the football stadium.

Mary and Bill Merrill
Columbus, Ohio

Saturday Treasures

Saturdays were always special for us since my dad was home from work. My parents always had the patience to let us "help" with projects around the house, even when we were very small. We planted shrubs, and each shrub belonged to one of us. We picked out stones in the woods for our parents to build a garden wall.

Our favorite Saturdays were when my mother had something to do that wouldn't get done if we "helped." On those days my dad took us hiking. He cut a marching stick for each of us and took us out to explore country roads. At every brook he carved twigs to drop for races under the bridge. We stopped and looked at everything and filled our pockets with treasures. Our friends might have had more things, but they always seemed jealous of our adventures.

Ginny Anton
Bridgeport, Connecticut

Manna In Memphis

We try to act out the scripture lesson for Sunday on the Saturday before. We do it in family teams and dress up in all kinds of things. My favorite experience was when my three-year-old son and husband used the pile of unfolded diapers to represent manna in the wilderness.

Andrea Wills
Memphis, Tennessee

Ministers Need Sabbaticals, Too

On January 1, 1987, Mel Williams, senior minister at Oakhurst Baptist Church, began a six-month sabbatical. Our church grants staff ministers a month toward sabbatical leave for each year worked. We do this in recognition of their need for study and growth, and for rest and reflection. This is also a way to express appreciation and support for their work and ministry.

In granting sabbatical leave we affirm faith in our ministers and in ourselves as ministers. The congregation is rewarded during the separation by challenging and stretching experiences, and after the sabbatical rewards come through a process of sharing our growth and renewal in the faith.

On the last Sunday before his sabbatical began we presented two simple gifts: a journal for reflections and a walking stick, handcarved by a member of the congregation. We used the following liturgy to commission Mel for his time away from us.

Leader:
He has showed you, O man, what is good
   And what does the Lord require of you?
But to act justly, and to love mercy
   And to walk humbly with your God.

Our brother, Mel, has led us in the ways of justice and mercy and humility. He has shown us what is good. We are grateful for his time with us.

Congregation: Keep us in thy way, O God.

Leader: He has brought light and laughter, kindness and love to us in our need.

Congregation: Keep us in thy way, O God.

Leader: Words of encouragement and affirmation have come constantly from his lips. He has taught us to believe in ourselves and each other.

Congregation: Keep us in thy way, O God.

Leader: His listening ear and his forgiving spirit have been faithful reminders of your love and mercy.

Congregation: Keep us in thy way, O God.

Leader: His concern for all—children, oldsters, blacks, whites, babies, young marrieds, youth—has kept us aware of your loving presence.

Congregation: Keep us in thy way, O God.

Leader: Mel Williams has been your faithful messenger. We send him

**"Everything that lives
Lives not alone,
nor for itself."**

William Blake

24

away with love, celebrating his presence with us and celebrating his rest-taking away from us.

All: Grant that this Sabbath time will bring strength and vision to Mel and this congregation. Teach us your way, O God. Help us to be your faithful ministers. And bring us back together in your mercy. Amen.

Rachel G. Gill
Stone Mountain, Georgia

Sabbath, Holy Communion and World Hunger

Eating together is among the finest of human activities. In many cultures around the world sharing a meal with friends and guests is a sign of intimacy, trust and love. Food provides sensual enjoyment and strength. It connects us to the earth and to each other as a family. Eating together and enjoying it glorifies God. It is a holy time.

Many influences in society cause us to devalue having a meal with others. We feel unable to successfully juggle heavy work loads, TV programs and free-time activities. More and more our diet consists of "fast food" which we eat alone or on the run. The art of conversation, laughter and listening are neglected when we don't give high priority to shared mealtimes.

The first Christians "partook faithfully in the teaching of the apostles and the support of one another in the breaking of bread and the prayers" (Acts 2:42), establishing a bond between the inward journey and the outward journey. Sharing food was important to their spirituality and solidarity with one another. The "breaking of bread" in the context of a meal, where the most basic human needs are met, was taken for granted in the early church.

Christians who come together on Sabbath days regularly celebrate Holy Communion. Often called Eucharist, meaning Thanksgiving, this is a meal with God and one another—a time of intimacy, fellowship, sharing and remembering. As instituted by Jesus, the Last Supper was an actual meal, not a ritualized worship that encouraged a privatized religion.

It will help us maintain the meaning and purpose of Holy Communion if we remember the setting in which it was instituted. Jesus shared the Passover meal with his disciples. They celebrated around food, remembering God's concern for and deliverance of those in Egypt whose lives were made bitter by oppression. In the Eucharist we follow Passover precedents by telling the story of God's liberating, saving acts.

Celebrating the Eucharist is an act of remembering, of sharing bread and of commitment. The simple, central action of the Eucharist is sharing food. It is a token piece of food to be sure, but it has enormous significance and meaning. To take bread and eat it without

25

remembering those who have no bread is not really celebrating the Eucharist. If we fail to feed the hungry or hesitate to support the oppressed, our celebration runs the risk of bringing judgment upon ourselves. We fail to discern the body of Christ. Every celebration of Holy Communion reminds Christians of their mission to a hungry world and offers encouragement for the task. We who identify with Jesus and receive his body must be bread for the broken world.

One does not have to wait for the church's observance of Holy Communion in order to have eucharistic celebrations. Having meals with family and friends can have some of the same sacramental significance as we give thanks, share food, build community and remember the needy.

Every Sabbath day should have at least one special meal when time is set apart for intimacy, communion, enjoyment of God's good earth and remembering our mission to others. Having this special meal on the Sabbath can bring added meaning to all other eating together. We remember the Sabbath day to keep it holy by our sacred eating times as well as our rest and worship times.

George Johnson
Minneapolis, Minnesota

2.
Advent, Christmas and Epiphany

While Sabbath is the original holiday, Christmas is the most widely observed holiday in Europe and North America. Christmas, "Christ's Mass," is observed each December 25 and commemorates the birth of Jesus Christ almost 2,000 years ago. The narratives of Jesus' birth in the first two chapters of the Gospels of Matthew and Luke, together with the more formal theological statement in the first chapter of John's Gospel, provide a rich tapestry of images and detail to remember on this holy day.

Although Christmas is not the most important holy day of the Christian calendar, the Christian year begins with Advent—a season of preparation. Advent begins on the Sunday nearest November 30 and includes the four Sundays before Christmas. In contrast to its general observance today, Advent (from the Latin *adventus* meaning "coming") was originally a season of solemn self-examination and repentance by the faithful, preparation for celebrating the birth of Christ. The themes of Advent include the Old Testament anticipation of the coming of the Messiah, as well as the New Testament anticipation of a second Advent when Jesus returns at the Day of Judgment.

According to the Christian calendar, the Christmas season ends on January 6 with Epiphany. Although the feast of Epiphany originally commemorated the baptism of Jesus, it is now remembered as the day the Magi arrived in Bethlehem and presented their gifts to the Christ child (Matthew 2:1-12). Some Eastern churches still observe Christmas on that day. Based on the role of the Magi in the Christmas story, the theme of Epiphany is the manifestation of Christ to the Gentiles.

In the United States, Christmas is the only religious holiday to be a national legal holiday. That it is both a religious and national holiday is an indication of its great popularity but also a clue to the current lack of clarity regarding the purpose of its celebration. In reality, the problem is an old one, going back to the beginning of the observance of Christmas.

Christmas in History: Mingling Cultural Traditions

Despite the fact that the Gospel of Luke links the date of Jesus' birth to a census in Palestine decreed by Caesar Augustus (Luke 2:1), nothing is known of the time of year of his birth. The first evidence of speculation about the date is in the third century when Clement of Alexandria suggested May 20. The earliest mention of observance on December 25 is in the Philocalian Calendar, representing Roman practice in the year 336. At about the same time, the Eastern Church began to observe the Nativity on January 6, the feast of Epiphany. By the middle of the fifth century, however, most Eastern churches had adopted December 25.

As with other Christian holy days, the date of Christmas appears to have been set to provide an alternative to one or more popular pagan festivals. December 25 was originally the date of the feast to the Sun God, Mithras. The cult of Mithras had spread from Persia into the Roman world in the first century, and by the third century was Christianity's main rival. December 25 also came at the end of the feast of Saturnalia, an ancient Roman festival commemorating the golden age of Saturn. Both of these festivals may well have been related to even earlier festivals marking the winter solstice.

Although Christmas was intended as an alternative to pagan festivals, the practices of those festivals were often simply incorporated into the Christian celebration. As Christianity spread through central and northern Europe, the accretions from local religions continued. As early as the fifth century, a small minority of Christian leaders expressed alarm at the growing pagan character of Christmas, a cause for concern that continued through the Middle Ages.

Christmas celebrations were not only enlarged by absorbing elements from local religions but from other Christian traditions as well, i.e., St. Nicholas. The association of Christmas with St. Nicholas came about in the Middle Ages, especially in Northern Europe. Little is known about his history except that he was Bishop of Myra in Asia Minor in the fourth century. Of the many stories about this saint, one of the most popular tells about his generosity in giving gifts anonymously to the poor. He became the patron saint of numerous countries, cities and groups—especially children. Because of this special relationship, tradition developed that he gave gifts to children on the eve of his feast day, December 6.

During the Reformation of the sixteenth century, many reformers wanted Christmas dropped as a Christian celebration. In their view, not only was there no biblical sanction for Christmas, but its popular practices still looked too much like the old Saturnalia festivals. In their general resistance to things Catholic, they also wanted St. Nicholas banished. For a few years in seventeenth century England, the Puritan-dominated parliament outlawed the feast of Christmas. At the same time, Puritans in Massachusetts passed similar legislation. Between the sixteenth and eighteenth centuries the widespread antipathy to Christmas as a holy day—especially by Puritans, Quakers, Baptists and Presbyterians—had important consequences, consequences which those religious groups could not have imagined.

Resistance to attaching religious significance to Christmas encouraged its growth as a secular holiday. For example, St. Nicholas was replaced by a more secular figure known as Christmas Man, Father Christmas and

"If it hasn't already done so, the church in the 1980's must recognize that it lives in a pagan society; it must seek for values and norms not shared by society. In short, it will either recover the Christian doctrine of nonconformity or cease to have any authentic Christian voice."

Doris Janzen Longacre

28

Papa Noel. The Dutch, reluctant to give up St. Nicholas, brought Sinterklass (St. Nicholas) with them when they came to America and honored him on December 6. In the seventeenth century, when the Dutch lost control of New Amsterdam to the English, Sinterklass gradually was anglicized into Santa Claus and acquired many of the accoutrements of Christmas Man, i.e, the workshop at the North Pole and the sleigh with reindeer. By the nineteenth century, when the formerly resistant Protestant groups began to celebrate Christmas, it was not only a religious holy day but a well-established secular holiday as well.

The Twentieth Century: Commercializing Christmas

Through the twentieth century in Europe and North America, the popular celebration of Christmas remains an amalgam of Christian and non-Christian traditions. The lack of clarity about the celebration's purpose has remained, accentuating a new factor in the twentieth century: the commercialization of Christmas.

More than just a mixture of diverse traditions, Christmas is now big business. While the Christian calendar calls for a solemn four- or five-week preparation to celebrate the birth of Christ, the "Christmas economy" overshadows even Halloween, with Thanksgiving Day serving as little more than a prelude to the greatest shopping weekend of the year. In 1939 President Roosevelt moved the date of Thanksgiving back to the third Thursday of November to expand the Christmas shopping season. With the survival of many businesses dependent on Christmas profits and half of the annual advertising dollar spent on Christmas-related advertising, it is not surprising that for some shoppers Christmas spending is regarded as a patriotic duty.

The commercialization of Christmas did not occur in a social vacuum. It is part of our society in which consumption for its own sake—regardless of need—is legitimated and encouraged. Without reluctance, consumerism exploits religious beliefs and deep emotions to persuade people to buy. Advertising's behavior modification specialists demonstrate that the strains of "Joy to the World" wafting throughout the shopping malls in December produce greater profits, and that "Silent Night, Holy Night" is even better. Using Christmas as a religion-sanctioned occasion for extravagant spending, business hopes that the $30 to $35 billion people spend on Christmas gifts in the United States is simply practice for greater spending throughout the rest of the year.

While it may be good for the economy in the short run, commercialized Christmas also has its costs. Preparations for observing the birth of one whose coming is "good news to the poor," are often displaced by the more financially attractive preparations to observe the coming of Santa Claus. Extravagant Christmas spending means fewer dollars available for those ministries and agencies addressing critical social and environmental problems. And the loss is more than dollars. The sense of exploitation that many feel at Christmas, the depression that comes when Christmas does not deliver the happiness popular hype promises and guilt from being willing participants in a religious fraud, all rob Christmas of its power to renew the human spirit.

Perhaps the greatest cost of commercialization at Christmas is paid by the poor. In our society the poor experience Christmas as a cruel hoax. Our pervasive cultural Christmas ideology is not Christology—celebrating Christ's coming as "good news to the poor," but what we might call "Santology," Santa Claus theology. The creed of Santa Claus theology is the well-known song, "Santa Claus is Coming to Town." According to this creed Santa is omniscient; like God, Santa knows all about us. There is also a day of judgment. It comes once a year when "good" children (and adults!) are rewarded with good things while the "bad" (i.e., the poor) get coals and switches. The truth is, of course, that gifts are not distributed based on who has been "good or bad" or "naughty or nice," but on what people can afford or get credit to buy. But that's not what our culture teaches children. What it teaches is bad for both poor and nonpoor children. Poor children are told that they don't receive gifts because they are bad, while the nonpoor are taught that they receive gifts because they are good. Both notions, equally reprehensible, are part of this culture's Santa Claus theology.

Commercial Christmas, its underpinnings of Santa Claus firmly in place, continues its spiraling growth. It seems evident that its cultural pervasiveness makes future change little less than a distant dream. It is also true that many Christians and congregations accept the distortion of their holy day without challenge. The reason, one suspects, is not so much an insensitivity to the issues, but rather a feeling of impotence—not knowing what to do or how to do it. Aware that slogans like "putting Christ back in Christmas" and ideas about "Christmas basket charity" are simplistic, many Christians opt to do nothing. Like the weather, commercialized Christmas is something everybody talks about but nobody does anything about.

> "We have met the enemy, and they is us."
> Pogo

Alternatives to the Commercialized Christmas

What can you do to make Christmas a joyful celebration of Christ's birth? How can the meaning of *Emmanuel,* "God with us," be made real at Christmastime?

RECOGNIZE at the outset that there are no quick fixes for miraculously transforming our Christmas celebrations. Christmas commercialization is deeply ingrained in this society. You can save yourself a lot of frustration by realizing that patience and perseverance are virtues needed in good supply for this venture.

Let Advent be Advent! Use the Advent season to develop a spirituality of cultural resistance to commercialized Christmas.

Turn down the volume of commercial Christmas hoopla. Before Christmas the airwaves, print media and shopping malls are saturated with messages to provide a "good" Christmas. Restrict exposure to this propaganda by watching television less frequently, making fewer trips to malls, and getting "Christmas" catalogues out of your house.

Tune in to activities that are less consumption-oriented. Set aside time in the weeks before Christmas for personal quiet and reflection, time for family and/or friends to work through an Advent calendar or the Gospel Bible readings for Advent, time for making gifts at home, time for household members to share in the pre-Christmas cleaning and cooking responsibilities.

EXPECT your religious community to provide resources and opportunities—through its church school, worship services and outreach committees—for members looking for ways to resist the pressures of commercialized Christmas. Then act to see that your expectation becomes reality. Consider organizing a community-wide alternative Christmas festival.

TAKE Santa Claus theology seriously. Perpetuation of the Santa Claus myth is an issue on which people of good will can and do disagree. Many—especially young parents—struggle with this issue alone because some congregations actively perpetuate Santa Claus theology, while others say nothing. Consider recovering the St. Nicholas tradition, thereby creating new celebration traditions that do not detract from celebrating Christ's birth.

REDISCOVER creativity in gift giving, both in what and where you buy. Recover the almost lost art of self-giving through gifts of time and skill, as well as presents made in the kitchen, workshop or at the desk.

INCLUDE in your congregation and family celebrations, those who would otherwise be alone. Celebrate Christ's coming as "good news to the poor" by sharing the joy and intimacy of your Christmas with senior citizens living alone, foreign students, street people, refugees and people who simply need hospitality.

GIVE to honor the birth of Christ. Do a cost analysis of your spending last Christmas. How much for presents? decorations? travel? food? Covenant with members of your household to take 25 percent of what you spent last Christmas and make that a "birthday gift" this Christmas. Give it to those who are working with and on behalf of the really needy.

PLAN for Christmas. Don't just be defensive. Find positive ways to react to society's idea of the "good" Christmas.

–During the summer, approach the appropriate committees in your church with ideas about how your congregation's celebrations might truly celebrate Christ's birth.

–Before Thanksgiving, write letters explaining your ideas about celebrating this year to family and friends with whom you ordinarily spend Christmas.

–Begin the gifts you want to make early enough to avoid being stampeded into buying at the last minute.

–Prepare your children early for an alternative Christmas. They need your help to resist the media's hard sell that begins right after Halloween.

Advent Promises

For your family's Advent celebration make a Promise Tree. Put a branch in a sand-filled pot. Each day in Advent write a promise to a family member and hang it on the tree. On Christmas Eve decorate your Promise Tree with hand-made symbols of Christ's birth.

Christmas Alternatives Catalogue
Our Saviour's Lutheran Church
Tucson, Arizona

Peace Notes at Advent

As a part of our Advent celebration we send international Christmas cards. On Christmas stationery we write a short note wishing peace and justice for our world. Then we invite friends to sign their names. The cards are mailed to national and world leaders to let them know our concerns as we anticipate the coming of the Prince of Peace. It is moving to receive notes from all over the world acknowledging our greetings.

Anne Broyles
Larry Peacock
Norwalk, California

"Navidad si
Consumismo no"
Graffiti on wall in Mexico City

Advent Workshop

In an effort to allow our small town of 2,000 to realize there are alternatives to Christmas gift-giving other than "shooting a wad" at K-Mart, we had an Advent workshop to encourage people to make some of their gifts.

We collected materials for making grapevine and pinecone wreaths, wooden candleholders, cutting boards, tree decorations and for decorating Christmas gift-wrapping paper. We tried to plan something for everyone, young and old. With volunteer supervisors to help with the rudiments of structure and design, we were able to charge just enough to cover the cost of materials.

As the price of admission participants brought a can of food to be used in food baskets distributed within our community at Christmas.

Sandra Ellingsen
Ellendale, North Dakota

33

St. Nicholas Day

We do all our immediate family gifts on this day. We hang stockings—simple, homemade muslin to which we add an embroidered symbol each year—on St. Nicholas Eve and remember the story of St. Nicholas and his gift of dowries to three young maidens. Then we play St. Nicholas for each other. We hang the stockings a while before bed, and everyone sneaks in to put gifts in each other's stockings. On St. Nicholas morning my two-year-old was so excited about what he had wrapped to give to *me* that he walked right past the rocking horse we had set out for him to get my gifts and put them in my lap.

When possible we share a common meal with others who also celebrate this way, followed by a visit from St. Nicholas himself. Complete with festive (borrowed) bishop's garb, St. Nicholas talks to the children, particularly emphasizing that he and God and their parents love them whether they "cry" or "pout", whether they're "good" or "bad." He then gives each of them a gold coin chocolate.

In the remaining weeks before Christmas we try to emphasize how nice it was to receive gifts. Now we do the same for others, for this is what God does at Christmas. So we bake, sew, glue and paste for grandparents, aunts, uncles and friends.

Ed, Andrea, Nathanael and Rebekah Wills
Memphis, Tennessee

St. Nicholas

A Puppet Play by Virginia Stevens

The St. Nicholas puppet play helps children and their parents understand the origin of Santa Claus traditions in the St. Nicholas legend. It challenges popular Santa customs and suggests that anonymous giving to people in need is more in keeping with the spirit of Christmas than the "getting" that goes with the Santa tradition.

The play addresses the ironic distortions which have occurred in the progression from St. Nicholas, who gave to the poor, to Santa, who gives only to those who can afford him. *St. Nicholas* is useful as a

church, community or home production; it can be the feature presentation at a Christmas festival; or it can be an important part of a workshop for parents who want to change Santa traditions in their homes and need a way to present the issue to their children.

Producing the play is a good way to involve youth groups in alternative Christmas activities.

Set: *The play was written with a Punch-and-Judy-type performance in mind, but with a few adaptations the new Muppet-style puppets and staging can also be used. It is also possible to use live actors.*

Sets are as follows:

For Scenes 1 and 3: Inside a poor home with a fireplace. The chimney should be visible outside the house on the roof (above the traditional stage; behind the large, open Muppet-style stage). A simple whitewashed background with a few painted-on cracks and a painted-on shelf with dishes would be sufficient. Although there were no windows in the homes of poor people during St. Nicholas' time, one may be painted on if it seems necessary to complete the feel of the inside of a house.

For Scene 2: Village square lined with medieval houses.

Props: *Broom, 2 small "oranges," bouquets of flowers (tiny dried flowers work well), money bag, table, 2 pallets.*

Puppets: *The Bilir Family*

ADA, *14 years old*	FATHER
OLIVIA, *16 years old*	NICHOLAS, *a young seminarian*
IDA, *12 years old*	JOHN, *Nicholas' colleague*
MOTHER	MRS. SAHED, *an unsympathetic neighbor*

Costumes: *Dress Bilir family in simple medieval costumes. For Nicholas and John use clerical collars and black shirts. A re-dressed witch gives a good "feel" for Mrs. Sahed.*

Scene 1

Inside Bilir home; table near front of stage.

ADA: [*Moves in back stage humming and sweeping; looks up at audience.*] Oh, hi! [*Moves toward front of stage.*] How are you? [*If no answer, she may prompt one.*] That's great! Say, I know there's a lot going on here today. I'm glad the organizers of this Christmas celebration let us have a part of the program. [*This can be modified to suit the occasion.*] By the way, my name is Ada Bilir. Any other Ada's here? Well, I want to tell you the story of my family. Let's see, there's my older sister Olivia and my younger one Ida. That makes three girls in all. Then we have a mother and a father. We live in Myra, a small village in Turkey. We have a pretty normal family, except we are very, very poor. And folks who are poor always have a rough time. But in Turkey in the fourth century, things are really rough because if parents don't have some money or jewels for their daughters, no one will marry them! Then the girls will have to become slaves. [*Shudders*] Oh-h-h. I wouldn't want to be a slave, would you? Uh-uh! [*Shakes head*] Not me. No way. But that's what is going to happen to Olivia and Ida and me because we don't have money or jewels for dowries. That's what they call the money and jewels—dowries. Our parents are so worried! What are we going to do? What *can* we do? [*Moves back a bit and resumes sweeping.*]

IDA: [*Runs in carrying two oranges.*] Ada, Ada! Guess what! I found two oranges today and they're only a little bruised. Aren't they wonderful? [*Puts oranges on table.*]

ADA: [*Moves forward to table.*] I'm proud of you, Ida. But, little sister, we need more than that to eat tonight. Maybe Olivia has also had luck and sold some flowers to the rich people in the village. Let's go find her. [*Puts broom in corner.*]

IDA: I'll bet I know where she is. Come on...[*Pulls her sister towards offstage "door"; Mother comes in wearily.*] Oh, hello, Mother. We're going to find Olivia. Be back soon.

MOTHER: Fine, girls. But don't be long. [*Girls leave.*] Now how shall I feed the family tonight with only a small piece of bread. [*Notices table.*] What's this? It looks like Ida has been out looking for food again. Well, at least we will have a bit to eat tonight. Maybe Anton has had a good day at work....

[*Knock at the door*]

MOTHER: Yes? Oh, come in, Mrs. Sahed. How are you today?

MRS. SAHED: [*Bustling in*] Terrible, Mrs. Bilir. Just terrible! My back! I cannot take a step without pain. No one suffers like I do! [*Notices oranges.*] My goodness, fruit! And only a *little* bit rotten! [*Sarcastically*] Well, you will certainly have a *feast* tonight, huh?

MOTHER: Yes, that's Ida's doing.

MRS. SAHED: Lovely daughters, you have. Of course, who *needs* daughters? Now, *my* sons...

MOTHER: They're good girls and...

MRS. SAHED: But they *are* girls. And you and your husband have enough problems without having three daughters.

[*Mother picks up broom and begins sweeping with her back to Mrs. Sahed.*]

MRS. SAHED: Now don't you ignore me. I know the story. There is no way your poor husband can earn enough money for those girls of yours to have dowries. No way!

MOTHER: Please...

MRS. SAHED: You have to face up to it. Your daughters have no dowries—no money, no jewels. Nothing! So no one will marry them. Olivia is already sixteen—time for her to leave home. You must know that you will have to sell her into slavery.

MOTHER: [*Angrily*] That's enough! There are plenty of problems without your reminding us. Now, I must fix dinner.

MRS. SAHED: I'm just trying to help. After all, plenty of girls end up in slavery because they are too poor to get husbands. But I can tell when I'm not wanted. [*Turns jerkily and strides out.*]

[*Mother puts her head down over her hands on broom and shakes as if crying.*]

CURTAIN CLOSES

Scene 2

Village scene. Scene begins with Ada in front of the closed curtains.
ADA: Our village is like many other villages, except we have a seminary. That's a special school where boys study to become priests in the church. There are many students in that school, including Nicholas and his friend John.

[*As she finishes, the curtains open and Olivia walks in front of houses at the back of the stage, carrying flowers. Ada moves off as curtains open.*]

OLIVIA: [*Calling out*] Flowers. Flowers for sale. Fresh from the countryside. [*Ada and Ida come hurrying up.*]

IDA: Hi, Olivia. I found two oranges that are almost fresh. Come on home now and see them! We will be eating soon.

OLIVIA: Yes, I'll come. I'm really tired—and hungry!

[*As the girls walk off back-stage left, Nicholas and John enter front-stage left and take note of them. Nicholas looks backward at them.*]

NICHOLAS: Aren't those the daughters of Bilir, the baker? They look so happy.

JOHN: That they are. But I've heard that their happiness will be gone soon. For Mr. Bilir has hardly enough money to feed his family. And nothing for a dowry. The oldest girl, Olivia, will soon have to go into slavery since no man will marry her without a dowry.

NICHOLAS: [*Disgusted and angry*] Such a stupid custom! Dowry indeed! As if a girl is like a pig or a cow to be bought and sold!

JOHN: Easy, easy! Don't get all over me. I didn't set up dowries. You've got to learn to accept life as it is, Nicholas. Besides we have plenty to worry about already. We will be having tests at school soon. There's too much to learn and too little time to do it.

NICHOLAS: [*Half listening*] Yes, yes, I know. It's important to serve God by doing well. But still...it's so unfair! Here *I* am. I have more than I need and those poor girls have nothing.... [*Thoughtfully*] It's just not right.

JOHN: Nicholas, I can't stand around here wasting time. We can pray for those girls and their parents—*after* we've studied for the Latin test tomorrow! [*Turns and leaves.*]

NICHOLAS: [*Pacing*] It's not fair. [*Turns to audience.*] Do you think it's fair that I have more money than I need and the Bilir family has almost nothing? [*Prompts response.*] Neither do I! What can I do? [*Stops as if in thought; children might respond, but it doesn't matter either way.*] Listen, listen. I am remembering some verses from the Bible. Why, yes, in St. Matthew it says that if someone has two shirts he ought to give one of them to another person who doesn't have any! And to share food, too. [*More excitedly*] And, oh, we just learned some verses last week in school. Let's see. What were they? [*Pauses*] I know, in First John it says that if someone has enough and doesn't help another person in need, the person with enough can't rightly say the love of God is in him. I want people to know God's love is in me. Don't you? Well, then I'll have to figure out a way to share with the Bilir family. But I must do it secretly because the Bible also says we are not to make a big deal of what we do for others. The Bilirs shouldn't feel like they owe *me* something just because I'm doing what God has told me to. I must make plans....[*Hurries off.*]

CURTAIN CLOSES

Scene 3

Inside Bilir house. Two pallets are in view. In one Father is tossing. Mother is beside him. In the other, the three girls are sleeping.
FATHER: What can we do? No matter how hard I work, there is never enough money to feed this family, let alone put together a dowry.

MOTHER: I know. We all do our best, but it just isn't enough. But if we don't get our sleep, we'll be in worse shape.

FATHER: Oh, I know. Well, good night. [*Makes motions as though turning over.*]

MOTHER: Good night.

   [*PAUSE—maybe with a few sleeping movements and sounds.*]

   [*Then scratching, like someone scaling a wall, is heard. Not terribly loud, but loud enough for audience to hear.*]

OLIVIA: [*Sitting up, speaking in a stage whisper.*] Ida! Ada! Do you hear that? Wake up!

ADA: [*Sitting up and looking around.*] What? What are you talking about? Are you awake?

IDA: [*If possible, she can pull blanket over her head; otherwise, she sits up.*] I hear it! Someone's climbing up the wall. I'm scared. Papa! Mother! Somebody's on the roof! Somebody's going to get us!

[*Nicholas appears moving across the "roof" carrying a money bag and cautiously approaching the chimney.*]

FATHER: Huh? Huh? [*Father and Mother sit up.*] What's the matter? [*Looks up at the roof.*] What next? If a robber has come to visit, he sure has made a bad mistake!

MOTHER: Quiet down. We must do something!

FATHER: [*Getting out of bed.*] Well, we've nothing here but a broom. Where is that broom? [*Looks around, but just at this moment Nicholas drops the money bag "down the chimney"; the sound of it hitting the floor should be heard. Nicholas looks down the chimney, then at the audience and smiles, then listens at the chimney.*]

[*At sound of money bag hitting, the girls scream. Mother goes to chimney and leans over and picks up money bag.*]

FATHER: What's that?

[*Everyone gathers near Mother and moves around excitedly with remarks like "What can it be?"*]

IDA: It looks like a sack of money!

MOTHER: That's exactly what it is. My goodness, it's heavy, too. Who would give us this fortune?

ADA: Yes, who could it be? [*Turns to audience.*] Do you know? Have you seen anybody?

[*Nicholas is almost hiding on the roof, but he shakes his head vigorously and puts his finger to his lips with a "shh." Ada and the others continue to try to find out from the audience. They may come to the front of the stage and look up, as if to the roof, but Nicholas ducks as they do. If the audience does name Nicholas, the family may look at each other puzzled, with statements like, "Nicholas?" "Who's he?" "I think there is a student named Nicholas studying to be a priest." "But it can't be him!" "Why should he care about us?"*]

MOTHER: Well, this certainly is a mystery. But one thing is sure. There is enough money for all three of you girls to have dowries. And so it is no mystery that God came to our house tonight.

[*Everyone hugs each other and bounces up and down—moving toward the back of the stage—except for Ada.*]

ADA: Yes, a special gift was given us that night. By someone who took seriously God's word to share what we have with others. Nicholas shared with us. Whom will you share with? Think about it.

CURTAIN CLOSES

(Virginia Stevens is the Presbyterian Hunger Action Enabler for Asheville, North Carolina. She is also the coordinator of an ecumenical hunger awareness group in Asheville, where she has helped to organize several successful Christmas festivals.)

Stuffed Ornaments
Find scraps of colorful material around the house. Cut two pieces in the same design (stars, circles, diamonds, etc.), turn inside out and sew around the edges, leaving an opening for stuffing. Stuff with cotton or suitable scrap materials and sew opening together carefully. This is a project the entire family can do for decorating or as gifts.

Jo Fleming
Orlando, Florida

Greetings From the Heart
For the past few years we have printed our Christmas cards. Two families share a small silk screen along with a supply of colored inks. Each family makes paper patterns and then we come together for an evening of designing cards. We use inexpensive colored paper for the cards and mail them in budget envelopes. Inside each card we write a personal message to family and friends. Our favorite designs are outlines of the three wise men and the dove of peace.

Mary and Bill Merrill
Columbus, Ohio

Our Richest Christmas

For Christmas last year we gave prayer to our friends and family. At the time, my husband and I worried that our gift might be misunderstood. Prayer, after all, doesn't sound like much. But it was given out of our need to make Christmas more meaningful. To our surprise it was received as a gift of great value, and it brought us, in return, the richest Christmas blessings we had known.

Our children took part in our prayers enthusiastically. Before the first devotion day arrived, our daughter noticed the craft supplies we had collected for illustrating the prayer cards. She volunteered to be in charge of crafts the first day, and thereafter she often planned that activity. Our son jealously guarded his role as acolyte and filled a basket with once lit candles to send with prayer cards. We wrote prayers together, and even after the holiday season ended, the children did not tire of devotions.

Then our friends and relatives showed us the grace of Christmas in the way they received our prayers. For one couple our prayers were the impetus for reestablishing a relationship. They came to our home to share their prayer day with us. Jewish friends invited us to join their Passover celebration in the new year. Several other friends planned special holiday dinners or concert trips with us. We were overwhelmed by the love and closeness of people.

Our alternative celebration permanently changed Christmas for us. It will always be a time when we remember that just as Jesus came as a gift to us, we are gifts to each other.

Co-Laborer, Winter 1986
Used by permission.

> **"A celebration is very different from a spectacle, where actors or musicians play to entertain an audience. In a celebration, we are all actors and all audience. It is not a true celebration unless everyone participates."**
>
> Jean Vanier

Merry Christmas, Beloved Stranger

A Kansas couple has been making Christmas more merry for strangers who don't have family to help them celebrate the season. A number of years ago, they set up a holiday help line. They placed an ad in the local newspaper and invited readers who might be spending Christmas alone to call them and make reservations for dinner at their house. Now, each year they host a holiday get-together for about 30 guests— strangers who have become friends.

Maybe you can't invite 30, but you could consider sharing your meal with one or two. Inquire at your church or local social service agency for names of people who would welcome such an invitation. If Christmas dinner doesn't seem appropriate, perhaps Christmas Eve or New Year's Day would be a suitable time.

Originally published in *Liguorian*
December 1983
Reprinted with permission

Simple Christmas Meal

In lieu of a traditional Christmas dinner (turkey, ham) we had a simple meal consisting of beans, tortillas and rice. We then gave a $25.00 contribution—representing what we would have spent on a traditional meal—to CROP, a hunger program of Church World Service.

The Miodunski Family
Barnhart, Missouri

New Orleans Church Bonds with Third World Parish

St. Joseph the Worker parish in New Orleans has "bonded" with a third world parish in a small mountain town in Chiapas, Mexico. Parishioners correspond with Mexican parishioners, providing needed financial assistance and exchanging pictures.

A member of the parish staff in Chiapas spent a week with the St. Joseph community sharing her own faith experience and learning more about her friends in the States. Her week concluded with the church's annual Christmas fair which exhibited many crafts from Chiapas.

> Brenda Broussard
> Baton Rouge, Louisiana

Love Thy Neighbor

Temple Isaiah of Lafayette cooked and served Christmas dinner for the Loaves and Fishes program, a hospitality ministry at St. Peter Martyr church in Pittsburg, freeing the church members and other volunteers to spend the day with their families. On December 24 Our Savior's Lutheran Church of Lafayette did the same. I feel this is a very real expression of the spirit of giving.

> Helen Wilson
> Pittsburg, California

Mission Mexico

Several years ago our family felt the frustration of observing Christmas in ways that failed to celebrate what God did in that wondrous moment. So we deliberately planned a Christmas that would serve a need with no way for the gift receiver to give back anything of material value and no expectation of the giver to receive anything of monetary value in return.

What began as our family's alternative has become an expression of the miracle of Christmas for hundreds of people. It started with our "five fish" (our five children) and we estimate at least 10,000 people were the recipients of the food, clothes, toys and other gifts we personally delivered into the desperately needy areas between Ciudad Acuna and Piedras Negras, Mexico's hill country.

Though most of the clothing and toys we take into these areas are used, we ask donors to make sure gifts are suitable and in good condition. Our criteria is to take only what we would feel good about giving. We also try to respond to community needs. One year we took gloves for street sweepers and policemen along with gloves and rubber boots for firemen who, we had observed the year before, had to work without them in the coldest weather.

As a result of these efforts, our group now receives full support and cooperation from local officials. The first year they were very skeptical, but after our third year border officials allowed us to cross without a search. Local police now escort us through the towns, our t-shirts communicating the message we bring more effectively than our halting Spanish: *Cristo Te Ama Y Yo Tambien*, which translated into English says, "Christ loves you and I do, also."

> Jerry L. Mash
> Guthrie, Oklahoma

Las Posadas

"Las Posadas," which literally means "the inns," highlights the plight of the refugees of Bethlehem. This custom was developed in the ancient Franciscan missions of Mexico and what is now the American Southwest. One of the high points of Christmas festivities in San Antonio and other towns with a strong Hispanic tradition, "Las Posadas" is a procession led by Mary and Joseph looking for shelter. As they arrive at various places they sing a song of entreaty, only to hear a song of rejection by those inside. Eventually, they are recognized by those in an "inn," and allowed to enter. Great rejoicing and feasting follows.

An English version of some of the songs for "Las Posadas" may be sung to the familiar tune of "Good King Wenceslaus" (see below). Reenactment of this festival might be used at a church supper where Mary and Joseph, looking bedraggled and dirty, seek shelter at different tables. When they are finally allowed in, all can join in singing the first stanza of "Gentle Mary Laid her Child," to the same tune. If possible, prepare traditional Mexican-American food for this occasion. The important point is for the congregation to see Mary and Joseph as

43

unwelcome travelers whom "decent" people would not let in and how this wandering couple resembles homeless refugees in our midst.

Las Posadas
(The Inns)

Verse 1
(Joseph and Mary sing:)
In the name of God we beg: will you let us enter?
We are tired and we are cold. May we please have shelter?

(The Innkeepers sing:)
You look dirty and you smell. Will you please keep moving?
For your kind there is no place, for our inn is decent.

Verse 2
(Joseph and Mary sing:)
It is not by our own choice that today we travel.
But the Emperor has said that all must be counted.

(The Innkeepers sing:)
For your reasons we care not. Every room is taken.
Can't you see the place is full? You are bad for business.

Verse 3
(Joseph and Mary sing:)
Will the child be born tonight out on a street corner?
Can't you find a place for him? Do you have no pity?

(The Innkeepers sing:)
Oh my goodness do come in. You can use the manger.
For the rooms that we do have are for a rich traveler.

Verse 4
(All sing:)
Holy Jesus you are still with the poor and homeless;
If we wish to do your will, we will bid them welcome.
Holy Jesus do forgive, in this Christmas season,
That the way in which we live, so beclouds our vision. Amen.

> By Justo L. Gonzalez
> Verses 1-3 translated and adapted from traditional words.
> Decatur, Georgia

How to Organize an Alternative Christmas Community Festival

An Alternative Christmas Festival is a concrete, exciting way to offer ideas and support for those who want to have more meaningful Christmas celebrations. It is also a positive way to introduce the need for change to people who have not yet thought about the problems connected with the way we celebrate Christmas. The size and scope of the festival you plan will depend upon the resources, talent and degree of commitment among those in your community.

What follows is a very brief "how-to." I share with you the learnings of several years of organizing a community festival. I hope this method has enough specifics to get you started in developing a festival coherent with the resources and needs of your own community.

1. GETTING STARTED. It is essential to have at least two or three very committed people to initiate and carry out the festival. These people

might be from a hunger or lifestyle group in the community, a denomination or a local congregation. Developing a core group and an ecumenical base is essential.

After this group has been identified, plan at least three sessions to develop clear understanding of the purpose and methods of the festival. The filmstrip, "Have Yourself a Merry Little Christmas," produced by Alternatives, can be used as a focus. Solicit volunteers for exhibits and other details of running a festival.

2. ORGANIZING THE FESTIVAL. Ideally there should be a Festival Coordinator with chairpersons of the following committees: a) exhibits, b) program, c) food, d) physical arrangement, e) publicity and f) finance. (In fact, we never have had six chairpersons.)

Exhibits are the heart of the festival. This is where visitors are given ideas and materials which guide them as they look for alternatives to unthinking compliance with the status quo. In order to maintain focus we think it extremely important not to sell anything, but you may want to make catalogues and order forms available for crafts and books. The exhibits chairperson position is an extremely important one as this person solicits appropriate exhibits and makes sure everything is ready at festival time.

You may want to consider some of the following for exhibits: Bread for the World, Heifer Project, Habitat for Humanity, Self-Help Craft Groups, On-the-Scene Craft Making for Children and Adults, Books, Celebrating Advent, Celebrating Epiphany, Children's Gifts, Game Room for Children, Gifts for Older People, Alternative Cards, Wrappings, Ornaments and Traditions of Christmas—especially dealing with Santa Claus.

3. PROGRAM. Have a printed program available for guests at the welcome area. If possible, get it published in the local newspaper before festival day. Enlist volunteers to perform musically and with skits, puppets, or storytelling. You may also include workshops or mini-workshops on special topics such as "How to Introduce the Christmas Alternatives Idea in Your Congregation."

4. FOOD. Serving a simple meal makes it possible for people to stay and enjoy an all-day festival. We have found soup the easiest since volunteers can make the same recipe in their homes and bring the finished product to the festival for reheating. We serve cheese, bread, apple slices and a drink along with the soup and charge a modest fee which more than covers the cost.

5. PHYSICAL ARRANGEMENTS. Choose a central location with which most people are familiar. Check for the availability of parking, kitchen and dining facilities, easy access to the building, and a supportive host who will donate use of the building, its facilities and equipment. Many church buildings fit these criteria.

6. PUBLICITY. The publicity committee's major work will be early in the planning process. Churches should be contacted at least three months before the festival so that it can be incorporated into their calendars of events. Design a poster for circulation throughout the community, making sure that all churches and sympathetic community organizations are included. Cost of the posters can be minimal if your group does what ours has done. We use Alternatives' "Whose Birthday Is It Anyway?" bulletin inserts as artwork on a construction paper background.

Whose Birthday Is It Anyway?

On the construction paper we carefully pen in pertinent festival information.

Use the media. Talk to the public service announcement representatives at radio and television stations to make sure the festival is included. Suggest coverage of the event to a local newspaper reporter and help the reporter with a good story angle.

7. FINANCES. From the outset have a clear understanding of how expenses will be covered. If simplicity is honored and ways to absorb the minimal expenses are devised, there should be little problem. These are some of the ways we have managed our financial matters:

a. With a start-up grant from our local hunger group, we rent films, buy printed materials for hand-outs, and purchase supplies which everyone uses.

b. We do not charge admission, but a donation box at the exit brings in a reasonable amount of money.

c. Grants of money, material and equipment from churches.

d. Lunch fees are mostly profit since most of the food is actually donated.

8. TYING THINGS UP. After the festival is over, do your very best to get written comments from each committee chairperson and all the exhibitors about what they did right and wrong, what might be changed in the overall design next time, etc. Also, have an evaluation form at the exit for guests to fill out. This provides excellent suggestions and possible workers for the next festival.

Start another folder for next year even before the festival is over. As you prepare, you will find useful ideas and materials too late for use in your current efforts. You will dream new dreams. But you will forget them unless you write them down now.

We have borrowed, modified and hopefully enriched the ideas and materials of countless others. Most we do not even know, but their creativity has spurred our own. Now we encourage you to do the same.

Virginia E. Stevens
Asheville, North Carolina

Editor's Note: This material is a brief adaptation of "How to Organize an Alternative Christmas Community Festival," a well-written, extensive guide to a Christmas community festival and a practical, life-changing response to commercialized Christmas. Virginia Stevens is the Presbyterian Hunger Action Enabler for Asheville, North Carolina. She has worked with an ecumenical hunger awareness group in Asheville to organize several successful Christmas festivals. Order the complete copy of "How to Organize an Alternative Christmas Festival" from Alternatives, P.O. Box 429, Ellenwood, Georgia 30049.

The Light
shines in the darkness,
and the darkness does not
overcome it.
John 1:5

A Litany for Christmas

Leader: O Lord, as we prepare to celebrate the birth of Jesus, we give thanks for the Light that has come into the world and given us hope. And we give thanks for those in every age who have been witnesses to the Light.

People: The light shines in darkness, and the darkness has not overcome it.

Leader: In the darkness of the threat of nuclear war, we are thankful for the witness of those of all classes, races and nationalities who have begun to say, "It does not have to be."

People: The light shines in the darkness, and the darkness has not overcome it.

Leader: In the darkness of hunger and homelessness in a world that has enough for all, we are thankful for the witness of those who feed the hungry, welcome the stranger, clothe the naked, and struggle for them in the halls of government and corporate board rooms.

People: The light shines in darkness, and the darkness has not overcome it.

Leader: In the darkness from unsafe streets to death row cells, we give thanks for the witness of those who remember that justice is not served by violence.

People: The light shines in darkness, and the darkness has not overcome it.

Leader: In the darkness of greed that is a sickness in our souls, we give thanks for the witness of those who dispel the illusion that life consists in the accumulation of things.

People: The light shines in darkness, and the darkness has not overcome it.

Leader: O God, forgive us when we are content to live in the shadows. This Christmas, strengthen our faith and renew our hope that we may be witnesses to the Light. Amen.

"Celebrations are ways to anticipate the future; they are managable times when the future envisioned in our ideals can be practiced in the present."

Whose Birthday Is It, Anyway?

In the land of Puzzling Tales there lived an eight-year-old boy by the name of Jason.

Now in this land and in the neighborhood where Jason lived, the unexpected always happened.

Instead of football they played kneeball; instead of the children "going to school" the teachers were busy "going to homes." In the summer time it was not uncommon to see water freeze and in the winter time leaves grew on trees. It was a funny, strange place.

One incident in the land of Puzzling Tales stands out. When it was time for Jason's ninth birthday, as usual, the unusual happened.

Jason's grandparents came from their home across the state to help celebrate, but of course when they got to Jason's neighborhood they went immediately to the Brown's down the street and visited and stayed there.

When Jason's mother baked the birthday cake she gave it to the letter carrier to eat.

And when all the neighborhood kids heard it was Jason's birthday they exchanged gifts with one another and, of course, Jason got none.

There was a blizzard of birthday cards. The post office had to hire extra workers and work longer hours to handle the deluge of cards. Of course, in the land of Puzzling Tales the expected was the unexpected and all the kids, the moms and dads, grandparents, even a couple of dogs and a parakeet got cards, while poor Jason got none.

Finally about nine o'clock, in a fit of frustration and anger, Jason went out of his house, borrowed the school cheerleaders' megaphone, rode up and down the street on his unicycle and shouted at the top of his lungs,
"WHOSE BIRTHDAY IS IT, ANYWAY?"

And the night was so silent that all night long echoes bounced off the mountain sides. "Whose birthday is it, anyway?" "Whose birthday is it, anyway?"

The baby Jesus will be kidnapped again this year and held ransom for millions of dollars. This year Americans will surrender more than thirty billion dollars to the stores to buy gifts to swap.

But it is Jesus' birthday! Jesus ought to receive the gifts. Jesus said, "Inasmuch as you have done it to the least of these my brethren, you have done it to me." We give to Jesus when we give to the poor, the weak, the hungry, the homeless, the refugees, the prisoners.

It will be a great birthday celebration when God's people begin in earnest to give once again to Jesus. For after all, it is His birthday, isn't it?

Rev. Arley Fadness
Harrisburg, South Dakota

(Printed on back of poster with artwork by Kathie Klein. Order from Alternatives, P.O. Box 429, Ellenwood, Georgia 30049.)

Light for the Dark Days

January and February are particularly long, dark months in Michigan. Our family has found that celebrating Epiphany at dinner time with each lighting a personal candle from the Christ candle we lit on Christmas Day, not only enriches our lives spiritually but also adds a good deal of light to some dark evenings!

Betty Voskuil
Holland, Michigan

3.
Giving and Receiving Gifts

The practice of gift-giving is as old as Adam and Eve. It may be the original basis for economics. Some authorities believe that in ancient societies gifts were a precursor to bartering, which in turn gave way to buying and selling. Lands and possessions were passed on to children as gifts, beginning a system of family inheritance which kept strict control on land distribution. Gift-giving to deities through sacrifices was an integral part of ancient religions. The purposes of sacrificial gifts were quite varied: to give tribute to the deity as king; to express gratitude; to gain favor; to establish or reestablish ties; to be purged of sin; or to provide sustenance for the deity's earthly visits.

In many ancient cultures there were special injunctions to make gifts to "strangers" or "sojourners." Some anthropologists suggest the reason for such behavior was that sojourners, who were thought to have special powers, were mistrusted. The gifts were to ensure the friendship of these transients. In the Old Testament, however, injunctions to care for sojourners are not based on fear but compassion: "...you were once sojourners in the land of Egypt." (Leviticus 19:33)

All of the world's major religions have provision for giving gifts—usually as alms—to the "poor and needy." However, little is said about this in the Old Testament. While Israel made it a practice to give alms to the poor, concern for them was expressed in broader terms, i.e. providing for their overall needs and protecting them against injustice. In one of the classic Old Testament texts the prophet Isaiah proclaimed that religious fasts were acceptable to the Lord only when they included freeing the oppressed, sharing bread with the hungry, bringing the homeless into one's own house, and clothing the naked (Isaiah 58). In the New Testament Jesus identifies himself with the poor and makes acting on behalf of the poor the standard by which the nations will be judged: "Inasmuch as you have done it to the least of these, you have done it to me". (Matthew 25:31-46)

Connections between gift-giving and ritual celebrations also began quite early. It was customary to exchange gifts on New Year's Day long before exchanging gifts at Christmas became tradition. On New Year's

Day Persians exchanged gifts of eggs—symbols of fertility—while Egyptians gave flasks to each other. Romans exchanged objects bearing the imprint of Janus, the god of two faces for whom the month of January is named. The Celtic-Teutonic Druids made gifts of their holy plant, mistletoe. Ancient peoples also celebrated birthdays and weddings with gifts. The Greek poet Aeschylus wrote about the custom of giving presents to children on their birthdays as early as the sixth century B.C.

The practice of gift-giving at Christmas has several origins. The early Roman feast of Saturnalia was already a well-established time for exchanging gifts when the date for celebrating the birth of Christ was set on the same date. But Christians had their own reasons for gift-giving at Christmas. Patterned on the gifts of the Magi—gold, frankincense and myrrh—brought to honor the birth of the Christ Child, gift-giving was a symbolic reminder of the great gift of God's Son.

As Christianity spread into different cultures and through time, various customs and traditions developed around giving gifts at Christmas. In Germany the Christ Child was said to bring small presents on Christmas Eve. Among the Dutch it was St. Nicholas who brought gifts to children on December 6, the eve of his feast. The practice of gift-giving at Christmas was firmly established in the nineteenth century when the traditions of the Christ Child ("Christkindl") and St. Nicholas ("Sinterklass") became anglicized into one—Santa Claus.

Gift-Giving in the Consumer Society

Gift-giving is no less important today than in earlier times. It is still viewed as an acceptable way to express love and to celebrate relationships. But gift-giving has a history of abuse, abuse that continues today. We abuse the practice of giving gifts in several ways: we use gifts to bribe or manipulate; we make gifts because of social pressure; we use gifts to alleviate guilt; we give gifts that are inconsistent with our highest values and ideals. While this abuse is not new, the practice of gift-giving has been affected by the consumer society. As even *The Amy Vanderbilt Complete Book of Etiquette* recognizes, "Today, in our materialistic society, the custom [of gift-giving] has grown to exaggerated absurdity,…"

Consider the consumer culture's values that have shaped our gift-giving practices:

• *Conformity is prized over individuality.* Despite society's rhetoric about individuality, the "if-you-don't-have-one-you-are-inadequate" message of mass culture relentlessly bombards the senses from the air waves and print media. Consumer society's emphasis is to create needs rather than creating products to meet needs we already have. This results in conformity in how needs are perceived and the ways we meet those needs. The more far-reaching result of our conformity, however, may be an absence of dissenting voices in today's mass culture.

• *Whatever is bought and sold is better than whatever isn't.* A broad assumption in the consumer society is that the only way to be happy is to accumulate things. Friendship, contentment, and security are significant only as they involve consumption. The way to express love and affection for another is by *buying* some *thing.* By implication, gifts that are not "bought things"—including things made with one's own hands—are not worth much. The restrictive nature of this assumption rules out a whole host of wonderful ways to give, i.e., gifts of time and skill. Not only does preoccupation with "buying to give" overlook other ways of giving, it also seems to make gift-giving less personal.

• *More and bigger are better. Less and smaller are chintzy.* In a society which produces consumer goods far beyond the needs of its members, consumption without restraint becomes an ideal. This society's extraordinary levels of consumption have resulted in unparalleled amounts of waste, thus earning the title, "the throwaway society." Unrealistic ideas that the earth has unlimited natural resources, cheap energy and adequate means of waste disposal have undergirded our consumption and waste, but all three of these assumptions are now known to be false. The issues raised by this knowledge are more than ecological. Recognition of our planet's limited resources forces us to address the question of a just distribution of goods and resources. New consumer values, ideals and practices are urgently needed so that all people can share in what the world has to offer.

As gift-giving practices have been symbols of the consumer culture's values and ideals, it is time to give voice to new values and ideals:

1. Give in ways that enrich human relationships, a process that requires the investment of self. Proper timing and creativity replace quantity and monetary value as the essentials of good giftgiving.

2. Give in ways that enable physical, mental and spiritual growth beyond the expectations and restraints of popular culture.

3. Give in ways that are life-supporting and conserving. Be aware of how your giving or nongiving affects people and the earth. Consider who profits from your purchase and who suffers. Think about the ecological cost of creation and disposal.

4. Give to those who work for those intangibles most needed by our loved ones and future generations: a world at peace, an inclusive society and a healthy environment. Let celebrations be occasions to reaffirm your relationship to the earth and all humankind.

As you think about ways your gift-giving can give voice to your ideals, consider:

• Time and skill. Gifts of time—especially to younger children or older relatives—are very important and can take many forms. Teach a skill—cooking, writing, carpentry, a foreign language, etc. Gifts of time and skill to justice organizations can be as useful as gifts of money.

• Home-made gifts. This nasty phrase in consumer society's vocabulary can be rehabilitated with personalized gifts from the workbench, kitchen

"To dig our heels in and say no to a present madness is a good thing, but to walk a new path and say yes is a better thing."

Jim Wallis, *Sojourners*

51

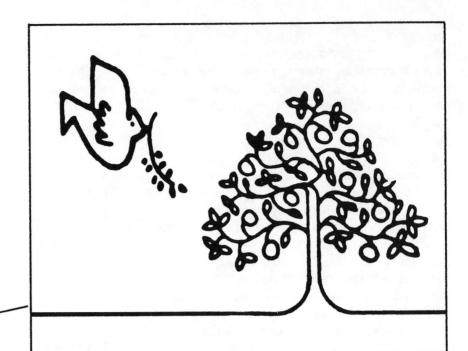

To celebrate this special time,
a gift has been given to

_____

in your name
by

_____

Similar cards are available from
The Institute for Peace and Justice,
4144 Lindell, #122, St. Louis,
Missouri 63108.

and desk. Planning and creativity, more than skill, are the essential requirements.

• Gifts from self-help craft groups. Consider the benefits. Your purchase helps keep alive old crafts. A larger percentage of the purchase price goes to the artisan than if you bought the same thing in the mall, and you are helping to provide employment for low-income people. Also, they make wonderful gifts! You will find a listing of self-help craft groups, many with customer mail order services, listed by states in the Appendix of this catalogue.

• Double-gift certificates. Unlike regular gift certificates that redeem items from a store, the "double-gift certificate" is two gifts for the price of one: a gift certificate to a non-profit charity in the name of a friend is a gift both to the charity and to the friend.

• Selective buying. Exercise your right *not* to buy from organizations that produce objectionable products or that exploit people or the earth. This is a vote for justice and a healthy environment in a consumer society.

• No-interest loans. Groups like Koinonia Partners and Habitat for Humanity solicit contributions in the form of no-interest loans. Donors may "call" the loans at any time; after a short waiting period the money is returned. This arrangement makes possible housing construction for low-income families without the usual high interest-bearing mortgage and cuts the actual owner cost of the house in half.

• Interest-bearing loans. Groups like the Southern Cooperative Development Fund pay interest on long-term loans. This money is then loaned to self-help development projects at low interest. Individuals and groups with savings accounts now have the option of supporting human justice organizations by depositing money in these kinds of development funds.

• Gifts in Life Estate. Your lawyer can advise you on how to make gifts of property to nonprofit groups. Life Estate allows you to use your property or income until your death, after which it goes to the group(s) you wish to help.

• Organ Donation. Even in death you can give the gift of sight or life through donating your organs to others. A signed statement indicating your desire to do this needs to be with you at all times. Many states provide a space for this on your driver's license.

DOUBLE YOUR GIFT OF LOVE

Retail store advertisers make a great effort to resolve all Christmas shopping problems. To make sure they don't lose the confused, uninspired shopper they go to great lengths to create gifts for the "man or woman who has everything."

You may not know anyone who has everything, but there may be friends or family members on your gift list who are not in need. Do something different for them. Make a gift to a church or charitable group in lieu of an unnecessary gift. We call this a double gift certificate: a gift to the charity and a gift to your friend or family member, a gift that complements a shared concern for a better world.

Send a card announcing your gift with your message of love for the card's recipient and your concern for peace and justice in the world. We have designed such a card for your use. Feel free to use our design for your cards or order them from Alternatives.

More Than a Tea Party

I decided to give a tea party for friends and at the same time do some education on hunger issues. Guests were invited to bring a mug to exchange with another guest and a contribution for Heifer Project International. Home-made goodies were served to friends who dropped in throughout the afternoon. We enjoyed visiting with each other while learning about and giving to a project that provides breeding stock to low-income farmers around the world. By the end of the party more than $700 had been raised.

Martha Brooks
Fort Worth, Texas

Cobbler Aprons Support Refugees

Many Hmong people from Southeast Asia have settled in Boulder. One way they support their friends and relatives is by selling beautiful embroidered fabric made by their people still in refugee camps. I designed a cobbler's apron featuring a block of this beautiful fabric which I bought for $5.00. I made five aprons as gifts for my three daughters, my daughter-in-law, and a friend. I also helped an older friend make an apron for a friend of hers.

Virginia McConnell
Boulder, Colorado

Jute Angels: Messengers of Hope

Our church offered little jute angels from Bangladesh to give as gifts in appreciation for contributions made to the Lutheran World Hunger Appeal. Lutheran Churches are using funds from the Appeal to establish a cottage industry for women refugees in Bangladesh. Along with information about the project, we sent a card with the angel. It said:

I've enclosed an angel for you. Please use it as a "messenger of hope." Hang it in your kitchen, in a window, or on your Christmas tree. It can also be an Easter reminder of the angel's message "He is risen."

In addition, I've also made a contribution to the Lutheran World Hunger Appeal. Let this angel remind you of the hope we have in life. Tell other people its story.

Last Christmas I sent an angel to my aunt. As a result, for my birthday this year she sent a check in my name to the World Hunger Appeal. So this one little angel has been a gift that has kept on giving—to feed hungry people around the world.

Eileen Ward
Mililani, Hawaii

Grandparents Make Talking Books

My husband and I sent books to our four-year-old granddaughter along with tape recordings of each of us reading the books to her. On the recordings we rang a little bell each time she was to turn the page. We not only read the words, but talked about the pictures as we would have if she were on our laps. We thought of the idea because she had lived with us and we had grown very close, but then she had moved far away. Our daughter reported that our granddaughter finds the voices so real that she carries on conversations with her "Grannie and Granpap" in absentia.

Joan Gauker
Norristown, Pennsylvania

Music for Parents Only

My husband and I are professional musicians. Our parents love it when we play and sing for them on our trips home, especially our original songs. Last Christmas we decided that the best gift we could give them was our music. We recorded a cassette tape full of songs for them. We put some original songs on the tape, and we also picked older songs that we knew they both loved. This year they have told us many times how much they continue to enjoy our gift, and that it was one of the best presents they have ever received. We got a great deal of joy out of giving it to them, and had a lot of fun sharing the recording together. The gift took a lot of time to make, but it was worth every minute.

Judy Leonard
Conyers, Georgia

Daddy's Calendar: A Priceless Gift of Art

Our three children make their father a very special Christmas present each year. During each December the children and I spend a day making a calendar. I fold large white drawing paper in half; on the top half the children draw pictures and I make the calendar on the lower half. Their father hangs it proudly in his office. The calendars are saved from year to year to show the change in the children's art work. It is a priceless gift which is cherished by their father.

Deborah Heaton
Enid, Oklahoma

Alternative Marketing: Nonprofit Gifts that Give Twice

Every time a handmade jute plant hanger, soapstone jewelry box, velvet Christmas ornament or painted trivet is sold from the SELFHELP Crafts warehouse in Akron, Pennsylvania, a needy craftsperson in Bangladesh, India, Thailand or El Salvador benefits. Through SELFHELP Crafts, North Americans are reaching out to brothers and sisters in developing nations who are victims of poverty, famine, unemployment, injustice and/or displacement.

SELFHELP Crafts, a nonprofit program of the Mennonite Central Committee (MCC), creates jobs for skilled craftspeople in developing nations by marketing their crafts in North America. The program began humbly in 1946 when a Mennonite woman, Edna Ruth Byler, traveled to Puerto Rico to visit MCC volunteers and brought back needlework made by needy rural women to sell to her friends and neighbors in Lancaster

County, Pennsylvania. Today, 40 years later, almost 3,000 items from 30 developing nations are sold throughout North America. Because almost everyone involved in the program is a volunteer, salaries are few and overhead expenses are low.

SELFHELP Crafts is one of a growing number of nonprofit Alternative Trading Organizations (ATOs) based throughout the world. Their merchandise works not for the bank accounts of rich multi-national corporations, but rather for peace, justice and global understanding. People who choose to buy items for gift-giving or for their personal/household use can be sure that a SELFHELP craft item gives twice: beauty and usefulness to the consumer; dignity, employment and a fair income to the producer.

Editor's Note. The above description of the Mennonite Central Committee's effort to work for peace and justice by providing a market for skilled craftspeople is different only in history and detail from many other self-help organizations. The philosophy of serving needy brothers and sisters throughout the world is basic to all such groups. In order to help you with gifts that give twice, we have included a listing by states of self-help craft groups in the Appendix of this catalogue.

Self-Imposed Tax on Celebrations: A Jewish Response to Hunger

The traditional Jewish response to blessing is to share it. It is this basic concept that triggered the beginning of Mazon, a new Jewish response to world hunger. Many American Jews are voluntarily putting a surcharge of three percent on celebrations such as weddings, bar or bat mitzvahs, birthdays and anniversaries, giving the money to Mazon.

A program still in its infancy, Mazon is already a great success. Leonard Fein, one of its founders and editor of *Moment,* a Jewish magazine, believes this idea struck a responsive chord among middle-to-upper class Jews who were looking for ways to share with others but needed a vehicle to do it. Estimates indicate that a minimum of $500 million per year is spent in North America on *simchahs* (celebrations), making Mazon's goal of $5 million a year a realistic one.

Giving something back to the world in gratitude for blessings—an idea with roots in the Jewish tradition—is a concept that Mazon's founders hope will catch on so that activities around celebrating and feeding the world's hungry are no longer seen as opposing each other. Mazon supporters also express the hope that churches and non-Jewish social organizations will adopt their idea of celebrating with conscience.

(Information on Mazon was taken from "A Jewish Response to the Hungry" which appeared in the *Los Angeles Times,* August 27, 1986.)

A Ministry With Scraps

For 25 years Wilma Watts Buchholtz made clothes for children she does not know. She created them out of remnants and scraps left from her regular sewing and from pieces others give to her. She then shipped the clothes to missionary friends or gave them to church clothes closets for nearby migrant camps. With creativity and resourcefulness she could make 40 or more children's outfits with materials bought with a $20 bill. One year, in response to the needs of farm workers in her community, she outfitted at least a dozen infants with gowns, diaper shirts and handmade quilts, besides making several stacks of children's clothes.

"The superfluities of the rich are the necessaries of the poor. Those who retain what is superfluous possess the goods of others."

St. Augustine

56

With five great-grandchildren to sew for, Wilma still sewed for her unknown friends. It delighted her to find just the right scrap of material to make a pretty piece of piping for a collar or unusual buttons on a worn-out blouse that added the perfect touch to a jumper. Each stitch and seam represented her gift of time, talents and loving concern for others. God has given everyone a gift—some can preach, some can sing, some can visit, and her gift was sewing. Wilma just sewed to the glory of God.

Lois B. Stone
Presbyterian Survey, March 1985

SOME ADVICE ABOUT GIVING TOYS

Toys ARE Us! A Parent's Perspective

The door before me opened soundlessly. But as I walked down the entrance hall, colors on the wall—geometrical patterns in vivid, angry colors—screamed at my senses. I rounded the corner to the display area and was completely overwhelmed by floor-to-ceiling shelves spilling over with merchandise for children. This was Toyland, 1986! My initial shock at the raucous enormity of the place was soon accompanied by nostalgia as I walked those aisles—remembering, with pleasure and pain, times when decisions about toys were an important part of my life, when the pulls between our children's programmed wants and our value-oriented perspective on their needs were often in conflict.

Certainly, my husband and I were not always successful in providing creative substitutes when we, with studied deliberation, questioned our children's wants. Specific toys were important cultural symbols in their world, and it was difficult to explain why we rejected those symbols. My brief visit to a toy store of the 80s convinced me that today's parents of young children face an even more difficult task. Giant shelves—stocked with violent dolls and grotesque monsters, along with perfect imitations of military and police weapons—included every imaginable accessory for creative destruction.

Those symbols of violence—even scaled down versions—gave off an oppressive, almost hallucinatory atmosphere. Children became "hyper" as soon as they entered the so-called "super action heroes" section. Their shrill screams of excitement could be heard throughout the store. Adults were affected, too. One mother walked up and down the aisles in a distraught state, lamenting loudly to anyone who would listen, "There's not a single puppet in the store! Can you believe it? Not a single puppet in the entire store!" That woman's anguished cry was real. And as I looked around me, her distress became mine. I realized that the absence of simple, creative playthings in that great toy

57

depository is not accidental. It is a fact that speaks with authority about today's world.

It is a lamentable truth that we feel surrounded by violence; we live in an atmosphere that not only tolerates but encourages violence. In television programming, movies and the print media—as well as current interpretations of America's role in the world—adults are surrounded by unspoken macho ideals like "might makes right" and "survival of the fittest," supported with military might. We are encouraged in insidious ways to deal with weakness in other people and with other countries from a position of strength and always with "our best interest" in mind.

It is alarming, but not surprising, how these ideas of power and domination have penetrated our children's world. As participants in those values, toy industries believe that self-interest dictates both their role to provide and their right to sell violent toys. And their profit indicators support their good business decisions. Since 1982 the sale of war toys has risen more than 500 percent! Adults must face the fact that it is not children who supply the toy industry with their profit margins; it is adults who buy for children.

Also, adults may be contributing to the violence factor for today's children by providing another disturbing wrinkle to this complicated mixture of children, toys and war games. It is possible that children who play violent war games are not simply victims of television advertising and an unscrupulous toy market. They also may be imitating adults with whom they live. This new phenomenon, The National Survival Game, is a complicated adult version of a child's game often referred to as Capture

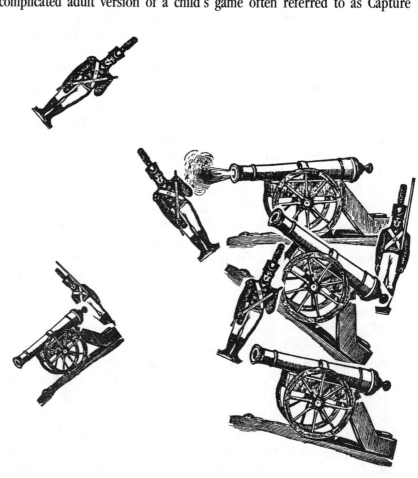

the Flag. Wearing camouflage trousers, jackets, gloves, heavy boots and often using face-masks, these weekend war-game players carry pistols whose pellets sting and raise welts, making it necessary to wear goggles. Players confess to getting hooked on the "adrenalin high" and "instinct toning" of a three-hour game, and many of them claim they have never felt so alive.

What does this mean? An admittedly simplistic analysis of these activities suggests that our society encourages adults to play like children and children to play like adults, with both groups using war games as a means for having fun. And on another level, national and international leaders also play at war with deadly games of "I dare you," in which nuclear holocaust—rather than the enemy's flag—is the prize of battle.

It may be a drastic leap in logic from the danger of war toys for our children and the specter of a nuclear holocaust. Unfortunately, the connection between the two may be more real than we want to believe. Today's adults and children are caught up in games that are far more frightening than those provided by the contents of shelves in a toy store. We have bought into our world leaders' obsessions with military solutions to people problems. And if we believe, with most child psychologists, that play is a child's work, we make our legacy to future generations when we decide to provide our children with up-to-date symbols of war. The values of our truculent, embattled society will become the norm for our children.

What can we do? To use words that come directly from war terminology, we can protect our children by providing them with a buffer zone—a "game against war" to which every thoughtful adult should be committed. But this means taking risks. We will certainly encounter the displeasure of our children if we interrupt their involvement with the symbols of their world. Even more than adults, children have difficulty trying to distance themselves from their culture. They are highly impressionable and easily conditioned to want what their friends have or what they see on television. Children who are allowed unrestricted exposure to mass-media hard sell—calculatingly and carefully designed by well-planned market research—are unlikely to want anything other than what they are told to want. Adults must assume some responsibility in determining when children's wants conflict with their needs.

Jesus once asked a question that may shed some light on this current dilemma with children. "Which one of you, if your child asks for bread, would give a stone? Or if he asks for a fish, would give him a scorpion?" We know the answer: no loving adult would feed a hungry child on a diet of stones and scorpions. But what is a parent to do if a child asks for a Voltron, a Gobot or a Rambo doll? We believe that responsible, loving parents will refuse to feed a child's hunger for play on a diet of violence and savagery.

Each Christmas we are faced with questions about gift-giving. What do we give our children? What is appropriate for celebrating the birthday of the Prince of Peace? With that as a point of reference, some disciplined thinking about creative substitutes for violent toys is certainly in order.

Rachel Granger Gill
Ellenwood, Georgia
Reprinted from *Alternatives Newsletter*
Fall 1986

On Buying Toys For Your Children

1. The best toys for your children, whatever the children's ages, are also those which are the safest and cheapest, and which involve a child in active, constructive play, rather than as a passive observer. To this end, avoid:

–*Any* toy that is battery operated.

–Cheap plastic toys. They're dangerous to your child's health.

–*Any* toy that is advertised on television with the message that it will make the child the "best," "fastest," "most popular," or "with the most friends" of any kid on the block.

2. Remember that adults have never invented a toy which can promote a child's growth as much as a toy created by the child himself or herself from materials which he or she has found around the home or neighborhood.

3. Remember, too, as you are barraged by commercial messages from the toy makers, that *no* toy can substitute for even a few minutes of warm, loving and supportive interaction between a child and his or her parent(s).

Dr. Michael B. Rothenberg
Professor of Psychiatry and Pediatrics
School of Medicine, University of Washington
Seattle, Washington

(Reprinted from "Values Through Toys," a brochure from The Peace Resource Center of San Diego, 5717 Lindo Paseo, San Diego, California 92115, 619/265-0730. Used by permission.)

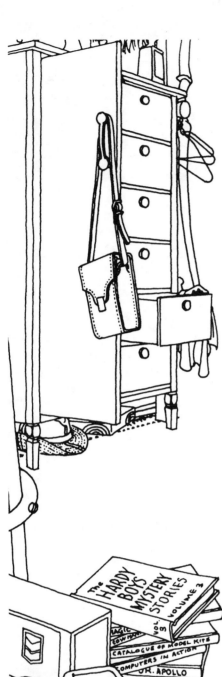

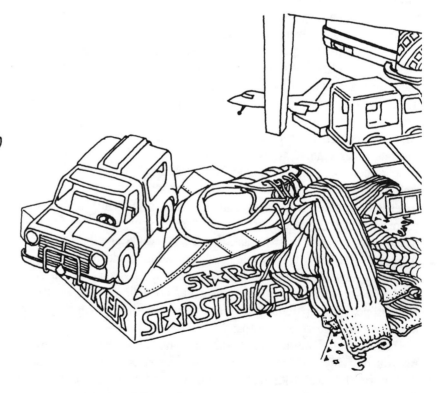

Questions To Ask Before You Buy Toys

Since there are so many violence-oriented toys today, it is impossible to list all of them by name or manufacturer; therefore, one might follow these principles or guidelines in selecting toys:

1. Look the toy over carefully and think about its purpose. What will the child be learning or imitating by using this toy?

2. Read the packaging! What is the attitude toward life promoted by this toy?

3. What is the toy's play value? Can it be used again and again in a variety of ways? Is it appropriate for this child's age level? Will it isolate the child in play or assist the child in social development?

4. Does it help the child to develop imagination without being lost in a world of overwhelming fantasy?

5. Does it assist the child in learning to cope with and bring order to the real world?

6. Would I feel comfortable involved in the child's play with this toy?

7. Are the concepts presented by the toy appropriate for a child?

8. Does the toy promote some kind of values? Does it promote concern for fellow humans? Does it promote concern for the earth? Does it allow for the development of values? Is it in tune with what I want my child to grow up to be?

> Mary Pliska
> Toy Project
> Wichita Falls, Texas

SOME OF THE BEST CHRISTMAS GIFTS

In the weeks before Christmas, our society goes into a shopping frenzy to find just the right gift—or any gift at all—for the people on our Christmas gift lists. Last year Americans spent more than $30 billion on gifts alone. Where is this consumption mania leading us?

Each year Alternatives pokes fun at the excesses of commercialized Christmas with a Best and Worst Christmas Gift Contest that receives nationwide press coverage. Winners receive a monetary gift contributed in their names to the nonprofit humanitarian organization of their choice. Contact Alternatives for more information about this contest.

The following are some of the best contest entries we have received over the years.

A Whole Week of Sewing

As a Christmas gift my mother gave me a week of sewing. Even though I enjoy sewing, my job requirements are such that I have little time to do it. I waited until August when the children needed new school clothes to use my mother's Christmas gift. Then we sewed together: I did the machine work and she did the handwork, pinning, and pressing. While I was at work, she ran errands and did chores so that when I was home we could concentrate on sewing. It was a wonderful gift. It meant so much to me because it was a gift of herself.

> Nancy Angerer
> Champaign, Illinois

A House Gift in Nicaragua

As their Christmas gifts to my sister and me and our families, my parents made a contribution to Habitat for Humanity. In our names, they gave enough money to enable this organization to build a house in Nicaragua. Since his retirement, my father has been volunteering on these house-building projects in the area where he lives and knows the

61

value of providing shelter for homeless and needy people. My parents could not have chosen a more wonderful gift to show their love for us and our families.

Karen L. Weidenheimer
Carson, California

Backrub Coupons: A Healing Gift

My sons, ages 14 and 16, gave me an unusual gift last Christmas. It was a "coupon" for three 5-minute backrubs per month, per boy. In other words, one-half hour of relaxation per month for me.

My life is very hectic, sometimes chaotic. I also have chronic back problems, the result of a childhood accident and genes. Their gift was marvelous for two reasons. First, it relaxes me and soothes my pained back. Second, it provides the two of us with undivided time. If nothing is on either of our minds, the backrub is only a physically healing event. But if there is something important to be discussed, the contact is there. That means the backrub may be over in exactly five minutes, or the conversation can last for an hour or more.

Virginia E. Stevens
Asheville, North Carolina

Michigan Mother Sees Ailing Son in Tennessee

My son has cancer. Three days before Christmas my relatives gave me a trip from my home in Michigan to my son's home in Tennessee so that we could spend Christmas together. Because I am disabled and live on a fixed income, I had not been able to see him in three years. It was the happiest, and saddest, Christmas ever.

Lavonda Teboe
Ypsilanti, Michigan

Family Trivia: Make a Game of It

The Drey family organized a family trivia game. Each member came to the family Christmas celebration with 20 trivia questions written out on index cards with answers written on the back. The questions were shuffled all together. Then, one by one, family members drew a card and tried to answer the question.

Since I am newly related by marriage, it was a wonderful way for me to get to know the family. Plus, it provided lots of laughs, a few tears and a general bonding of family members as the past was remembered and enjoyed. This was the best gift I received for Christmas last year!

Janet Drey
Des Moines, Iowa

Busy Mother's Gift: Christmas Day Out of the Kitchen

The best gift I received last Christmas was given by a wonderfully thoughtful son and daughter-in-law. To understand why it meant so much to me you need to know that I have been the wife of an Episcopal priest for some thirty years and have raised four children, now joined by two grandchildren.

Christmas for me has meant, in addition to the usual family activities and responsibilities, assisting wherever needed with the Christmas services. Since we could not be away from church at Christmas we also entertained all four grandparents, necessitating extra cleaning, cooking, preparing sleeping accomodations, etc.—all of this while coping with excited children. Christmas day, while wonderful in its own way, has always been hectic for me.

Last year our son and daughter-in-law, who live about fifty miles away, approached me some weeks before Christmas with the suggestion that I take the day off. Their proposal included planning, shopping for, preparing, and serving all the meals on Christmas day for all of us, as well as cleaning up afterwards. I was told to stay out of the kitchen all day. They arrived on Christmas Eve with baskets and bags containing everything from home-made coffee cake for breakfast to turkey for dinner, along with all the table decorations for a festive day. Needless to say, I had the most enjoyable holiday ever.

> Jean Carson
> Hillsboro, Ohio

Grandma's Cross-Stitch

My best Christmas present was made by my oldest granddaughter. At age nineteen she designed and created an original modern sampler. Embroidered in the tiniest cross-stitches in Old English black letters is the word "Grandma" on a white background. Over each letter are little figures of my 12 grandchildren (ages 6-19) done in the same tiny cross-stitching, each in a pose depicting his or her interest—diving, dancing, playing soccer, gymnastics, drama, gardening, relaxing. The little figures are embroidered in different colors atop the letters of "Grandma." Even the children's hair is their true coloring.

The four families live great distances from me so having this lovely picture on my kitchen wall is a wonderful and constant reminder of each of them.

Anne B. Macosky
Hamden, Connecticut

Surprised by Love Notes

Christmas was a fun-filled day with loved ones, children, grandchildren and great grandchildren in my home. After goodbyes were said, they all left for their homes in distant places. What I didn't know is that they had written and hidden little love notes for me that I found over the next weeks. Those notes made me feel loved and needed. This was my best Christmas.

Mrs. Edward Schreur
Orange City, Iowa

Vintage Video

My husband found an old film in my mother's attic. Covered by years of dust and discarded clothing, it proved to be the movies of my parent's wedding in 1932. He took it to a lab where he had it titled and turned into a video tape with background music. This was my Christmas gift, a gift beyond price, and better than the finest store could provide.

Anne M. Coyle
Fort Washington, Maryland

SERRV
Self-Help Handcrafts
P.O. Box 365
New Windsor, MD 21776
(301) 635-6464, ext. 189

SERRV Self-Help Handcrafts

HANDS...theirs, ours, yours...hands working together to weave the fabric of human justice.

Hands creating...earning the dignity of self-sufficiency.

Ecumenical hands choosing... selling handcrafts made by struggling people.

SERRV, an economic development program of the Church of the Brethren, provides a fair market for producers in nearly 40 countries.

Send $3.00 to order your catalog or write for information.

Carver—McKean Leprosy Rehabilitation Institute

An Open House for Christmas Breakfast

For several years two friends have opened their home and hearts to folks who have lost a loved one and are alone on Christmas morning. They felt that people are usually included in gatherings later in the day, but Christmas morning can be very lonely and a difficult time of day to get through.

They invite acquaintances from past years and anyone they find who will be alone to share breakfast in their home. They make them welcome with a breakfast of pancakes and sausage served by a warm fire, making a lonely time of the day comfortable and friendly.

I lost my husband four years ago and have no children to spend time with at Christmas. I will never forget that first invitation. Each year they call with another invitation which I accept with great pleasure. They give much more than breakfast.

Blanche Buchter
Lancaster, Pennsylvania

Crafts and creative alternatives in Central America. Nonprofit. Cooperatively produced cashews from Honduras, exquisite Guatemalan weavings, handmade clothing, blankets. Handmade furniture, hammocks from Salvadoran refugees, children's goods, gifts.

Free Catalog

Name_____

Address_____

City_____

State & Zip_____

Pueblo to People
1616 Montrose Blvd #5606
Houston, TX 77006
(713) 523-1197

FREE CATALOG
1-800-843-5257 Ext. 5606

Pueblo to People
A Non-profit Organization
1616 Montrose
Houston, TX 77006
(713) 523-1197
1-800-843-5257

The Desert Homestead

ALL HANDCRAFTED AND DIRECT FROM OUR CRAFTS PEOPLE

Hickory Rockers and Stools, Wooden Toys, Quilted items, Baskets, Woven Rag Rugs, Stuffed Animals, Pottery, Soap, Jams, Applebutter, Herbal Teas, Stone-ground Flour and so much more.

3 miles South of Loudonville, Ohio off of State Route 3.
On site with Pine Run Grist Mills.
Consignments and/or inquiries welcome.

The Desert Homestead
c/o the Family McCardel
3175 State Rt. 3
Loudonville, OH 44842

Koinonia Partners
Americus, GA 31709

Koinonia, established in 1942, is an experiment in meeting human need. Right now about 75 people are living on 1400 acres of Georgia red clay, swamp, and forest—permanent residents, children, and volunteers who have come together in varying degrees of involvement in fellowship and work.

Koinonia Partners is committed to living out the radical teachings of Jesus: peace, kindness, sharing, and simplicity. Friends around the world have supported us in our ministry over the years through the purchase of quality pecan and peanut products. We will be happy to send you more information about our life and work.

Friends of the Third World
National Resource Center
611 West Wayne Street
Fort Wayne, IN 46802

FRIENDS OF THE THIRD WORLD, INC

Be part of an International Alternative Trading Network

Natural Soap
from Bangladesh

Clothing
from Guatemala

Arabica Coffee
from Tanzania

Wild Lake Rice
from Minnesota

**Products at Fair Prices from Producer
Cooperatives in Latin America, Asia and Africa**

• Organize a Third World Shoppe or Fundraising Project
• Attend the Annual ATO National Conference
• Send for Catalogs of Food, Crafts or Books
• Be a Volunteer Sales Representative

Since 1972

**611 West Wayne Street
Fort Wayne, IN 46802-2125
(219) 422-1650**

Our 15th Year

We are a nonprofit membership group. Join Today.

©1987 Friends of the Third World, Inc.

66

Development through Fair Trade

Despite their poverty craftspeople from Turkey, Bangladesh, Bolivia, the Philippines, Guatemala, Paraguay, Thailand and many other third world nations are united in hope. Their mutual struggle for self-sufficience through craft production has revived their innate dignity and self-respect.

Third World Handarts helps destitute craftspeople to help themselves through dignified labor. A non-profit organization, we provide an essential marketing outlet for handcrafts made by thousands of people who have no other source of income. In light of the inequitable distribution of our world's resources and of the need for human interdependence, Third World Handarts' promotion of person-made crafts tangibly stimulates personal growth through the judicious use of human energy and creativity. Hand art production is labor-intensive. Because it requires few tools other than the artisan's own hands and creativity, it affords those who have the least with the opportunity to earn a just wage through meaningful, life-sustaining employment.

HANDARTS ARE AVAILABLE YEAR-ROUND:

* AT OUR GIFT SHOP

* AT CONSIGNMENT SALES THROUGH CHURCHES
  (write for info on how you can sponsor a sale)

* THROUGH THE ADOPT-A-CO-OP PROGRAM
  (write for info on this wise use of your tax-deductible donations)

* THROUGH MAIL ORDER
  ($1.00 requested for our current catalog)

Third World Handarts
465 N. Anaheim Blvd., Orange, CA 92668
(714) 634-1685

Third World Handarts
465 N. Anaheim Blvd.
Orange, CA 92668

67

Heifer Project International

You'll Love the Good it Gives

Headquarters:
P.O. Box 808
Little Rock, AR 72203
(501) 376-6836

Northeast:
R.R. 1, Box 174-A
Rutland, MA 01543-9761
(617) 886-2221

Mid-Atlantic:
P.O. Box 188
New Windsor, MD 21776
(301) 635-6161

Southeast:
159 Ralph McGill Blvd., NE
Atlanta, GA 30308
(404) 659-0002

Great Lakes:
P.O. Box 767
Goshen, IN 46526
(219) 642-3096

Great Plains:
P.O. Box 4527
Topeka, KS 66604
(913) 267-3818

South Central:
P.O. Box 808
Little Rock, AR 72203
(501) 376-6836

Rio Grande:
9400 N. Central Exp.
L.B. 123
Dallas, TX 75231
(214) 373-4343

Northwest:
P.O. Box 126
Ceres, CA 95307
(209) 537-8996

Southwest:
P.O. Box 1968
Whittier, CA 90609
(213) 693-7757

Give a Living Gift

Show your love to family and friends and give hope to the hungry of the world.

Heifer Project International is an interfaith, nonprofit organization dedicated to alleviating hunger by helping low-income families in the U.S. and around the world to produce food for themselves and their communities. For over four decades, Heifer Project has been providing livestock and the training to needy rural families in 107 countries.

Each family that receives an animal agrees to pass on one or more of the offspring to a needy neighbor. In this way, the helpless become the helpers and receivers become givers and a hunger-breaking cycle is begun.

You give hope to the hungry and honor loved ones on special occasions by giving a "living gift" in their name.

How Your Gift Helps

$1 . . . . . . buys a day-old chick or duck. $10 . . . buys a beginning flock.
$25 . . . . . buys a package of bees that quickly multiply to several hives.
$60 . . . . . buys a trio of rabbits which can produce 150 lbs. of inexpensive meat each year.
$75 . . . . . buys a local goat in Honduras.
$150 . . . . buys a goat that gives a half-gallon of milk a day, or a sheep that grows wool for warm clothes, or a mother pig that produces up to two tons of pork a year.
$200 . . . . buys a superior buck, ram or boar to assure continuation of top-quality offspring.
$300 . . . . provides a draft ox for a farmer in Ethiopia or starts an aquaculture project that produces fish, an inexpensive source of protein.
$900 . . . . pays for a heifer that gives five gallons of milk a day, plus a calf every year.
$1000 . . . supports an animal technician for a month.

Heifer Project International

You'll Love the Good it Gives

Headquarters — P.O. Box 808 • Little Rock, Arkansas 72203

Call 1-800-442-0474

**Honor a loved one and at the same time send a gift of life to a family in need. Give your love where you'll love the good it gives.
Give us a call.**

GIFTS THAT GIVE TWICE.

The purchase of a gift from SELFHELP Crafts does more than brighten the day for someone close to you. It brightens the prospect of self-sufficiency for a needy artisan far away.

The sale of SELFHELP Crafts in North America provides vitally needed income for some 30,000 craftspeople in 30 developing nations.

SELFHELP Crafts are sold at over 70 shops listed in the state-by-state list on pages 219–223. And through display sales hosted by church and civic groups.

Call or write for information on how to sponsor a SELFHELP Crafts sale in your community. Wholesale inquiries are also welcome.

 Crafts

SELFHELP Crafts
Department A
704 Main Street
Akron, PA 17501
(717) 859-4971

Mountain Maid
Self Help Project

Fermathe, Haiti

EMBROIDERED CLOTHING
NO IRON LINENS
USEFUL/DECORATIVE WOOD
MUCH MORE

Send for a copy of our Mail Order Catalog. Please enclose $3.00 to cover costs and postage.

U.S. Forwarding Address:
Mountain Maid
Box 15650
W. Palm Beach, FL 33416

Haiti's Best Values

An Outreach of the Baptist Haiti Mission

Mountain Maid
Box 1386
Port-au-Prince, hAITI

U.S. Forwarding Address:
Box 15650
West Palm Beach, FL 33416

69

Habitat for Humanity International
Habitat and Church Streets
Americus, GA 31709

Join the grass-roots movement to end poverty housing!

Habitat for Humanity International, a nonprofit Christian housing ministry, works in partnership with poor people throughout the world to improve their inadequate shelter by building simple, decent houses and selling them with no-interest mortgages.

This Christmas — or anytime during the year — give the gift of shelter in honor of family and friends. Habitat for Humanity will send a full-color card to the person or persons you choose. To the right are the approximate prices of supplies for homes built in the U.S. and overseas.

United States		Overseas	
10 Blocks	$10	10 Bricks	$5
Window	$50	Window	$20
Toilet	$50	Latrine	$125
Door	$60	Door	$40
Wall	$60	Wall	$50
Paint	$120	Paint	$50
One Room	$350	One Room	$200
Floor	$600	Floor	$100
Roof	$2,500	Roof	$500
Foundation	$3,000	Foundation	$265
House	$25,000	House	$2,500

Please specify whether you want us to send a Christmas card, memorial card, or all-occasion card.

 HABITAT FOR HUMANITY
INTERNATIONAL

Enclosed is my gift of $_____ ($5 minimum). ☐ *Christmas card*
☐ *Memorial card _____ (deceased)*
☐ *All-occasion card _____ (occasion)*

_____
TO (PLEASE PRINT)

_____
ADDRESS

_____
CITY/STATE/ZIP

_____
FROM

_____
ADDRESS

_____
CITY/STATE/ZIP

If you wish to honor more people, please enclose a list with their names and addresses typed or printed legibly. All gifts are tax deductible.

☐ *Please send more information about how I can become a Habitat partner.*

Make check payable to: Habitat for Humanity International, Inc. and send with this order form to Habitat and Church Streets, Americus, GA 31709.

AC

4.
Food and Celebrations

Food has been an important part of celebrations for people of
various cultures and religions from earliest times to the present.
Museum exhibits of ceremonial bowls and goblets used by the ancient
Greeks; Latin writings describing Roman banquets; religious documents
giving instructions for feasts and festivals; traditions of native Americans
for sharing meat from the hunt—these are reminders that festive food
has been an integral part of celebrations throughout history.

The Bible includes accounts of many special meals; in fact, food is a
recurring theme in scripture. In the story of the prodigal son, the
"fatted calf" is killed and prepared for his homecoming feast. And when
Jesus becomes aware that the time of his arrest and death are near, he
makes careful preparations for one last intimate sharing of the Passover
meal with his disciples.

For twentieth-century North Americans, as well as for those living in
other times and places, food and celebration seem to go together. Even
a casual look at most bookstores' cookbook sections or a glance at space
given to describing holiday meals in newspapers and magazines will
reveal the keen interest our culture takes in food. Special meals for
national, religious or family celebrations add variety and zest to our
daily routine. They afford opportunities to share family anniversaries, to
recognize important events, to affirm or to comfort a family member or
friend, to increase our understanding and enjoyment of many holidays.

How can we emphasize the creative and joyous aspects of celebrations
and avoid both the anxiety of having everything "just right" and the
extravagance of preparing and eating foods that are too rich and too
expensive? In this chapter we will suggest some answers to these
questions and will include some hints, menus and recipes to help you
follow the suggestions.

1. **Share responsibility.** Invite members of the household to take
part in planning, shopping, preparing and serving a special meal. This
change from a pattern of assuming that one person, usually the wife
and mother, will do it all may not be easy. Sometimes the person

usually responsible likes being in charge and feels threatened by having others do her/his jobs. Conversely, members of the household may not want to take on additional tasks. But if planning is done far enough ahead, if new ideas are considered, if there is some choice about who does what and when and if a team spirit can be developed, then sharing responsibility is more plausible. The investment of time and energy into this kind of joint planning and job sharing is worthwhile because it can yield exciting dividends.

The first dividend goes to the one who has customarily taken responsibility for the meal. That person will be less tired, less anxious, less resentful and, therefore, more able to enjoy the celebration. The Best Christmas Gift of 1985, in a contest sponsored by Alternatives, went to a woman who is a mother, grandmother, minister's wife and annual hostess of her large family's Christmas dinner. A few weeks before Christmas her son and daughter-in-law notified her that their gift to her would be a "Kitchen-Free Day" on December 25th. They planned, shopped for, prepared, served and cleaned up breakfast, lunch and dinner for the whole family. On that day she did not feel torn between duties at the church, visiting with family and friends and kitchen tasks. She was a guest in her own dining room.

The second dividend goes to the children and adults who help with the meals. Because they are involved from the beginning, they are spared those vague feelings of guilt about one person "slaving over a hot stove;" they share credit for the results—especially their own dishes—and feel more a part of the festivities. Talents might be discovered and later tapped for regular family meals.

The third dividend goes to the guests. They join wholeheartedly in a celebration atmosphere where nobody seems worn out or uptight. In the rush and strain of daily routines, the gift of a leisurely visit with friends is enjoyable and renewing.

Another way of sharing responsibility for a meal is by asking those coming to bring part of the food. This can be a true potluck, with guests bringing whatever they like, or a planned potluck, where each guest is asked to bring one part of the meal (salad or vegetable, etc.). Or, the hostess or a committee can ask each guest to bring a specific item—for example, a broccoli casserole—and will furnish a recipe if that is desired. One real advantage of a meal where guests bring part of the food is that participants share the expense as well as the work.

Gifts of food can be a part of special occasions in many ways other than meals at home. A gift of food, especially a favorite recipe, can be taken to the celebrant for a special occasion. If the person is a friend of the family, preparation of the food can be a joint endeavor. Church and neighborhood groups traditionally take food to bereaved families, an effort that is really helpful and received with gratitude. Members of the North Decatur Presbyterian Church in Decatur, Georgia, have a tradition of packing goodie-filled Valentine boxes for students away at college.

2. **Work ahead.** The most crucial step in arranging food for celebration is planning. First, choose a workable, affordable menu. Divide up such tasks as shopping, advance preparations and cooking on the day of the event. Children enjoy making table decorations if they are not rushed and if they are allowed to use their own creative ideas. They are also tireless helpers for a cookie-making project, but the project supervisor must be sure to allow enough dough for preparty sampling! Members of the household with demanding work schedules can make cook-ahead dishes like breads, desserts or salads, and they can prepare ingredients for dishes to put together later (shell and chop nuts, cut up dried fruits, prepare raw vegetables). Advance preparation frees the kitchen from last-minute congestion, allowing family members and guests to enjoy each other in a more leisurely manner.

3. **Keep it festive but simple.** Set a festive table with attractive mats or tablecoth, a pretty centerpiece of cut flowers or a bowl of fruit and a special card or gift for the guest of honor. Have an eye for color—parsley, cocktail tomatoes or pimento are pleasing garnishes. Serve the food in bowls and platters different from those used every day. Keep the meal simple by serving fewer dishes. Even for a party meal a hearty main dish, fresh vegetable, salad, bread and light dessert are enough. Prepare a sufficient quantity of each dish. Try new recipes, but include some familiar ones, especially if there are children in the group. If those who share the feast leave the table feeling pleased and satisfied, but not "overstuffed," those who prepared the meal deserve to be complimented.

Some meals are fun to eat! Set up your own Salad Bar, Rice and Toppings, Potato Bar or Pocket Bread Sandwich Bar. Look at the section on Menus in *Simply Delicious* and *More-with-Less Cookbook.* Young people seem particularly pleased with food they put together themselves.

In the spring of 1980 the moderators of the then two main branches of the Presbyterian Church were to join in leading worship at Second Presbyterian Church in Richmond, Virginia. The hospitality committee wanted to plan a time following the service when members of the congregation and visitors could greet the moderators. It was not feasible to serve a regular meal unless a sizable number of people missed the church service for kitchen duties. The committee came up with a plan

**"O God,
To those who have hunger
Give bread;
And to us who have bread
Give hunger for justice."**

73

that worked out very well. A large quantity of rice was prepared ahead of time in the church kitchen. Members of the congregation were asked to bring any kind of vegetable, meat, fish or cheese sauce that would combine well with rice. Those unable to prepare a cooked sauce were asked to bring peanuts, raisins, coconut or other toppings. The pastor of one of the congregations in the city opened his remarks of appreciation for the event by saying, "We Koreans like rice!" That was a plus for the menu that the committee had not even considered. Since rice is a staple in so many parts of the world, it is a good choice for meals prepared for people from other countries.

4. **Invite others to share the meal.** In planning a dinner for Thanksgiving, Christmas or any special occasion let members of the household suggest persons they would like to invite: foreign students, friends who have no family members nearby or persons they have met from the church shelter. For a birthday dinner, a child might want to include a scout master, church school teacher or a new friend from school. For a wedding anniversary a couple might want to invite friends who attended them or the minister who performed the ceremony.

Each Christmas I enjoy thinking of friends who joined our family celebration in past years and of the special contributions each made to the occasion. I recall:

• A young couple from Kenya, students in Louisville, Kentucky, were away from their families at Christmas for the very first time. They good naturedly played a game of shuffleboard on the front walkway with our four children.

• A mother and two young children wore traditional Japanese dress for our special celebration. They spoke no English and we spoke no Japanese. Fortunately, a cousin visiting from Chicago acted as interpreter. When my husband asked the little boy if he would like more turkey, the question was repeated by the cousin to the mother, by the mother to the son who said one word in Japanese which must have been "Yes" because the plate was passed along with the cousin's very polite, "Yes, thank you very much."

• A couple from Lesotho, Africa and their four children were political refugees. The father had to flee for his life in the middle of the night when government soldiers shot into his house and ordered him to come out. It was not until the next morning that the wife discovered that one of the bullets had killed their little grandson. The family managed to escape to Kenya and from there came to the States for a rest. After dinner we sang carols around the pump organ. They sang in Sesotho and we in English, but the tune was the same. Then, with the mother beginning in a very high voice and the others coming in with different parts, they sang their beautiful national anthem. With great depth of feeling they sang this haunting song of a country from which they were exiles.

• A Japanese mother and three-year-old daughter decided on Christmas Eve to accept our invitation, if the father could come later when he had finished his duties at the hospital. One of our sons was at home for Christmas. He shared our loneliness for the other members of our family—children and grandchildren. When he heard about the guests, he perked up immediately. He went shopping to fill a small stocking and offered enthusiastic help in the kitchen. The visit from that family was our best Christmas present that year.

Children who grow up in families where guests from other countries and cultures are often in the home find it easy to relate to persons from different backgrounds. Money cannot buy the kind of educational experience that growing up with friends from different places provides.

Change IS Possible

Experiencing the beauty and variety of other cultures in their growing up years is a privilege not many adults can claim. But most of us are aware of a thread running through every culture: humanity's common need to celebrate—those occasions when we commemorate important events in our lives. A second commonality is a penchant to organize celebrations around good food and warm friends amid pleasant surroundings. As noted earlier, we have done it this way for centuries. But recent history tells us that millions of the world's people are in a constant struggle simply to survive. With this in mind it seems no longer appropriate to celebrate by imitating opulent, self-indulgent, Roman-style feasts.

It is not necessary, however, to give up celebrating in order to be sensitive, compassionate world citizens. However, celebrations that take into account the world's hungry people and the earth's finite resources demand discipline and commitment to ethical eating, and changing our style of living to consider all who inhabit the earth. If the way we live includes good habits in food buying and preparation on a daily basis, our festive occasions will be easier to plan and execute within the context of responsible living. And we will be rewarded for our efforts by nutritious meals that attest to our involvement with the world's hungry people and celebrations that are both life-giving and life-enriching.

Almost everyone agrees that certain changes in our diet may be to our benefit. Studies by the Senate Select Committee on Nutrition and the U.S. Department of Agriculture suggest that we should (1) consume fewer calories; (2) eat more fruits, vegetables and whole grains; and (3) eat less fat, especially saturated fats (butter, red meat, hard cheese) and cholesterol (animal products, egg yolks, ice cream). Doris Janzen Longacre in the *More-with-Less Cookbook* also urges avoidance of over-processed foods, convenience foods, large amounts of refined sugar and saturated fats. But change is difficult—or, at least, we think it is—and, oftentimes, we resist. Three statements are frequently made when new approaches to eating are discussed:

1. It is too time-consuming;
2. It's hard to find those ingredients;
3. The members of my family won't eat it.

So in recognition of these concerns, the recipes here take no longer than it would to corral the children, drive to a fast food place and get served. They are also short, easily followed and tasty.

Try to shop where there is an advantage to quantity buying, less packaging, fewer preservatives, a wide variety of whole grains, fresh fruits and vegetables and bulk herbs and spices. Family cooperation is sometimes achieved when each member helps in the planning and decision making. Those who accept responsibility for meals (husband, wife, children, etc.) have a better chance of success if there is a firm conviction about the benefits to be reached—better health, lower cost, greater satisfaction, more to share and happier memories!

Dare to experiment! Make a few changes at first. The daily papers and monthly magazines are full of practical suggestions for new dishes—pastas, stir-fries, frittatas, Oriental and Eastern vegetable dishes, quick

"We thank you much for bread to live, We thank you more for bread to give."

Robert Davis

breads, unfamiliar fruits (kiwi, papaya, mangoes), lentils, etc. Many communities have good farmers' markets and some have stores featuring "health foods." Even traditional grocery stores are becoming more responsive to demands for brown rice, rye flour, spinach noodles, bulgar wheat, pita bread, snow peas, carob candy and fresh pineapple.

Celebrations are more joy filled when, in conjunction with good fellowship and delicious, simple meals, we carry out commitments to conserve resources, share our bounty and follow good health practices.

Shopping

Good shopping habits trim the food bill, save time and help change eating patterns. First, get a cookbook that encourages thrift, good health and awareness of the world. Doris Janzen Longacre's *More-with-Less Cookbook* is a basic. Read it until you are saturated with the fact that what *you* do at the market and in the kitchen matters!

Think about meals as a testimony of faith, not just an act of survival. Enjoy planning, reading food ads, making a few new menus and thinking ahead so that meal time is a joy and a celebration.

Rearrange storage space so that buying and storing a few items in bulk is possible; for example, whole wheat flour, brown rice and a variety of pastas. Get rid of those things in your refrigerator that you have not used in weeks and stock bulk yeast, unflavored gelatin, fresh herbs (ginger, dill, mint), fresh fruits and green vegetables in the newfound space. Cut down on canned items which usually are heavily salted and sugared. Stock a few new spices on your pantry shelves. Try oregano, basil, thyme, rosemary and whole nutmeg. Buy spices loose at one tenth the price and keep them in small labeled bottles. I built a small shelf by the stove where spices can be easily seen and reached.

Find a store that caters to the "new you." Farmers' markets and health food stores are good sources for these foods. Or, if you live in an area where such markets are not available, ask your grocer to stock these items. Wherever you shop, do two things: (1) Make a list; and (2) Have an eagle eye for bargains.

Prepare for shopping by doing three things: (1) Read weekly food ads; (2) Mark "specials" that fit agreed-on standards (omitting Cool Whip, Jello, frozen pies—meat or sweet), sugared cereal, etc.; and (3) List items needed for selected menus. Do incidental shopping by keeping the list in your purse and stopping by the store when you are in that area. Be firm about steering clear of sections of the store that tempt you to binge on sugary doughnuts or to indulge in impulse buying. But be flexible enough to snap up a bargain.

Cooking

Experiment with stir-fry cooking. Children usually love it, especially if they can help. Try new soups—cheese broccoli, corn chowder, fresh spinach, gazpacho, or even cold fruit soups. Make enough for more than one meal.

Discover pasta salads, using raw marinated vegetables and a variety of salad dressings. Serve hot pasta with bits of beef or chicken; I have not served a whole beef roast in years. Chop fresh vegetables for a salad. Use homemade dressings which are cheaper and free of additives. Cut down on the number of different items on your menu—hot pasta, vegetable salad and fruit dessert are adequate and nourishing.

For dessert, try to stick with fresh fruit, simple puddings or healthful cookies. Find simple, reliable recipes for making a batch of cookies or a sheet cake on Saturday afternoon and hide it to use during the week. Breads are delicious but high in calories—presenting a problem for many, but they may be eaten sparingly. Hot breads with bran, nuts or raisins furnish protein and make an ordinary meal special.

New Kinds of Cookbooks

If we are looking for responsible kinds of cooking, we now have many alternatives to those put out by P.T.A.'s, Garden Clubs, churches or money-making groups. Health and world hunger organizations have prompted numerous individuals to publish cookbooks with specific ideas for changing diets while preparing attractive, wholesome meals. These books do more than present new recipes. They provide incentive to change by making us aware of the dangers of additives and preservatives, giving us a new appreciation for natural foods and enlisting us in the war against needless starvation in the world. Some of the books are general in nature, covering a range of foods and kinds of preparation. Others are specifically directed toward certain kinds of food, for instance, making mouth-watering desserts. All ages can profit from these exciting, challenging books. No one is too old to change or too young to begin right!

SUGGESTED COOKBOOKS

- *Better Than Store Bought* by Helen Witty and Elizabeth Schneider Colchie. New York: Harper and Row, 1979. $8.95, Paperback, 325 pages.
   A basic resource for those wanting to really cook "from scratch."
- *The Enchanted Broccoli Forest* by Mollie Katzen. Berkeley, California: Ten Speed Press, 1982. $11.95, Paperback, 307 pages.
   This is the second vegetarian cookbook which Ms. Katzen has written and illustrated in a delightful manner.
- *Fast and Natural Cuisine* by Susann Geiskopf and Mindy Foonay. Ashland, Oregon: Quicksilver Production, 1983. $8.95, Paperback, 255 pages.
   Vegetarian and seafood recipes which take less than 45 minutes to prepare and serve.
- *Flavors of Stony Point* by Deonne Barkley. Stony Point, New York: Stony Point Center, 1982. $3.50, Paper, 71 pages. (Order from Stony Point Booktique, Stony Point, New York 10980.)
   Contains family-size recipes based on nutritious and flavorful dishes served at the Stony Point Center, conference center of the Presbyterian Church (U.S.A.). Charmingly illustrated by the author, this book is a good choice for a wedding present or hostess gift.
- *Jane Brody's Good Food Book* by Jane Brody. New York: W. W. Norton and Company, 1985. $19.95, Hardback, 700 pages.
   A treasury of healthy eating by the Personal Health Columnist of *The New York Times*, this selection of recipes leans heavily toward carbohydrates.
- *Keep It Simple, Thirty-Minute Meals from Scratch* by Marian Burros. New York: William Morrow & Co., 1981. $3.95, Paperback, 386 pages.
   Burros is the award-winning food editor of *The Washington Post* and author of several cookbooks, including the best-seller *Pure and Simple*. This book includes a 40-page section on "Prepare-Ahead Mixes." The heart of the book is a 250-page section on "30-Minute Meals—Menus and Recipes."
- *Loaves and Fishes* by Linda Hunt, Marianne Frase and Doris Liebert. Scottdale, Pennsylvania: Herald Press, 1980. $6.95, Paperback, 168 pages.
   This attractive cookbook for children includes recipes for snacks, picnics and celebrations and also gives recipes from other countries. Many of the illustrations were drawn by children.
- *Moosewood Cookbook* by Mollie Katzen. Berkeley, California: The Ten Speed Press, 1977. $11.95, Hardback; $8.95, Paperback, 221 pages.
   Vegetarian recipes adapted from quantity recipes used in the

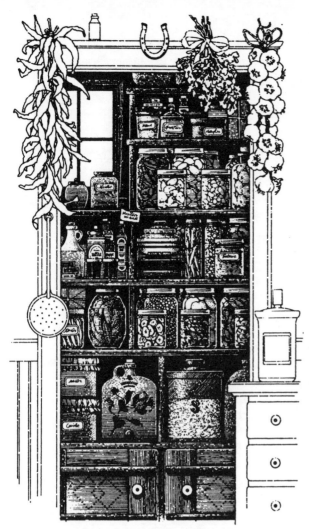

Moosewood Restaurant, Ithaca, New York. Charming illustrations and hand lettering by the author.

● *More-with-Less Cookbook* by Doris Janzen Longacre. Scottdale, Pennsylvania: Herald Press, 1976. $5.95, Paperback, 315 pages.

Includes a discussion of eating patterns in North America as compared with those in other parts of the world, a discussion of foods required for good health and suggestions about changes in our diets, as well as helpful charts and tables. Contains more than 500 practical and consistently good recipes in all categories.

● *Naturally Delicious Desserts and Snacks* by Faye Martin. Emmaus, Pennsylvania: Rodale Press, 1978. $16.95, Hardback, 408 pages.

The author bases dessert recipes in this book on her favorite traditional recipes. The 300-plus revised recipes contain no additives, artificial coloring or bleached white flour. The result is recipes for delicious and healthy foods.

● *Simply Delicious* edited by Grace Winn. Ellenwood, Georgia: Alternatives, 1983. $5.50, Paperback, 109 pages.

Designed especially for large church groups who want to reflect concern for world hunger and proper nutrition in their meals together, this cookbook contains more than 150 recipes to feed large groups.

● *Uncommon Fruits and Vegetables* by Elizabeth Schneider. New York: Harper and Row, 1986. $24.50, Hardback, 544 pages.

A common sense guide to using the new ethnic vegetables and fruits brought to us by recent immigrants from Asia.

"A healthy farm culture...nourishes and safeguards a human intelligence of the earth no amount of technology can satisfactorily replace."

Wendell Berry

79

RECIPES

Christmas Punch

1 large bottle (64 oz.) cranberry cocktail
1 quart ginger ale
1 large can (64 oz.) pineapple juice

Mix and serve over ice in punch bowl decked with holly boughs.

Crumb-Topped Fish

3 Tbs. plain bread crumbs
1 Tbs. butter
1½ Tbs. grainy mustard
Juice of ½ lemon
Salt and pepper to taste
1½ pounds fish fillets

Saute bread crumbs in butter briefly, then stir in mustard, lemon juice, salt and pepper. Let cool, then spread over top of fillets. Bake fillets at 350 degrees for 15 to 20 minutes or until fish flakes. Serves 4.

Green Beans in Hot Vinaigrette

¾ pound fresh green beans
1/3 c. chopped green onion
2 Tbs. snipped parsley
2 cloves garlic, minced
1 Tbs. red wine vinegar
1 tsp. Dijon-style mustard
3 Tbs. olive or cooking oil
Salt and pepper to taste

Trim beans. Cook green beans and onion, covered, in a small amount of boiling salted water 5 to 6 minutes or until crisp-tender. Drain vegetables well and return to saucepan. For sauce: In mixing bowl combine parsley, garlic, vinegar and mustard. Gradually add oil, stirring mixture with a whisk. Add dash salt and dash pepper. Stir until well blended. Pour sauce over vegetables in saucepan; heat through. Serves 4 to 6.

Oriental Stir-Fry of Celery and Turkey

1 c. brown rice
1 bunch celery (6 cups 1-inch pieces)
2 Tbs. cornstarch
2 tsp. sugar
1½ tsp. ginger
¼ tsp. garlic powder
¼ tsp. salt
Dash pepper
1½ c. chicken broth
3 Tbs. vegetable oil
2 c. diced, cooked turkey
½ c. roasted peanuts

Christmas Party for Neighbors
Christmas Punch
Spinach Dip with
  Raw Vegetables and
  Pumpernickel Bread
Fresh Fruit with Coconut-
  Honey Dip
Granola Snack
Peanut Butter Bars

Welcome Home Dinner
Continental Chicken Stir-Fry
  with Brown Rice
Lemon Glazed Carrots
Winter Fresh Fruit Salad with
  Winter French Dressing
Orange Muffins

Trim-the-Tree Party
Broccoli-Cheese Soup
Halloween Old-Fashioned
  Pumpkin Muffins
Peanut Butter Apple Bars

Thanksgiving Feast
Beef and Snow Peas with
  Noodles
Garlic-topped Tomatoes
Broccoli Salad
Six Weeks Bran Muffins

Spring Brunch
Sinful Scrambled Eggs with
  Tomatoes
Zesty Fresh Asparagus
Oatmeal Biscuits
Fresh Apple Cake with Honey
  Frosting

Cook rice while you prepare celery and turkey. Remove leafy tops from celery, wrap in plastic and refrigerate for use in soups or stews.

Wash and dry celery ribs and cut on the diagonal into 1-inch pieces. In a bowl, combine cornstarch, sugar, ginger, garlic powder, salt, pepper and chicken broth.

Heat oil in a large skillet or wok. Add celery and stir-fry until barely tender, about 7 minutes. Add turkey and stir-fry another minute or two. Add peanuts and stirred-up seasoned chicken broth. Cook and stir until mixture in skillet boils and thickens, about 1 minute. Serve over hot cooked rice. Serves 4.

Fruit with Honey Dressing

Dressing: Mix
½ c. honey
2 Tbs. lemon juice
1 Tbs. snipped candied ginger
1 Tbs. finely shredded orange peel

Peel four oranges and slice crosswise. Pour dressing over oranges and chill overnight. Drain. Save dressing. In a bowl arrange layers of orange slices, blueberries, melon cubes, sliced strawberries or any other fruit you choose. Pour remaining dressing over all. Top with whole strawberries, sliced kiwi or blueberries.

Garden Pasta Salad

1 c. salad dressing
¼ c. chopped parsley
1 tsp. dried basil leaves, crushed
1 garlic clove, minced
8 oz. natural cheddar cheese, cubed
2 c. broccoli flowerets, cooked
1 c. (4 oz.) tri-color corkscrew noodles, cooked, drained
2 medium tomatoes, cut into thin wedges
½ c. chopped walnuts (optional)

Combine salad dressing, parsley, basil and garlic; mix well. Add cheese, broccoli and noodles; mix lightly. Chill. Arrange tomatoes on platter; top with salad. Sprinkle with walnuts. Serves 6.

Herbed Avocado Spread

1 large avocado, seeded, peeled and pureed
½ c. butter or margarine, softened
3 Tbs. minced parsley
3 Tbs. minced chives
1 Tbs. minced fresh basil or 1 tsp. dried basil
4 tsp. lemon juice

Combine avocado with butter, parsley, chives, basil, lemon juice and season to taste. Blend until smooth. Makes about 1 cup.

Meal-on-a-Muffin

1 Tbs. peanut butter
1 English muffin, lightly toasted

New Year's Family Party
Crumb-Topped Fish
Green Beans in Hot
    Vinaigrette
Tabouleh
Stewed Fruit

Teenage "After Exams"
Celebration
Pizza Pita Sandwiches
Garlic Buttered Broccoli
Whole Wheat Brownies

Late Saturday Buffet
Whole Wheat Pancakes with
    Honey
Strawberries with Yogurt

Halloween Supper Party
Baked Potato with Hamburger
    Topping
Lettuce Salad with Italian
    Dressing
Apple-Oatmeal Bars

"Grandma's Here" Dinner
Herbed Chicken with
    Vegetables
Fruit with Honey-Lemon
    Poppy Seed Dressing
Ever-Ready Bran Muffins
Quick Fruit Cobbler

Saturday Clean-Up Day
Lunch
Frankfurter a la Reuben
Cabbage Slaw with Vinaigrette
    Dressing
Baked Pears

2 slices juice-packed pineapple rings, drained
¾ oz. cooked ham, halved
1 oz. low-fat yellow hard cheese, halved

Spread peanut butter evenly over each half of toasted muffin. Layer pineapple rings, then ham and cheese over peanut butter. Place under broiler until cheese has melted. (Microwave: high for 15 seconds.) Serves 1.

Pizza Pita Sandwiches

1 lb. ground turkey
½ c. chopped onion
1 clove garlic, minced
1 tsp. Italian seasoning
1 8 oz. can tomato sauce
1 2¼ oz. can sliced olives, drained
Salt to taste
3 large pita breads
1½ c. shredded lettuce
1 large tomato, chopped
¼ c. shredded mozzarella cheese

Brown turkey with onion and garlic. Drain any excess fat from skillet. Stir in Italian seasoning, tomato sauce and olives; cook for 5 minutes. Taste and add salt if necessary. Cut pitas in half, open to form pockets. Fill with shredded lettuce, spoon meat mixture over and top with chopped tomato and cheese. Serves 6.

Lemon-Glazed Carrots

1 lb. carrots
1 lemon
½ c. water
2 Tbs. sugar
2 Tbs. butter

Easter Brunch
French Onion Soup
Herbed Avocado Croissants
Fresh Fruit

Movie Night
Meal-on-a-Muffin
Carrots and Celery Strips
Oatmeal Cookies

Fourth of July Dinner
Meat Loaf
Zucchini and Corn
Bran Muffins
Fresh Sliced Peaches

Dad's Birthday
Broiled Chicken with Mustard
Quick Tomato Aspic
Fettucine with Asparagus
Ice Cream

Herald Press
Department ALT
616 Walnut Avenue
Scottdale, PA 15683

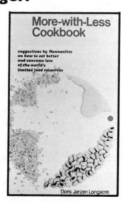

A cookbook that helps people respond to world hunger.

More-with-Less Cookbook
by Doris Janzen Longacre

". . . a large contribution to the store of knowledge on world hunger and what the individual can do to alleviate it."—U.S. Senator Mark Hatfield

Over 500 recipes from Mennonite kitchens and tested by professional home economists. Recipes from around the world as well as traditional favorites. Spiral-bound for easy use.

Order from your bookseller or from Alternatives. **$11.95** plus shipping
Herald Press, Dept. ALT, 616 Walnut Avenue, Scottdale, PA 15683

82

Trim, peel and quarter carrots into 3-inch lengths. Grate the rind, then squeeze the juice from lemon. Place the grated peel, juice, water, sugar and butter in a small saucepan. Bring the mixture to a boil, add the carrots. Simmer covered for 20 minutes; then uncover and continue cooking until the glaze is thickened. Serves 4.

Brunswick Stew a la Dorothea

1 chicken, whole or cut up
3 medium potatoes, chopped
3 medium onions, chopped
Water for cooking and/or chicken stock, if available
2 qts. tomatoes, home canned preferred

Simmer these ingredients together until chicken is almost done. If not enough flavor add several chicken bouillon cubes. Season to taste. Then add:
20 oz. package frozen lima beans
20 oz. package frozen corn

Simmer several hours. The stew seems to acquire more flavor if left overnight and reheated before serving. Thicken with potato flakes, if desired. Use care so stew doesn't stick. Stir frequently. Water may be added if necessary, especially if no stock is available. Serves 12-15.

These recipes were collected from and used by permission of the *Atlanta Journal and Constitution* and various individuals.

Summer Supper
Garden Pasta Salad
Oatmeal Muffins
Baked Apple with Raisins and
  Nuts

After Thanksgiving Party
Oriental Stir-Fry of Celery
  and Turkey
Brown Rice
Cranberry Sauce
Pineapple Sherbet

After Christmas Celebration
Sliced Turkey with Avocado
  Sandwich
Ratatouille
Make-Ahead Pumpkin Chiffon
  Pie

The Hunger Action Fund
■ Dealing with poverty through direct aid and development
■ Advocacy of responsible public policies at every level
■ Education and mobilization to alleviate hunger

**Hunger Action
  Coordination
United Church of Christ**
475 Riverside Drive
16th Floor
New York, NY 10115

83

United Methodist Committee on Relief
General Board of
   Global Ministries
475 Riverside Drive
New York, NY 10115

Miracles do happen

And that's what it takes –

a miracle to prevent 18 children from dying of hunger each minute

You can help through...

United Methodist Committee on Relief

If you gave to Oxfam America last year, here's your reward:

If not, here's your chance:

Find out how you can help the world's poor to help themselves.

Call today, toll-free:

800-225-5800

Please send for:
- Info on our color-photo notes and postcards
- Educational resources brochure
- Current issue of the *OA NEWS*

You can make a world of difference.

Oxfam America

Practical ways to help the world's poor.

Oxfam America
115 Broadway
Boston, MA 02116

513 Valencia Street
San Francisco, CA 94110

Please pass the potatoes

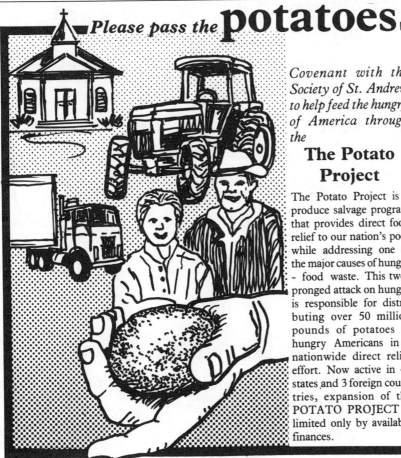

Covenant with the Society of St. Andrew to help feed the hungry of America through the

The Potato Project

The Potato Project is a produce salvage program that provides direct food relief to our nation's poor while addressing one of the major causes of hunger - food waste. This two-pronged attack on hunger is responsible for distributing over 50 million pounds of potatoes to hungry Americans in a nationwide direct relief effort. Now active in 47 states and 3 foreign countries, expansion of the POTATO PROJECT is limited only by available finances.

Society of St. Andrew
State Route 615
P.O. Box 329
Big Island, VA 24526
(804) 299-5956

Rural Crisis Issue Team
Domestic Hunger and
Poverty Project
NCC/Division of Church
and Society
475 Riverside Drive
Room 572
New York, NY 10115
(212) 870-2307/2308

RURAL CRISIS:
A call for Justice and Action

"AS A PEOPLE OF GOD, STRUGGLING TO BE HONEST TO THE CALL TO DISCIPLESHIP IN RURAL AMERICA AND ALL THE WORLD, WE HAVE PLEDGED OURSELVES TO HEED THE CALL FROM THE PEOPLE OF THE LAND."

DIVISION OF CHURCH AND SOCIETY

National Council of Churches of Christ in the U.S.A.

5.
January and February

NEW YEAR'S DAY: ENDINGS AND BEGINNINGS

The first day of the calendar year is celebrated as a holiday in almost every country. After the adoption of the Gregorian calendar in the 1500s, January 1 was generally recognized as New Year's Day in the western world. The Chinese, Egyptian, Islamic, Jewish and Roman years all begin at different times, but in every culture the first day is marked by special celebrations.

In ancient Rome there were occasions as early as 45 B.C. when New Year's Day was celebrated on January 1. Janus—the god of gates and doors, of beginnings and endings and for whom the month of January was named—was honored on that day. He had two faces; one looked ahead and one looked backward. On that day people looked back to the happenings of the past year and thought about what the coming year might bring. Comparative religions historian, Mircea Eliade, has observed that New Year rites in ancient societies were intended to abolish the past, so that creation could begin anew. In many societies heavy drinking on New Year's Eve was a personal reenactment of the old year's chaos that would give way to a recreated world in the new year.

In the fourth century, Christians of the Eastern Church began to observe the Feast of the Circumcision, a festival commemorating the circumcision of Jesus on the eighth day after his birth (cf. Luke 2:21). Its observance on January 1 was not established at Rome until the ninth century, over four centuries after December 25 had become the accepted date of Christmas. Its late introduction to the western calendar has been attributed to the unwillingness of the Roman Church to introduce a festival on a day already characterized as a day of rioting and drunkenness.

The old tradition of sweeping out the old year with excessive partying and drinking has persisted. The notion of "turning over a new leaf" for the New Year has also persisted, if often in very superficial terms. It is ironic that the idea of paying off one's debts before the end of the old year, so that the new year could be started debt free, has been reversed

★ **New Year's Day**
  (January 1)
★ **Emancipation Day**
  (January 1)
★ **Epiphany**
  (January 6)
★ **Martin Luther King Day**
  (January 15)
★ **Ground Hog Day**
  (February 2)
★ **Valentine's Day**
  (February 14)
★ **Day of Remembrance**
  (February 19)
★ **Lincoln's Birthday**
  (February 12)
★ **Washington's Birthday**
  (February 22)
★ **Purim**
  (February/March)
★ **Chinese New Year**
  (January/February)

by the use of credit cards and the commercialization of Christmas. Many now greet the new year burdened by their greatest indebtedness of the year.

In the spirit (but not the letter) of the writer of Ecclesiastes, "There is a time for frivolity, and a time for seriousness." Times for reflection and personal planning often seem to be casualties of the fast paced life in our consumer society. An extended Christmas vacation or a couple of days off for New Year may offer possibilities for some quiet time. Times for reflection and planning will not only enrich New Years' holidays but can also make a difference in the way we live the rest of the year.

New Year's Eve Watch Night Services

In 1770 "watch night" services on New Year's Eve were started by St. George's Methodist Church in Philadelphia. Designed to provide an alternative to secular New Year's Eve celebrations, watch night services are still observed in many churches. The evening may begin as a festival, but it always concludes at the midnight hour in contemplation and usually includes the observance of the Lord's Supper.

Reviewing the Old Year with Friends

On New Year's Eve, or sometime in the week between Christmas and New Year's Day, I join some of my friends to talk about the old year. Sometimes we watch one of the network, year-end news reviews and then talk about the major events. After reflecting on how we have been affected by the big events of the year, as well as other changes that have taken place in our personal and family lives, we also talk about our hopes for the new year. We joke about our New Years' resolutions, but this annual evening helps me keep things in perspective. It is also a way to reaffirm old friendships.

Unknown Contributor

New Year's Day

A rite for New Year's Eve or New Year's Day: Write down—with suggestions from family members—a very brief outline of outstanding events of the previous year. Make it personal, but be concise.

Decide on a storage place: desk, file cabinet or safety deposit box. We call our list "We Remember" and include births, deaths, graduations, marriages, employment changes, moves, etc., also losing friends or gaining new ones.

We borrowed this idea from the Pat Boone family back in the 60s, and it has given us a rich family history.

Era T. Weeks
Dunwoody, Georgia

EMANCIPATION DAY: HOPE FOR SLAVES

On January 1, 1863, President Lincoln issued the Emancipation Proclamation, freeing slaves in all areas claimed by the Confederate States. This Proclamation, however, did not change the status of slaves outside the Confederacy, nor did it have much immediate effect on slaves within the Confederacy, except to give them a glimmer of hope. It was almost three years later, on December 18, 1865, when the Thirteenth Amendment became law of all the land, that the complete abolition of slavery in the United States was finally achieved. Even that act was but one more step on the long road to realize the truth of the Declaration of Independence that "All [people] are created equal."

Emancipation Day provides an excellent opportunity to begin studies and activities on the history of Black people in the United States, culminating in special observances of the birth of Martin Luther King, Jr. on January 15.

Tabletalk for Emancipation Day

Talk about how important New Year's Day was for slaves in 1863. Someone, perhaps a child, can tell the story of Harriet Tubman, an escaped slave who brought more than 300 slaves to freedom by way of the "underground railroad." Offer a prayer of thanks for Harriet Tubman and all of those who worked to end slavery.

MARTIN LUTHER KING, JR.'S BIRTHDAY: THE DREAM LIVES ON

In 1985 Congress declared the birthday of Dr. Martin Luther King, Jr. a national holiday. Born January 15, 1929, and assassinated in Memphis, Tennessee, on April 4, 1968, Dr. King was recognized as leader of the Civil Rights Movement, a black-led nonviolent protest which brought about the passage of the Civil Rights Act of 1964. Dr. King was more than a civil rights leader. He called for the United States to live out its ideals of freedom and justice, whether in the arena of civil and economic rights for its own citizens or in foreign policy.

"Stony the road we trod,
bitter the chast'ning rod,
Felt in the days
when hope unborn had died;
Yet with a steady beat,
have not our weary feet,
Come to the place
for which our fathers sighed?
We have come over a way
that with tears
has been watered,
We have come,
treading our path thro'
the blood of the slaughtered,
Out of the gloomy past,
till now we stand at last
Where the white gleam of
our bright star is cast."

James Weldon Johnson,
"Lift Every Voice"

89

Because this new holiday enjoys widespread popularity, those planning Martin Luther King (MLK) Day activities are tempted to ensure that popularity by selective celebration: focusing on those things for which King is now publicly acclaimed and ignoring other less popular and less understood ideas for which he was often assailed. While his role in the Civil Rights Movement should be remembered and celebrated, so should his uncompromising stands on those peace and economic justice issues that were not so popular. Too much effort has been invested in getting this holiday recognized to allow it to degenerate into a day of platitudes about racial harmony. Make these celebrations important occasions for developing interracial solidarity in the continuing struggle for equal rights and economic justice for the world community.

> As we go with you to the sun,
> as we walk in the dawn,
> turn our eyes
> Eastward and let
> the prophecy come true
> Great God, Martin,
> what a morning that will be.
>
> From "A Letter to Dr. Martin Luther King"
> by Sonia Sanchez
> from *Graterfriends,*
> Vol. III, #1, Feb., 1985.

Family Celebration of Martin Luther King, Jr.'s Birthday

These are suggestions of how families can make Martin Luther King, Jr.'s birthday celebration on January 15 an important learning time through studying his life and listening to his words. These are activities in which most family members may participate.

1. TV SPECIAL/LISTEN TO TAPE. Plan a family time to watch a televison program about King's life or listen to a cassette tape of one of his speeches. Follow this event by a short discussion on what you have viewed and/or heard, carefully including the views of all age groups present. "I Have a Dream" is probably the best known speech and could lead to discussions about the kind of world family members imagine for the future.

Resources:
- Current television specials
- *Free At Last,* Gordy Records
- *Great March to Washington,* Gordy Records
- *A Knock at Midnight,* Creed Records

2. FAMILY READING. Spend family time reading a book about King's life and the Movement associated with him. Choose a reading level that young family members understand. Schedule enough time for discussion and encourage questions.

Resources:
- *Martin Luther King, Jr., a Picture Story* by Margaret Boone Jones, (Ages 4-8) Available through Alternatives Resource Center.
- *Martin Luther King, Jr.* by Beth P. Wilson. (Ages 8-10)
- *Stride Toward Freedom: The Montgomery Story* by Martin Luther King, Jr. (Ages 12 and up)
- *What Manner of Man: A Biography of Martin Luther King, Jr., 1929-1986* by Lerone Bennett, Jr. (Adults)

3. DRAMATIZE THE ROSA PARKS STORY. Recount and then act out the story of Rosa Parks, the courageous Montgomery, Alabama woman who refused to obey seating requirements for blacks on a city bus and started a revolution against segregation.

Resources:
- *Rosa Parks* by Eloise Greenfield (Ages 6-10)
- *Stride Toward Freedom: The Montgomery Story* by Martin Luther King, Jr. (Ages 12 and up)

4. FAMILY CONFLICT RESOLUTION. Nonviolent change was the cornerstone of Dr. King's philosophy and work. He believed in applying that concept to interpersonal conflict as well as to societal conflict. Developing a set of family rules on "fighting" nonviolently is one way to implement King's philosophy in our own families.

Resource: Learn four basic nonviolent communication skills helpful in family conflict resolution.

(1) Use the other person's name.

(2) Tell how you feel.

(3) Identify the problem.

(4) Tell what you want. Example: John, I really feel angry when you call me stupid. Please stop. (Taken from *Fighting Fair: Dr. Martin Luther King, Jr. for Kids,* produced by the Grace Contrino Abrams Peace Education Foundation, Inc., P. O. Box 19-1153, Miami Beach, FL 33119. This resource includes an 18-minute video, plus an excellent curriculum guide. $69.95 plus postage. A valuable resource for family ministry groups.)

5. POVERTY AND RACISM. It is important for privileged children to relate to those who are victims of poverty and racism. Put children into contact with people or groups who struggle to maintain their cultural identity or who publish materials fostering a sense of pride in their group as well as correcting misperceptions about themselves.

Resources: Plan family field trips to a minority run community center; a street festival in minority community; church services in minority community.

This section on family celebrations of the King holiday is provided and used by permission of:

Baptist Peace Fellowship of North America,
222 E. Lake Drive
Decatur, Georgia 30030
Ken Sehested, Director

"Compassion constitutes a radical form of criticism, for it announces that the hurt is to be taken seriously, that the hurt is not to be accepted as normal and natural but is an abnormal and unacceptable condition for humanness."

Walter Brueggemann

VALENTINE'S DAY: SWEETHEARTS AND PRISONERS

Like many holidays, the origins of Valentine's Day are shrouded in mystery and legend. While Valentine's Day is observed on the feast day of two Christian martyrs named Valentine, the origins of today's festival of romance and affection are probably linked to Lupercalia, an ancient Roman festival observed every February 15 honoring Juno, the Roman goddess of women and marriage, and Pan, the god of nature.

In 496 A.D. Pope Gelasius changed the date of Lupercalia to February 14 and renamed it Saint Valentine's Day, giving Christian meaning to a pagan festival. According to Christian tradition, there were two Saint Valentines. One, a priest who lived in Rome during the third century, was jailed presumably for aiding persecuted Christians and credited with curing his jailkeeper's daughter of blindness. Legend holds that on the night before his execution he gave the jailkeeper's daughter a note of affection signed, "Your Valentine." Another St. Valentine, bishop of Terni, was martyred in Rome in 273 A.D., supposedly for converting a Roman family to Christianity.

Little is known about the tradition of giving "valentines" before the fifteenth century when young people in England chose their valentines by writing names on slips of paper and then drawing them, by chance, from a vase. The practice of giving special Valentine notes of affection on this day has continued until the present. For the card, candy and flower industries, Valentine's Day is one of the more lucrative days of the year. Discovering alternatives to buying these prepackaged expressions of affection for lovers, relatives and friends is one of the fun challenges of Valentine's Day.

In recent years, there have been attempts to incorporate the tradition of the two original St. Valentines into what has become a festival of romance by including a focus on prisoners, prisoners of conscience and the criminal justice system. In some denominations, the Sunday nearest February 14 is designated "Criminal Justice Sunday." Without taking away from the importance of celebrating human relationships, this day can also be a time of learning about and remembering those in prison.

Human Rights: An Affair of the Heart

All over the world people are imprisoned because of their politics, beliefs, religion, ethnic origin or sexual preference. Torture is carried out in the name of national security. Executions, official and unofficial, are justified in the name of law and order. People considered dangerous to those in power are detained without trials, while others simply disappear.

IN GERMANY THEY CAME FIRST FOR THE COMMUNISTS;
I DID NOT SPEAK OUT BECAUSE I WAS NOT A COMMUNIST.
THEN THEY CAME FOR THE JEWS;
I DID NOT SPEAK BECAUSE I WAS NOT A JEW.
THEN THEY CAME TO FETCH THE WORKERS, MEMBERS OF THE TRADE UNIONS;
I DID NOT SPEAK BECAUSE I WAS NOT A TRADE UNIONIST.
AFTERWARD, THEY CAME FOR THE CATHOLICS; I DID NOT SAY ANYTHING BECAUSE I WAS A PROTESTANT.
EVENTUALLY THEY CAME FOR ME,
AND THERE WAS NO ONE LEFT TO SPEAK...
—MARTIN NIEMOLLER

92

When Valentine, on the eve of his execution, wrote a note of thanks to the jailer's daughter who had shown him kindness during his imprisonment and signed it "Your Valentine," he probably started the tradition of sending cards to loved ones on this day.

But St. Valentine's gesture had deeper meaning than an expression of personal affection. His life and death upheld the right of individuals to act according to their consciences and deeply-held beliefs, despite larger or higher national and political concerns. His action symbolizes the strength of human feelings and relationships as a source of resistance to injustice and depersonalization.

On Valentine's day we can celebrate the importance of relationships by demanding that those in power respect basic human rights:

- Write a letter of thanks to someone whose friendship has helped you to overcome the effects of a depersonalizing situation.
- Form a group to discuss possible human rights violations in your community. Raise questions about what constitutes a "human right." Have a copy of the Bill of Rights handy to help with the discussion.
- Invite someone from an organization like Amnesty International to explain how your group can encourage international consensus about acceptable standards for arrest, detainment and punishment.

Prison Bars Don't Stop Love and Appreciation

Grand Rapids, Michigan—One critic offered blunt and outspoken sentiment when Cascade Christian Church began its "Operation Open Hearts." "Valentines for a bunch of punk jailbirds? You've got to be kidding, Reverend. Why should we spend thousands of dollars assembling Valentine treats for those bums that have mugged, robbed, assaulted and murdered our neighbors and friends?"

But with most of the congregation, the idea of Valentine treats for the 650 inmates of Kent County Jail struck a responsive note. Since 1982, through Operation Open Hearts, the church has put together individual gift packages for each prisoner, including mixed nuts, candy, toothbrush and toothpaste, perfume for the women and shaving lotion for the men, a meditation card and two stamped Valentines for the prisoner's personal use. Each packet costs more than five dollars, and the total expense each year is more than $3,000.

The Kent County sheriff was somewhat reluctant about the whole idea initially. But things went so well the first year, he now welcomes the church with open arms. Inmates express time and again their appreciation for the congregation's thoughtfulness as lay chaplains hand the plastic bags through the bars. Thank you notes are in abundance. A note from the "girls on block two" reads: "God bless your congregation for thinking of us at Kent County Jail on Valentine's Day. Here, the days are long and uneventful and your gifts were like a breath of heaven."

Raymond Gaylord, *The Disciple.*
Journal of the Christian Church
(Disciples of Christ),
St. Louis, Missouri.
Used by permission.

DAY OF REMEMBRANCE: PAINFUL MEMORY

Celebrations are not always joyful. Like Memorial Day, past events are sometimes celebrated so that a particular past might not be repeated. The "Day of Remembrance" is such a day. Just three months after the Japanese bombed Pearl Harbor, President Franklin Roosevelt—in response to our nation's war hysteria—signed Executive Order 9066. This unprecedented act gave the army the power to arrest, without warrants or indictments or hearings, every Japanese American on the West Coast—110,000 men, women, and children. These Americans, three fourths of them born in the United States, were taken from their homes and transported to camps in the interior of the country where they were kept under prison conditions for more than three years. And they have yet to be reimbursed for property that was confiscated during this time of citizen disenfranchisement. In the September 1945 issue of *Harper's Magazine*, Yale Law Professor Eugene V. Rostow wrote that the Japanese evacuation was "our worst wartime mistake."

"...since justice is indivisible, injustice anywhere is an affront to justice everywhere."

Martin Luther King, Jr.

94

February 19, the Day of Remembrance, is observed by Japanese Americans and their friends with candlelight services. It is a good day for all Americans to remember.

Tabletalk on Remembrance Day

Remember the story of Japanese-American internment during World War II. Try to imagine what it would be like for you to be suddenly evicted from your home and placed in a concentration camp. Find out what attempts have been made to provide compensation to those who lost their homes and businesses. Decide if you want to write a letter to your Congressperson and Senators about this matter.

PRESIDENTS' DAYS: CELEBRATING POLITICAL LEADERSHIP

When the late Professor Arthur M. Schlesinger of Harvard University surveyed historians to rank the Presidents, they selected Lincoln and Washington as the greatest, in that order. Their birthdays are in the same month: Washington was born on February 22, 1732, while Lincoln was born on February 12, 1809. Washington's birthday is a federal holiday, observed on the third Monday of February. A legacy of ill will from the Civil War is the main reason why Lincoln's birthday is not a national holiday and why seventeen states do not recognize it.

The Presidents' Days offer an opportunity to remember two great Presidents and, in the process, to consider important qualities of political leadership. Getting beyond romanticized images of both men—considering their blind spots as well as their vision, their failures as well as successes—can be helpful in a needed reassessment of the role of the Presidency in this country.

PURIM: CELEBRATING SURVIVAL

First observed in the fifth century B.C., perhaps with roots much earlier in Babylonia, the Festival of Lots (*pur* means "lot" in Hebrew), or Purim, is a light and fun-filled festival about Jewish survival. Observed on the 14th day of the lunar month of Adar (in February or March), celebrants read the story of Esther from the Bible, exchange gifts, and sometimes dress up in appropriate costumes. The story tells how Esther, a Jewish woman who becomes queen to a Persian king, saves her people from destruction. Purim is regarded as a minor festival because the directive for observance is in the book of Esther, not the Torah. Beneath the frivolity of the festival, there is a serious undertone of concern about the Jews' status as a minority people. It is the only Jewish holiday that deals specifically with anti-Semitism.

Purim is an occasion for Jews and non-Jews alike to remember the frightful consequences of anti-Semitism in Western history. It is a time for renewed commitment to resist anti-Semitism and any other ideologies that justify the oppression of peoples of whatever race or religion.

Tabletalk on Purim

What is "anti-Semitism?" What are some current examples of it? What are other ideologies that justify the oppression of peoples (white supremacy, apartheid, etc.)? Make a contribution to one of the agencies working to counter these ideologies, perhaps your denomination's office for racial justice.

CHINESE NEW YEAR

For Chinese people everywhere, Chinese New Year is the most important holiday of the year. Those who can, celebrate for a week or ten days. The beginning of the year is based on a lunar calendar with origins in the twenty-seventh century B.C., which places the day anywhere between January 21 and February 19 in a given year. While colorful and loud festivities are planned to sweep out the evil spirits of the old year, visiting with friends may be the single most important part of the New Year celebrations. A part of the tradition is to present children with gifts of money in red envelopes.

Chinese New Year can be an occasion to appreciate the rich cultural heritage of Chinese and other Asian peoples and to learn more about their history in this country, especially the prejudice they have faced during the nineteenth and twentieth centuries.

Tabletalk on Chinese New Year

Over a meal of Chinese food—which you have learned to cook or at your favorite Chinese restaurant—talk about Chinese contributions to this society. Decide to get acquainted with some Chinese Americans or Chinese in your community.

6.
March and April

LENT: PREPARING FOR DISCIPLESHIP

Originally a season of fasting and penance for new converts preparing for baptism on Easter Eve, Lent is a period of 40 weekdays from Ash Wednesday to Easter and corresponds to Jesus' 40-day fast in the wilderness in preparation for his ministry. Actually, Lent is a period of 46 days because Sundays, as days when fasts could be broken, were not included in the 40 days. The season of Lent includes many special days marking particular events in Jesus' ministry as he approached his death: Ash Wednesday, Passion or Palm Sunday, Maundy Thursday, Good Friday and Holy Saturday.

When Christianity became the state religion of the Roman empire in the fourth century, the church was endangered by throngs of new untutored members. To counter the paganism of these new converts, the Lenten fast and practices of self-renunciation became requirements of all Christians. Fasting and self-renunciation were symbolic ways to identify with the suffering of Jesus. Lent became a time of recommitment; a time to ward off the threat of assimilation into the popular culture.

As a time for disciplined reexamination of one's baptismal vows—leading to repentance—and reflection on the cost of discipleship, Lent culminates naturally and directly in the celebration of the resurrection on Easter Sunday and its implications for participation in Jesus' ministry.

Another Kind of Fasting

Our most important family alternative celebration occurs during Lent. We used the following idea one year and, at our children's request, have repeated it.

We had become aware of the severely limited budgets of families living on welfare. In order to know how that feels, our family decided to observe Lent by choosing to live on the amount of money a welfare family receives for food. The first year I actually took out the entire amount of money we had to spend on our welfare budget so the children could watch it being spent. Even with the normal amount of

★ **Lent**
(40 days before Easter)
★ **Easter**
(March/April)
★ **Passover**
(March/April)
★ **Ramadan**
(variable date)
★ **International Women's Day**
(March 8)
★ **St. Patrick's Day**
(March 17)
★ **First Day of Spring**
(March 20 or 21)
★ **Central America Week**
(week of March 24)
★ **April Fool's Day**
(April 1)
★ **National Farm Worker Week**
(two weeks before Mother's Day)

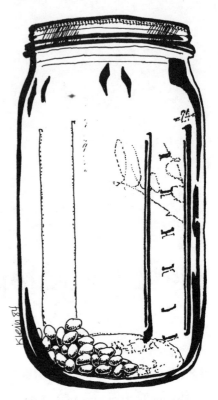

food on hand at the beginning of our Lenten experience, during the last week we had some very unusual meals.

We celebrated Easter with a feast, using money carefully saved from our welfare budget. The next day the children and I went to the grocery store, using the money we had saved from our regular food budget to purchase food and take it to our local food pantry.

Although this is not like having to live on a restrictive budget day in and day out, it provides a "hunger" experience and several family discussions on hunger. This also provides the family with the experience of giving up and giving to others.

Deborah Heaton
Enid, Oklahoma

Homemade Cinnamon Rolls

Every Sunday morning, except during Lent, our family enjoys homemade cinnamon rolls as a symbol of resurrection. On Easter Sunday morning our favorite cinnamon rolls reappear on our table, this time in the form of the resurrection lamb.

Betty Voskuil
Holland, Michigan

Stations of the Cross

One year for Good Friday our family did a living Stations of the Cross. We visited places where Jesus suffers today: abortion clinic, welfare office, unemployment office, military weapons manufacturer.

The next year we did this on a simpler scale, doing things in which our children could be involved. We visited a hospital and took books for its nursery and visited in a senior nursing home. We then collected food for the local food pantry.

Mary and Bill Merrill
Columbus, Ohio

Lenten Lifestyle Assessment

Lent is a time for expectation, reflection and self-examination. A group of concerned people from our congregation decided it was important for us to evaluate our lives as Christians and determine if we were living them to the fullest. The result was a family calendar indicating daily Bible readings, along with thoughtful activities for each day during the six weeks in Lent.

As an attempt to gain support for each other, a tree was set up near the pulpit to be used for families to write their experiences on "ornaments" to be placed on the tree. After three weeks of the experiment, a pot-luck dinner was held for participating families to share their joys and frustrations.

A Lenten Lifestyle Assessment Program gave focus to each week's activities with concrete suggestions for changes in our use of the earth's resources as well as individual gifts and resources. We were challenged to practice and to experiment with voluntary simplicity in television watching, auto and energy use, the way we spend our time, foods we choose, recreation and leisure activities, and the ways we choose to serve others.

Participating families were asked to sign a Lenten Covenant to

1. Engage in daily scripture reading and prayer;

2. Focus on specific activities each week, as suggested in the packet.

3. Pray for members of the congregation who are participating in the Lenten project;

4. Share activities with others via the tree near the pulpit;

5. Share the idea of this Lenten Covenant with at least one other person during the Lenten period.

> Mt. Hope Lutheran Church
> Address unknown

SYMBOLS AT THE FAMILY TABLE ADD MEANING TO HOLY WEEK

Just as the Advent wreath gives children a better understanding of the spiritual meaning of Christmas, setting your table with Easter symbols can illustrate the events of Holy Week. Collect simple household items that depict the events surrounding Christ's death and resurrection. At family worship around the table use Bible passages to further explain what happened during Holy Week.

PALM SUNDAY. Place a palm leaf, fern frond or even a green paper leaf in the center of a table. The table itself, representing the one where Christ served his disciples the Last Supper, can be your dining table or another space reserved for these symbolic objects. Read from John 12:13. "So they took branches of palm trees...."

MONDAY. Add a small bowl of water with a folded napkin or towel. Read John 13:5. "...and [Jesus] began to wash the disciples' feet and wipe them with the towel." Talk about the humility and service that Jesus showed by these acts.

TUESDAY. Place on the table a picture or molded clay figure of praying hands. Read Luke 22:41. "And he withdrew from them about a stone's throw and knelt down in prayer." Sing "Sweet Hour of Prayer."

WEDNESDAY. Add a picture or ceramic figure of a rooster. Read Luke 23:61. "...Peter, the cock will not crow this day until you three times deny that you know me." Fear of personal reprisal, Peter's reason for denying Christ, is still a reality for Christians. Conclude by praying together or singing a verse from the hymn, "Stand up, Stand up for Jesus."

THURSDAY. Make a crown of thorns by twisting rough twigs, a rose stem or weed stalks together. Take turns feeling the crown before it is placed on the table. Emphasize that this symbol of power and royalty was used to mock Jesus. Read Mark 15:17. "...and plaiting a crown of thorns, they put it on him." Sing or repeat the words to "Oh, Sacred Head, Now Wounded."

FRIDAY. Make a small cross of sticks. Read Luke 23:26-33. "And when they came to the place which is called the Skull, there they crucified him." Explain that Christ chose the way of suffering to show love for us. Sing or repeat together the words to the third stanza of "Oh, Sacred Head, Now Wounded" which begins, "What language shall I borrow to thank thee, dearest friend...."

SATURDAY. Gather around the table filled with Holy Week symbols. After a period of silent meditation, join hands and sing the spiritual, "Were You There?"

EASTER. Place a lily or other blooming plant in the center of the other symbols. Read John 11:25. "I am the resurrection and the life...." Center discussion around the lily bulb that is buried in dirt but which grows into a beautiful plant in the spring. Compare Christ's burial and resurrection with the lily. Use this time to separate the Christian from secular observance of Easter. Conclude the Holy Week family worship by singing one of the joyful Easter hymns.

> Joy dawned again on Easter Day,
> The sun shone out with fair array,
> When to their longing eyes restored,
> The Apostles saw their risen Lord.
>
> O Jesus, King of gentleness,
> Do thou thyself our hearts possess
> That we may give thee all our days
> The willing tribute of our praise.
>
> (5th century Latin carol)

For Parents, March-April 1982

100

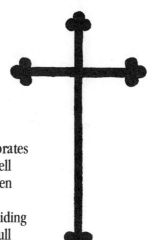

EASTER: CELEBRATING THE RESURRECTION

Easter, the most important festival of the Christian Church, celebrates the resurrection of Jesus from the dead. The Feast of Easter was well established by the second century, but controversy developed between the Eastern and Western Churches over the proper day for its observance. In 325 the Council of Nicaea settled the dispute by deciding that Easter would be celebrated on the Sunday following the first full moon after the vernal equinox, making it fall on variable dates each year between March 21 and April 25.

We celebrate Easter on Sunday because it is the day of the week when Jesus rose from the dead. The Council's decision to time the celebration with the vernal equinox, however, suggests that the day replaced one or more pagan rebirth festivals observed at the time of the vernal equinox. (See article on **Spring** near the end of this chapter.)

The derivation of the word "Easter" is not clear. The Venerable Bede, an early English historian (672-735), connected Easter to *Eostre,* an Anglo-Saxon spring goddess whose festival was celebrated at the vernal equinox and whose symbols were the hare and the egg. It seems likely that the hare and egg traditions of the goddess Eostre became the Easter bunny and Easter eggs.

Still other pagan practices came to be associated with the feast of Easter. For example, sunrise services, while having some basis in the early dawn visit of the women to Jesus' tomb (Luke 24:1), were also part of traditional vernal equinox rites which welcomed the sun and its power to bring new life.

One wonders if the popular preoccupation with Easter as a time to celebrate hope for life after death also has its roots in ancient rites of

spring. The New Testament clearly links hope for a general resurrection to Jesus' resurrection (I Corinthians 15, et al); however, the spring and rebirth symbols often used in churches at Easter may actually distort the meaning of resurrection. These symbols (e.g. butterflies) suggest natural cycles of life, death and rebirth. Resurrection in the New Testament sense is not natural. Rather, it is a radical action contravening nature for God's own purposes.

Although the resurrection theme of life after death is certainly valid, the larger significance of the resurrection is often ignored: that is, God raised Jesus from the dead to validate his ministry on earth—a ministry of healing, teaching, preaching and suffering on behalf of the poor and outcast that did not end on the cross. Through the resurrection that ministry became the universal ministry for those who would follow Jesus. As Jesus said to the fearful unbelieving disciples on that first Easter, "Peace be with you. As the Father has sent me, so I send you." (John 20:21)

The commercialization of Easter makes it difficult to keep the real purpose of the resurrection celebration in perspective. In addition to the annual Easter clothes, card, flower and candy blitz, attempts by business interests to make Easter a "Second Christmas" have spawned an Easter-oriented toy industry and a massive live-animal business selling millions of rabbits, baby chicks and ducks each year.

There is another significant level of concern with our Easter celebrations. Although many attempts have been made to link the Easter bunny and Easter egg traditions to the resurrection, those traditions actually divert attention away from celebrating the resurrection. "What happened on the third day?" asked the church school teacher to a group of preschoolers one Easter morning. "The Easter bunny brought eggs," was the immediate and unequivocal reply. As children grow and learn that the Easter bunny is a myth passed on to them as truth, they have less reason to believe what is taught them as truth about the resurrection.

Better Than Chocolate Eggs

Consider placing a book in your child's Easter basket—one that expresses the love and sacrifice represented by the observance of Easter.

Signs of Faith

At Easter we help our children understand the significance of the season by adorning our home with signs of faith—a dove sculpture or crucifix hung on our wall only during this season, or a banner with an Easter message hung temporarily on our refrigerator or front door.

Since Easter is our family's most festive occasion, we celebrate with an all-day Open House. Two homemade grapevine baskets (no chocolate Easter eggs, no Easter bunny) are filled with dogwoods, violets, daffodils—whatever is blooming—as a symbol of new life. Gifts for the children specifically celebrate life. Last year they got umbrellas to play in the life-giving spring rains. We end Easter day with the Paschal vespers at dusk.

Ed, Andrea, Nathanael & Rebekah Wills
Memphis, Tennessee

Easter in the Philippines

In the fresh air of the Philippine countryside, *Index* families met in the early morning to read together from the Easter text. After a short period of meditation each family offered symbols of new life—plants, seeds, eggs, handpainted butterflies and a pair of booties! These symbols were put on dry twigs to make an Easter tree. Older children planted quick-sprouting mango seeds in an earthen pot and were told to watch carefully for an amazing demonstration of new life.

Ana Maria Clamor
Social Development Index
Quezon City, Philippines

103

Easter Seder: We Remember

Easter is the most sacred holy day in the Christian church. It marks an extraordinary event—the resurrection of Christ—and is supposed to remind us of the meaning of that event. Commercial interests, pushing Easter bunnies, new clothes, cards, baskets, candy and toys, sometimes make it hard to stay focused on the real purpose of celebrating Easter. The Easter Seder helps us remember.

The idea for the Easter Seder comes from the Jewish Passover Seder. Jewish people observe the Passover, which commemorates the Israelites' liberation from slavery in Egypt, about the same time of year that Christians celebrate Easter. At the heart of the Jewish festival is the retelling of the story behind the Passover meal which is called the Seder, or "order":

"When your children say to you: 'What do you mean by this service?' Then you shall say..." Exodus 12:26 (KJV).

In response to a set of questions from the children, the different generations at the table recount the story and the meaning of the observance. The rite has proved to be an important way to keep the significance of this celebration before the children and the whole family.

The following questions and answers, using the form of the Jewish Seder, attempt to retell the story of the death and resurrection of Jesus, helping us understand what that event 2000 years ago has to do with the way we live now. The Easter Seder is designed for use by families or other groups on Easter Sunday. If you decide to use the Seder in a worship service or with a group at church, also consider using it at home when you have your traditional Easter meal. This Seder, like the Jewish one, assumes the presence and participation of more than one generation. The younger generations ask the questions and the older generations answer and explain.

Feel free to adapt the following Seder to your liking. Create one that you will use year after year so that the Seder becomes an Easter tradition in your family.

The Youngest Child: Why is this day different from all other days?

An Elder: On this day, almost 2,000 years ago, God raised up Jesus from the dead. Jesus was crucified. His friends took his body down from the cross and placed it in a tomb. Early in the morning, three days after he was buried, some women went to his tomb. When they got there, they found the stone that sealed the tomb had been removed and the body of Jesus was gone.

A Child: What happened to his body?

An Elder: The women thought his body had been stolen. But an angel appeared and told them not to be afraid. The angel brought the good news that Jesus was alive! He had been raised from the dead, just as he had promised, and he would see his followers later. The women ran to tell Jesus' other disciples what they had seen and heard. Some of the men didn't believe the women's story until Jesus actually appeared to them. Then, they knew he was alive.

A Child: Who killed him?

An Elder: Roman authorities executed Jesus because of his claim to be King of the Jews. The Romans had occupied Judea for almost a hundred years, but the Jews never stopped trying to regain their freedom. Since Jesus was a very popular figure, the Romans were afraid if he became King he would be successful in driving them out of the country. Some of the religious leaders who had received special favors from the Romans were also afraid of Jesus. Together with the Roman officials, they cooperated in a plan to bring Jesus to trial and have him executed.

A Child: Why were the religious leaders afraid of Jesus?

An Elder: For three years, Jesus and his twelve disciples traveled all over Judea, preaching, teaching and healing people. Great crowds followed wherever they went. Jesus taught that God loves all people and that to love God and to love neighbor are the two most important commandments. He enlarged the meaning of neighbor to include the poor, the outcasts and even one's enemies. He spent most of his time with society's rejected, giving them hope.

But religious leaders did not like Jesus' teachings, and he was often in trouble with them. His teachings about accumulating wealth, injustice to the poor and needy and religious hypocrisy were hard words for those who were neither poor nor outcast and had no concern for the destitute. In his manner of living and in his teaching Jesus sided with the poor, exposing the religious leaders in their selfishness and bringing fear that they would lose their privileged positions.

A Child: Were all of the religious leaders opposed to Jesus?

An Elder: No, not all of them opposed Jesus. Some were amazed at his healing, his teaching, his courage in confronting authorities and believed that he was sent from God. But those religious leaders who feared him conspired with the Roman authorities to put him to death.

A Child: Did God really raise Jesus from the dead?

An Elder: The New Testament tells us that the risen Jesus appeared to his followers on the seashore, on the road and in a house where they had gathered to pray. One of the stories tells about a disciple who doubted that Jesus was really alive. But after Jesus appeared to him and invited him to touch his wounds, he believed. These stories also make it clear that the risen Jesus appeared to be different.

Whatever the differences, his followers recognized him when he appeared to them. Their sense of his presence was so real that they began doing the things he had done during his lifetime, although they knew that could mean suffering, persecution and even death.

A Child: Why do *we* celebrate Easter?

An Elder: God's Son, Jesus, was sent into the world to bring God's good news of love and forgiveness for all people, including us. Because Jesus included the poor, the outcasts and even enemies of the people in the circle of God's love, he was persecuted and finally killed.

God raised Jesus from the dead as a sign of approval for the work he had done on earth. His preaching, teaching, healing and his identification with the poor was the work God intended. For two days after the crucifixion, Jesus' followers were desolate. It seemed that all Jesus had done was nothing more than a beautiful, fleeting dream. But that was not the end! God raised up Jesus as if to say, "The words he spoke in my name are true! The deeds he did are my deeds! And they are now the work of all who follow him." When Jesus appeared to his followers after the resurrection he told them, "As the Father has sent me, so I send you."

And so we are called!

Children: THE LORD IS RISEN!

Elders: THE LORD IS RISEN INDEED!

All: Hallelujah! Amen!

PASSOVER: FREEDOM FROM SLAVERY

Passover, or *pesach* in Hebrew, is the Jewish festival commemorating the Exodus. Passover refers to the night before the Hebrew slaves were to leave Egypt, when an angel of the Lord would kill the first-born of the Egyptians. The Hebrews had been warned that only houses marked with lamb's blood on the doorposts would be spared. These houses the angel would "pass over."

The directive for observing the Passover is in the twelfth chapter of Exodus. An eight-day festival, Passover begins on the eve of the fourteenth day of the lunar month of Nisan—usually between mid-March and mid-April—with a Seder in the home. This ceremony, celebrated with family members around a special Seder meal, is a retelling of the Exodus story and has been done in the same way for hundreds of years. A child asks four questions and the elders answer, recounting why Passover is such a significant occasion. (See Exodus 12:25-27) Although the Seder is the central part of the Passover festival, there are many observances, activities and special foods for the other days.

The Passover has long had significance for Christians. On the night he was arrested, Jesus celebrated the Passover with his disciples, using that sacred feast to institute the Eucharist—sometimes called the Lord's Supper or Holy Communion (Matthew 26:17-30, et al). Beyond that unique connection to Passover, many Christians observe the Passover Seder as a way of affirming their own Jewish heritage. Given the long and tragic history of Christian persecution of Jews, such affirmation is most appropriate.

RAMADAN: MONTH-LONG FAST FOR MUSLIMS

Ramadan, commemorating the revelation of the Koran to Mohammed, is the most sacred celebration in the Muslim world. The observance begins on the eve of the ninth month of the lunar year. Since the lunar year is eleven or twelve days shorter than the solar year, the incidence of Ramadan moves through all the seasons of the year in cycles of approximately 33 years. In 1987 Ramadan begins on April 29, in 1988 on April 19, in 1989 on April 9, etc.

Celebrated for 30 days, the observance affects a large portion of the Third World. According to Islamic law, fasting from sunup to sundown is required of every able-bodied Muslim. The fasting is meant to 1) help keep the observance in mind, 2) encourage spiritual discipline, 3) create an identification with the poor and 4) remind people of their ultimate

106

dependence on God. Popular celebrations of Ramadan sometimes involve lavish feasts after the sun goes down, but this custom does not represent the holiday's true spirit, to bring about inner strength through austerity.

Tabletalk for Ramadan

Islam is a religious tradition little understood by most Westerners, perhaps because of its intense politicization in the East. During one meal identify popular stereotypes of Muslims. Then do some reading. Better still, make the acquaintance of some Muslims in your community. Then, at another meal, try to go beyond the stereotypes to real people.

INTERNATIONAL WOMEN'S DAY

International Women's Day, a day to honor working women, is widely celebrated throughout the world—especially in socialist countries. Set on March 8, the day commemorates a march of women garment and textile workers in New York City in 1857. Little known or observed in the United States, International Women's Day is a national holiday in the Soviet Union and the People's Republic of China, where women workers are given special recognition.

"I know that it feels a kind o' hissin' and ticklin' like to see a colored woman get up and tell you about things, and Woman's Rights. We have all been thrown down so low that nobody thought we'd ever get up again; but see if we don't; we'll have our rights; and you can't stop us from them; see if you can. You may hiss as much as you like, but it is comin'.... I am sittin' among you to watch; and every once and awhile I will come out and tell you what time of night it is...."

Sojourner Truth at the
Fourth National Woman's Rights
Convention in New York, 1853

Tabletalk for International Women's Day

Throughout history women have made wonderful contributions for the betterment of humankind. Study the lives of women who have made an impact in various fields: i.e., Mother Teresa, Golda Meir, Beverly Sills, Susan B. Anthony. Talk about *why* women work. Discuss their dual responsibilities of home and job. Discover ways women are discriminated against in the job market and on their jobs.

ST. PATRICK'S DAY: WEARING THE GREEN

St. Patrick's Day is an Irish religious holiday. Celebrated on March 17, this holy day commemorates the contributions of that country's fifth-century patron saint. Like many other Irish religious figures, St. Patrick was believed to have a special rapport with nature which helped him to convince the pagan Irish that he was in touch with God. Forsaking the religious significance of this day, commercial interests in the United States trade more and more on the ethnic stereotype of the "hard-drinking" Irish to make St. Patrick's Day an occasion for revelling. Irish societies in the United States are working to counteract this stereotype by conducting alternative St. Patrick's Day celebrations.

In addition to "wearing the green" and cooking special Irish recipes, this is a good day to overcome stereotypes by recalling the contributions that Irish Americans have made to this country. It is also a day to mourn the civil strife that plagues Northern Ireland and the divisive role that religion has played there.

Tabletalk on St. Patrick's Day

Around the dinner table, talk about a "Who's Who Among Irish Americans," beginning with Patrick Henry and remembering John F. Kennedy.

SPRING: LIFE AFTER WINTER

In different parts of the world the signs of spring differ dramatically, but astronomers can tell exactly from the earth's motion around the sun when one season ends and the next one begins. The vernal equinox marks the beginning of spring, in the Northern Hemisphere coming between March 20 and 21. On this day, the center of the sun appears

directly above the equator, so that along the equator there are 12 hours of daylight and 12 hours of darkness.

Ancient people knew that at the vernal equinox winter was giving way to spring. Many rites of fertility and rebirth were observed at the time of the vernal equinox, as in the festival of Eostre in Britain (See **Easter** above). Even though the manifestations of spring are different in different places, the first day of spring is a good time to celebrate the

108

ending of winter and the renewal of life in nature. It is much better than mixing the coming of spring with the celebration of the resurrection.

In 1979 another important dimension to the celebration of spring was added when children rang bells at the United Nations at the exact hour of the vernal equinox, inaugurating Earth Day. It is a day for celebrating nature and learning about the interdependence of all life. Implicit in that celebrating and learning is the recognition of the threat waste and pollution pose for the fragile ecological balance which makes life possible on the planet.

"The least movement affects all nature; the entire sea changes because of a rock."
Pascal

Tabletalk for the First Day of Spring

Read, and then discuss, the following words of Wendell Berry from his book, *The Unsettling of America: Culture and Agriculture*:

...The earth is what we all have in common, it is what we are made of and what we live from, and we cannot damage it without damaging those with whom we share it. There is an uncanny resemblance between our behavior toward each other and our behavior toward the earth. By some connection we do not recognize, the willingness to exploit one becomes the willingness to exploit the other.... It is impossible to care for each other more or differently than we care for the earth.

Celebrate Spring by Celebrating Life

This is the water, celebrate the water
May you always drink your fill.
We can save the treasure
if we stand together
and celebrate the water.
Don't think we don't need you; we need you.
Don't think we don't hear you; we hear you.
Those who care just lift your voices
and join us as we sing.
Save our planet, keep our planet green

This is the air, celebrate the air,
May you always breathe your fill.
This is the music, celebrate the music
May you always sing your fill.
These are the people, celebrate the people
May you always love your fill.
This is your life, celebrate your life
May you always live your fill.
We can save the treasure
if we live together
and celebrate life.

Neal Gladstone
Corvallis, Oregon

A Rite for Spring: Begin to Recycle

Anyone can—and should—participate in recycling. Practically every community has an organization that accepts recyclable material: a junk dealer, a municipal or private drop-off center, a charitable organization that operates a paper drive. Find out what materials can be easily recycled in your area. Then keep those materials separated from your trash and recycle them as they accumulate.

To make a serious impact on our country's solid waste problem, we need community-wide recycling programs. Private citizens can play key roles in initiating and supporting recycling programs; without them, solid waste professionals typically underestimate the potential of citizen participation and lean toward high-technology options for dealing with the problem. So investigate what is happening in your own community. If there is a recycling program, support it by participating in its efforts, by promoting it to friends and neighbors and by supporting it at the governmental level. If no recycling program is planned or in operation, take the initiative by writing to the newspaper, talking with public officials or even forming a citizens' group to press for recycling.

Community recycling programs not only reduce the trash disposal volume to more manageable levels but also contribute to more effective use of scarce resources on our Spaceship Earth.

Earl Arnold
Eco-Justice Task Force
Ithaca, New York

CENTRAL AMERICA WEEK: THE SPIRIT OF ARCHBISHOP ROMERO

Commemorating the life and witness of El Salvadoran Archbishop Oscar Romero, Central America Week is observed in the week around the anniversary of his assassination. While saying mass on March 24, 1980, the Archbishop was shot and killed. In his final homily that day, he said,

I implore you, beloved brothers and sisters, to seek a better world from an historical vantage point, to have hope, joined with a spirit of surrender and sacrifice. We must do what we can. All of us can do something...

Sponsored by many Catholic, Jewish, Protestant and secular agencies, Central America Week has become a time to mobilize concern about Central America. Religious communities are urged to set aside the first

Sabbath and Sunday services of the week to lift in prayer and to celebrate the sufferings and joys common to North and Central Americans of faith. They are further encouraged to plan special events through the week to focus attention on that region's struggles.

For scheduled events and resources contact the Inter-American Task Force on Central America, 475 Riverside Drive, Room 563, New York, NY 10115. Tel. 212-870-3383.

NATIONAL FARM WORKER WEEK

National Farm Worker Week, observed each year during the second week before Mother's Day, is a celebration of the achievements of the United Farm Workers (UFW). The United Farm Workers, organized in 1962 by Caesar Chavez, has given farmworkers hope. Victories for them have not come easily, but they now have some important ones. Chavez' strict adherence to the principles of nonviolence, even in the most violent situations, has won respect and admiration from people around the world.

Numbering more than a million, farm workers are on one of the lowest rungs of the economic ladder in the United States. There is still much to be done in this area. National Farm Workers Week is an appropriate time to remember farm workers all over the world—how they contribute to this economy and at what price.

For more information, contact the National Farm Worker Ministry, 111-A Fairmont Avenue, Oakland, CA 94611; and Agricultural Missions, 475 Riverside Drive, 6th floor, New York, NY 10115.

Tabletalk for Farm Worker Week

Few fruits and vegetables arrive on our dinner tables without the labor of farm workers. This week, see if you can find out where the fruits and vegetables on your table come from, and how they got there. Consider making a contribution to one of the agencies working with farm workers in an amount equal to the cost of the fruits and vegetables you and your family eat this week.

NATIONAL FARM WORKER MINISTRY

Felipe Franco is six years old. He was born without arms or legs. His mother worked in the grape vineyards of California until the eight month of her pregnancy. She thinks pesticides are the cause.

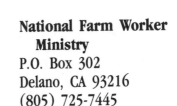

We are called to build a new heaven and a new earth and to make choices that will prevent needless suffering. You can respond to that call and make a difference in the future of all creation.

Become an Associate Member of the National Farm Worker Ministry Among Pesticide Victims. Pledge $1 a week for a year. (Make checks payable to NFWM).

National Farm Worker Ministry
P.O. Box 302
Delano, CA 93216
(805) 725-7445

Society of St. Andrew
State Route 615
P.O. Box 329
Big Island, VA 24526
(804) 299-5956

Society of St. Andrew
HUNGER MINISTRIES

THE POTATO PROJECT is a produce salvage program that provides direct food relief to our nation's poor while addressing one of the major causes — food waste. During the first four years of operation, this two-pronged attack on hunger has been responsible for distributing over fifty million pounds of otherwise wasted potatoes to hungry Americans in 47 states and the District of Columbia. Expansion of the Potato Project is currently limited only by available finances.

THE HARVEST OF HOPE is a gleaning/study project with rich Biblical roots. Aimed at the salvage of produce left in the fields after harvest, the Harvest of Hope, like the Potato Project, is a two-pronged attack on hunger. The second major emphasis of the program is the education of participants to the realities of world hunger. Combining work and study, the Harvest of Hope is the ideal way to actually do something for the hungry.

Evergreen Society
Box 222
Grand Rapids, MI 46588

EVERGREEN SOCIETY

"The Gift That Keeps on Giving"

$10.00 will plant ten fruit trees in a developing nation in the name of your loved one who will receive a letter acknowledging your contribution in his or her honor.

$100.00 contribution will plant 100 trees and be acknowledged by a beautiful plaque.

Evergreen Society
Box 222
Grand Rapids, MI 46588
(616) 956-0075

112

THE RURAL ADVANCEMENT FUND
THE NATIONAL SHARECROPPERS FUND

Since 1937, dedicated to family farms and justice for rural people.

For information about our projects, please contact:
RAF/NSF
2124 Commonwealth Avenue
Charlotte, NC 28205
704-334-3051

RAF/NSF
2124 Commonwealth Avenue
Charlotte, NC 28205
(704) 334-3051

RED BIRD MISSIONARY CONFERENCE

THE UNITED METHODIST CHURCH
QUEENDALE CENTER

BEVERLY, KENTUCKY 40913
606-598-5915

A Witness for Christ in the heart of Appalachia

Churches & Outreach Ministries   Henderson Settlement

Red Bird Mission   Red Bird Medical Center

Red Bird Missionary Conference
The United Methodist Church
Queendale Center
Beverly, KY 40913

NEW CREATION INSTITUTE

The Institute works in the spirit of II Cor. 5:17 to renew the earth and its people. Recommended reading on the subject of earthkeeping:

● *A Worldly Spirituality: The Call to Take Care of the Earth*
By Wesley Granberg-Michaelson, Harper & Row, $12.95. Alerts the church to its Biblical task of earthkeeping and demonstrates practical ways in which Christians can participate in the care of the earth.

● *Tending the Garden: Essays on the Gospel and the Earth*
Edited by Wesley Granberg-Michaelson, Eerdmans, $8.95.

Order by sending your check to The New Creation Institute, 518 South Ave. W., Missoula MT 59801. Tax deductible gifts are also needed to further our earthkeeping efforts.

The New Creation Institute
518 South Avenue West
Missoula, MT 59801

Agricultural Missions, Inc.
475 Riverside Drive
Room 624
New York, NY 10115
(212) 870-2553

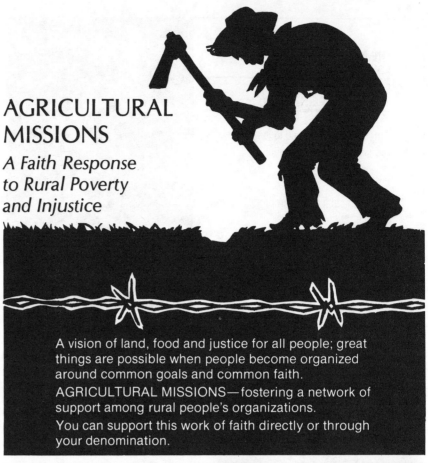

AGRICULTURAL MISSIONS

*A Faith Response
to Rural Poverty
and Injustice*

A vision of land, food and justice for all people; great things are possible when people become organized around common goals and common faith.
AGRICULTURAL MISSIONS—fostering a network of support among rural people's organizations.
You can support this work of faith directly or through your denomination.

United Farm Workers
La Paz
Keene, CA 93570

FOR OUR FUTURE, AND FOR YOURS — BOYCOTT GRAPES

300,000 farm workers are poisoned each year by pesticides used on the food we eat.

The pesticides used on table grapes are among the most dangerous.

The United Farm Workers Union is boycotting fresh grapes until growers agree to ban the most dangerous pesticides and agree to free and fair elections and good faith collective bargaining for farm workers.

What you can do:
- **Boycott California fresh table grapes.**
- **Send a contribution to support the boycott.**
- **Join the UFW's full-time volunteer staff.**

 Write: **Cesar Chavez, United Farm Workers**

114

7.
May and June

MAY DAY

Although not much celebrated in the United States, May Day has roots in prehistoric times as a spring festival, marking the revival of nature after winter. Maypole dances and flowers still mark the celebration in some places.

Meeting in Paris in 1889, a congress of world socialist parties voted to support the United States labor movement's demands for an eight-hour work day and chose May 1, 1890, as a day to demonstrate in favor of the eight-hour day. That action set a precedent, and May 1 became the traditional time for labor demonstrations in Europe. In the Soviet Union May Day is a national holiday marked by giant banners, patriotic speeches and military parades.

Tabletalk for May Day

If spring comes late to your area and March 20 or 21 goes by without any visible signs of new life, celebrate its coming today. If possible, spend some time outside. Consider how different your life is because the labor movement won the struggle for an eight-hour work day.

PENTECOST: DESCENT OF THE SPIRIT

Pentecost (from Greek *pentekoste* meaning fiftieth) celebrates the postresurrection descent of the Holy Spirit on Jesus' followers (Acts 2:1-6), a miracle that took place on the Jewish Pentecost which is observed fifty days after Passover (See **Shavuot** below). On this day a group of frightened disciples in hiding in Jerusalem were empowered to become fearless witnesses, even in the face of opposition by the civil authorities. For that reason, Pentecost is said to be "the birthday of the church."

While setting the Christian observance of Pentecost on the existing Jewish feast day was probably intentional, the two days have only the name and date in common. Also known as Whitsunday, Pentecost was celebrated as early as the third century, with celebrations sometimes

★ **May Day**
(May 1)
★ **Ascension Day**
(forty days after Easter)
★ **Pentecost**
(fifty days after Easter)
★ **Shavuot**
(fifty days after Passover)
★ **Mother's Day**
(second Sunday in May)
★ **Memorial Day**
(last Monday in May)
★ **Father's Day**
(third Sunday in June)
★ **Beginning of Summer**
(June 20 or 21)

including the whole fifty days. Because it was a feast of joy, any kind of penance was forbidden.

The Lent/Easter season concludes with Pentecost, celebrating a universal ministry empowered by God. According to the story of Pentecost, many nationalities were represented in the crowd that listened to the disciples preach the good news of Jesus that day, but they all heard the message in their own language. Pentecost is a good time to hear the message in your "own language" and to consider what participation in Jesus' ministry means for you.

Tabletalk for Pentecost

Recall heroes of faith who were empowered to participate in Jesus' ministry despite great personal cost. Of well-known public figures, would you include any of the following: Dietrich Bonhoeffer, Dom Helder Camera, Dorothy Day, Martin Luther King, Jr., Mother Teresa, Desmond Tutu? Who else? What lesser known people would you include?

SHAVUOT: FIRST FRUITS AND THE TORAH

Meaning simply "weeks" in Hebrew, Shavuot is observed seven weeks (50 days) after Passover. Other names describe its character: Harvest Festival, Festival of the First Fruits and Festival of the Giving of the Torah. Originally an agricultural festival, Shavuot was one of three occasions when people were required to go to the Temple in Jerusalem with offerings from their farms. After the destruction of the second Temple in the first century, the people could no longer bring their offerings to the Temple so the festival was designated as the anniversary of the reception of the Torah at Mt. Sinai. While the agricultural theme has not been removed entirely, the central focus is on the Torah. At the synagogue service the Ten Commandments are recited and the book of Ruth is read.

Tabletalk on Shavuot

Tell the story of how God gave the Law to Israel (Exodus 19:17-20:21). Repeat the Ten Commandments and discuss their meaning. If you have not already done so, spend some time memorizing the Commandments.

MOTHER'S AND FATHER'S DAYS: HONORING PARENTS

Mother's Day, observed on the second Sunday in May in the United States, has its origins in the different concerns of two women: Julia Ward Howe and Anna Jarvis. Julia Ward Howe—writer, lecturer, social reformer and author of "The Battle Hymn of the Republic"—made the first known suggestion for Mother's Day in 1872. She wanted to observe Mother's Day on June 2 and dedicate the day to peace. For several years she sponsored an annual Mother's Day meeting in Boston as a way of connecting her ideals of motherhood and peacemaking.

Anna Jarvis had a very different reason for honoring mothers. Never a mother herself, she spent most of her adult life caring for her mother in Grafton, West Virginia. Her concern was for mothers who needed care and whose adult children were neglecting them. Out of this concern, in 1905 Anna Jarvis started a campaign for an annual religious celebration honoring mothers.

116

Although others started Mother's Day celebrations in their areas, Anna Jarvis is responsible for making it a nationwide observance. In 1914 Congress passed a resolution providing that the second Sunday in May be designated as Mother's Day, and President Woodrow Wilson issued a Mother's Day Proclamation.

Anna Jarvis envisioned Mother's Day as a time of recommitment to honoring and caring for mothers, especially mothers who were no longer able to care for themselves. But she was dismayed to see the way the holiday was celebrated. She lived to see Mother's Day become the victim of commercialism, when honoring mothers was reduced to giving flowers, cards and gifts. She died in 1948, disappointed and disillusioned that her work had been so trivialized.

A special day to honor mothers has ancient and world-wide precedents, but a special day to honor fathers seems to be unique to the United States. Many different people contributed to the creation of Father's Day, all of whom were likely influenced by Mother's Day. The first Father's Day service was probably conducted at a church in Fairmont, West Virginia, at the request of Mrs. Charles Clayton. But the person most responsible for getting the day started was Mrs. John Bruce Dodd of Spokane, Washington. The idea came to her during a Mother's Day sermon in 1909. She remembered her father who had raised six children after his young wife's death. Only one year later, on the third Sunday of June 1910, Spokane became the first city to honor fathers with a special day. Although widely observed since that time, it was only in 1972 when President Nixon signed a Congressional resolution putting it on the same basis as Mother's Day.

The founders of Mother's Day and Father's Day would probably not be pleased with the lot of many of today's elderly people. Part of what

"you have touched me
you have cradled me in your
security
until i found my own
given me words
when they were unknown to
me
tenderly you have held my
heart in your hands
your firmness has given me
strength
life itself wrapped in love
was your first gift to me
to love you is to love myself
to love myself is to love you"

Mary Eleanore Rice

they were responding to in the early part of this century was more than a simple desire to honor their parents. They feared that the emerging pattern of small nuclear families would contribute to a growing neglect of elderly parents and bring about a growing social disorder: the economic and cultural marginalization of the elderly. Theirs was a prophetic vision. They identified a problem with which this society has yet to come to terms in any serious way.

Mother's Day and Father's Day remind us to honor our parents in special ways. Beyond that, however, calling attention to the plight of the elderly in this society and pressing for serious attention to their problems may be the best way to honor them. Hopefully, the blatantly commercial creation of "Grandparents Day" will die a commercial death, and the genuine concerns for the elderly which moved the founders of Mother's and Father's Days will find expression on those days.

Although the founders had elderly parents in mind, there is no reason why younger mothers and fathers and the special problems they face should be excluded from these observances, including the growing phenomenon of single parents.

Although it didn't catch on as part of traditional observances, Julia Ward Howe's idea for making Mother's Day (or Father's Day) a day dedicated to peace makes sense. Those who bring life into the world and nurture it to adulthood have a special stake in seeing that those lives are not senselessly destroyed in war. Mother's Day cards with peace messages may not be available anytime soon, but you may want to combine honor for parents and the desire for peace in your celebration.

Tabletalk on Mother's Day

Recognize and acknowledge that those who care for small children occupy a very influential place in society. Whether at home, in elementary schools or in daycare centers, the kind of care given to small children determines the direction of our society.

Use Mother's Day as an occasion to speak on behalf of better daycare arrangements for the growing numbers of mothers who work and for better prenatal care for poor mothers. Consider the struggles of mothers trying to support families on inadequate welfare allotments and of elderly women whose social security benefits do not meet their costs for living.

Mothers Mourn in El Salvador

Throughout many countries in the world, Mother's Day is an occasion for mothers to spend with their children, celebrating motherhood and family. But in my country of El Salvador, motherhood has taken on another meaning. After six years of war, 60,000 deaths and more than 6,000 disappearances of our loved ones, we Salvadoran mothers pass Mother's Day as we do any other day, mourning for our missing children and husbands. While mothers everywhere spend sacred moments with their children, we only have our sorrow to embrace. For us, the greatest homage on Mother's Day would be the liberation of our incarcerated children and the declaration of the whereabouts of our disappeared ones.

America Sosa
COMADRES
Washington, D.C.

Mother's Day: A Celebration of Love; a Festival of Peace

Mother's Day was initiated in the 1870s as a call to women to work for peace in the world. In that first Mother's Day proclamation, Julia Ward Howe wrote:

> Arise then, women of this day! Arise all women who have hearts. We women of one country will be too tender for those of another country to allow our sons to be trained to injure theirs. From the bosom of the devastated earth a voice goes up with our own. It says, "Disarm, Disarm!"
>
> As men have often forsaken the plow at the summons of war let women now leave all that may be left of home for a great and earnest day of counsel with each other as to the means whereby the great human family can live in peace, each bearing after his own time the sacred impress, not of Caesar, but of God.
>
> I ask that a general congress be held to promote the alliance of the different nationalities, the amicable settlement of international questions, the great and general interests of peace.

On this day we honor our mothers for their constant love. Motivated by that love let us also make an earnest search for peace.

Center for Disarmament Education
Baton Rouge, Louisiana

Older Adults: A Nonrenewable Resource

A television commercial features an older man on his first day at work at a local fast-food hamburger restaurant. The scene moves quickly from his young coworkers' skepticism at his arrival to their frank amazement when they see how effectively he does his work. When he returns home in the evening, he says confidently to his questioning wife, "I don't know how they ever got along without me."

The first time I saw this commercial, I thought the message was good: not only is this man able to do good work, but the quality of his work is recognized by the younger generation. I have since had second thoughts. What does this commercial suggest about a society where selling hamburgers at minimum wage is an appropriate use of a senior citizen's skills and experience?

It is my hope that this commerical will be viewed as a parable about the contribution older people can make to all facets of life in this society. The skills and experience of these people are like nonrenewable resources. When they are gone, they are gone forever. How long can our society afford to waste this critical resource?

Prayer of Thanksgiving and Intercession

God of all ages and every generation, whose wisdom extends beyond the horizon and whose care reaches the furthest depths of the sea, we give thanks that we abide in the shelter of your encompassing love.

We thank you for the wisdom and gifts of our elders, their insights and skill gained through the years. Teach us that same maturity as we grow in faith. May they remind us of the obedience of Christ to the One who sent Him into the world. Help our elders to teach us what it means to live at peace with one another, and give us some measure of their wisdom as we seek to be faithful.

We pray that you will surround them with your care and mercy. Let us not exclude them from our thoughts and prayers. They have stories to tell us; help us take time to listen. They are proud of their accomplishments; give us the grace to honor them. They are sometimes frightened and lonely; we pray for compassion and patience as we sit by their side. Cleanse us of whatever foolishness that causes us daily to ignore or betray them. As you grant them long life let us embrace them with honor and dignity.

O God, you have been our "dwelling place in all generations....So teach us to number our days that we may get a heart of wisdom." Amen.

Rev. James G. Kirk
Presbyterian Church (U.S.A.)
Reprinted by permission.

Litany to Honor Older Adults

Call to Worship

(L-Leader, R-Responder, A-All)

L: Sovereign Lord, I put my hope in you; I have trusted you since I was young.

R: I have relied on you all my life; you have protected me since the day I was born.

L: You have taught me ever since I was young, and I still tell of your wonderful acts.

R: Now that I am old and my hair is gray, do not abandon me, O God!

A: Be with me while I proclaim your power and might to all generations to come.

Psalm 71:5-6, 17-18 (TEV)

Prayer of Adoration

Lord, you have made so many things!
    How wisely you made them all! The earth is filled with your
    creatures.
All of them depend on you to give them food when they need it.
    You give it to them, and they eat it;
    you provide food and they are satisfied.
When you turn away, they are afraid.
    When you take away your breath,
    they die and go back to the dust from which they came.
But when you give them breath,
    they are created;
You give new life to the earth.

I will sing to the Lord all my life;
As long as I live I will sing praises to my God.
Praise the Lord, my soul!
Praise the Lord! Amen.

Psalm 104:24, 27-30,33 (TEV)

Prayer of Confession

O Lord, you have always been our home.
Before you created the hills or brought the world into being,
    you were eternally God, and you will be God forever.
You place our sins before you,

"The test of a people is how it behaves toward the old. It is easy to love children... But the affection and care for the old, the incurable, the helpless, are the true gold mines of a culture."

Abraham J. Heschel

120

our secret sins where you can see them.
Our life is cut short by your anger;
  it fades away like a whisper.
Seventy years is all we have—
  eighty years, if we are strong;
Teach us how short life is,
  so that we may become wise.
Fill us each morning with your constant love,
  so that we may sing and be glad all our life. Amen.

Psalm 90:1-2, 8-10, 12, 14 (TEV)

Assurance of Pardon
God says, "I will save those who love me
  and will protect those who acknowledge me as Lord.
When they call to me, I will answer them;
  when they are in trouble, I will be with them.
I will reward them with long life; I will save them."

Psalm 91: 14-16 (TEV)

Presbyterian Office on Aging
Presbyterian Church (U.S.A.)
Used by permission.

"Linking Generations"

*Here—for you. This is what I lived for. I give you back
my years.*

Nash Buckingham, 1945

Tom Siler, papa of two sons, has turned the Father's Day tables this year.

He's doing the gift-giving.

Like the best of presents, his comes straight from the heart. It's homemade. Spawned with love, forged through hours of labor, polished into an heirloom the lads can treasure when they are gray of beard. Titled simply "To Tom Jr. and Charlie," it is a 61-page history of their old man's early life.

How-things-were-when-I-was-a-child is a popular topic around many a family. Has been for hundreds of years. But it's more meaningful today than ever before, because the farther and faster we race into the computer age, the wider the gap between generations grows.

That's what makes Siler's gift unique. In the span of a single generation, his world leaped from the horse-drawn surrey he rode to church to jumbo jetliners that carried him to international sporting events.

"This is something I've been meaning to do for a long time," said Siler, retired *News-Sentinel* sports editor and columnist. "At 76, I'm old enough to be the boys' grandfather. For years, the boys and my wife had been after me to preserve the stories they'd heard at family gatherings.

"Finally, Tom Jr. sat me down last Christmas and said, 'Dad, if you don't do it soon, you never will.'"

"That hit home. That's when I put the first sheet of paper into the typewriter."

What was it like to grow up in Jellico during the early coal mining days? Let these Silerisms paint the picture:

—I never gave sex education much thought. After all, a boy who is around chickens and pigs and takes a cow for a "visit" with the bull doesn't need pictures drawn for him.

—The revenue agents gave us occasional excitement. All very hush-hush, but somehow many knew that the agents were in town. I recall one night when the word got out that the "law" had a rendezvous with the moonshiners on Pine Mountain. They did. Three men were shot to death that night, one officer and two of the whiskey runners.

—Before you could drive, you had to learn to start the car, which meant cranking it. The trick was to grasp the crank firmly but without wrapping your thumb around it. Thus you could let go quickly if it recoiled. Otherwise, a broken arm was possible.

—Most churches were quite rigid on dancing. But it was all around us anyway. Such as a dance held in Jenkins' Garage on Main Street. I can't vouch for this, but rumor has it that our pastor went down and looked through the garage window, checking to see if any of his church folks were there.

—Chickens have no stamina. All one does is pick out the luckless fowl and begin trotting after him. Don't let him stop and rest. Just trot him. He will soon be exhausted. Pick him up, grab him by the neck, whirl the bird in a circle a few times. The chicken will fall to the ground, headless and flopping around briefly. Deliver the carcass to Mama and anticipate a breakfast of fried chicken, gravy, hot biscuits and homemade jelly.

—Did you ever work in sweet potatoes? The hills are elevated and the vines cover the ground. One must bend over and hold up the fragile vines while working the hoe with the other hand. Mama would just laugh when I told her how my back ached, reminding me how good the potatoes would taste in December.

So what does all this have to do with Father's Day in Knoxville, this year?

Plenty.

If you're a father, you owe it to your kids to preserve your family stories, too. And don't give me that business about not having Tom Siler's tools or skills. A blue-line tablet and a Bic pen will suffice.

Forget about an outline and spelling and punctuation. One rough draft is all you need. You can even record conversations on tape, if you like.

Don't worry about spit and polish. All that matters is that the job gets done.

Because when you finish, you'll have a gift that lasts forever.

Sam Venable
Knoxville News-Sentinel, June 15, 1986.
Used by permission.

MEMORIAL DAY: THAT OTHERS MAY NOT DIE

Memorial Day is a day to honor lives lost in all military conflicts. Originally, it was a day to commemorate those who lost their lives in the Civil War. According to one tradition, the day began when some Southern women chose May 30 to decorate the graves of both Confederate and Union soldiers killed in the Battle of Shiloh. More than remembering war dead, the day was to help bring reconciliation to a bitter, scarred and sharply-divided nation.

Popular celebrations of Memorial Day tend to emphasize the

importance of military strength and military preparedness. The day might be more appropriately observed as a time to resolve old hostilities and work for peace, so that there will not be more war casualties.

Patriotic Questioning

On Memorial Day, quiet, manicured lawns lined with orderly rows of white crosses invite us to peaceful reflections honoring our nation's heroes—those men and boys who fought and died for our country's honor. Peaceful military cemeteries somehow soften the horror of death on the battlefield. While it is our purpose to honor our war dead, do we instead glorify war?

What problems are solved because soldiers die? Is our world a better place because we are willing to give our young on the altars of national security?

What about those who are now filling graves for tomorrow's "peaceful" cemeteries? Are bereaved families comforted by the honor they receive?

What about war? Does it bring peace and life or death, destruction and empty ceremonies?

Children of War

This Memorial Day let us celebrate life. Let us honor the survivors of war in our time—the children of war.

In 1986 the Children of War Tour brought young people who had grown up in war-torn areas of the world to the United States. Joined by North American teenagers they toured cities across the country, telling their stories:

"Children have an ability to forgive and forget. We are less sure that we are absolutely right. Adults who are sure they are absolutely right, they make war over their absolute rightness. Now, look at us, look at us. We represent the places in the world where men are killing each other and yet we are living together."

—Arn Chorn, Cambodia

"We believe that wars are not the solutions in our countries. We must learn to live together because we are the future. We've been learning from old people, and old people is [sic] teaching us to kill."

—Hector Recino, El Salvador

Said a 15-year-old boy to his Minneapolis hosts, "We don't call this a basement where you play Ping-Pong. We call it a bomb shelter."

—Marwan Najjar, West Beirut, Lebanon

Confirming the importance of the young people's mission, Nobel Prize winner Archbishop Desmond Tutu accompanied the children on their visit and told them: "When you go back home and walk down the street and people ask 'Who is that?' you tell them, 'I am a sign of hope.'"

(The above quotes are taken from "Brave Bearers of Hope, the Children of War Tour" by Judith Thompson, Coordinator of the Children of War Program at the Religious Task Force, Mobilization for Survival, Brooklyn, New York. Used by permission.)

SUMMER: LONG DAYS AND VACATIONS

In the Northern Hemisphere summer arrives on June 20 or 21, when the summer solstice occurs. On that day the sun is high in the sky and there are more daylight hours than on any other day.

Traditionally, summer is the time to take vacations. Since ancient times people have recognized the importance of changes in routine to help restore minds, bodies and spirits. While festivals and celebrations helped to provide them with brief changes in routine, vacations—as we know them today—were generally available only to the wealthy.

The nineteenth-century labor movement is responsible for the now widespread practice of vacations with pay, the only way most working people can afford to take time off from their jobs. With children free from school for a couple of months, vacations came to be associated with summertime.

While the idea of taking a vacation is still a privilege accorded to relatively few people in the world, the tourist business is now recognized as the world's largest industry. Although widely viewed as an ideal form of development for poor areas both in this country and abroad, there are many questions about whether tourism aids or inhibits development.

Regardless of the time of year they are taken, vacations should be occasions for rest and renewal. But unless vacationers exercise care, they can also be self-destructive and exploitative of others. Like other celebrations, vacations can be times to restore the human spirit without sacrificing concerns for other people and the environment.

"Los Niños 'Vacation' in Mexico, a Gloriously Different Experience"

Have you ever dreamed of a vacation "south of the border?" At the sound of this phrase, the mind sketches scenes of sunny beaches, tropical weather, and plush resorts. At least, that was my first impression and experience of Mexico—waterskiing in Acapulco, sunbathing in Cancun. Recent experiences, however, have provided a different "vacation:" three summers in poverty-stricken neighborhoods, crowded orphanages and a squalid jail. And I wouldn't trade those experiences for all the luxurious tourist resorts in the world!

This atypical vacation was possible through "Los Niños"...no, it's not a travel agency or a Mexican airline. Los Niños, which means "the children," is a nonprofit organization that provides direct aid, education and development service to the impoverished people of Tijuana and Mexicali, Mexico.

The program has a powerful three-fold goal: 1) to provide direct help to meet the basic needs of impoverished children and families in a way that respects their dignity and human worth; 2) to catalyze cooperative efforts among the poor so that they might discover and develop their own resources for change; 3) to educate the affluent about the need for personal responsibility and structural transformation in a hungry world.

Volunteers are invited to spend a weekend, week or summer working on the Mexican-American border. They are encouraged to deepen their educational experience by participating in social justice seminars, sharing sessions and ecumenical worship services.

Working out of two barrack-style buildings in San Ysidro, California, the two-year volunteer staff and short-term volunteers commute daily into Tijuana, Mexico, just minutes away. The stark contrast often shocks new volunteers. Gone are the lush southern suburbs of affluent San Diego. Instead, one finds dirty city streets surrounded by the dusty, crowded confusion of shouting vendors and beleaguered beggars.

In the morning, the Los Niños van struggles up steep and rocky unpaved roads to *Panamericana Alta,* a neighborhood built on a former city trash dump site. The inhabitants live in dwellings of rearranged refuse, made from discarded scraps of metal, wood and cardboard. Nothing is wasted—even an old, ragged mattress frame makes a sturdy wall.

The people here make their living at the nearby functioning dump, wading through smelly, smouldering rubble to collect bits of glass, aluminum cans, scrap metal and bottles—all to be resold for a mere pittance of pesos. Some families have traveled hundreds of miles to work in this dump—"to feed my children," as one woman explained.

After two summers of helping out in this neighborhood, I find myself this summer as *directora,* or principal, of the small summer school operated by Los Niños. "School," for us, is a dirt floor shack with two wobbly tables and too few chairs. Since the community is without running water or electricity, we learn to innovate: removing a few boards from the walls provides natural light and "air conditioning."

The purpose of the school is to supplement the education that some of the children receive at nearby Mexican schools and also to teach those who are unable to attend these schools. At Los Niños, education is a concrete tool that can, we hope, provide a way out of the vicious cycle of poverty.

The children's needs are so basic that volunteer teachers feel extremely useful, teaching math and reading and writing skills. Though we teach in Spanish, the non-Spanish-speaking volunteers also feel needed in helping children print the alphabet and write their names, and organizing craft and recreational activities.

Although rewarding, the days are not without frustration. Stray dogs and chickens wander in and out of the schoolroom during classes. The student body magically doubles from 25 to 50 within the first two weeks! One class is moved outside and another class into the van; the chickens stay.

The painful challenges never cease. But inspirations outweigh frustrations. In our seven-week program, a 10-year old learns to add and subtract for the first time; a 14-year-old child proudly learns to read; and yet another, at age 8, holds a pencil for the first time and finally learns to print his name.

It is ironic to be placed in this "teacher" role. I feel more like a student! In a few months, the children have taught me far more than my years of formal education.

I have learned not only how to live without plumbing or electricity, but I have also realized the countless number of gifts I take for granted: abundant, purified water and reliable, nutritious meals each day.

I have learned some of the great joys possible that can't be derived from material possessions: the healthy, wholesome ecstasy of a child's hug and the glad comfort of a loving, affirmative family.

And, most precious of all, I have gained a revealing view of myself from Third-World eyes. I now realize what a marvelous gift it is to have my basic needs met and my rights as a human being respected. And I now see that along with this comes the responsibility to help others secure the same.

Mev Puleo
Los Niños
San Ysidro, California

"What You Shouldn't Leave Home Without: Ethics and Tourism in the Third World"

Travel changed my life. My traditional Mississippi Delta background provided me with a set of stereotypes about life, people and the world; and though I questioned those values at an early age, I learned to accept their teachings and adjusted my behavior accordingly. But my first trip away from home challenged all that. As a college student I spent a summer working for the United Methodists at a camp in Hawaii.

Everything was different—food, foliage, friends. And for the first time I met people prejudiced against me because I was white.

But I was enthralled by what I saw and felt, and this first experience of tourism became one of the most profound learning experiences of my life. The way I saw myself in the world was radically changed, so I decided to see more of the world in order to have a better understanding of my place in its great diversity. Throughout the rest of my formal schooling, I chose summer jobs with people whose culture was different from my own. After graduation I became a travel agent—a job that enables me to help others have the broadening, life-changing experiences I have enjoyed since that first trip to Hawaii.

Tourism is now the largest industry in the world. To disassociate ourselves from it is almost impossible. But the more I learn about this international business, the more concerned I become about its ethics and the more I question the effect of this giant industry on our world. The ethics of tourism are highly undeveloped. Church offices and boards—with their huge travel budgets—are among the greatest supporters of this industry, largely without questioning the industry into which they invest so much money. The truth is, tourism is no longer a frivolous, middle-class issue; it encompasses human rights and justice causes throughout the world. As supporters of the industry, individuals and institutions must take ethical questions into account.

What are these questions? Last year I attended a conference sponsored by the Center for Responsible Tourism in San Anselmo, California. There I heard reports from people who constantly deal with difficult issues forced upon their countries by the demands of tourism. In Tahiti, tourists consume precious water resources, making water tables sink dangerously low. Hawaiians live on beaches because of insufficient housing on islands sporting luxurious hotels. In South Africa, government officials boast that tourists will not be affected by ongoing racial strife. Puerto Rico's fishermen and land owners are displaced so that hotels and resorts can be built. And in the Philippines, along with other Asian countries, tourism for prostitution is big business.

Stories about tourism's abuses seem endless. Why do these things happen? An important reason is that poor nations are encouraged by world banking institutions to promote tourism as a way out of poverty. Now, however, many countries realize that profits from tourism go out of their countries, back to outside investors. As host countries they are left with their lands defaced, their people put into degrading roles and their way of life changed forever.

The Ecumenical Coalition on Third World Tourism was formed in response to these burdening concerns. Meeting several times in the past few years, this group has developed an important concept for responsible tourism: a code of ethics for tourists, helping guests to be respectful and gracious in their visits to other countries.

While tourism presents many problems, the industry also provides an opportunity for people from different cultures to meet—crossing political, social and religious barriers. However, in order for this human encounter to take place, those of us who travel must be willing to treat people with dignity. While at seminary I wrote a paper comparing the influx of northerners in the South after the Civil War to U. S. intervention in Central America. I made that comparison to help people understand the powerlessness and frustration felt by citizens in other countries when touring Americans fail to treat them with respect.

This past year I had the opportunity to help a youth group in San Anselmo, California, make their travel plans for a work project in Jamaica. The group was very careful to make sure all Jamaicans that helped with arrangements for the group were adequately compensated. In addition, a group of Jamaican young people were invited to work alongside the young people from California. Together they created a much-needed playground for the village. Tourists in this instance treated hosts with complete dignity, and the experience for everybody was very fulfilling.

A number of organizations are helping travel consumers meet recreational and educational needs in ways that are not dehumanizing to people in host countries. For help in this area you may want to contact the following:

Center for Responsible Tourism, 2 Kensington Road, San Anselmo, California;

Contours, P. O. Box 11-357, Bangkok 10110, Thailand.

Terre Balof
Atlanta, Georgia

A Code of Ethics for Tourists

1. Travel in a spirit of humility and with a genuine desire to meet and talk with local people.
2. Be aware of the feelings of the local people to prevent what might be offensive behavior. Photographers, particularly, must be respectful of subjects.
3. Cultivate the habit of listening and observing, rather than merely hearing or seeing.
4. Realize that other people may have concepts of time and thought patterns which are very different—not inferior, only different.

5. Instead of seeing only the "beach paradise," discover the richness of another culture and way of life.

6. Get acquainted with local customs and respect them.

7. Rather than knowing all the answers, cultivate the habit of listening.

8. Remember that you are only one among many visitors. Do not expect special privileges.

9. If you want a "home away from home," why bother traveling?

10. As you shop and bargain, remember the poorest merchant will give up profit rather than dignity.

11. Make no promises to new, local friends that you cannot implement.

12. Spend time reflecting on your daily experiences in order to deepen your understanding. What enriches you may be robbing others.

The Christian Conference of Asia, 1975

Justice, Liberation and the Gospel
Travel opportunities to Central America
The Caribbean The Philippines The Middle East

The Center for Global Education coordinates travel seminars to several regions of the world where struggles for justice and liberation provide valuable learning experiences for U.S. citizens. The seminars are designed to challenge participants to expand their world view, through meetings with poor people and representatives of governmental and development agencies. Issues are explored within the context of the Christian gospel. Special trips can be organized for your group, or individuals may join any of our scheduled trips. For more information, contact the Center for Global Education, Augsburg College, Minneapolis, MN 55454, 612/330-1159.

Contributions to general operating expenses or travel seminar scholarship fund are welcome.

Center for Global Education

Center for Global Education
Augsburg College
731-21st Avenue South
Minneapolis, MN 55454

Phonefriend...
An **Alternative** way to serve latchkey children and their parents!

On-site after-school programs are wonderful—but you may not have personnel, facilities, or skills for that.

PHONEFRIEND is a telephone "warm-line" that can be set up with only a table, roladex file, call-forward and call-wait system on your phone, and volunteers to cover a few hours a month. Children can then call YOU when they are lonely, frightened, or just need someone to take a problem to.

A PHONEFRIEND Manual and Replication Packet (developed by the American Association of University Women in State College, PA) is available with complete details on how to set up this alternative to on-site care for latchkey children (0128P) $20.00. (Free descriptive brochures are also available (Q180L).

Discipleship Resources, The United Methodist Church, General Board of Discipleship, P.O. Box 189, Nashville, TN 37202.

Discipleship Resources
The United Methodist Church
General Board of Discipleship
P.O. Box 189
Nashville, TN 37202

St. Martin's Table
2001 Riverside Avenue
Minneapolis, MN 55454

Nein! **St. Martin's Table**
books · food · conversation

**A restaurant/bookstore owned and managed by the Community
of St. Martin, dedicated to peacemaking and social justice.**

Interested in books on simplicity of
lifestyle, peace/war, Central America, women's and
men's issues, spirituality, books for children?

Catalog available for mail order service.
To order catalog, please send name, address and
$1.00 to cover handling and postage
(will be refunded with first order.)

2001 Riverside Avenue   •   Minneapolis, MN 55454   •   612 / 339-3920

Faith and Life Press
718 Main, Box 347
Newton, KS 67114
(316) 283-5100

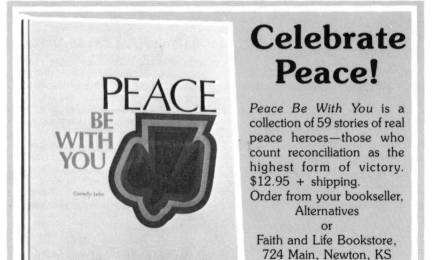

Celebrate Peace!

Peace Be With You is a
collection of 59 stories of real
peace heroes—those who
count reconciliation as the
highest form of victory.
$12.95 + shipping.
Order from your bookseller,
Alternatives
or
Faith and Life Bookstore,
724 Main, Newton, KS
67114.

**Baptist Peace Fellowship
of North America**
499 Patterson St.
Memphis, TN 38111

The Kingdom first?

☐ Yes. Inconveniently so.

☐ The Baptist Peace Fellowship of North America is a network of
Baptists involved in a variety of justice and peace issues.

☐ We believe the church's calling consists of giving its life for the
sake of the weak, the poor, the forgotten—
all those for whom the world has
little or no use.

☐ Won't you come wage peace
with us? Members ($15/yr.)
receive our bimonthly newsletter.
(Ask for the "Kingdom first?"
poster, free to new members.
Single copies, $2.50.)
BPFNA, 499 Patterson Street,
Memphis, TN 38111.

*The Kingdom of God FIRST? Really
FIRST?? . . . How inconvenient!*

Resources for Christians

Sermons by Martin Luther King, Jr.,
"Strength to Love," with a foreward by Coretta Scott
King; $6.00

Women and Worship
"No Longer Strangers," globally inclusive litanies, prayers,
affirmations of faith; $5.50

Transcultural Worship
"Cantemos! Let's Sing!" Spanish hymns and liturgical music
used in Cuernavaca, Mexico. Tape and book; $8.50

Southern African Liberation
"Freedom Is Coming," Songs of protest and praise from
South Africa. Tape and music book for mixed choir; $17.50
"Why, O Lord?" Psalms and sermons from Namibia; $5.00

...who care about justice
Write Lutheran Human Relations for complete resource list.

Lutheran Human Relations
2703 N. Sherman Blvd.
Milwaukee, WI 53210
(414) 871-7300

PEACE AND JUSTICE RESOURCES

AVAILABLE FOR

- Parenting
- Teachers
- Hunger
  - Economic Justice
  - Racism
    - Sexism
      - Peacemaking

WRITTEN MATERIAL FOR SALE ...

- Educating for Peace and Justice
  National, Global, and Religious Dimensions
- Parenting for Peace and Justice
- Solidarity with the People of Nicaragua
- Hope Springs from God
- Puppets for Peace and Global Family Puppets

AUDIO VISUALS FOR SALE...

- Building Shalom Families Videos
- Donahue Video on Parenting for Peace and
  Justice
- Families in Search of Shalom Filmstrip
  - Christian
  - Black American
  - Jewish
  - Spanish

FOR MORE INFORMATION WRITE OR CALL

The Institute for Peace & Justice
4144 Lindell #122, St. Louis, MO 63108
or (314) 533-4445

**The Institute for
Peace and Justice**
4144 Lindell #122
St. Louis, MO 63108
(314) 533-4445

What About the Russians?
A Christian Approach to U.S.-Soviet Conflict
Edited by Dale W. Brown

What are the Russians really like? Are they
believers or atheists? Why are we afraid of
them? How widespread is their influence in
the world? How should Christians respond
to communism?

These are some of the questions dealt with by
authorities in Russian history and culture and
by those who have travelled extensively in the Soviet Union. Writers include William Sloane Coffin, Jr., Richard Deats, Senator Mark Hatfield,
George Kennan, Bishop Leroy T. Matthiesen, Ron Sider, John Swomley,
Jr. and Jim Wallis. $6.95 plus $1.00 postage and handling.

Brethren Press, 1451 Dundee Ave., Elgin, IL 60120. Call toll free 800/323-8039.

Brethren Press
1451 Dundee Avenue
Elgin, IL 60120

Discipleship Resources
P.O. Box 189
Nashville, TN 37202
(615) 340-7285

DISCIPLESHIP·RESOURCES
MATERIALS FOR GROWTH IN CHRISTIAN FAITH AND LIFE

Books, Booklets, Manuals, and Audiovisuals
for
Ministries
in

Christian Education • Church and Society • Ministry of the Laity
World Methodism • Age-Level/Family • Ethnic Concerns • Evangelism
Higher Education and Ministry • United Methodist Men
Stewardship • Worship

AVAILABLE TITLES INCLUDE

Hungry Decisions (7844C)
We Can Break the Cycle of Child Abuse (DR021B)
Stress: How Christian Parents Cope (DR032B)
Fork in the Road: Young Adult Decisions (DR042B)
Youth Servant Team Handbook (2038C)
The Society of St. Stephen Handbook (LA015K)
We Don't Have Any Here—Planning for Ministries with
People with Disabilities in Our Communities (DR030B)

Free Catalog Available with Information on
Resources for All Aspects of Congregational Ministries

P.O. Box 189 • Nashville, TN 37202 • Phone (615) 340-7285

Cooperative Disaster Child Care Program
P.O. Box 188
500 Main Street
New Windsor, MD 21776
(301) 635-6464

COOPERATIVE

DISASTER CHILD CARE

. . .reaching and touching children in traumatic disaster settings

Responding to children in dealing with their fears, anger, and confusion at the time of a disaster is the main focus of this ecumenical program of trained volunteers.

Our goal is to have a state by state network of child care givers.

To reach this goal we need your help!

. . .attend a workshop and become a trained child care giver.

. . .your gift of money will help train more volunteers and provide funds for expenses incurred while on disaster response.

FOR INFORMATION CONTACT:
COOPERATIVE DISASTER CHILD CARE PROGRAM
P.O. BOX 188, 500 MAIN STREET
NEW WINDSOR, MD 21776
(301) 635-6464

8.
July and August

DOMINION DAY: CELEBRATING A UNITED CANADA

Dominion Day, one of Canada's most important national holidays, is celebrated on July 1 to honor the day the provinces of Canada were united in one government. The Dominion of Canada was created on July 1, 1867, by the terms of the British North America Act.

INDEPENDENCE DAY: REMEMBERING NATIONAL IDEALS

On July 4, 1776 the Continental Congress adopted the Declaration of Independence. The anniversary of that event, Independence Day, is regarded as the birthday of the United States. John Adams, one of the signers of that historic document, expressed what many feel is the spirit of the occasion:

> I am apt to believe that it will be celebrated by succeeding generations as the great anniversary festival. It ought to be commemorated as the day of deliverance, by solemn acts of devotion to God Almighty. It ought to be solemnized with pomp and parade, with shows, games and sports, guns, bells, bonfires and illuminations from one end of this continent to the other, from this time forward, forevermore. You will think me transported with enthusiasm, but I am not. I am well aware of the toil and blood and treasure that it will cost us to maintain this Declaration and support and defend these States. Yet, through all the gloom, I can see rays of ravishing light and glory. I can see that the end is worth more than all the means.

Out of the collective memory of those who came to America fleeing religious persecution and oppressive governments in Europe, Samuel West tempered Adam's enthusiasm with a warning:

> Unlimited submission and obedience is due to none but God alone.... To suppose that God has given a set of men power to require obedience to that which is unreasonable,

★ **Dominion Day**
(July 1)
★ **Independence Day**
(July 4)
★ **Hiroshima Day**
(August 6)
★ **Assumption Day**
(August 15)
★ **Women's Equality Day**
(August 26)

133

cruel and unjust is robbing the Diety of justice and goodness.

Black orator and editor Frederick Douglass spoke for slaves, Native Americans and other minorities who did not experience the freedom and justice proclaimed in the Declaration:

> What to the American slave is your Fourth of July? I answer, a day that reveals to him more than all other days of the year the gross injustice to which he is the constant victim. To him your celebration is a sham; your boasted liberty an unholy license....

Let neither West's nor Douglass' statement discourage celebrating the birth of this nation. Rather, let them be reminders that while the creation of this nation is unique in human history, it is also a very human and imperfect creation. To disregard the latter is to negate that uniqueness. An alternative July Fourth celebration may be informed by two considerations: First, unlimited loyalty is due only to God, not the nation. Second, legitimate patriotism requires that the nation be continually called to live out its vision of liberty and justice for *all*.

"Independence Day Could be a Real Bang"

The fourth of July is over. I admit, I'm glad. Frankly, I dread the holiday. When five days or so of *pop* and *bam* and *kaboom* finally grind to an end with the last illegal "bomb" at 1:30 a.m., I settle into restful sleep giving thanks that it will be 360 days until this mess comes again.

That's sad. Independence Day for a nation of people should be a glad occasion for me. Freedom from foreign domination is a longing of every human; it's a treasure many a nation dreams of this very day.

Two things interfere with my celebrating. Obnoxious, disturbing-the-peace, dangerous firecrackers are the first. (I am specifically talking about those items, often lit and thrown, whose sole purpose is noise, not beauty.) The second is our lack of any genuine celebration of independence or freedom. It seems to me that once a year we make a lot of racket and cloak it in hollow slogans about freedom.

I find it contradictory that we choose to acknowledge the fragile, priceless gift of national freedom by doing something as irrelevant to freedom and ofttimes costly to health and home as going around setting off explosives. I watch children, only a bit conscious of what they have hold of, casually lighting whatever's in the sack, barely getting it away in time, throwing it toward another person or into traffic for entertainment. I watch animals hide in fear. I hear people complain. I read stories of fires and accidents and injuries. This is celebrating?

But we persist. Exploding explosives is how we celebrate freedom. Surely we will wake up one day and stop it. Like so many ills and addictions, it will likely require some serious accident or alarming statistic to end what could have been stopped if we had used common sense.

So what is the heart of this holiday? Is it not remembering and reaffirming freedom—the right of a nation's people to govern themselves, to establish an economy that strengthens their security, to enjoy life with dignity and promise for future generations? We enjoy those blessings. We rebel when those principles are violated in our

"The care of human life and happiness is the first and only legitimate object of good government."

Thomas Jefferson

134

neighborhood, our church, our city or our nation's capital. So how can we celebrate freedom in a way that truly recalls, reminds and teaches its true character and the struggles required to achieve it?

What if one year in our own town the Fourth of July celebration was planned by our librarians, our high school and college history teachers, our museum director, and our refugee neighbors who know first hand freedom's high price. These people would be gifted in history, in its important lessons for today, and in the saga of freedom not only in our country but elsewhere on the globe. What if for one day radio stations played only songs of protest, of freedom, or courage, of believing in something enough to die for it—just like we hear Christmas carols all day December 25. What if churches and schools dramatized the lives of individuals whose faith and courage have shaped our national character, inspiring us to be strong and free. What if our national leaders were challenged on this day to look across the earth and name other nations whose struggle for independence today is akin to ours over 200 years ago.

I can imagine an incredible celebration with dance and drama and music and story-telling replacing explosives in the alley. I can picture immigrants and elders telling us of freedom in ways we would not forget. If in this way we could learn and relearn what our freedom really is and how we got it, we would better understand other nations and peoples struggling this very day for that same treasured quality of life. We might even see that 200 years ago, from another country's viewpoint, we were the guerillas and revolutionaries trying to disrupt the status quo.

You know, Independence Day could give me a real bang.

> Terry Woodbury
> *Silver City Record*
> Kansas City, Kansas
> July 11, 1985
> Used by permission.

> "The true standard by which to gauge a culture is the extent to which reverence, compassion, justice are to be found in the daily lives of a whole people, not only individuals."
>
> Abraham J. Heschel

Celebrate the Fourth by Welcoming Strangers

The United States is a nation of foreigners. Since colonial times, over 50 million immigrants have landed in this country.

"Give me your tired, your poor, your huddled masses yearning to breathe free," reads the inscription on the Statue of Liberty. Safe harbor for those seeking asylum is a national ideal worth recalling on the Fourth of July.

Are there too many people taking advantage of this offer? Some think so. According to the U.S. Attorney General, "We are losing control of our borders." This is not a new opinion. King George tried unsuccessfully to restrict immigration to the colonies. His action prompted one of the grievances leveled against British rule in the Declaration of Independence.

Actually, we have never had control of our borders. If the first Americans had controlled their borders, most of us would not be here. Perhaps we are afraid that newcomers to the U.S. will treat us like our ancestors treated Native Americans.

Knowing what to do about foreigners in need of refuge is not easy. The social and economic implications of immigration are complex, both for U.S. citizens and for those who come from abroad. But this

country's ideal of justice for all should be protected as a national goal.

With regard to those who are already here, the Bible's mandate to us is clear: welcome strangers and help them get settled in their new homes. Many churches are recognizing their responsibility and persevering in a climate which sometimes questions even the presence of foreigners in the United States.

Celebrate this Independence Day by recalling why you or your ancestors came to America and compare the reasons people are coming today. Discover all you can about this complex problem. But don't stop there. Find practical ways to welcome and assist those who are already here.

HIROSHIMA DAY: REMEMBERING THE PAST FOR THE SAKE OF PEACE

Hiroshima Day commemorates the first use of nuclear weapons on August 6, 1945. Peace Day, as it is sometimes called, recalls the insight of Mahatma Gandhi, who said that nuclear weapons would make peace a necessity. The bomb dropped on Hiroshima killed more than 100,000 people instantly. Three days later another 50,000 died when the second bomb was dropped on Nagasaki. Tens of thousands died more slowly from radiation poisoning. Survivors—their children and grandchildren—continue to be affected in ways that are not yet understood.

Although the events behind this observance are unpleasant to recall, the possibility that nuclear weapons might be used again is making this day an important time for people all over the world to say "Never Again!"

Sadako and the Thousand Paper Cranes

In 1955, a 13-year-old Japanese girl died of "atom bomb disease," radiation-induced leukemia. She was one of many children to suffer the aftereffects of the bomb dropped on Hiroshima in 1945.

During her illness, Sadako Sasaki buoyed her spirits by folding paper cranes. Japanese legend says that cranes live for a thousand years, and that the person who folds a thousand paper cranes will be granted a wish. With each paper crane she made, Sadako wished for recovery from her fatal disease. Before her death she had folded 644 paper cranes. Classmates completed her task so that she was buried with a thousand cranes.

Stories of this brave Japanese girl spread quickly. Sadako's friends collected money from children all over Japan to build the Children's Peace Monument. Today, standing in Hiroshima Peace Park is a statue of Sadako; her outstreched hands hold a golden crane. The inscription reads:

This is our cry,
This is our prayer,
Peace in the world.

Sadako and the Thousand Paper Cranes
by Eleanor Coerr
Used by permission.

Middlebury, Indiana to Hiroshima, Japan

Students, teachers, administrators, aides and media center personnel made it happen—from Middlebury, Indiana to Hiroshima, Japan! Highlight of the year for Jefferson, Middlebury and York Elementary School media centers was the story, project and journey of the paper cranes.

It all began with a story hour featuring *Sadako and the Thousand Paper Cranes*. Students and teachers at the three Middlebury elementary schools were challenged by this moving story of Sadako's faith and courage and her friends' dedication to peace. Then each school adopted an origami project, the art of Japanese paper folding, honoring Sadako by re-enacting her story and sharing their concerns about nuclear war and their hopes for world friendship and peace.

At each school students worked hard to reach their goal of folding 1,000 gold and silver paper cranes which were displayed for several weeks as mobiles in the media centers. Most students folded at least one crane; some folded many more to achieve the objective. Principals, teachers and parents also lent their skill and support.

Plans were made to send the completed cranes by a nine-year-old girl and her six-year-old brother who would be spending the summer with their aunt, a former community teacher now living in Tokyo. Included in each school's carefully packed box was a photo of the mobile as displayed in the media center with the following laminated message:

To: Children's Peace Monument
Peace Park, Hiroshima, Japan
To honor Sadako Sasaki and to share our hopes
for peace in the world.
From: The students of...(name and address of each school).

Taking the cranes to Hiroshima's Peace Park was described in a letter by their teacher friend to the children of Middlebury in this way: "Your 3,000 paper cranes are at home now under the statue of Sadako Sasaki in Hiroshima's Peace Park. We went straight to the Peace Park and

unpacked the beautiful, shiny cranes. We tied each thousand together, attaching the message from each school. A reporter from Hiroshima's *Chugoku* newspaper asked questions and took lots of pictures. Thousands and thousands of paper cranes were laid carefully around the monument. What a beautiful sight—rainbow colors, patterned origami, silver and gold—all together, made in hopes of peace."

From this activity came rewarding experiences in teaching, learning and teamwork. In many classrooms, Japanese culture and folklore were featured, with projects in haiku poetry and other origami projects. Besides learning to work together, many students experienced a memorable and positive way to deal with the bombing of Hiroshima. In 1985, the fortieth anniversary of the bombing, 3,000 cranes from the three Middlebury elementary schools made their dramatic plea for peace.

Elizabeth Johnson
Elementary Media Coordinator
Middlebury Community Schools
Middlebury, Indiana

How to fold a paper crane

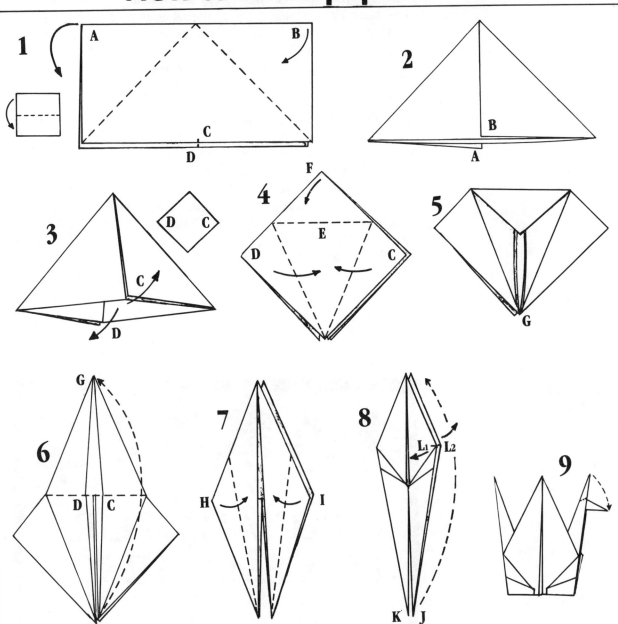

1. Fold a square piece of paper in half horizontally. Then fold **A** back to bottom center (*D*), and **B** *forward* to front bottom center (**C**).

2. Your paper should look like this.

3. Pull **C** (the front) and **D** (the back) apart all the way until you have a flat diamond (as in small diagram).

4. Fold top layers of **C** and **D** inward to center line at **E** and fold down **F** along dotted line.

5. Your paper should look like this.

6. Now here's the tricky part: Unfold step 4. Take top layer *only* at **G** and pull it up making use of the crease (dotted line). This allows points **C** and **D** to fold back to center line along creases. Turn paper over and repeat steps 4, 5 and 6, ignoring new flap topped by point **G**.

7. With split at bottom, fold **H** and **I** inward so that edges meet center line. Turn paper over and repeat.

8. Temporarily open flaps at **L1** and **L2**. Pull J up to top between flaps and close flaps (**L1** and **L2**). Repeat with **K**. Fold down head. Fold down wings.

Alternatives, P.O. Box 429, Ellenwood, Georgia 30049

WOMEN'S EQUALITY DAY: VICTORY FOR WOMEN'S SUFFRAGE

Women's Equality Day commemorates the victory of the Woman's Suffrage Movement which won women the right to vote. On August 26, 1920, those rights were secured by the ratification of the Nineteenth Amendment. Despite the many changes in the status of women since that time, full equality with men is yet to be achieved.

Women's Equality Day celebrates the history of women's struggles for status and rights.

Tabletalk for Women's Equality Day

Achievement of the right to vote in the early twentieth century did not come easily. Advocates were ridiculed, harassed and sometimes beaten. The infamous practice of force-feeding was practiced on hunger-striking women, jailed for protesting their denial of the right to vote. How many of the leaders of the Woman Suffrage Movement can you name (e.g., Susan B. Anthony, Carrie Chapman Catt, Julia Ward Howe, Lucretia C. Mott, Elizabeth Cady Stanton, Sojourner Truth)? What are the important women's rights issues today?

Fellowship of Reconciliation
Box 271
Nyack, NY 10960-0271

ESPECIALLY FOR PEACEMAKERS

Celebrate happy occasions, holidays, friendships, and love with cards, calendars, books, T-shirts, or a subscription to *Fellowship* magazine.

For a holiday catalog and a sample copy of *Fellowship*, write to:

Fellowship of Reconciliation
Box 271
Nyack, NY 10960-0271

DOROTHY DAY

"the woman who changed the sensibility of American Catholicism"
—F.A. Homann, S.J.

LOVE IS THE MEASURE, *Jim Forest.* "Jim Forest has written with candor, with great skill and greater love, a life of Dorothy Day that is radiant. The spirit of this unlikely and splended woman shines, red-hot from the refiner's fire, on every page."
—*Pax Christi*
Cloth $14.95

MEDITATIONS/DOROTHY DAY, *edited by Stanley Vishnewski.* Over one hundred meditations of our times by a leader of American Christianity. Reissued edition.
Paper $3.95

PAULIST PRESS
997 Macarthur Blvd., Mahwah, N.J. 07430
1-201-825-7300

Paulist Press
997 Macarthur Blvd.
Mahwah, NJ 07430

For two decades we have worked at the grassroots level in rural communities around the South. Through community based cooperative economic development efforts, we, our member cooperatives and credit unions have worked to generate new income, jobs, services, training, awareness and a spirit of self-help and change for many low income and economically exploited people in some of the most depressed and per-persistently poverty stricken rural counties in America.

We need your tax exempt contributions to continue to organize poor people to address their own problems.

**Federation of
Southern Cooperatives/
Land Assistance Fund**
P.O. Box 95
Epes, AL 35460

100 Edgewood Avenue, NW
Suite 1228
Atlanta, GA 30303

Co-op America
2100 M Street, NW
Suite 310
Washington, DC 20063
(202) 872-5307
1-800-424-2667

We Don't Just Talk About It...

We Do It!

Co-op America is taking the *first* critical steps to build an economic system which lives up to our values. Co-op America is a non-profit national membership association linking hundreds of progressive organizations and thousands of equally concerned individuals.

We want you to join with us to build an economic alternative . . . a marketplace where social values and community accountability are as important as the bottom line.

Building Economic Alternatives

As a Co-op America member, here are some of the action-oriented benefits you receive:

- A **Catalog** with hundreds of products that will delight and challenge you—natural fiber clothing, political books, furniture, Appalachian crafts, gift items, Third World products, music, and much more—all from Co-op America member organizations.

- Access to an innovative **health insurance plan** that provides you with excellent protection and benefits as well as socially responsible investment of premiums and input into plan changes.

- **Socially responsible investment** information—how to receive a secure and strong return on your money and feel good about it.

- *Building Economic Alternatives*, the quarterly magazine that provides practical strategies to help you integrate your politics, lifestyle choices and values.

- -

☐ **Please send me more information on membership and the many services available to members.**

☐ **I want to join Co-op America; enclosed is $15.**

Name_____ Phone (_____)_____

Address_____ County_____

City_____ State_____ Zip_____

Co-op America, 2100 M Street, NW, Suite 310, Washington, DC 20063.
1-800-424-2667 or (202) 872-5307

402

9.
September and October

LABOR DAY

Peter J. McGuire, president and founder of the United Brotherhood of Carpenters and Joiners, instituted Labor Day to recognize the contributions of laborers and acknowledge the role unions have played in protecting workers from exploitation. He chose the first Monday in September because he saw it as the most pleasant time of the year—midway between the Fourth of July and Thanksgiving—and it filled a wide gap in the chronology of legal holidays. Labor Day is a holiday in all fifty states and the District of Columbia.

Labor Day weekend has become a time for final outings and vacations before students return to school. Leisure activities are particularly appropriate since paid holidays and vacations are possible, in large part, because of the labor movement. Labor Day provides a chance to learn more about the productive history of the labor movement as well as its recent history of decline. This is a day to be grateful for those who labor. It is also a day to be more aware of those who want to work but remain jobless because of current problems in American industry.

AUTUMN BEGINS

Although Labor Day marks the end of summer social activities, autumn officially begins on September 22 or 23, when the autumnal equinox occurs. On this day, like the vernal equinox which marks the beginning of spring, the sun appears directly above the equator.

Learn about the changing seasons. Teach children—with a walk in a park, in the back yard or out in the country—about what happens in nature. Autumn is the time when nature prepares for winter: flowers die; trees lose their leaves; animals develop warmer coats. In areas without four distinct seasons, children can learn why these changes do not occur where they live.

★ **Labor Day**
(first Monday in September)

★ **Autumn Begins**
(September 22 or 23)

★ **Rosh Hashana**
(September/October)

★ **Yom Kippur**
(September/October)

★ **Sukkot**
(September/October)

★ **Columbus Day**
(second Monday in October)

★ **Canadian Thanksgiving**
(second Monday in October)

★ **World Food Day**
(October 16)

★ **United Nations Day**
(October 24)

★ **Halloween**
(October 31)

★ **Reformation Day**
(Sunday nearest October 31)

143

ROSH HASHANA: JEWISH NEW YEAR

Rosh Hashana, celebrated on the first day of the lunar month of Tishri, falls sometime in September or October. In contrast to the frivolity associated with many New Year's Day celebrations, Rosh Hashana, or Jewish New Year, is a most solemn holiday. On that sacred day, according to Jewish tradition, the world is created anew and set right by God's power. Ancient ritual for worship dictates that the *shofar*, a ram's horn, be blown to call the faithful to purify themselves. Those who are not totally right with God and their fellow humans have ten days, the Days of Awe, before Yom Kippur to make reparations through fasting, prayer, penitence and righting wrongs.

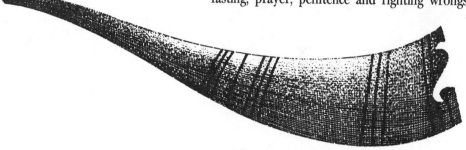

YOM KIPPUR: DAY OF ATONEMENT

Yom Kippur, Judaism's highest holy day, is held in such high regard that it is known as "a Sabbath of Sabbaths." According to tradition, on this day Moses descended from Mount Sinai with the Ten Commandments after God forgave the Israelites for worshiping the golden calf.

Yom Kippur is a day of strict fasting for everyone except children and sick people. No business is transacted and normal routines are suspended. The entire day is devoted to self-examination and repentance.

Atonement themes found in Scripture are read on that day: Leviticus 16, Numbers 29:7-11, Isaiah 57:14-58:14, and finally, the book of Jonah. When Yom Kippur was observed in the Temple in Jerusalem, the emphasis was on seeking forgiveness from God through the mediation of the High Priest. Since the destruction of the Temple, the emphasis is on praying directly to God for forgiveness.

Yom Kippur ends with the longest and loudest cry of the ancient shofar, sounding a note of hope for the new year. Almost another year goes by before the shofar is heard in the synagogue again.

Both the personal and communal goal of the ten days of purification is to begin the new year in harmony with God. A Jewish legend says: "It is out of kindness toward his creatures that the Lord remembers them year after year on Rosh Hashanah, that their sins may not grow too numerous...[Otherwise] their sins would grow to such an extent as to doom the world, God forbid. So this revered day assures the world of survival."

Tabletalk for Yom Kippur

In addition to recognizing that this is Judaism's most important holy day, it is also a good day to recall the common roots of modern Judaism and Christianity. Read and discuss Isaiah 57 and 58, scriptures that are immensely important for both traditions.

144

SUKKOT: FESTIVAL OF BOOTHS

The Jewish Festival of Booths is celebrated for eight days beginning with the fifteenth day of the lunar month of Tishri, fifteen days after Rosh Hashanah and five days after Yom Kippur. Originally a harvest festival, this day is increasingly being observed by synagogues as a time to share food with those who need it. The custom at Sukkot is to build and live in a hut made of branches and boughs in order to recall times of Jewish homelessness and uncertainty (Leviticus 23:42-43). Sukkot also marks the end of the solemn period of the high holy days.

Tabletalk for Sukkot

Recall times of homelessness and uncertainty in your family history and remember those who are homeless on this day—those in refugee camps or on city streets. If you are not already doing so, consider joining the efforts of those working with homeless people and other refugees.

COLUMBUS DAY: "DAY OF THE RACE"

Columbus Day is celebrated each year on October 12—the federal observance coming on the second Monday in October—to commemorate the discovery of America by Christopher Columbus in 1492. First observed in the United States in 1792, the day is also remembered in Latin America, Canada, Spain and Italy. Although Columbus Day is not a national holiday, it is a legal holiday in several states. Since the late nineteenth century, it has had special meaning for American citizens of Italian descent.

In Latin America, Columbus Day is called Dia de la Raza (Day of the Race). This date commemorates the birth of a new "race" of people, born of the mixture of Europeans and native Americans. The tragic irony of this celebrated day is that so little discovery took place. There was no time for discovery, only arrogant confrontation by the Europeans. The European conquest began a new age of dominance over native Americans from both hemispheres. That they should observe this day more with mourning than rejoicing is understandable.

Celebrate this day with your own efforts to discover the two peoples who came together, European and native American, and the new race born out of their confrontation. This is the heritage of Hispanics living in this country. Like St. Patrick's Day and other days identified with

particular ethnic groups, Columbus Day is a time to chip away at stereotypes of Hispanics and Italian Americans.

WORLD FOOD DAY

On October 16, in the midst of the traditional harvest season, over 150 nations observe World Food Day. Established by the United Nations in 1980, its purpose is to mobilize concern about the systemic dimensions of food production, food distribution and world hunger. A wide variety of educational resources for use on or around World Food Day are available through the World Food Day National Committee, 1001 22nd St., NW, Washington, D.C. 20437.

UNITED NATIONS DAY: HOPES FOR WORLD ORDER

On October 24, 1945, the United Nations Charter was approved by a majority of its member nations. In 1947, the UN General Assembly passed a resolution designating October 24 as United Nations Day. The importance and hope for peace attached to the UN was so great that the National Council of Churches moved the date of World Order Sunday, a time for churches to reaffirm their responsibility for world peace and justice, to conform to United Nations Day—even before the UN General Assembly had made that day official.

United Nations Day presents an important opportunity to remember how interrelated the world has become, and how critical the need for international cooperation if humankind is to survive. The fact that the United Nations has been severely attacked by some in the United States magnifies the need to learn more about this institution, including its successes and its failures.

HALLOWEEN: ALL SAINTS' EVE

Halloween means the evening before All Hallows or All Saints' Day and is celebrated on October 31. The origins of the day come from the Druids' New Year celebration. Along with other groups, the Druids believed that on the last day of the year the dead came back to mingle with the living. In the eighth century Pope Gregory III moved All Hallows to November 1, probably an attempt to provide an alternative to the popular pagan festival. All Saints' Day was in honor of all the saints who had died, whether or not the church had yet offically canonized them. During the Middle Ages, All Hallows Eve became known as a special time for witches and sorcerers.

The tradition of Halloween as Mischief Night, when pranks of all sorts were played on the unsuspecting, likely originated with the old belief that on All Hallows Eve ghosts roamed the countryside playing tricks. Pranks could thus be blamed on the ghosts.

While Halloween is very popular with children, several factors compel us to reexamine current practices in celebrating Halloween. First, more candy is consumed by children on Halloween and the day after than in any other 48-hour period of the year; second, the return of Mischief Night, with malicious and destructive pranks especially in urban areas; and third, trick-or-treaters find harmful things like razors and poison in their collected goodies.

Creativity and planning, combined with moderation and safety, can make Halloween fun.

Halloween Lock-In

For their traditional Halloween Lock-In our Youth Group discussed Halloween and its connection to the festival of All Saints. Then each person received an unlighted candle before processing quietly to the chancel area of the dimly lit church building. Seated on the floor around the marble steps by the altar, we remembered people, now deceased, who had touched our lives in special ways. We recounted ways we continue to be connected to these people in "the communion of saints."

The large Paschal candle by the baptismal font had been lighted, symbolizing Christ's resurrection. With that symbol of resurrection assurance filling our thoughts, we shared the name of the person for whom our candle was lighted and what that person's life meant to us. Then, lighting our candles from the Paschal candle, we placed them in front of the altar.

The light of our candles flooded the church, just as the people they represented continue to illuminate our lives. During a time of quiet prayer we thanked God for the lives of these people, praying that we would be faithful to the light they had shared with us.

Pastor Richard L. Schaper
Lutheran Church of the Redeemer
Atlanta, Georgia

Community Pumpkin Patch

For Halloween we have a community Pumpkin Patch. Our local social service agency has a volunteer-operated community garden. Garden plots for individual use are free, but all takers must help plant and harvest one crop in the community garden to provide fresh produce for the food pantry. These community gardens are located on city land used as a leaf dump, and we have found that pumpkins grow well in uncultivated leaf mounds.

Just before Halloween our harvested pumpkins, supplemented by others we purchase, are placed in the Pumpkin Patch where customers trade cans of food for pumpkins—two food items for a small pumpkin; four for a medium pumpkin, etc. These canned goods are given to the local food pantry.

We make money for the food pantry by selling homemade pumpkin baked goods and apple cider. Two local residents set up their apple press and make fresh cider, stimulating sales by giving out free samples. In addition, volunteer artists paint a cute or scary face on pumpkins for 25 cents. For entertainment the zoo brings animals to pet, and the recreation center provides clowns for face painting.

The Pumpkin Patch has become quite a tradition in our community. It raises several hundred dollars for our food pantry and contributes many pounds of canned goods. This project requires little work and lasts one Saturday from 9 a.m.–1 p.m.

Mary and Bill Merrill
Columbus, Ohio

All Hallows Eve

We celebrate All Hallows Eve with a hot dog roast and bonfire. Everyone is encouraged to dress as a saint, but no draculas are turned away. We play games like "Pin the Crown on the Saint" and sing "I Sing a Song of the Saints of God" (Episcopal hymnal). We end with the service for All Hallows Eve around the bonfire.

Ed, Andrea, Nathanael & Rebekah Wills
Memphis, Tennessee

Fall Festival

We hosted a family party encouraging everyone (not just children!) to come dressed as Bible characters or saints. As folks gathered we sang fun, campfire-type songs. Then we all told who we were and were given the prize of a bookmark.

Afterwards the adults played table games (And they must have really enjoyed it, staying as late as they did!) while the kids had their choice of face painting, guessing the number of pieces of candy in a jar, bobbing for apples, bean bag toss, ping-pong ball toss or drawing faces on balloons. We had trouble getting people to leave, so perhaps we'll have another celebration next year!

Susan M. Landis
Orrville, Ohio

Family Halloween Celebration

Dress the whole family in costume and visit a pediatric ward. Get permission for your visit in advance, making sure your planned gifts to the children there are appropriate. Balloons, coloring books or comics may make better gifts than candy or gum. Or, if the hospital has no objections, bake cookies together and take them. Visit a few rooms briefly. The joy you bring to the patients and their parents is a real gift.

Joel E. Shirk
Cheshire, Connecticut

Finding Acceptable Alternatives

Although our four children at home—aged 7 to 11—were reluctant to give up costumed trick-or-treating, my wife and I had decided that the quantity of candy ingested and the risks to the children warranted stopping the tradition. As an alternative, we proposed a Halloween party at our house. After the children compiled their guest list, I called the invitees and their parents. Guests were to come dressed as historical heroes. Costumes were to be simple and made with whatever was available at home. Each person was to learn some factual data about the hero chosen, part of which would be required for admission to the party. They were instructed to keep their identity secret from the other participants until it would be revealed in a special game of charades. During the game they gave prearranged clues to their identities and acted out their characters. Among the heroes they chose were Joan of Arc, Sitting Bull, Martin Luther King, Jr., and Abraham Lincoln.

In addition to the hero-related activities, we did some of the more traditional things: bobbing for apples, eating homemade cookies prepared by their parents, and going through a haunted house designed by our kids in the loft of the barn.

In the spirit of ghosts and goblins, we took the kids out back of the barn in a small pasture where we sat down and talked about the spirits of the people who might have lived at this place many years ago: Indians, slaves, slave owners, tenant farmers and others. While we tried to make it a little scary, it was more an opportunity to remember those who had been there before us.

149

This party required a lot of planning as well as time, but the kids did not feel cheated out of Halloween. The next year, we enlarged the party to include the fifth and sixth grade class from our church.

Milo Thornberry
Ellenwood, Georgia

REFORMATION SUNDAY

On October 31, 1517, Martin Luther nailed his "Ninety-five Theses" to the church door in Wittenberg, Germany. Reformation Sunday, celebrated on the Sunday nearest October 31, celebrates that event as the official beginning of the Protestant Reformation. With this act Luther publicly protested practices of the Church which he believed to be wrong. He was especially incensed by the sale of "indulgences," a practice which led followers to believe they could buy forgiveness of their sins with cash. Resistance to reform by the Church at Rome, together with growing nationalism in northern Europe that was eager to reject Roman authority were key factors in igniting the biggest rupture in the Christian Church since the schism between the Roman and Eastern Churches in 1054.

Reformation Sunday should give perspective to the Reformation. As in any quarrel, points at issue are often distorted and oversimplified. Sometimes, a quarrel results in new insights for both parties. Without taking any joy in the division of the Church that occurred in the Reformation, celebrate the diversity and unity between the two traditions.

Peace Corps Partnership Program
806 Connecticut Avenue, NW
Washington, DC 20526

The Gift of New Horizons . . .
PEACE CORPS PARTNERSHIPS

Peace Corps Partnerships are about new horizons. For overseas communities they can mean assistance in improving water supplies or building a schoolhouse. For your family and friends it can mean entering a new world through contact with the Peace Corps Volunteer and community members involved in the project.

Partners select from a variety of projects around the world. And they know that *all* of their gift is applied to material project costs. but it is the communication and active participation with the overseas community that truly makes the gift of a Partnership a gift of new horizons.

For More Information and Free Loan of Films
Call 800/424–8580, ext. 227, or Write:
Peace Corps Partnership Program
806 Connecticut Avenue, N.W.
Washington, D.C. 20526

The Presbyterian Hunger Program

I want you to share your **Bread** with the **hungry**, open your homes to the homeless **poor**, remove the yoke of **injustice**, Let the **oppressed go free.**

Isaiah: 58

Eunice Cudzewicz

RESPONDING
TO HUNGER AND POVERTY
IN THE UNITED STATES AND
AROUND THE WORLD THROUGH

- Education
- Direct Food Relief
- Development Assistance
- Influencing Public Policy
- Lifestyle Integrity

Presbyterian Church (USA)
100 Witherspoon St.
Louisville, KY 40202-1396
(502) 569-5000

The Division of Overseas Ministries
The National Council of the
  Churches of Christ
  in the USA
475 Riverside Drive
New York, NY 10115
(212) 870-2175

What In The World Are You Doing?

In a world of painful images: hunger, disease, homelessness, illiteracy, injustice war, despair.

The Division of Overseas Ministries serves as a witness to Christ, through the loving and life-giving work of communities at home and abroad.

In Partnership with churches around the world that proclaim and live the Gospel;

In Solidarity with people's movements and communities in the pursuit of justice;

In Support of fundamental human rights—the right to food, shelter, clothing, health care, education, information;

In Education and Advocacy for change of attitudes and policies in the United States that affect the lives of people all over the world:

JOIN US IN THIS MINISTRY

Contributions or requests for information to D.O.M.
475 Riverside Drive, Room 606, New York, N.Y. 10115

Alternatives
P.O. Box 429
Ellenwood, GA 30049
(404) 961-0102

Celebrate Life

Become a Supporting Member of Alternatives. For $25 you'll get:

- a year's subscription to the Alternatives' Newsletter;
- a 10% discount on all Alternatives-produced resources;
- samples of new resources;
- opportunity to elect at-large Board members.

Alternatives, P.O. Box 429, Ellenwood, GA 30049

Live Responsibly

152

INVEST IN LIFE

RELIGIOUS NEWS SERVICE PHOTO

Your prayers and your gifts to the Evangelical Lutheran Church in America's Hunger Appeal enable poor and hungry people to improve their lives. Your contribution can provide an avenue for:

- Immediate food relief, plus long-range development assistance, both here and overseas;

- Advocacy in the halls of government, business, and the church itself for people who are poor;

- Talking with and listening to poor people and those who produce and distribute food;

- Raising awareness of our lifestyles and how they affect people around the world;

- Helping each other understand and alleviate the basic root causes of hunger.

Please contribute regularly either through your congregation or directly to the ELCA Hunger Appeal.

☐ Enclosed is my gift of $_____

☐ Please send me a brochure about the ELCA Hunger Appeal.

Please send regular offerings or inquiries through your congregation or directly to:
ELCA Hunger Appeal, Evangelical Lutheran Church in America, 8765 W. Higgins Road, Chicago, Illinois 60631, (312) 380-2700

Name_____

Address_____

City_____ State_____ Zip_____

**ELCA Hunger Appeal
Evangelical Lutheran
Church in America**
8765 W. Higgins Road
Chicago, IL 60631
(312) 380-2700

153

Bread for the World
802 Rhode Island Avenue, NE
Washington, DC 20018

Bread for the World

An Idea Worth Supporting

Bread is basic to life. But not everyone has enough. Four hundred and fifty million people — including many U.S. citizens — will go to bed hungry tonight.

Tens of thousands of U.S. Christians think our nation should take the lead in finding ways to remedy this outrage. They press the issue hard with our nation's leaders, and they are making a difference.

You can join them. Call **1-800-82-BREAD** toll-free for information on membership in Bread for the World.

You can also help by sending a financial contribution. Every dollar you send will be multiplied *hundreds of times over* for hungry people.

To make a gift in someone's honor, send their name and address along with your check, and they will receive a special Bread for the World gift card.

If you need tax deductibility, make out your check to BFW Educational Fund. Otherwise, send your gift to:

Bread for the World
802 Rhode Island Avenue, N.E.
Washington, D.C. 20018.

10.
November and December

THANKSGIVING

Harvest festivals have been a part of human history since the beginning of agriculture. With harvesting completed and food stored away for the winter months, those early tillers of the soil celebrated the results of their labor. They also recognized their dependence on elements and forces beyond their efforts that made harvest possible. Ancient cultures held harvest festivals in honor of the Earth Mother; the Greeks honored Demeter, and the Romans Ceres. Jews celebrated harvest in several periods throughout the year. In medieval times many Europeans observed the Feast of St. Martin of Tours on November 11, and Harvest Home celebrations began with the reign of James I in England. Today Thanksgiving Day is observed on the second Monday of October in Canada, while in the United States it is on the fourth Thursday of November.

The "first" Thanksgiving in America is subject to debate. One of the first observances was entirely religious and did not involve feasting. On December 4, 1619, 39 English settlers arrived at Berkeley Plantation on the James River in Virginia. Their charter required that their arrival date be observed yearly as a day of thanksgiving to God.

Most people, however, associate the first Thanksgiving with the Pilgrims at Plymouth. Escaping religious persecution in Europe, these colonists attempted to reach the Virginia colony. Their sixty-seven day voyage ended instead at Cape Cod's Provincetown Harbor on November 11, 1620. At a recently vacated Indian settlement, they discovered corn set aside for spring planting. Already on a starvation diet, they were more concerned about their immediate need for food than for anyone's future crop so they took ten bushels of the Indian's seed corn in order to survive the winter.

In the summer of 1621, less than a year after their arrival and after a terrible winter when half of the colonists died, hope was renewed by a good corn crop. Squanto, a Patuxet Indian, helped the colonists during that first winter and spring, showing them how to prepare the fields and

★ **Thanksgiving**
(fourth Thursday in November)
★ **Hanukkah**
(November/December)
★ **Feast Day of Saint Nicholas**
(December 6)
★ **Festival of the Virgin of Guadalupe**
(December 15)
★ **Winter Begins**
(December 21 or 22)
★ **Christmas Day**
(December 25)
★ **Kwanza**
(December 26-January 1)

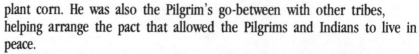

"Celebration is a forgetting...of ego, of problems, of difficulties, in order to remember the common base that makes another's sufferings mine and in order to imagine a relief of that suffering. There can be no compassion without celebration and there will be no authentic celebration that does not result in increased compassionate energies."

Matthew Fox

plant corn. He was also the Pilgrim's go-between with other tribes, helping arrange the pact that allowed the Pilgrims and Indians to live in peace.

The first corn harvest brought rejoicing, and Governor William Bradford decreed that a three-day feast be held. Chief Massasoit was invited to share the celebration, and share he did. Ninety braves came with him—probably to celebrate their traditional harvest feast. They brought five deer to add to the Pilgrim's collection of wild geese, ducks, lobsters, eels, clams, oysters, fish, berries, biscuits, breads, corn cooked in a variety of ways, and puddings of cornmeal and molasses. Sweet strong wine from wild grapes supplemented the feast.

These were great days of celebration. Women cooked meals, children played, men showed off their marksmanship with firearms, while the Indians demonstrated theirs with bows and arrows. The feast lasted for days, with little attention to religious services. Some believe that the Pilgrims chose to keep their harvest festival secular because they disapproved of mingling religious and secular celebrations. It seems to have been a one-time occasion, with no thought to future celebrations.

Serious questions have been raised about the nature and purpose of Thanksgiving Day observances in the subsequent one hundred years. William B. Newell, a Penobscot Indian and former chairman of the anthropology department at the University of Connecticut, says that the first official Thanksgiving Day was proclaimed by the Governor of Massachusetts Bay Colony in 1637 to celebrate the massacre of 700 Indian men, women and children at their annual Green Corn Dance (their Thanksgiving). For the next 100 years, says Newell, "every Thanksgiving day ordained by a governor was to honor a bloody victory thanking God for the battle won."

On November 26, 1787, President George Washington issued a proclamation for a day of thanks. In the same year the Protestant Episcopal Church announced the first Thursday in November would be a regular yearly day for giving thanks, "unless another day be appointed by the civil authorities." But for many years afterward there was no regular national Thanksgiving Day in the United States.

In 1863, during the darkest days of the Civil War, President Lincoln proclaimed Thanksgiving a national observance. That he did so was largely due to a campaign by Sarah Josepha Hale, the editor of *Godey's Lady's Book,* the most widely circulated women's magazine in the late nineteenth century. For nearly 40 years, Hale publicly promoted the idea of a national Thanksgiving. Even in the midst of Civil War, she urged that the celebration not be austere. Fasting, she warned in her magazine, only pointed to the terrible "condition of the country and the deeds of men," while feasting exalted God and the culinary prowess of women.

Each year, for the next 75 years, the President of the United States formally proclaimed that Thanksgiving Day should be celebrated on the last Thursday of November. In 1939 President Roosevelt set it one week earlier; he wanted to help business by lengthening the Christmas shopping season. Finally, however, Congress ruled that after 1942 Thanksgiving would be observed on the fourth Thursday of November and would be a legal federal holiday.

If celebrations give voice to the ideals by which we are trying to live, how should we observe Thanksgiving? It may be easier to think first of how we ought not observe it. It ought *not* be

- a day for thanking God for affluence while others go hungry. The notion that it is God who gives affluence to some and poverty to many not only ignores the role humans have played in arranging patterns of affluence and poverty but flies in the face of the Biblical God of love and justice.

- a time to claim God's special blessing on any nation. As a minority religious group, the Pilgrims knew only too well the problems that occur when the interests of God and nation are identified by a dominant religious group.

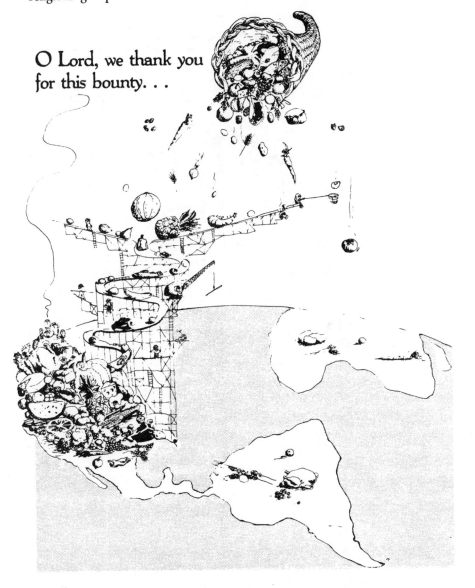

O Lord, we thank you for this bounty. . .

- an occasion to romanticize the cooperation between the Indians and the settlers, unless to recall in sorrow the subsequent centuries' genocide of Native Americans.

- a day of rest before the two largest shopping days of the year, when giving thanks is swept out the back door so Christmas commericalism can come in the front.

As a day that gives voice to our highest ideals, Thanksgiving can be a time to

- remember with gratitude and humility that we alone are not responsible for whatever bounty is in our lives;

- confess that part of our bounty has come at the expense of others, including Native Americans, slaves, farm workers and hosts of others we do not even know;
- share what we have with others, and include in our celebrations those who would otherwise be alone;
- commit ourselves to creating a world where hungry children are fed, the homeless are provided with shelter, and those who suffer discrimination because of race, sex, religion or age are respected.

A Thanksgiving Litany

(L-Leader, P-People, A-All)

L. We thank you, God.

P. We thank you, God, for who we are.

L. Some of us look like the people who lived here long ago, so close to this land that their arrival is not recorded. With them we are pilgrims in this land.

P. We thank you, God, that you are a pilgrim with us.

L. Some of us look like the Spanish, who came in big ships. They took the land from the Indians, and thought it was theirs. With them we are pilgrims in this land.

P. We thank you, God, that you are a pilgrim with us.

L. Some of us look like the English, who also came in big ships. They took the land from the Indians and the Spanish, and thought it was theirs. With them we are pilgrims in this land.

P. We thank you, God, that you are a pilgrim with us.

L. Some of us look like the Africans, who also came in big ships. They did not choose to come, and they had no land and no freedom. With them we are pilgrims in this land.

P. We thank you, God, that you are a pilgrim with us.

L. Some of us look like the Asians, who came in big ships across the other ocean. They came looking for work and freedom, and many found discrimination and injustice. With them we are pilgrims in this land.

P. We thank you, God, that you are a pilgrim with us.

L. All of us are different. No two of us look exactly alike. But we are all made in the image of God, who came to earth that we might be one.

A. Together with pilgrims past and those yet to come, we thank you, God, for who we are, and we pray that you show us what we are to be. Amen.

(Inspired by essays of Puerto Rican school children in New York City and published by the Foundation for Change.)

Justo and Catherine Gonzalez
Decatur, Georgia

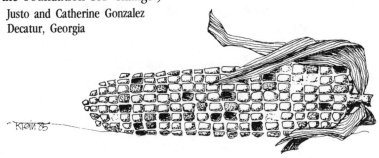

Five Grains of Corn

In early New England at Thanksgiving time it was customary to place five grains of corn at every plate. This served as a reminder of those stern days in the first winter when the food of the Pilgrims was so depleted that only five grains of corn was rationed to each individual at a time. The Pilgrims wanted their children to remember the sacrifices, the sufferings, the hardships which made possible the settlement of a free people in a free land. They did not want their descendants to forget that on the day on which their ration was reduced to five grains of corn only seven healthy colonists remained to nurse the sick, and nearly half their number already lay in that windswept graveyard on the hill.

Plymouth Congregational U.C.C.
Des Moines, Iowa

Thanksgiving in the Woods

Thanksgiving has always been a special time for my family in Suwanee, Florida. Twenty-five years ago, along with various relatives, we began celebrating Thanksgiving in the woods because our homes were too small to include everyone. My father, brother and other men in the family enjoyed hunting after the crops were harvested. Since they were camping in the woods, this seemed to be the place to meet for our celebration.

Some years there was so much pain in our lives that attempting to celebrate Thanksgiving seemed a farce. I particularly remember the year my husband and I separated. From miles away my mother was trying to comfort me with scripture and song, all to no avail. But Thanksgiving was a glorious day with a vibrant blue sky and warm weather so, as usual, we ate outside. All the people who loved me most were there to affirm that life goes on, even in the midst of the deepest pain.

Then came the year we celebrated without my father, who had helped to start the tradition. As we gathered for the meal, our sense of loss at his death was tremendous and giving thanks was difficult. However, we gave thanks for the memories that are left to us, for the father who never failed to give thanks and for the many ways that God meets our needs and cares for us. We celebrated in the way we have grown to love—in the woods with the sound of rushing water nearby, the smell of outdoor fires, dogs barking, birds singing, and people laughing and talking—remembering the Creator who made us all.

Kay Deen Mann
Decatur, Georgia

"To Rest Without Care"

An old man once asked me, "Why do you people, French and Portuguese, come from so far away to seek wood to warm you? Don't you have wood in your country?" I answered that we had plenty, but not of that quality, and that we did not burn it as he supposed but extracted a dye from it for dyeing, just as they did to their cotton cords and their feathers. The old man immediately replied: "And I suppose that you need much of it?" "Yes," I answered, "for in our country there are traders who own more cloth, knives, sissors, mirrors and other goods than you can imagine. So one single trader buys all the brazilwood carried back by many loaded ships." "Ah," said the old man, "you are telling me marvels. But this very rich man you are telling me about, does he not die?" "Yes," I said, "he dies like all the rest." But savages are great debaters and generally pursue any matter to its conclusion. He therefore asked me: "When he dies what becomes of what he leaves?" "It is for his children if he has them...or for his closest brothers and relatives." "Indeed," continued the old man, who as you can see was no fool, "I now see that you French are great madmen. You cross the sea and suffer great inconvenience, as you say when you arrive here, and work so hard to accumulate riches for your children or for those who survive you. Is the land that nourished you not sufficient to feed them too? We have fathers, mothers and children whom we love. But we are certain that after our death the land that nourished us will also feed them. We therefore rest without further cares."

Jean de Lery, 16th-century French cleric in Brazil
Hemming, John, *Red Gold: The Conquest of the Brazilian Indians, 1500 - 1760.* Cambridge, Massachusetts: Harvard University Press, 1978. Page 16.

"Any 'Christians' who take for themselves any more than the plain necessaries of life, live in an open habitual denial of the Lord. They have gained riches and hell-fire."

John Wesley

160

HANUKKAH: FEAST OF DEDICATION

This annual Feast of Dedication for Jews (*hanukkah* means "dedication" in Hebrew) is celebrated for eight days, beginning on the twenty-fifth day of the lunar month of Kislev, falling normally in December. Hanukkah was first celebrated in 165 B.C. when a little band of Jewish patriots defeated the hated Syrian army which occupied their land. Syria had tried to Hellenize the Jews through a series of repressive decrees, including turning the Temple in Jerusalem into a house of worship for the Greek god Zeus. When this small group of Jews succeeded in driving the Syrians out of Jerusalem and recovered the Temple, an eight-day festival to rededicate the Temple to the service of God was proclaimed.

Since the military victory was only temporary, the observance was transformed into an eight-day Festival of Lights. Each evening during Hanukkah a candle is lighted in a special eight-branch candelabrum, the menorah, until on the eighth day all the candles are lighted. Legend has it that as the Temple was being prepared for the original eight-day festival only one container, providing one day's supply of oil for the Eternal Lamp, could be found. Miraculously, the one day's supply lasted for eight days, enough time to prepare additional oil so the lamp in the Temple did not go out, in keeping with sacred Jewish law. The lights are a sign of God's presence.

Hanukkah's significance lies in the struggle of Jews to preserve their integrity against social pressure for assimilation. It is ironic that its popular celebration in Jewish homes today is often an example of just such assimilation, thanks to the tremendous cultural and economic forces swirling around Christmas. Because Hanukkah comes during the Christmas season in the United States and celebrations of the two holidays have become similar over the years, it is sometimes erroneously thought of as a "Jewish Christmas." This is a good time for Jews and Christians to resist the commercialization of their holy days and to reaffirm their commitments to the concept that people be allowed to worship God as they wish.

Combining Hanukkah and Christmas

The convergence of Christmas and Hanukkah should not become an occasion for alienation between Jews and Christians. On the contrary, I think both face a common moral dilemma as a result of the vast commercialization of both holidays.

I ask Jews to study the history and meaning of Hanukkah. Hanukkah was always a beautiful, but quite modest, holiday. It focuses primarily on the inspiring story of how the Maccabees fought the first struggle in human history for religious freedom.

The Hanukkah tradition of giving gifts to children was not meant to overindulge them. The idea was to give gifts to the poor. The central theme was not spoiling kids but to instill a deep sense of social responsibility. I think that holiday has to be recaptured. Rather than spending $400 on toys that are discarded in a week or a month, give the children money and let them give it to the poor or the homeless.

Jews tempted to integrate Christian symbols into their holiday should consider that decision carefully. If one wants to become analytical, it reduces the meaning of both holidays to the lowest common denominator. Because if one takes Christianity seriously, then Christmas celebrates the birth of Jesus as Lord and Savior. And if you don't share that theological conviction, then you are really engaging in a false act or reducing the core idea of Christianity to some kind of social ritual. You're making it on the level of Santa Claus and Rudolph the Red-Nose Reindeer.

Rabbi Marc Tanenbaum
New York, New York

Hanukkah: Challenge for Contemporary America

Even though a distinctly Jewish festival, Hanukkah, nonetheless, has a challenge for contemporary America. Our nation's strength has been in its avowal of pluralism and respect for all religious traditions. The First Amendment and other important documents have created a wall of separation between church and state so that no one's religion is entitled to special privileges or status, and no doctrine may be elevated above the others. For more than two centuries, this tradition of granting credibility to all religious expressions has served us well.

This tradition, sadly, is under attack these days. Zealots within the Religious Right openly admit that their goal is to have our public institutions reflect that the majority of Americans are Christians. Hence, the pressure for prayers in the public schools and for teaching the first two chapters of Genesis as an alternative scientific theory to evolution. Hence, the insistence to place creches on public property and to affix Christian symbols in city halls and in other government buildings. Hence, the cry of fundamentalist church leaders that elected officials and appointed judges be "true believers." Hence, the behemoth crusade against secular humanism—code words for all views inconsistent with a fundamentalist Christian outlook.

Hanukkah is a timely context in which to focus on the message of religious liberty and of the right of all faith communities to enjoy equality before the law. Religious conformity, whether it be imposed by force, as in the days of Antiochus, or by law or judicial decree, as attempted in our day, must cause darkness to descend upon our society. The hope for light, implicit in the Hanukkah ritual of adding candle to candle, affirms that only the ongoing commitment to pluralism and to protecting the rights of all to worship—or not to worship—can keep America strong.

Rabbi Arnold M. Goodman
Atlanta, Georgia

FESTIVAL OF THE VIRGIN OF GUADALUPE

A major celebration in Mexico on December 15, this festival commemorates the appearance of the Virgin Mary to a poor Indian peasant on his way to mass in the early 1500s. According to the story Mary not only appeared to the peasant, she spoke to him in his Indian language. After Spain's devastating military and cultural conquest of Mexico, the Virgin's appearance came to have a special meaning for Indians and the poor, the affirmation of their worth as human beings. It is said that church authorities in Mexico were reluctant to believe that Mary would appear to an Indian. Only a miracle—the peasant brought roses in the dead of winter to the bishop—convinced the authorities that the peasant was telling the truth. Especially popular with the poor and Indians, the festival is celebrated with parades, relay races and fireworks, as well as religious observances.

WINTER BEGINS

The season of winter in the Northern Hemisphere begins on December 21 or 22, when the winter solstice occurs. On that day, the sun is very low in the sky and there are fewer hours of daylight than on any other day.

KWANZA: AN AFRO-AMERICAN FESTIVAL

A new holiday, Kwanza (a Swahili word for "first") is an Afro-American celebration that begins on December 26 and ends on New

Seeking social justice in Appalachia

CORA

Commission on Religion in Appalachia
P.O. Box 10867
864 Weisgarber Road, NW
Knoxville, TN 37919
(615) 584-6133

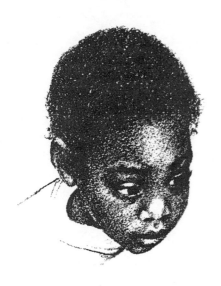

Year's Day. The festival was started in 1966 in California by black nationalist Maulana Ron Karenga. Although rooted in traditional harvest celebrations in Africa, Kwanza is an alternative to the commercialized Christmas in the United States. The focus of the observance is on African and Afro-American history and culture, as well as on seven principles of Kwanza: unity, self-determination, collective work and responsibility, cooperative economics, purpose, creativity and faith.

Each night there is a ceremony involving lighting the day's candle by children, passing a unity cup, and discussing the principle for that day. Prayers of thanksgiving, songs, folk tales and resolutions for the future are often part of the celebration. After the seventh principle has been discussed on the seventh day, the holiday ends with gifts, a feast, singing and dancing. The emphasis for gifts is on small handmade items with special meaning that will help the recipient get through the next year.

Kwanza is a celebration for blacks of all religious and nonreligious persuasions. While Kwanza was born of a desire to celebrate African roots, Christians should also note that it was born of the conviction that a celebration of principle was needed to counter the moral bankruptcy of the commercialized Christmas.

United Methodist Church
General Board of Global
Ministries
World Program Division
475 Riverside Drive
Room 1516
New York, NY 10115

The Time Is Now!
AFRICA
Church Growth and Development

The ever-increasing number of African Methodists need our support NOW in these areas:

EVANGELISM	(008235-2 A-T)
LEADERSHIP DEVELOPMENT	(008237-4 B-T)
CHURCH GROWTH/REPAIR	(008231-7 A-N)

Designate your gift, "Africa Church Growth and Development," and indicate one of the above numbers, or the general number (008233-0 H-T).

World Program Division
General Board of Global Ministries

164

WILL YOU PUT HIM ON YOUR CHRISTMAS LIST?

Photo by WCC/Peter Williams

REFORMED CHURCH WORLD SERVICE

We're the Reformed Church in America. We came over in 1609 with Henry Hudson. And that makes us the oldest denomination in the country with a continuing ministry.

We're a mission-minded church . . . and part of our mission is to minister to people in need . . . whatever the need, wherever the place.

Reformed Church World Service is our program for responding not only to immediate relief needs, but also for seeking solutions to long-term problems through development, rehabilitation and advocacy. A famine in Africa, an earth quake in Mexico, hunger and homelessness in the United States . . .

Reformed Church World Service is there . . . with the hungry, the sick and the homeless.

TO: Reformed Church in America—Room 1827
475 Riverside Drive, New York, N.Y. 10115

I want to help! Enclosed is my gift of *$_____.
(Please make checks payable to REFORMED CHURCH WORLD SERVICE.
Thank you.)

NAME _____

ADDRESS _____

CITY _____ STATE _____ ZIP _____
REFORMED CHURCH WORLD SERVICE   *All gifts are tax deductible.

Reformed Church in America
475 Riverside Drive
Room 1827
New York, NY 10115

165

**Interfaith Center on
Corporate Responsibility**
475 Riverside Drive
Room 566
New York, NY 10115
(212) 870-2295

Executive Director
  Timothy Smith
Director of Publications
  Diane Bratcher

JOIN US IN CHALLENGING CORPORATE POWER

ICCR has been called the
"conscience of American business"
with good reason!

ICCR coordinates research & action
by Protestant and Roman Catholic
churches pressing corporations to
be socially responsible.

We work on major social issues:

- Investment in apartheid
  South Africa

- The corporate role in Star Wars
  and the nuclear weapons race

- Equal employment opportunity

- Alternative investments in
  community development

- Infant formula marketing abuse

Through ICCR's newsletter,
"THE CORPORATE EXAMINER"
you can discover
how to challenge corporate power.
Write for a free sample and for our
literature list.

Please send your
tax-exempt contributions
to support campaigns for
corporate social responsibility.

INTERFAITH CENTER ON CORPORATE RESPONSIBILITY

475 Riverside Drive, Room 556, New York, New York 10115

166

SPONSOR A THIRD WORLD VILLAGE

HELP YOUR NEIGHBORS
IN THE DEVELOPING COUNTRIES
TO HELP THEMSELVES

Pax World Foundation's **VILLAGE VITALIZATION PROJECT** helps provide the elements communities need — a convenient, safe water supply; basic health care; rudimentary educational facilities; a supply of trees for firewood; know-how for improving farm crops and curbing soil erosion. All of these developmental components are carried on simultaneously, by the villagers themselves. They work with technicians furnished by international agencies, missionaries and volunteers, with support from Pax World.

Your $500 can make safe water available to most villages, or help establish a health clinic. Your $100 can provide thousands of seeds of fast-growing trees to help preserve the soil, provide firewood, curb erosion. Your contribution will be pooled with others to help villagers make the changes needed to better their lives. We have supported villages in Ghana, Kenya, Sierra Leone, Tanzania, Nepal, Bangladesh, India, Thailand, Bolivia, Honduras, and Dominican Republic. You will receive periodic village progress reports.

- -

I wish to SPONSOR A VILLAGE which needs my help.

☐ Enclosed is my check for
       ☐ $500   ☐ $100   ☐ $50   ☐ Other _____
☐ Please send an information package.

Name_____
                    (Please Print)

Address_____

City_____ State_____ Zip_____

Gifts are tax deductible, if itemized. No more than 10% of the sponsor's contribution will be used for fundraising and administration expenses. The Foundation pays **no** executive salaries nor receives any government funds.

Pax World Foundation
4400 East-West Hwy.
Suite 130
Bethesda, MD 20814

ADVISORY COUNCIL

Peter G. Bourne, M.D.
Betty Bumpers
Robert F. Drinan, S.J.
Arthur S. Flemming
Jerome Frank, M.D.
Arvonne Fraser
Bishop Thomas J. Gumbleton
J. Harry Haines
LaDonna Harris
Paul F. McCleary
George McGovern
Esther Peterson
Sen. Paul Simon
Earnest A. Smith
Bishop C. Dale White
William Winpisinger

167

Church World Service
P.O. Box 968
Elkhart, IN 46515

From the time we can walk, each of us yearns for the joy that comes from being able to do for ourselves. Church World Service recognizes this important aspect of human dignity in its commitment to provide not just the immediate necessities of life to the people of the world but to work in partnership with them to prepare for the future.

For updated information about the work of Church World Service, call the CWS Hotline.
1-800-223-1310 (NY 1-800-535-2713)

Part Two:
Rites of Passage

Rites of passage are those rituals or celebrations that mark the passage of a person through the life cycle, from one stage to another, from one role or social position to another: birth, puberty, marriage, etc. In the pre-modern world, these rites served at least four functions:

- *Safe Passage*. Rites of passage integrated biological reality (birth, reproduction and death) with cultural and religious experience. Passages are anxiety-producing life crises. The rites not only "gave permission for"—or legitimated—the anxiety, but they allayed it by giving meaning to the experience. They made the "passage" from one life stage to another safe and clear.

- *Moments of Learning*. Although some rites of passage occur at great moments of anxiety (life crises), all provide an atmosphere in which learning can take place. By calling attention to the particular life change, rites of passage might actually increase anxiety, but did so in a context where important learning occured that assisted in the transition. For example, acknowledging the reality of death in a funeral or memorial service may increase anxieties already being experienced. But that ritual acknowledgement may also aid friends and relatives in accepting life without the one who has died.

- *Connection to Community*. Rites of passage celebrated the connecting of individuals to a community. The physiological fact is that one is born and dies alone, unique and separate. But each one is also a member of a community, a group that has particular values and understandings of life. Rites of passage connected the individual experience to the understandings of the group in such a way as to give meaning to that experience. While Christian rites of infant baptism, christening and dedication are performed for different reasons, they have in common celebrating linking the individual to a group.

- *Transformation Experiences*. Not only did these rites help to facilitate passage from one stage to another, but the rites actually shaped and manipulated biological imperatives as well. The message from ancient societies is that women and men are not simply born, nor do

they merely procreate and die; what they are is in part what they are "made" through rites of passage. In some societies, girls became "women" when they went through puberty rites whether or not they had begun to menstruate; and adolescent boys became "men" when they went on the hunt or were circumcised whether or not they had gone through puberty. As Mircea Eliade has put it, one may become what one performs. Rites of passage were transformation experiences.

Do They Have a Place in Modern Society?

The place of rites of passage in a modern society such as ours is not clear. Some anthropologists have expressed doubt that rites of passage can have much meaning in a society so complex, so secular and so fragmented. Gail Sheehy's best-seller, *Passages: Predictable Crises of Adult Life* has called attention to the reality of life passages for adults and to the various cultural and psychological problems that result from them. She does not, however, consider the importance of "rites" to these junctures in life.

Few, however, doubt the need for such rites or the cost of not having them. In a society which so prizes individuality over community many find it necessary to adjust to life's transitions quite alone. Increasingly our lives are entrusted into the hands of experts and anonymous agencies or individuals who care for only a small part of our human needs. We are born, for the most part, in hospitals, and we usually die there. For many, the most profound events of their lives have become merely secular affairs and left uncelebrated. Beyond the traditional passages, there are in this society numerous forms of crisis and transition: menopause, surgery, "empty nests," graduation, career change, divorce, retirement, leaving the family home for a retirement home, etc. Traumatic, exciting and anxiety-provoking, these passages regularly go unobserved. As early as 1897 in his classic study on suicide, Emil Durkheim wrote that one of the consequences of the lack of social connection and unacknowledged existence in modern society was suicide. Others have since pointed to the relationship between mental illness and going through passages alone and uncelebrated.

Our consumer culture has also had its impact on the observance of rites of passage, especially by making them occasions for greater consumption. Under pressure to do "what society expects," some people spend beyond their means and end up resenting the occasion itself. Moreover, when the focus of the celebration is on consumption, the critical functions of safe passage, learning, connecting to community and transformation become distorted or obscured altogether.

The absence of "community" in a traditional sense makes observing the rites of passage in families, immediate communities and religious communities all the more important. If you don't have suitable rites for the passages in your life, create them! But don't stop there. *Resist the pressures of the consumer society* and *observe the rites* in ways that enable you to recover the renewing and maturing power they are intended to have by focusing on:

- *People.* Focus on the people in passage, their anxieties and the real issues they face in the new stage, instead of the gifts and other paraphenalia used to aid or celebrate the transition. In this way, those in passage can be brought "safely" through to a new stage of maturity.

- *Values and Ideals.* Instead of mindlessly celebrating to anesthetize the person(s) to the trauma of transition, focus on values and ideals needed for the next phase of life can make the occasion a critical moment for learning.

- *Community.* Instead of the consumer culture's narcissistic privatization of life transitions, focus the rites on the mystery and wonder of our place in community. These can be critical times to experience support from those relationships as well as times to mature

"In rites of passage [people] are released from structure into *communitas* only to return to structure, revitalized by their experience of *communitas*. What is certain is that no society can function adequately without this dialectic."

Victor W. Turner

171

in our understanding of the community which sustains us. While "fragmentation" rather than "community" may characterize twentieth-century society, we are more than ever part of a world community, dependent on one earth and a fragile eco-system for survival.

Just as the rites in ancient times moved those in passage toward their new responsibilities in the community, so today's rites of passage must celebrate our relationship to the larger community and to the eco-system, and aid in moving us toward assuming the responsibilities incumbent on us because of those relationships.

• *Change.* By focusing on the life changes that are required in the particular passage the rites can help make the passages transformation experiences. Rites help people visualize the desired outcome of the passage and to see themselves on the other side. As such, rites become occasions of transformation.

11.
Birth and Death

BIRTH

From the earliest times birth has been regarded not only as a rite of passage for the baby, but for the parents and community as well. While modern science can explain in clinical detail the reproduction process, mystery and wonder still surround every pregnancy and birth. In ancient societies, this life transition required many different rites: taboos that related to pregnancy and birth; rites to ward off evil spirits and to protect from witchcraft; rites to make delivery easy and safe; rites to secure good fortune for the child; rites to admit the child to society; and rites to readmit the parents back into society in their changed state.

In today's world many of the functions of the old rites have been dropped altogether or are performed by doctors and other health care professionals. The contribution of modern medical science and technology to the biology of the reproductive process has been incalculable. It is lamentable, however, that our modern world has not been as successful in replacing those ancient rites relating to cultural traditions—those traditions which assured parents and children of acceptance and support by the larger community. The functions of those early rites are now provided by friends, parents, classes and books. One birth rite that continues is the baby shower. A shower is more than an occasion to provide physical necessities for the new baby. It can be a time when friends gather around the mother-to-be in a ritual circle of support for the coming event, wonderful yet shrouded in mystery and uncertainty.

Like all other passages in the consumer society, births present opportunities for excessive consumption. Baby industry promoters play on pride, insecurity and ignorance to convince parents and their friends that the new baby must have a whole host of superfluous products. An ad for designer diaper covers maintains, "It's never too early for your child to learn the importance of class." Providing necessities for the new baby—clothes, blankets, diapers, etc.—is an important part of getting ready. There are also other ways to help prepare for this important passage. Consider giving more personal gifts of time and skill: painting

> "When the child is born,
> it screams and cries,
> and with that crying,
> joy surges forth again."
>
> Julia Esquivel

173

"Advertising serves not so much to advertise products as to promote consumption as a way of life. It "educates" the masses into an unappeasable appetite not only for goods but for new experiences and personal fulfillment."

Christopher Lasch

the nursery, preparing some meals or caring for other children in the family around the time of the birth. Gifts of books on baby care are common, especially if this is a first child. Equally appropriate is a book like *Parenting for Peace and Justice* by Jim and Kathy McGinnis. If the family is adequately supplied and cared for, gifts made in the name of the family to projects which help less fortunate children are particularly appropriate.

Christening, dedication and infant baptism are rites that celebrate the connecting of the child to a religious community. As these rites call attention to the responsibilities of the parents and the members of the community for the spiritual nurture of the child, they also recognize the new status of the parents in the community. In some families baptism anniversaries are observed just like birthdays. Except in subsequent birthday celebrations, there are no generally used rites to celebrate the entrance of the child into a family; however, you may want to create a rite to use with immediate family and close friends when mother and baby come home from the hospital.

It is unfortunate that the practice of naming godparents for a new baby is now largely symbolic. Traditionally, godparents not only had responsibility for the child in the event of the parent's deaths, but they also had special responsibilities for the child's spiritual nurture. It was their responsibility to guide their godchild in the ways of faith by teaching the Ten Commandments, the Lord's Prayer, and the Apostle's Creed. In this time when grandparents may be far away, the traditional godparent role could provide active support and nurture to parents and children alike.

Roots for a New Arrival

When my first grandson was born seven years ago, I gave considerable thought to what might be an appropriate gift for him. His other grandparents had generously supplied everything imaginable that would be needed for his care and entertainment. I found it rather frustrating that whatever I mentioned as a possible gift for him was something he already had.

What I came up with was something I did not have to shop for, except in the recesses of my memory and in a journal I had kept for many years. My gift took the form of a letter to our little Noah to be read to him at some suitable time in his growing up years. This was the life story of certain family members with whom he would find his own identity.

In a radio interview, Alex Haley, author of *Roots* made the following poetic statement: "Grandparents sprinkle stardust in the lives of their grandchildren." My "stardust" letter included our family's welcome to Noah, something of what we felt as he came into the world. There was some informal genealogical information, but quite a few special stories of his own father (our son Daniel), covering Danny's birth, position in the family, early experiences related to such things as nature, prayer, family and school.

Then came information about my husband and myself, our childhood and youth, experiences in school and church, influences that led us into our life's work. Much of this section showed definite interest and involvement with moral or religious matters which were part of the formation of our faith.

174

The response to this letter was more than I had dreamed possible in terms of communication with my son, his wife, and her family. Danny said there were things in the letter which he had never known. His wife now had a better understanding of who we were and from where we came; her grandmother, with whom she shared Noah's letter, told me that it was one of the most beautiful things she had ever read. Yet this was not a pietistic, sentimental presentation. It was simply something I wanted to share with my grandson about some of the people in his life, and some of those who lived before us.

Mary Lou McCrary
Atlanta, Georgia

Handmade Muslin Gifts for New Baby

When my grandmother had her children there was no such thing as a baby shower. The word of an impending birth spread naturally to family members and a few close friends. Aunts, sisters, cousins, nieces, grandmothers, and close friends each made one article—such as a baby quilt or small gown—as a gift from their own families. The gifts were not wrapped and they were not given to the expectant mother. They were given to the grandmother-to-be who took them with her when she went to help prepare for birth.

Since the mother-to-be received the gifts in private, there was no embarrassment for the giver who was unable to make a beautiful or expensive gift. My grandmother received some beautiful little muslin gowns with delicate embroidery, cleverly designed with many tucks and with long hems to be let out as the baby grew. She also was given quilts and knit sweaters, bonnets and booties.

Sheryl Craig
Warrensburg, Missouri

Quilting for Baby

For a special baby blanket/quilt have people who attend a shower for the expectant parents sign their names onto a solid-color square of flame-retardant flannel. Embroider all names and back it with a printed material square of flame-retardant flannel. You may wish to put quilting material inside.

Missy Thomson
Santa Fe, New Mexico

We Make Showers a Community Affair

Frustrated by the typical ladies-only-sweet-dessert-type showers, our church hosts family-oriented wedding and baby showers. We usually hold these following the Sunday morning worship service when most family members are together. We share a pot-luck meal and have some songs and games to involve everyone. Helpful hints, words of wisdom or a favorite Bible verse may be written on an index card and read aloud as part of the shower program, as well as given to the honored couple. We emphasize practical and humorous gifts. For parents-to-be we might include books and magazines about parenting, coupons for babysitting or for a meal to be brought to the home soon after the baby's birth, cloth diapers and recycled baby clothes.

Anne Hall Shields
Cooperstown, North Dakota

Homemade Frozen Dinners Make Fantastic Gifts

I belong to an eating group that has shared Monday dinners together for more than four years. During that time there have been three births among our members. For each birth the eating group hosted a shower, including the couple's other friends. For our collective gift each adult member prepares a one-dish meal which is frozen and delivered around the day of the birth. With the number of members this provides the family with dinners for about two weeks.

A recipient as well as a preparer, I know this is a fantastic gift.

Kathie Klein
Atlanta, Georgia

Siblings Are Proud, Too

New babies can be announced with homemade cards featuring artwork by older siblings proudly announcing the arrival of their new baby brother or sister.

Meryl A. Butler
Virginia Beach, Virginia

Tree Planting Commemorates Birth

"It is with [people] as it is with trees—one must grow slowly to last long." Henry David Thoreau

This inscription accompanies a small Japanese red maple tribute tree. It was planted in August of 1982 in commemoration of the christening of our son Benjamin Blair, and grows in the Dawe's Arboretum in Newark, Ohio. We wished to emphasize to our son and our family and friends attending his christening our connection with Mother Earth and the many blessings and responsibilities which are a part of that connection. This concept of a life token, found among folklores and legends of many countries and cultures, is not new. For instance, it was formerly a Jewish custom to plant a tree at the birth of a child, a cedar for a son and a pine for a daughter. When a couple married, their

respective trees were then cut down to make their *huppah*, or bridal bower.

As loving family and friends encircled Benjamin (and Dr. Pete who helped deliver Bemjamin into the world) and his tree, the baptism waters nourished the young sapling.

Water is what God uses to wash and nourish the earth. It is what we use to wash and nourish ourselves. God uses water to cleanse us spiritually and to initiate us as Christians.

In addition to scriptures, selections from an anthology of Native American spiritual thought and Thoreau's writings were read.

Jennifer Kinsley
Baltimore, Ohio

Prayer of Blessing

At our church it is important to welcome new babies into our community and to assure parents of the community's support. A tradition for doing this developed around a symbol reintroduced to this country by the televised rendition of *Roots*.

On the first Sunday the mother and baby are able to come to service—often on the way home from the hospital—the parents bring the baby to the front of the church as deacons present the collected offering. A black minister in our congregation prays a prayer of thanksgiving for the child and the parents. He then lifts the baby high, as if in offering to God, asking God's blessing on the new life and God's guidance for the parents and church community as we accept our shared responsibility for nurturing the child in the faith.

The "Prayer of Blessing by Jim Brooks," as it has come to be called, is an important birth rite, a rite that surrounds the family with our love and support and enables us to share in their joy.

Rachel G. Gill
Stone Mountain, Georgia

Baptism Day Stoles

Each member of our family has a homemade baptismal stole with the person's name, a baptism symbol and whatever else has special meaning for that person embroidered or appliqued on white material. On the anniversary of each baptism day the celebrant chooses a special food for dinner. Then we all put on our stoles, light the baptism candle and have a prayer of thanksgiving. We remember the symbols of baptism on our stoles and talk about what baptism means.

Our oldest child will soon make her first communion so a eucharist symbol will be added to her stole at that time. We have also made and given baptism stoles to our godchildren.

Rodger and Mary Beth Routh
Ankeny, Iowa

Prayers for Sarah

Sarah, our first daughter, had been showered with gifts since the day we had even announced her coming! We wanted her baptism to be a prayerful presence (not presents!) celebration. The invitations invited family and friends to write a short prayer for Sarah and bring it as a gift for the occasion. We asked that prayer be the only gift to celebrate this holy time in her life. We provided the prayer sheet, simple paper decorated with her name and the date of her baptism. It was a marvelous time when we realized that most people did exactly that...no gifts, just the gift of prayer! We prayed the prayer-gifts during the ceremony. We celebrate the day of her baptism each year with dinner shared with her godparents and the priest who baptized her and a short reading of those prayers.

Nancy Parker Clancy
Troy, Michigan

Naming Ceremony Celebration

Within a few minutes after our daughter's birth in an Alternative Birth Center, we shared in a celebration for her birth with two close

178

friends. Using the service we had prepared earlier, we gave thanks, sang, spoke her name out loud for the first time and prayed. We four "worship professionals" (all United Methodist ministers) were teary eyed and could barely sing because of the deep emotions this service called forth.

Prayer of Thanksgiving
Sing to our God, all the earth,
Break forth and sing for joy.
Sing praises to God with the harp,
and with voices full of joyous melody.
With trumpets and the sound of the horn,
Sing out to God.

Antiphon
Thank you God for the gift of birth,
For love made flesh to refresh the earth.
For life and strength and length of days,
We give you thanks and praise.

Prayer of Thanksgiving
Let the sea roar in all its fullness,
the whole world and all its inhabitants.
Let the floods clap their hands,
and the mountains sing for joy
Before God and the nations. (Psalm 98)

Repeat Antiphon

Hymn: "Now Thank We All Our God"

Prayer
O God, like a mother who comforts her children, you strengthen us in our solitude, sustain and provide for us. We come before you with gratitude for the gift of this child, for the joy which you have brought into this family, and the grace with which you surround them and all of us. As a father cares for his children, so continually look upon us with compassion and goodness. Pour out your spirit. Enable your servants to abound in love and establish our homes in holiness. Amen.

Naming
A name has power. It distinguishes us from another, yet it connects us with our Christian roots and our family heritage. "Fear not, for I have redeemed you. I have called you by name. You are mine. When you pass through deep waters I will be with you, your troubles will not overwhelm you. Fear not, I am with you. I have called you by name." (Taken from Isaiah 43)

Giving of the Name

Prayer
Loving God, sustain this child with your strong and gentle care. May the life of (child's name) be one of happiness, goodness and wisdom. Grant that (child's name) may seek after peace and justice, compassion and joy for all of creation. Amen.

> Anne Broyles
> Larry Peacock
> Norwalk, California

"**The need to celebrate is rooted deeply in what it means to be human.**"

The Passage of Pregnancy Loss

Modern medical technology has made it possible for the bonding process, that series of interactions through which we humans come to know one another, to begin much earlier in pregnancy than ever before in human history. It is, for example, possible to know one is pregnant within days of conception, to know the sex of the baby before mother "begins to show," and to see fetal responses to the mother's voice and activity even before she can feel movement. These dramatic yet commonplace developments and today's drastically reduced childhood mortality give the impression that prenatal and infant death are relatively rare. Unfortunately, the common perception is illusory. Far from being an infrequent event, perhaps as many as one fourth of all pregnancies end in death before birth.

The death of a child before birth is a crisis of unrealized magnitude; it remains a frequent family crisis in modern life. These deaths can be very lonely times for the bereaved parents. In these lonely and painful circumstances, the opportunity to worship is an opportunity to challenge God for answers, to forgive and be forgiven, to share one's grief with others, to remember and celebrate special moments, and to hear a word of hope.

Marilyn Washburn, M.D., M.Div.
Avondale Estates, Georgia

Editor's Note: Little is known about how families make it through this passage. We would like to know about your experience with pregnancy loss. What helped? What hindered? Write to Dr. Washburn in care of Alternatives.

DEATH: THE LAST PASSAGE

Given the inevitability and definiteness of death, it is not surprising that the idea of dying has captured the thoughts and imaginations of human beings in every culture. As much as death is a natural part of life, so is resistance to it. The resistance to death is related less to the pain that can accompany it than to the mystery of it, the broken relationships with the survivors and the idea of the decomposition of the body.

Death is not a purely individual act, any more than life is. Like every great milestone in life, death is celebrated by a ceremony whose purpose is to express the individual's solidarity with family and community. In ancient societies, funeral rites had several functions: – Rites recalled the beliefs of the community regarding the future of the departed, whether or not death was perceived as a transition, deliverance or the end of the person.

– Rites attended to the surviving relatives and friends, mourners who needed to be consoled and reassured.

– Rites were a revitalization of the group that has been disturbed by the death of one of its own.

The needs of the grieving family and community continue in modern society, but cultural changes in the twentieth century have made meeting those needs more difficult. In contrast to early societies, this pluralistic society lacks one coherent view of life after death. Our communities— even religious communities—are made up of people with widely differing beliefs about life after death. Even though each religious community has its own beliefs about life after death, the pluralism of modern culture has undermined the power of the unanimous affirmation of those beliefs at death.

Just as there is no unanimous affirmation about life after death, so also is there no one routine to follow at death as there was in earlier times. Survivors have to make many decisions under emotional duress: which funeral home, what manner of interment, what kind of funeral or memorial service, what official notices of death to give to whom, etc.

The mobility of modern society is changing the traditional practice of being buried in one's home town. Not only is one much more likely now to die a long way from that home town, but the notion of "home" town does not mean what it once did. There is little assurance that the deceased's survivors will continue to live in the same place, so the reason for burial in that place has been diminished. While lack of burial space has not been a significant factor in the growing practice of cremation in the United States, as it has in some other countries, modern mobility and the lack of attachment to a "home place" apparently has.

The common place of death is no longer the home. Fewer and fewer people die at home: more die at the hospital after "heroic" efforts of medical personnel to prolong life. The time of death can often be lengthened to suit the doctor. Sometimes this prolonging of life becomes an end in itself, and hospital personnel refuse to discontinue the treatments that maintain an artificial life. While the contributions of modern medical science to longevity are truly remarkable, those advances have contributed to contemporary culture's perception that death is not a part of life, but a failure of medical science. It is often regarded as a defeat both for the one who dies and the attending medical personnel. Not only is death viewed as failure, but by making the hospital the place of death, death is also more solitary and lonely.

With the hospital the place of death, and the immediate transfer of the body to a funeral home, the home is bypassed. Scheduled hours for viewing the body or greeting the family at a funeral home have replaced the traditional wake. The wake was a time at home when relatives and

"Let us endeavour so to live that when we come to die even the undertaker will be sorry."

Mark Twain

181

friends sat up with the body until the funeral. Not always solemn, wakes were unhurried opportunities to adjust to the death in the company of loved ones.

Not unrelated to its fixation on youth, this culture denies death. In what he calls "the pornography of death" in modern Western society, Geoffrey Gorer argues that death has become as shameful and unmentionable as sex was in the Victorian era. Death has been removed to a distance. People are not only no longer present at the deathbed, but presence at funerals and burials has diminished greatly. Where once communities paused when one of their members died, now little note is taken.

Signs of mourning have fallen away because they are unseemly. The need to grieve has been interrupted by this society's distaste for death. In the name of providing privacy for grieving, many funeral home chapels have walls that separate the family from their friends who attend. In his history of attitudes toward death in the West, *The Hour of Our Death*, Philippe Aries has put it graphically: "The tears of the bereaved have become comparable to the excretions of the diseased. Both are distasteful. Death has been banished."

Finally, like other celebrations and rites of passage, death has been commercialized. Not including the cost of a cemetery lot, a vault or a headstone, funerals in the United States average over $3,000 each. Funerals, along with houses, weddings and cars, are among the most expensive items purchased in this culture. As a study for the Wharton School of Business concluded,

> ...[we] can think of no parallel case where such a large consumer expenditure is contracted for under such pressures of time, by persons having so little knowledge of the area in which they are dealing, who are not in the fullest possession of their normal judgment.

While dealing with death in this culture has been made more difficult by the cultural factors we have been describing, there are now some positive changes under way. First, through the efforts of Elisabeth Kubler-Ross and others, the demands for restoring death to its place as a normal part of life have been widely acclaimed. Kubler-Ross' book, *On Death and Dying*, has become a classic. The development of the hospice movement and the increasing availablity of hospices—specialized health care programs for the terminally ill, making the family the unit of care through both the dying and the period of bereavement—now offer humane alternatives for the dying and their families.

Second, the critique of the commercialization of death in this culture and the dissemination of information about ways of dealing with death that are humane, less costly, and life-supporting have given people alternatives. While Jessica Mitford's best-seller, *The American Way of Death*, provided a far-reaching critique of the funeral industry, Ernest Morgan's book, *Dealing Creatively with Death: A Manual of Death Education and Simple Burial*, provides the necessary detailed information about simple burial, memorial societies, anatomical gifts, and other related concerns. (Celo Press, Burnsville, NC 28714. Also available from Alternatives.)

Third, many churches and secular educational organizations now offer death education classes, where people are encouraged to view death as a part of life, learn how to plan ahead for death, and the alternatives open to them for disposition of the body. Some religious communities now require that a standard cloth pall cover the casket at funerals. The pall not only has liturgical meaning, but it prevents the expense of the casket from being an issue in the service. Having the funeral or memorial service in a worshipping community provides part of the sense of community so absent in this culture.

Unlike other life passages, you don't usually know when death will come. You can't prepare for it as you are going through it. More than all other life passages, it is important that you prepare beforehand: a will, wishes about the use of life-support systems, what you want done with your body at death, instructions for the funeral or memorial service, etc. You can approach this passage with greater peace of mind and be of immeasurable help to your survivors if you plan for this passage.

The American Way of Dying

At age 76 Mom had a stroke, putting her in a wheelchair and seriously impairing her hearing, eyesight and speech. She also lost control of her bodily functions and had to wear a diaper. Although she regained her speech and learned to read lips pretty well, she felt her time was up and she was ready to go. She did not understand why God was punishing her by making her stay when she was ready to go.

Last fall, at age 83, she had another stroke. When she was put in the hospital, a new sparkle came to her eyes. Hope! God was giving her a chance to beat the system and die, she told me. And she was going to take it. When they gave her pills, she spit them across the room. When they tried to feed her, she jammed her lips shut. And when they tried to feed her intravaneously, she pulled the needle out. She lasted two weeks.

When she died our feeling was relief, even joy. As the attending doctor said, "She finally got her wish." Something is really wrong with a system that insisted on making my mother's dying a war of wills between her and the doctors, a war that left the family caught in the middle.

Jack Shuford
Marietta, Georgia

Living With Loss

When Todd died I wondered if I'd ever be happy again. The absence of our vibrant 15-year old son left a hole in my heart and in my life. A deep, dark, vast hole. Today, a few years later, I'm glad to be alive once again. The drag in my step has given over to a skip. The tight rope around my chest has dropped away, allowing free and easy breathing. The iron hand squeezing my heart has released its grip. Facial lines of worry and fatigue have softened to make room for the crow's feet of crinkled smiles. Once again I respond to people and things. Life is good!

What made the difference? How does one move from the devastation of loss to a rich and full life? When we experience loss we have a choice. We can choose to be hateful and bitter or to grow and develop and become contributing members of society. In examining my personal loss and in conducting workshops where I've observed and counselled others going through grief, the following insights for constructive coping have emerged.

- Loss occurs frequently—learn from it.
- Loss drains the spirit—seek solitude and sociality.
- Loss can be put to work—help others.
- Life is short—get on with your goals.
- Life is NOW—enjoy this moment.

These insights don't erase a loss, but they do assist us in using loss for good. However, they're mere words unless they're woven throughout by a common thread—that of hope. When hope is present one can face loss. For Christians, that hope lies in knowing God is with us. My favorite symbol of hope is that of the caterpillar. In his furry coat, he crawls over the earth's hills and valleys, constantly facing obstacles, but trudging on. His hope lies in someday soaring over the obstacles in his new-found freedom as a butterfly. My prayer is that in our losses we may experience such hope: the hope of a caterpillar waiting to become a butterfly.

Vivian Elaine Johnson
Minneapolis, Minnesota

(Adapted from "Living With Loss," *Faith at Work,* April 1979.)

"One who knows sorrow
For a long or little while
Learns a new language."

Jean Fox Holland

Memorial Societies: What They Are and How They Work

Memorial societies are cooperative, non-profit, democratically run consumer organizations that help members get simplicity, dignity and economy in funeral arrangements through advance planning. They are not run by funeral directors.

These societies act in an advisory capacity and often have contracts or agreements with funeral directors, helping members get exactly the services they want at reasonable cost. Although a few of the large societies have paid secretaries, the work of the societies is usually done by unpaid volunteers. Memorial societies do collectively what few individual families are prepared to do—they inquire around, compare services and prices, then share this information with their members. They do *not* collect payment for funeral services.

There are memorial societies in some 200 cities in North America with a combined membership of more than one million people. Most societies charge a one-time membership fee of $10 to $25, and some have a small "Records Charge," which they collect from the family at the time of death, via the funeral director. Families moving to another city can transfer their membership at little or no charge. Likewise, when a death occurs away from home, the society in the host city and its cooperating funeral director will assist the family.

Memorial society members commonly save fifty to seventy-five percent of usual funeral costs. The savings are in part due to collective bargaining by the societies, but more from the simplicity that members are encouraged to practice.

The success and popularity of memorial societies have led to imitations. Private companies calling themselves societies have entered the funeral service business. If someone from a "society" tries to sell you something or offers you a prepayment plan, investigate carefully. Memorial societies have no commercial interests and rarely charge membership fees over $25. The societies are an outstanding example of how consumers, by democratic group effort, can empower themselves at the grassroots level.

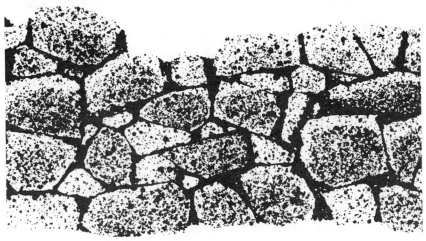

"Memorial societies constitute the most important lay movement of our time relating to funeral practices and death ceremonies."

Ernest Morgan

Nearly all bona fide societies in the United States and Canada are members of their respective national organizations. If you have doubts about a society, check to see if it is a member of the national association. For more information about memorial societies, where the nearest one is to you, or how to organize one, contact one of the two national associations:

Continental Association of Funeral and Memorial Societies, 2001 "S" St. N.W., Suite 530, Washington, D.C. 20009. Tel. (202) 745-0634.

Memorial Society Association of Canada, Box 96, Station A., Weston, Ontario M9N 3M6.

(Adapted from *Dealing Creatively with Death: A Manual of Death Education and Simple Burial*, by Ernest Morgan and published by Celo Press, Burnsville, NC 28714.)

Hospice Care: Dying With Dignity

The hospice movement in the United States grew out of several concerns of the 1960s and early 1970s. The hospital environment was no longer one of "hospitality," but of impersonal technology; the cost of care began the skyrocketing course on which it continues; and many people sensed an absence of any control over their own lives once they entered the foreign territory of hospital rules and regulations.

In an effort to reclaim an opportunity for intimate personal relationships, reduce the costs, and once again make dying a significant life passage, especially at the point past which medical technology has little to offer, dying people simply went home. In many situations, however, nursing, pastoral, social, and to a lesser extent, medical support were needed for the comfort of dying persons as well as their family members. So, the home-based hospice was born.

Studies revealed that hospice patients lived longer, with more comfort and dignity, while their care cost far less than that of hospitalized patients. There remained, however, many of the terminally ill whose family members could not care for them at home, so only a couple years after the beginning of its home-based program, the first "free-standing" hospice was built by Connecticut Hospice. As more patients began to choose hospice care, and as health care workers grew increasingly familiar with its benefits, hospitals began to develop hospice units or wards—islands of alternative care within traditional hospital settings. This movement back into the hospital has resulted in the diffusion of hospice learnings and philosophies. Now health care providers themselves are wondering why people have to be dying to get hospice care.

And the learnings are many. We have proven that family-given care is more intense as well as loving; that the opportunity to care for a loved one can be healing to the family as well as to the dying person; that families can almost always learn to manage necessary "high-tech" equipment—including ventilators and intraveneous pain medications. The costs are lower and pain is better controlled. Health care professionals have worked together as interdisciplinary teams, establishing new relationships and new respect for one another's contributions. All these developments and more offer a great deal to health care delivery in many situations.

But, there are concerns as well. Because of the cost efficiency of hospice care, federal legislation made hospice care Medicare-reimbursable, and many "third party" insurance companies have followed suit. While this has made hospice care available to many persons who could not otherwise afford it, this development has also opened the door to the possibility of "for-profit" care for the dying, and threatens to divorce the hospice concept from its very personalized, grass-roots origins. Only a great deal of vigilance will protect the fledgling institution of intimate personal care from commercialization.

Marilyn Washburn, M.D., M.Div.
Avondale Estates, Georgia

Editor's Note: For more information about hospices write to: National Hospice Organization, 1901 N. Fort Myer Drive, Suite 402 Arlington, VA 22209.

Hospice: Stewardship of the Rites of Passage

The most devastating reality of terminal illness is the continued loss of control over daily life. Accordingly, the goal of hospice care is to give dying persons and their loved ones as much agency over, and autonomy in the midst of, their situation as possible.

Hospice, then, is spiritual care inasmuch as caregivers explore what gives meaning and order to the living, dying and grieving of those they serve. Hospice structures this meaning and order by supporting rites of passage which will enable them to journey along an uncharted path; rites fashioned from their family tradition, cultural milieu and religious heritage.

Consequently, hospice doesn't *do* things for those who suffer. Rather, hospice allows persons to continue to *be* in the midst of their suffering.

William E. Wallace
Director of Hospice, Grady Memorial Hospital
Atlanta, Georgia

Preparing for Release

In July 1982, Elaine and her husband, John, received a devastating blow when they learned that their younger daughter, Adele, had an inoperable brain tumor. After a brief period of hope that radiation therapy might save her life, relapse began. As the paralysis spread and Adele lost all means of verbal communication, her world became progressively narrower, and so did her mother's. John had an outlet in his job and their older daughter, but Elaine devoted herself almost entirely to providing home care for Adele. This could have become a heavy burden; instead, her spiritual world broadened during the long silent hours she had to reflect on the gift of life.

Adele died peacefully at home on January 15, 1984, surrounded by her family and a special adult friend. Elaine prepared herself for releasing Adele by doing something tangible. A wood-working friend had made a simple pine casket at John and Elaine's request. Using a dainty pink calico fabric, Adele's favorite color, Elaine had lined the box and covered the lid herself. This object, at first a "vessel of horror," had gradually become familiar as she worked on it with her hands. At the same time, the reality of Adele's impending death and Elaine's own need to surrender her to God had also become more acceptable. Lining the casket had helped prepare Elaine to release her little girl to God's trust.

Ann C. Sherwin
Raleigh, North Carolina

(Adapted from "Standing in a Garden," *Christian Living*, August 1984.)

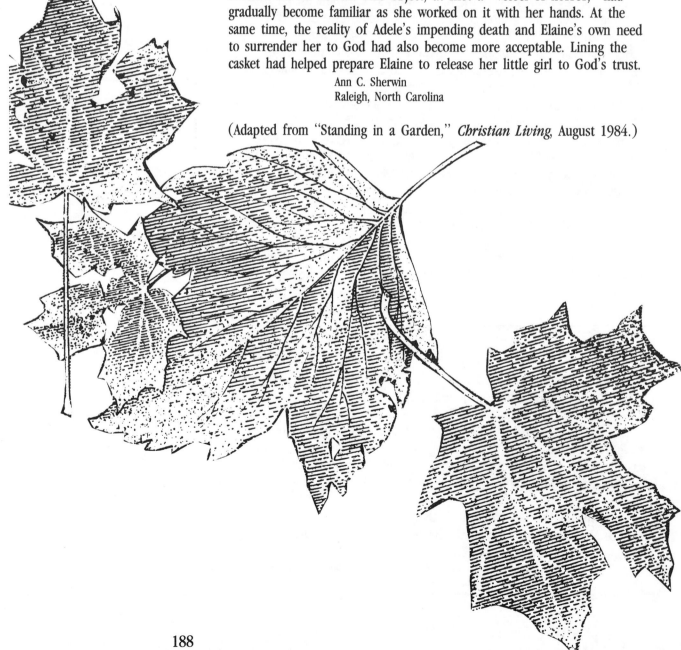

Ancient Rite Helps Grieving Process

My husband died very suddenly of a heart attack on the summit of Torrey's Peak, one of Colorado's highest mountains. He died in our youngest daughter's arms, although our son and members of a rescue squad tried several hours to revive him.

When our family went to the mortuary, I asked for a pan of water and a cloth to bathe my husband's body before cremation. I had just read about an ancient rite where the person nearest to the deceased bathes the body, a custom that is still practiced in many cultures. Although we had never had this kind of experience before, it felt right. It was an important part of a grieving and healing process for me and a very special way to say goodbye.

> Virginia McConnell
> Boulder, Colorado

Sugar Cookies Make Wonderful Memories

After the memorial service for my grandmother, who had died several months earlier, a number of people came back to our house for a meal and conversation. My sister had baked two of my grandmother's most often used recipes—one was her legendary sugar cookies and the other a loaf-style chocolate cake. It was a lovely way to remember as everyone there had at one time or another tasted these special goodies from Grandma's kitchen.

> Jane Ander
> Rock Island, Illinois

Open House Memorial

Several months after my wife died, our family decided to have an Open House as a memorial to my wife. Guests were invited to bring finger food and a recollection or comment for a Memory Book. We showed family slides and with the warm comments and memories shared by friends, it was a true celebration of her life.

> Robert K. Marsh
> Berkeley, California

The Dead Helping the Living: Anatomical Gifts

The day will come when my body will lie upon a white sheet tucked neatly under the four corners of a mattress, located in a hospital busily occupied with the living and the dying. At a certain moment a doctor will determine that my brain has ceased to function and that for all intents and purposes my life has stopped.

When that happens, do not attempt to instill artificial life into my body by use of a machine and don't call this my deathbed. Let it be called the bed of life and let my body be taken from it to help others lead fuller lives.

Give my sight to the man who has never seen a sunrise, a baby's face or love in the eyes of a woman. Give my heart to the person who has nothing but endless days of pain. Give my blood to the teenager who was pulled from the wreckage of his car so that he may live to see his grandchildren play. Give my kidneys to a person who depends upon a machine to exist from week to week. Take my bones, every muscle fiber, every nerve and try to find a way to make a crippled child walk. Explore every corner of my brain, take my cells, if necessary, and let them grow so that some day a speechless boy will shout at the crack of a bat or a deaf girl will hear the sound of rain against her window.

Burn the rest and scatter the ashes to the wind to help the flowers grow.

If you must bury something, bury my faults, my weaknesses and my prejudices against my fellows. Give my sins to the devil, give my soul to God.

If by chance you wish to remember me, do it with a kind deed or a word to someone who needs you. If you do all I have asked, I will live forever.

Robert Test

(Quoted in *The Bank Account*, January 1987, published by The Living Bank, P.O. Box 6725, Houston, Texas 77265, Tel. 1-800-528-2971. Reprinted by permission of The Living Bank.)

Editor's Note. For information about anatomical gifts write or call The Living Bank. Ernest Morgan has also included detailed information on the need for such gifts, how to make a "living will" and comprehensive lists of banks in *Dealing Creatively with Death*.)

190

12.
Marriage and Divorce

MARRIAGE

Getting married is a rite of passage in which two people determine to live together in close relationship as wife and husband. In every known society, marriage is the culturally prescribed way of expressing adult love and establishing a family. Marriage gives both permanence and responsibility to the relationship, as well as responsibilities for the children of this relationship.

More than the socialization of reproduction, marriage is a relationship that offers the possibility of respect between equals, deep experiences of fidelity, trust in another person, self-acceptance, growth in intimacy and nurturing new life. It is belief in a relationship with these profound ideals which moves two single people to join in a covenant of marriage.

Marriage as an institution into which two people enter voluntarily as equals—both in the sight of law and the faith they hold—is relatively new in Western civilization. As in most other civilizations, marriage in western tradition is an institution which rationalizes and enforces the subordination of women through its religious and legal systems. Neither the Old Testament emphasis on justice in human relationships, nor the New Testament emphasis on mutual love for both husband and wife has been sufficient to transcend the culture's prevailing belief that women should be subordinate to men.

Marriage was considered a sacrament in the medieval period, but negative views of women and sexuality made celibate life in a religious order morally superior to marriage. The Protestant Reformation brought about basic changes in the Church's way of viewing women and marriage. When Martin Luther, an ex-monk, forsook his vows of celibacy and married Katy, a former nun, he made a dramatic statement about the sanctity of marriage. He accepted marriage as the normal life intended by God and, therefore, not morally inferior to celibacy. He saw women and sex as fundamentally good, a radical change from the tradition that viewed women and sex as evil. Despite religion's attitudinal change, tradition and vested political and economic interests continued to treat women as less than equals in marriage. A strong current of public opinion that the wife's place is in the home as the primary care provider, and the husband's place—with less parental responsibility—is outside the home as primary bread-winner continues to pressure couples to fit into these traditional roles. Unfortunately, in this society when two people determine to enter a covenant of marriage based on respect for each other as equals, it is still a counter-cultural commitment.

While the issue of equality is an old one, there are new realities that affect marriage. Many assume that social conditions now exist for a new intimacy between women and men: freeing sex from procreation makes it possible for people to value the erotic life for its own sake; the shrinking family size makes it possible for women and men to respond more easily to each other's needs; and the loss of the binding character of the marriage contract makes it possible to ground sexual relations in something more than legal compulsion. The "new intimacy" may be an illusion and the eagerness for it the symptom of a serious sickness in our culture.

In his classic work, *The Culture of Narcissism: American Life in An Age of Diminishing Expectations*, Christopher Lasch argues that one of the key characteristics of the narcissistic culture is the inability "to take an interest in anything after one's own death." The need for close personal encounters in the present, the avoidance of self-investment in a life-long covenant, and the demand for instant gratification have undermined genuine intimacy between men and women and also between parents and children. In this culture, women and men who enter a covenant of marriage based on a life commitment, the equality of both partners, self-giving and sacrifice, are taking a truly radical stance. Our culture pays lip service to the institution of marriage, but prevailing cultural values with stress on the primacy of self-gratification, novelty and excitement work to undermine it.

Legitimate anxieties which accompany such an important life passage are exacerbated by consumer society's definition of the value of the wedding and related rites by the quantity of consumption. According to *Bride's Magazine*, the average cost of a wedding in the United States is now almost $7,000—$2,300 for the reception, $800 for rings, $470 for pictures, $350 for bride's dress, $300 for rehearsal dinner. "It's sort of an ego-building thing," said a consultant who plans weddings from New York to Texas. "If we are going to spend $150,000 on baby sister's wedding, we do it to build egos and to show that we have good taste. And secretly, I think they love to have people discuss how much they spent on it."

Marketing people in the industry speak of "bride-generated" purchases. To understand what this means, you need only pick up a copy of one of the bridal magazines to find page after page of ads for china, crystal, and silver—to say nothing of vacuum cleaners, luggage, electric cookware, photographers, tuxedos, and bridal gowns. The travel industry is also there with "Days You'll Always Remember." While brides-to-be represent only three percent of the population, they account for a disproportionate share of household purchases in many categories: sterling-silver flatware, crystal, small-kitchen appliances, etc. A promotions director for *Modern Bride* explained, "They don't want to wait any more to get things. In effect, these new brides have become upscale."

It is sad that such expenditures bring little happiness on the wedding day or after, nor do they offer any assurance for the success of the marriage. Sadder yet is the fact that the consumptive aspects of the celebration often overshadow the religious and personal significance of the rite itself. The good news is that some can and do reject this tradition and create alternatives that better express their values, ideals and commitments.

Alternatives

How do you plan an alternative wedding? There are no formulas, because there is no one "right" way to do it. A good way to begin your plannning is to talk about the kind of lifestyle you expect to lead, the mutual goals you have and your priorities. Think about how your engagement and wedding ceremony can reflect these values. Talk with friends, clergy or other advisors. Be sensitive to the wishes of your parents or relatives, but don't let them decide for you. And if you are serious about being equal partners in marriage, don't assume that it is the bride's prerogative to decide what kind of wedding it will be, or that her family will pay for it.

Engagement. The engagement period is historically one in which the couple has time to prepare for marriage—getting to know one another and their respective families better. It is an important time to discuss in depth the shape you expect your lives to take, the priorities each of you have and the goals you want to work for. Don't let preparation for the wedding ceremony get in the way of preparing for the marriage.

Rings. The custom of giving an engagement ring may have originated at a time when marriages were arranged—as they still are in some

"The kingdom of heaven is like a wedding feast.' Each small celebration in our communities has to be this sign too."

Jean Vanier

parts of the world—and a groom gave a ring as a down payment on the agreement. Neither the engagement ring nor the wedding ring is a requirement. If rings are important to you, there are alternatives to the traditional diamond. You may wish to exchange family rings or rings found at auctions or antique jewelry stores. You may have a local craftsperson make a ring that is less expensive than a diamond and has special meaning.

Parties, Showers. These social occasions are good opportunities for couples to feel the support of their friends and families. They serve the useful function of helping supply a couple's household needs, but they can also create an unnecessary financial burden for friends and relatives who may feel obligated to give a wedding gift as well. The new couple needs more than things. Consider giving ideas: recipes, information and hints can be cleverly packaged and shared. You might give an IOU for a dinner or some other service you will provide for the couple later.

Invitations. According to bridal magazines, invitations are key status indicators. Consider making your own invitations or simply use handwritten notes. Inviting friends by phone may be the most personal way. For larger numbers of guests, consider inexpensive methods of duplicating such as quick-copy. Whatever way you choose, be sure to give your guests an idea of appropriate gifts and attire. The more information they have the more comfortable they will be and the more festive your celebration.

Gifts. It is perfectly all right to suggest the kinds of gifts you would like. Your friends usually want to give something you will find useful or beautiful. If you have enough things and would like donations made to a favorite group, give them the name and address of the organization.

Rehearsal Dinner. Consider carefully whether you want—or are able to afford—an expensive dinner at a restaurant. Friends may be delighted to help prepare such a meal as a wedding gift.

The Wedding Day. Like any other event, a wedding must be carefully planned or it may turn into a catastrophe for everyone concerned. That does not mean you have to hire a wedding consultant. A friend or two are usually available to help with the required organizing. Take the time several weeks—or months!—ahead of the wedding to sit down and talk about the day with the person you choose to help you.

Place. Wedding ceremonies and receptions are held just about anywhere—from a great hall to a barnyard—provided arrangements are thought out and made well in advance. The high costs of receptions have more to do with status projection than with the discovery of a place that has special meaning for you, your family and friends. If the church family is the major support community for your marriage, then the wedding should be in the church. Wherever you decide to have the wedding and reception, be sure that your guests know how to get there.

Dress. Many brides—or perhaps more accurately, many brides' mothers—wouldn't feel they were married without the traditional bridal dress and veil. If owning a new wedding dress is not important to you, you may want to use your mother's or a friend's dress. Consider buying a dress that can be used on other occasions. You may even want to consider renting a dress. What is true for bridal dresses is also true for attire for grooms and attendants. Men don't have to wear matched tuxedos; in fact, they don't even have to wear suits. Nor do the brides' attendants have to wear matching dresses. Decide what you really want.

Dress does make a statement. What kind of statement do you want to make?

Decorations. It is possible to have a wedding without decorations, but just as a lifestyle of responsibility would be drab without celebrations, so celebrations would be drab without decorations. That doesn't mean that "more is better." Simple, carefully thought-out decorations can convey the spirit of the occasion.

The Ceremony. Your wedding ceremony should say what you want it to say. Work with the person you choose to perform the service. There may be fewer requirements than you think. All that is required by law in the United States is the signature of a validated marriage license by a clergyperson, judge, sea captain or other qualified person. Most denominations have certain requirements for the service, but most clergypersons will work with you to make the service meaningful for you.

195

"A wedding is a time when all that is divine seems to meet all that is most human in joy."

Jean Vanier

Keep in mind that while the wedding is a joyful occasion, it is also a time for grieving. When their children marry, parents say goodbye to a special relatedness to their children and children to their parents. Family and friends must give up the old before they greet the new. Find ways to express the grief as well as the joy.

The Reception. This most expensive item in the average wedding cries out for rational thought. How much of your parents' or your own money are you prepared to spend for this occasion? It does not have to be expensive to be fun and for you to receive congratulations and good wishes from friends and family. If you want to keep it simple, light refreshments or a covered-dish dinner will not lessen the joy and fun of the occasion. Music can often be provided by friends who want to make their music a special gift to you.

An Inclusive Wedding Shower

My daughter wanted to have a nonsexist wedding celebration. Her efforts to that effect began when a friend suggested a bridal shower. After finessing an invitation for her fiance, she was asked to provide a list of her friends she would like to invite. On this list she included both male and female names. A couple of her male friends were taken aback when they received a standard shower invitation. A more serious problem was when one of the hostesses panicked on hearing the bride wanted to invite men. "What will they eat?" she worried. "We are only having finger food." As it turned out the men who came enjoyed the finger food immensely...using their fingers to stuff it into their mouths with great gusto.

Sara Lee Schoenmaker
Iowa City, Iowa

Alternative Wedding Registry

As we thought about the wedding gifts we would receive, we decided to keep the *things* and to give away the *money* we received to three nonprofit organizations. We knew a number of relatives who hadn't met us would want to give gifts but didn't know our tastes. To help them we commissioned a set of dishes from our favorite potter. It was like a wedding registry at a store—people ordered place settings or serving dishes—and the potter, not a store, made the profit. Our wedding date is inscribed on the backs of all our dishes, a great memory when cleaning up after supper.

Kathie Klein
Atlanta, Georgia

It's All in the Family

At the home of an older friend, I recently saw a beautiful friendship quilt. When she became engaged, each female relative embroidered one white muslin square with her own name in the middle along with birds, flowers or any design she chose. An elderly aunt who was blind wrote her name in pencil and her daughter embroidered it for her.

The squares were assembled into a quilt top and quilted by her mother and sisters. It made a beautiful, lasting, practical and inexpensive gift, although it took some effort. Each member of her family had one as it was always their gift to each other.

Sheryl Craig
Warrensburg, Missouri

A Variety of Special Gifts

Some special monetary gifts for our wedding were made to the Heifer project and to a Christmas angel program which supplies gifts to poor children at Christmas. Our organist donated the gift of music for the ceremony; a woman loaned her lovely silver trays for our reception; my aunt and uncle made the mints for our wedding reception; and Russ' brother made a clock for us. And we made a gift of our wedding flowers to another couple who were married the day after our wedding.

Karen Greenwaldt
Nashville, Tennessee

When Wedding Plans Don't Go Smoothly

Harsh words, tension-filled moments and decisions that were seen as selfish all stood in the way of our wedding being a grace-filled moment. In order not to make a mockery of the love we were about to celebrate, we decided to have a service of reconciliation.

Family and wedding party were invited to the church for rehearsal. After the traditional practice, we invited everyone to take part in a short prayer time focusing on the theme of reconciliation. We prayed a common prayer asking for forgiveness and spoke a greeting of peace to each other. Finally, we joined hands and prayed together the Lord's prayer. This experience was a necessary and prayerful part of our marriage.

Nancy Parker Clancy
Troy, Michigan

Back Porch Elegance

At our son's wedding we decided to extend the rehearsal dinner to include family members who were coming to Georgia from as far away as California and Oregon. Having the dinner in a local restaurant was rejected because it was too expensive for our values and budget, and because we wanted this occasion to be a personal expression of our family.

As their wedding gift, close friends of our family made their large, screened back porch available for our party and agreed to serve the dinner and clean up. Our nutritionist hostess helped us plan a meal that was both reasonably priced and delicious. We did all the food preparation the night before. Four of us gathered in her small kitchen and wrapped marinated chicken breast in phyllo dough for hours! We were very tired at the end of the evening, but we had a good time as we did it. We agreed that a less complicated recipe would have been more practical, but the chicken was delicious and elegant. The rest of the menu was quite simple: garden salad, steamed broccoli, whole wheat rolls baked by another friend, and sherbet. On the day of the dinner a neighbor cooked some of the chicken in her oven so at dinner time it arrived hot and steaming.

We borrowed tables and chairs from our church, but since this was to be a family party we used our own china, silver and linens. A friend brought colorful flowers from her yard, and our hostess made beautiful arrangements for each table. Carefully planned seating helped members from the two family groups get to know each other. The relaxed atmosphere afforded by our host family helped the tired feelings from all the preparation slip away. The gratitude of our son and new daughter, and the support we felt from our gathered families made this a highlight of our celebrations.

Rachel G. Gill
Stone Mountain, Georgia

International Dinner

Since Dennis and I were both seminary students and we felt our community at that point in our lives was there, we decided to be married on campus. Since we had both served as short-term mission volunteers—he in Nigeria and I in Paraguay—and several of our friends and professors had also worked overseas, we decided to have an international dinner with costumes. Friends made West African stew, a festive meal, served on African tablecloths at the home of one of our professors. As table decoration we bought several variegated plants which doubled as gifts for members of the wedding party.

Paula Meador Testerman
Wake Forest, North Carolina

Remember My Name

When I got married I kept my own name. I wanted to communicate this decision to our relatives. Our friends' experiences with either not specifically announcing it or being subtle and understated had not met with success—many relatives ignored the womens' use of their own names. We didn't expect such a reaction from close family but wanted to inform more distant relatives. We decided to use the invitation/announcement to let people know.

With my choice of words I wanted to address several points. I wanted to make it sound as unsurprising for me to keep my name as for my husband to keep his. It was not my purpose to be strident, aggressive or alienating in tone nor to seem critical of any who made a different choice. I did want to indicate some expectation that others would honor our decision.

As the folded invitation was opened, the wedding information was on the right-hand side. On the left side at the bottom we put: We will continue to be known by our own names. Your cooperation will be appreciated.

Kathie Klein
Atlanta, Georgia

Wedding Fiesta in Taos

We wanted to help my daughter make every aspect of her wedding significant. She began by choosing to have the wedding in the place where she had grown up rather than the place where she or the family was currently living. The date of the wedding coincided with local fiestas and Pueblo Indian dances.

Following the wedding a supper party and dance were held at our little adobe house. After the festivities were over many of the guests camped out in the beautiful field by the river—some in sleeping bags under the star, some in tents.

As a part of our larger celebration we planted a tree in memory of her father who had died two summers earlier. The children presented a romantic play, "The Owl and The Pussycat" and had fun swinging at a homemade pinata. Candles and a big bonfire of pinon logs gave soft light to the house and added beauty and warmth to an unforgettable occasion.

Virginia McConnell
Boulder, Colorado

Incorporating Different Perspectives and Pot-Luck

A major issue in planning our wedding was to create a common and congenial form from two very different perspectives—Cliff and his family are militantly secular and my family and I are rooted in faith. We scrutinized each element of the ceremony to determine how to shape it to express our particular meaning, and to respect the integrity of our differences.

In our planning with Mike, my colleague and our wedding celebrant, we imagined the ceremony as concentric circles with ourselves in the middle. The inner circle was family, spreading out to friends and the larger community. In the church, to bridge the space between the straight rows of seats and where we stood facing those seats, we placed a semi-circle of chairs for our immediate families.

Our parents were involved in the ceremony at two different points which we arranged to make sure each parent had a role. After Mike and we welcomed everyone, my mother welcomed Cliff into our family and Cliff's father welcomed me. They wrote their own greetings—my mother's included a prayer and Cliff's father's was a story—each standing on its own terms. Later, my father and Cliff's mother brought us the rings to exchange.

199

For the reception we organized a gigantic pot-luck dinner (there were over a hundred guests). One close friend's gift to us was to coordinate it. We provided hams and a core group made particular items at our request. The rest was pot-luck. Since it was spring and since there was no stove in the church basement, we asked only for salad-type dishes or ones that required no heating.

Kathie Klein
Atlanta, Georgia

The Second Time: Children Participate

Milton and I wanted to share our expressions of love and commitment with our children, our families and friends. Since this was a second marriage for both of us, it was important for our children—who through our wedding were becoming part of a blended family—to feel as much a part of the service as we did.

Unlike our first traditional weddings, we were determined to have a ceremony that was an expression of ourselves. We chose an open-air stage in a local park with benches in the shade of oak trees. We decorated the stage area with borrowed hanging baskets of begonias and ferns. A small table covered with a white linen cloth and adorned with candles and daisies served as an altar, and hanging on the wall behind the altar was a rustic cross made by our friend who officiated at the wedding. Other friends made paper cranes and hung them as mobiles on each side of the stage.

It was a casual wedding. A friend played the recorder as everyone gathered for the ceremony. Accompanied by our children, each of us walked to the altar where each child declared his support of the marriage. Family members from both sides and friends also pledged their support and lighted candles as a symbol of their promises. After we said our vows to one another, we marched out to an old fiddle tune played by a musician friend.

Dinner on the grounds followed. We supplied barbecue and punch bowls with iced tea and lemonade while guests brought their favorite dishes. Wedding cakes were gifts from friends. After dinner we had an old-fashioned barn dance. Our casual dress (I chose a peasant dress and Milton wore dress slacks with a knit shirt.) and that of our guests enabled everyone to dance until their feet ached.

As we had hoped, it was a wonderful, fun-filled day and uniquely our own. We will always cherish those memories, including the pack of dogs that roared through the park and helped themselves to one of the pans of barbecue.

Janie Howell
Ellenwood, Georgia

A Family Affair

Wedding anniversaries are a family affair, especially if children were part of the wedding (not rare anymore in this age of blended families). This can be a special time of celebrating the birth of the family unit with family-oriented activities or gifts. Candles from each family member's birthday cake can be melted down into one big candle for this occasion.

Meryl A. Butler
Virginia Beach, Virginia

"For every woman who is tired of acting weak when she is strong, there is a man who is tired of appearing strong when he feels vulnerable."

Nancy R. Smith

200

Happy Anniversary to You!

On our twenty-fifth wedding anniversary we sent out the following card to friends and family: "In celebration of God's providential care through twenty-five years of marriage and in honor of your friendship, we have made Edmarc Children's Hospice, Suffolk, Virginia the recipient of a gift in your name."

Virginia and Dick Bethune
Pulaski, Virginia

Food Bank Shares in Anniversary Celebration

A couple in our church celebrated their fiftieth wedding anniversary with an open house in the church fellowship hall. They asked that no gifts be given to them. Instead, they asked their friends and neighbors to remember the poor and needy.

Some of their friends took this a step further. The friends asked everyone who came to the open house to bring a can of food to share with the needy through the local City Rescue Mission Food Bank, the favorite charity of the anniversary couple.

The response was overwhelming. More than 30 bags of food were collected. This food was greatly needed since we live in an area that has been hard hit by plant and steel mill closings. The opportunity to share a little of their blessings was a thrill for the couple and the church.

Jacquelyn S. Thompson
Pulaski, Pennsylvania

Friends Tell All

When my parents celebrated their fiftieth wedding anniversary, my family and I wanted to give them some special remembrances of their life together. On a formal anniversary celebration announcement friends were asked to bring stories instead of gifts. The invitation read, "If you would like to present a gift other than your presence, we suggest a written account of a special time spent with our parents as a reminder of the richness each of you has added to their life together."

Kay Goodman
Lexington, Virginia

201

DIVORCE: WHEN MARRIAGE DOESN'T WORK

Next to death, divorce is probably the most traumatic life passage. Although not universal like death, the increasing divorce rate in this society makes one wonder if it might not become universal for all who marry. That it is now so commonplace does little to alleviate the pain, suffering and sense of failure often felt by the wife and husband, their children and other family and friends. The reasons for divorce are as

many and complex as the people involved, but prevailing values in the consumer culture almost insure a high rate of divorce.

There are numerous rites with which to move through the passage into marriage—engagement, showers, wedding—but, apart from legal proceedings, there are almost no rites to move individuals and their families through the passage of divorce. Perhaps one of the reasons for the absence of divorce rites is the assumption that to provide such rites would be to encourage the incidence of divorce. Moreover, newly divorced people often find themselves isolated from former friends— especially couples. Sometimes the isolation is selfimposed, perhaps out of shame. Sometimes it is because friends are not able to cope with the experience themselves. The reality is that many people are left to pass through this nightmare alone. Not only the former spouses suffer, but their children as well.

Although few rites exist for the divorce passage, they serve a real purpose for families, friends and within religious communities. As in marriage ceremonies, there is a need for expressions of grief as well as joy at changing relatioships, so also in divorce. There is a need for the divorced person to recognize the death of a particular relationship and the sadness that brings as well as to celebrate the joy and excitement of entering a new life. Like funerals, such rites would provide a medium for family and friends to grieve and to offer support when words are inadequate.

Divorce: A Service of Ending and Beginning

Leader: It is Christian tradition for the church to gather and to surround major events in the lives of its members with worship—with songs and prayers and expressions of mutual support in the presence of God. We observe marriage with weddings, birth with baptism and blessing, and death with funerals.

Divorce is a major event, similar in many ways to death. We are only beginning to learn to put it into a public worship setting—much like a funeral—in which we can deal with our guilt and our grief, our gratitude and our hope, in the healing fellowship of the Christian community. There is no long tradition here, no established guidelines, but with reverence toward God and with kindled affections and tender hearts toward those who have suffered a grievous loss, let us worship God.

Hymn – "Be Still My Soul"

Call to Confession – In his time on earth our Savior encountered many people whose relationships were tangled and who suffered from a sense of failure and guilt. He invited them: "Whoever comes to me I will in no wise cast out." He forgave them: "I do not condemn you. Your sins are forgiven." Let us bring our tangled relationships, our failures and our guilt to him.

Unison Prayer of Confession – Dear Lord, we all start out with high hopes and good intentions, especially in our marriages. When we take our vows we mean them sincerely. But sometimes communication breaks down. Sometimes we are betrayed and sometimes we ourselves betray. Love is so wounded that it dies and loveless marriage becomes a living lie and a source of endless pain, blocking any meaningful future. And in the friction between adults, children are hurt. Have mercy on us, O God, in the shame and guilt and failure that we feel. We do not ask that you approve of us, but only that you forgive us. Forgive us all, for when a marriage fails in the Christian community, we are all involved. Amen.

Silent Personal Confession

Assurance of Pardon – Hear the comforting words of our Savior: "Whoever comes to me I will in no wise cast out....Your sins which are many, are forgiven. Go and sin no more." Amen.

Response – You are the Lord, Giver of mercy.

A Prayer of Thanksgiving – Great God, giver of every good gift, we thank you for all that was good about _____ and _____ marriage. For their first love, for years of faithfulness through good times and bad, for the wonderful children who came to bless their home: _____, _____, _____, for the way each furthered the work of the other, for joys and sorrows shared that are too numerous to name, we give you thanks. As we value the lives of loved ones who have died, help us to value all that was good in this marriage that is ending. You are the giver of all good things, and we praise your name. Amen.

Hymn – "If Thou but Suffer God to Guide Thee"

> "All celebration is like a great 'Alleluia' and song of thanksgiving, in which we remember before God all those who cannot celebrate."
>
> Jean Vanier

203

Unison Prayer of Grieving – God of all comfort and mercy, hear our grief. Something very precious has died and we want to cry, to wail, to mourn, perhaps to scream in our anguish. You know our pain and sorrow and you hear our anger and distress. Our brother Jesus wept, and we know that weeping is a part of our humanity. So we offer you our tears and beg for your comfort. Comfort us, O God. In Jesus' name. Amen.

The Old Testament Lesson – Psalm 46

Unison Prayer of Hope – Creator God, you make all things new. And you can give to _____ and _____ and their children and to all of us a new future, a time full of hope and of unforeseen possibilities. We pray that in your wisdom you will prepare us and lead us into that future one day at a time, one step at a time. Your love is in our hearts. And we rest assured that if our hope comes from you, we will live in your light. Praise be to you. Amen.

The New Testament Lesson – II Corinthians 5:16-19

Expressions of Concern and Support – We now invite the friends of _____ and _____ and their children to stand and speak simply from the heart your concerns and your support.

Hymn – "Blest Be the Tie that Binds"

Benediction – May the God of hope fill you with all joy and peace in believing, so that by the power of the Holy Spirit you may abound in hope. Amen.

North Decatur Presbyterian Church
Decatur, Georgia

Help for Children

When my parents divorced I was only 11 years old. The divorce was hard on my mother, and I spent a lot of time at home trying to console her. My reaction to my situation at home was to cause trouble at school. My mother had the foresight to know this might happen, so she spoke with my teachers letting them know about the divorce and the tough time I was having at home. This simple alerting process helped my teachers respond to me in positive ways. They helped me at school by allowing me to do things alone so I would not make trouble with the other students. This enabled me to deal with the divorce without spending a lot of time in trouble.

Divorce has many implications for children, but one I have become aware of is the loss of the parent without custody. The child might spend time with this parent, but it is not the same relationship the two once had. In my case, my father moved out of our house. He saw my brothers and me on weekends, but he could no longer discipline us the way he once had. He talked with us, but he did not reprimand us for fear we would not want to see him.

My mother was busy with work and her night classes so she had little time to spend with us. My dad could spend time only on the weekend, so he became more like a friend than a parent. Though I love him we will never be able to have the same relationship we once had as parent and child.

Joe Hayes
Morrow, Georgia

Celebrating in Single-Parent or Blended Families

We like to think of celebrations as times that affirm the strength of family ties. But often they lead to conflicts about how to spend the limited time, whose traditions to follow, whether or not to attempt changes in celebration and how to proceed. The fact that these issues are commonplace does not make them any easier. In single-parent or

205

blended families—combined families with stepparents and stepchildren—where children's time must be divided among former spouses, celebrations can be especially difficult. Tension between former spouses—often compounded by differing values—can make celebrations times of extreme anxiety.

There are no easy answers! It doesn't help much to rail at the high divorce rate or the fragmentation of the nuclear family. If celebrations are to be occasions for nurture and fun, these problems must be acknowledged with sensitivity. The following suggestions may help you avoid holiday tensions:

1.   Talk with an ex-spouse about a coming celebration only after you have a clear idea of what the significance of the event is to you.

2.   Let family members and ex-spouse know about your ideas well in advance of the event.

3.   Discuss with your children, in a sensitive manner, the different perspectives and practices they may encounter in celebrations with their other parent. The same discussion would be appropriate for plans to celebrate with grandparents or other relatives.

4.   Resist cultural pressure to out-spend the other parents in order to prove your affection. Extravagance may soothe a troubled conscience, but it cannot compensate for separation. Try talking to your children about this difficult issue.

5.   Eliminate a tone of self-righteousness about your new way of celebrating.

6.   Be flexible in the dates of your celebrations. Alternative approaches can also apply to the day you celebrate.

7.   Finally, even though your immediate family unit may not get much support from other parents and relatives, hold fast to your own plans for alternative celebrations.

Milo Thornberry
Ellenwood, Georgia

13.
Other Passages

BIRTHDAYS

Observing birthdays, especially for children, is a relatively new phenomenon. The practice of marking an individual's exact date of birth came into existence only with the reckoning of time by a fixed calendar. Even then, birthday observances were usually reserved only for gods, kings, and nobles. Some societies did not note the day of birth at all, fearing that such knowledge in the hands of evil spirits was dangerous. Others were careful to mark the hour of birth as well as the day, especially those societies where astrology and horoscopes were thought to reveal special influences on the infant because of the particular planetary configuration at the hour of birth.

Birthdays celebrate entry and continuing place in the family: a time to recall the birth and significant events of an individual's life and a way to highlight the honored one's uniqueness.

While each birthday may be considered a rite of passage, some are clearly more universally important than others. For many years the first significant life transition happened at the age of six when a child left home to go to school for the first time. Today, with the preponderance of working mothers and the increase of preschool care and kindergarten, this is less true. At age 13 Jewish children are ushered into adulthood with a formal celebration of Bar/Bat Mitzvah. At age 16, children in most states are considered old enough to become licensed drivers—a first step into adult responsibilities for many; and at 18, young women and men become eligible to vote and young men register for the draft. Throughout adulthood, the decade birthdays—30, 40, 50—are important passages for many people, but the sixtyfifth birthday—the standard retirement age—is another of the more universal passages in this culture. While all of these are usually happily celebrated occasions, they may also be anxiety-producing passages. These life transitions need to be celebrated with a focus on whatever makes them special, including new responsibilities to be undertaken.

Seventh Was Best

Our family prefers outings for birthday celebrations. Some were memorable occasions, but the very best birthday party we ever had was in honor of our daughter's seventh birthday. I gave her the choice of an outing with one or two of her friends or a backyard barbecue with anyone she liked. She chose the barbecue and invited her family, a few friends her own age, several neighbors including adults, and at least two infants. In addition, she asked if she could invite the young man who taught her swimming class at the local pool.

I felt sure she would be disappointed but that charming young man accepted her invitation, appeared at the party, ate a hamburger, and gave her his second-best lifeguard whistle as an aboslutely memorable gift for a seven-year-old.

We made hand-cranked ice cream and had bowls of soap suds for blowing bubbles. There were no games. The children ate and ran about and watched the stars come out. Everyone enjoyed it.

Carolyn K. Willett
Larchmont, New York

Forty More Years

The fortieth birthday party for a friend of mine was depressing. His pride was his physical strength and he thought of this birthday as a milestone to physical deterioration. He cried, his wife was miserable and a pall settled over all of us.

208

My fortieth birthday came soon afterwards, and I was determined to celebrate in a positive way, forestalling any thoughts or feelings I might otherwise develop about my declining physical prowess. The theme I came up with was "Forty More Years," and I used the occasion to assure both my friends and myself that I planned to be vigorously involved in the things I loved for many years to come. This celebration brought optimism about my place in the world and the feeling that I can accomplish some things that are very important to me during the rest of my lifetime.

> Brian Sherman
> Decatur, Georgia

Picture-Perfect Birthday

My brother and I no longer live close enough to spend birthdays together. I wanted to let him know I was thinking of him so for his birthday, I sorted through family photographs and had copies made of some of my favorite ones with my brother in them. I put together a scrapbook of his growing-up years and added favorite quotes. It is something he will always cherish, and I relived some wonderful memories creating it.

> Patti Wilson Marcum
> Oxford, Mississippi

A Triple Celebration

The invitation read: "Can you join the Olsens and Santos' on Sunday afternoon, August 17 from 3-7 p.m. at Mark Keir's Kids 'N Stuff Nursery School. We're honoring two birthdays: Granddaughter Cristina's 13th, Elmer's 80th and Kate's and Elmer's 50th anniversary as partners and pals. No presents, please, except the pleasure of your presence. Bring a dish for a pot-luck meal (A-I dessert, J-Q casserole, R-Z salad) and folding chairs, beach blankets, balls, games, photo albums, slides. It will be a do-it-yourself fun afternoon, an instant celebration."

The nursery school, with its fenced, tree-filled yard, was a wonderful place for our intergenerational affair. Two local folk singers led a sing-along after the meal, aided by song booklets illustrated by Cristina and her eight-year-old brother. We used banners with a "Good Luck" message on which guests pinned colored slips of paper with messages for each honoree.

> Kate Olsen
> Martinez, California

"Celebrations are ritualized interruptions in daily life that give focus to life."

Adoption Day: Our Special Time

Our family—father, mother, two daughters and one son—love celebrating birthdays. For our children, whose birthdays are all in the first 20 days of December, this causes a lot of rushing around with other seasonal activities.

The fact that our oldest daughter and our son are adopted gave us a perfect reason to create a celebration that has become special to us. Since 1976 we have observed a day in March or April, a less hectic time of year, as our family's Adoption Day. This lets us all celebrate an occasion that we appreciate and talk about freely in our family.

Actual arrival for our adopted children was in March so it is appropriate to observe our day then. All of us are involved in planning and preparing for the occasion which we celebrate in a variety of ways:

having a romp in the park and eating at a fancy restaurant; picnicking at a state park; visiting a new town and going to a movie. Whatever our plans or activities, we always spend time talking about each child's "special story": what the children looked like, where we first saw them, what we did the first day, etc. As the children get older the stories are repeated over and over and we add details of the "first mother" as they are appropriate and as the children are ready to hear them. Sometimes we laugh so much over past incidents that we can hardly continue. It's a very happy time for our family.

Larry Miller
Macon, Mississippi

New Twist on Family Trivia

Each year my family tries to think up something creative and fun for our birthday celebrations. For my aunt Catherine's surprise party—to which nonfamily members were invited—we decided to make our own trivia game. A friend and I agreed to do the necessary research. This included going to the library to read microfiche newspaper articles on the date of my aunt's birth and for each decade birthday. We also looked up references to "Catherine" in encyclopedias, history books and maps.

We devised questions relating to important events on her birthdays. We also had questions on "Catherines" in history and geography. Cards with one question on each were given to the guests. Then they took turns asking the questions on their cards. The participants would try to guess the answers. If no one else knew the answer, my aunt was allowed to guess. It was great fun! Everyone there probably learned something they didn't know about the life and times of my aunt. For Catherine, the effort that went into preparing the game was an affirmation of her importance to us.

Ondina Gonzalez
Decatur, Georgia

At 75, She's the Talk of the Post Office!

For my mother's seventy-fifth birthday my sister and I gave her a card shower. We felt that things were unnecessary and cumbersome at that point in her life, but renewing old associations and friendships would be truly joyful for her.

With this in mind, I heisted her address book (a tricky deal!) and copied down every single name and address. Since she has a penchant for saving addresses, we had a wealth of information. We printed a letter bringing friends up to date on her activities and asked them to share in the celebration of her birthday by sending a card to arrive on her special day.

At a family birthday dinner a few days before her birthday, we announced the surprise by reading the letter that had gone out. Then the mail began to arrive—170 birthday cards from all over the country and from people she had not seen in years! Her postman said she was the talk of the post office.

This gift gave her hours of fond remembrance and it was satisfying for my sister and me, as well, for I don't think anything else could have given her as much pleasure and happiness.

Ronice E. Branding
Florissant, Missouri

210

EARLY PASSAGES

Tooth Rites. When a child loses the first tooth, the event is usually noted with a ritual visit from the Tooth Fairy. This stage of development is symbolic of leaving babyhood behind. Planting a tree or bush with the child to symbolize new life and growth and giving the child new privileges and responsibilities are ways that this time might be made more meaningful.

Starting School. Entering the first grade at the age of six is no longer the universal passage it once was in this society. Now many parents place their children in day care as early as their first year and many children attend preschool and kindergarten. Whenever a child first leaves home, it is an important passage. It may be a time of joy for the new level of maturity reached by the child, but it also may be a time of great anxiety for the parents and the child. The child experiences anxiety at being left alone for significant periods without the family support system, and the parents worry about whether or not the child will make the passage successfully and about the quality of care the child will receive. For the parents there is also great concern about the values and ideals to which the child will be exposed outside the home. This is such an important life passage that it ought to be observed in the family, both for the sake of the child and the parents.

PUBERTY

This period of rapid growth marks the end of childhood and the beginning of physical and sexual maturity. The bodies of boys and girls change noticeably, as do many of their feelings. While in pre-modern societies puberty was often marked by elaborate celebration, there are no commonly used rites for this passage in our culture. With many parents reluctant to discuss—let alone celebrate!—this development, boys and girls often make this passage with only advice from peers and information gained from television and sex education classes at school.

Not a Curse, but Blessing!

One of my fondest memories of time spent with a warm, creative family occurred several years ago. Their eldest daughter had experienced her first menstrual period, and her mother and I were particularly concerned that this be greeted with a positive attitude. For us, as well as for many generations of women who preceded us, menstruation was regarded as a curse—certainly not a blessing. We wanted to help this young woman avoid that experience and also set a pattern for her two younger sisters.

Like women's rites held so sacred in earlier times, all the females gathered—her mother, myself, another unofficial "aunt" and the two younger sisters. We presented the "initiate" with a bouquet of rosebuds with which we wished to express budding womanhood. At a special dinner that evening, her father made a short speech acknowledging this new stage of development, a life passage many more of which would follow.

The same ritual has been observed for each of the sisters and all have spoken warmly of the importance of that occasion in their lives.

Kathleen Timberlake
Ann Arbor, Michigan

BAR/BAT MITZVAH AND CONFIRMATION

Bar Mitzvah ("son of the commandment") is a special confirmation ceremony for Jewish boys—for Jewish girls it is Bat Mitzvah ("daughter of the commandment"). Conducted in the synagogue, usually around age 13, the celebration signals the young person's assumption of adult religious duties.

Confirmation is a rite observed in many Christian traditions that also signifies a spiritual coming of age. Usually for teenagers who were baptized as infants, the rite celebrates the assumption of adult responsibilities in the Christian community. In some traditions this may also mean taking an additional name, a name of a favored saint with whom the child chooses to identify.

Bar/Bat Mitzvah in Kibbutz

A creative joint Bar/Bat Mitzvah took place in an Israeli kibbutz. During the thirteenth year the boys and girls engage in 13 creative projects (field trips, directing a play, writing poems). The year-long process of creativity instead of a crash event symbolizes the rite of passage into responsible adulthood.

Art Waskow
Washington, D.C.

212

Belated Bar/Bat Mitzvah

I believe that Bar Mitzvah ceremonies for 13-year-olds are premature and would be far more meaningful at an older age. A senior at Brandeis University had his Bar Mitzvah as a part of the Sabbath morning "havurah." Thirty friends joined in the singing, "davening" and Torah reading, and the young man's "derasha" (preaching) on the covenant highlighted the event. The "Kiddush" was catered by his friends.

Other alternative ways of celebrating Bar/Bat Mitzvah include designing and making invitations at home; serving homemade food or sharing the task of food preparation with the congregation; having joint services with other families to share expenses and joy; creating decorations at home; using puzzles, games and rented movies for entertainment.

A growing number of rabbis are setting spending limits on weddings and Bar/Bat Mitzvahs for the sake of simplicity and religious integrity. An alternative is to give money to worthy causes in honor of these observances and celebrants.

Rabbi Albert Axelrad
Boston, Massachusetts

Editor's Note: For further information on celebrating with integrity you may wish to read "Self-Imposed Tax on Celebrations: A Jewish Response to Hunger" found in Chapter 3.

GRADUATIONS

From kindergarten to graduate school, graduations are important passages that recognize the graduate's growth and accomplishment and acknowledge the role others played in making the graduate's educational experience possible. For the graduate this is a time to accept responsibility for making a positive contribution to society. Although graduation ceremonies bring joy at achievement and accomplishment, they may also bring anxiety about the future: Can I get a job? Can I get into graduate school? Am I ready to assume responsibility for my life? It is not enough to leave these important passages to commencement rituals nor to treat them as new occasions for needless consumption. Observances at home, with friends and in one's religious community can give these passages the attention they merit and aid the graduate to move on to life's next stage.

"Knowledge, if it does not determine action, is dead to us."

Plotinus

213

RETIREMENT

In many premodern societies aging was regarded as a natural part of life and the elderly were treated with respect, if not reverence. The high esteem accorded the elderly was based both on the fact that they had survived to be old as well as the wisdom accumulated from many years of living. Moreover, the sense of interdependence within the community made respect and care for the elderly a natural expression of gratitude for their earlier contributions.

In modern Western society the passage from middle age to old age is generally perceived to be at retirement. The idea of retiring at a particular age—whether at 65, 70 or some other age—is new. It is an outgrowth of industrialization when machines began to produce a surplus of products and, combined with increased longevity, created a surplus of laborers. At the turn of the century only 39 percent of the people in the U.S. could expect to reach the age of 65. Now more than 70 percent can expect to reach that age. Of course, people retired before the industrial revolution, but there were no standard ages at which retirement began. In earlier times, the age for retirement had more to do with an individual's health or financial status than with chronological age.

Some people eagerly anticipate retirement. For them it offers a break from heavy work schedules and time to do things they have wanted to do: spend more time with family, travel, pursue avocations, etc. Others dread retirement. Some see it as a symbolic inauguration of deteriorating health. For others it means an unwanted change in routine, the loss of job satisfaction, too much leisure time, decrease in social contacts and reduced income.

While the consumer culture offers many comforts and conveniences to the aging, its prevailing values undermine respect for older people. In an aging society the consumer culture idolizes youth. To people living on reduced and fixed incomes, having money to spend is touted as the source of happiness and satisfaction. For those most in need of community, individualism is prized above the common good.

As is the case in all passages, more than the individual is involved. Births are passages not only for the baby but the parents. Getting married is a passage not only for the bride and groom but for parents and friends. Death is not only a passage for the deceased but for the survivors. Retirement and other later passages—selling the family home, entering a nursing home, etc.—are not only passages for the individual but for the surrounding family and community as well.

Most retirement ceremonies point to the accomplishments of the honoree and look forward to the positive side of retirement. Recognition of the community's indebtedness to the retiree should be coupled with recognition of the community's new responsibility to and for the person. Somewhere—in the family and/or in the religious community—there need to be rites that anticipate the joys *and* the sorrows of the next phase of life. Rites are needed, not unlike a wedding, that celebrate the new relationship with the rest of the family and community and call attention to family and community responsibilities in this new relationship.

> "...overindulgence in recreational activities aggravates rather than ameliorates a condition it is trying to deal with, namely, the trivialization of existence."
>
> Abraham J. Heschel

214

Time to Get Deeper into the Fray

What is coming up for me is not retirement *from* anything, as I see it. It is advancing. When you live in an industrialized country where the majority of the poor are little children, you have to think about moving deeper into the fray. For dozens of years I've made my living consulting with a smorgasbord of anti-poverty groups. When I stop consulting I intend to keep right on working with some of these groups as a volunteer.

Gene Sylvestre
Minneapolis, Minnesota

Grandpa's Room

Great-Grandpa was too old to live alone and was coming to live with us. We fixed up his room with comfortable, used furniture and a clock; we selected our best pictures for the walls and made new curtains. We put lace doilies and fresh flowers on all the tables so the room wouldn't look empty when he came, but we left room for the things he would bring with him.

He arrived with two suitcases and his violin. In the suitcases he brought his clothes, some pictures and his Bible. He put his things away and we had supper. It was a special meal to welcome him, but it was just his family.

It was clear from that first day that this, like a good marriage, was a "till death do us part" arrangement. He was immediately part of the decision-making process and was made privy to all household and family matters. Everything was done beforehand to make him feel he had just come home. I think the simplicity of the occasion and the homey, readied room—which we were already calling Grandpa's room—made it easy for him to slip into the family.

Sheryl Craig
Warrensburg, Missouri

Homer's Heifer Celebration

Our pastor retired after many years of service to our congregation. For many he was the only minister they had ever known. For his retirement celebration, the children's choir led the congregation in singing "The Farmer in the Dell." After one verse the director asked the congregation to continue singing with word changes she would suggest, beginning with "Homer (our minister's name) needs a cow." As the congregation sang, two of the children carried in a life-sized cardboard cut-out of a cow. The congregation continued singing, "Homer needs a goat; a chicken; a rabbit; a pig; some bees." With each verse children brought in cardboard facsimilies.

After the song a prompted questioner rose to ask, "What will Homer do with all these creatures since he is moving to a very small house in the city?" In response, all the children chorused, "He can give them to needy people through the Heifer Project." And that is what he did. All the creatures we sang about represented gifts to the Heifer Project that had been solicited to celebrate our pastor's retirement.

H. J. Kopke
Cleveland, Ohio

Retirees Make Hospital Possible

In the small North Carolina town in which I grew up, there was a desperate need for a new hospital. With the complexity of federal regulations about funding, the necessity to raise a large amount of money locally, and the demands to find suitable administrative personnel and additional medical personnel, the job was mammoth and time consuming. I watched from a distance as two men and a woman, all retired, took on the job and succeeded. Only retired people could have given so much time to combine with their wisdom and experience. One of the men was my father. I flew there for the grand celebration of the hospital opening and his eightieth birthday.

Julia T. Gary
Decatur, Georgia

Washboard Band Scrubs Myths About The Aging

The Northside Shepherd Center's Washboard Band began more than eight years ago. Jane Carrier, leader of the band and emcee at their performances, has been a professional musician in the country music field since the 1930s. A member of the Atlanta Country Music's Hall of Honor and senior citizen herself, Carrier understands the need of older people to stay involved and to feel useful.

As Program Director at the Center, Carrier leads the band and teaches the rudiments of performance—including complicated rhythms and high-kicking dance routines. Performances are greeted with appreciative whistles, enthusiastic cheers and standing ovations. And currently, the band is adding occasional radio and television invitations to its busy schedule.

"If I had known having grandchildren was so much fun, I would have had them first."

216

In addition to providing happy times and purpose to its members, the Washboard Band is beginning to provide some financial support to its home base. A modest fee for performances allows the band to contribute to the Center's varied programs for community elders.

The Washboard Band is but a reflection of the larger community to which it belongs. It is, in fact, a microcosm of this community—a caring, energized, productive and happy group of folks who happen to be elders. Housed in the basement of Tenth Street United Methodist Church, Northside Shepherd Center is patterned after and affiliated with the Shepherd Center in Kansas City, an organization founded in 1972, to help older people stay in their own communities.

The Northside Center is a place where elders are actively engaged with each other, and in the process they are building community. These elders are still learning how to live.

Rachel G. Gill
Stone Mountain, Georgia

Editor's Note: For further information on the Shepherd Center concept, contact the Shepherd Center, 5218 Oak St., Kansas City, Kansas 64112.

Rite to Retire

Minister: Retirement is a perfect time for taking a serious look at this gift we call life. It is also a time to examine our relationship to our Creator. With retirement, there is time to think, to study and to pray; there is time to see life in a new perspective, to be thankful. And most of all, there is time to live!

For many of the significant transitions in our lives, there is a ceremony—a ritual, a rite of passage—in which we cast off an old status and assume a new one. In the presence of family and friends we take on new responsibilities. From birth we go through personal, educational and professional changes that indicate beginnings. Baptism, confirmation and marriage are religious rites in our church. Jews celebrate Bar and Bat Mitzvah, marking the passage of boys and girls into manhood and womanhood and adult religious responsibilities.

Today, we shall begin a new rite in our church, a service that I hope will become an annual event. Those in the congregation who are 65 years of age or more and who wish to redirect their lives to renewed growth and service may come to the altar for a time of celebration and dedication. The congregation is invited to join in a litany of support for their redirection.

In this community of faith, love and service, we come to celebrate a time of passage for some of our members—a passage through retirement to redirection.

All: We believe that we are created in the image of God; that we are intended for a special relationship with God through Jesus Christ and, thereby, for service to all humankind. At this moment we, of all ages, reaffirm this statement of the purpose and meaning of our lives.

Minister: Retirement is a gift, a wonderful gift of increased personal freedom and time. Our friends at the altar come now to ask for God's guidance and help in redirecting their lives.

Seniors: We pray that we may be open to new direction, new insights, and new opportunities for service.

Minister: This congregation challenges you as mature and experienced

> "May I suggest that...old age be regarded not as the age of stagnation but as the age of opportunities for inner growth."
>
> Abraham J. Heschel

elders among us to use your gift of time and freedom to increase your understanding of a life lived for God and in close relationship with God.

Seniors: We pledge ourselves to increased study of the scripture, to regular times of meditation, and to prayer.

Minister: We recognize your accomplishments and contributions as members of this congregation and affirm your experience and knowledge. We need your continued involvement in this fellowship and actively seek your wise counsel.

Congregation: As a congregation, we applaud the accomplishments of our senior members and are grateful for their contributions to this community of faith. We celebrate their passage into a new phase of life and offer our support.

Minister: Let us pray. Dear God, you are mother and father to all; you defend, nurture, and support us as we seek to serve you. We thank you for our friends and loved ones standing here, for their past service to you in their business, professional and family lives. We celebrate their entry into this new phase of life, a time for renewal in the faith, for growth and service.

For the new challenges and opportunities that will come to them and for the new roles that they will assume, we seek your nurture and support. As a congregation, we pledge our help in this time of passage, knowing that your divine guidance is always there. Let this be a time when our congregation, your church, will grow in its mission as we work together—all ages, in keeping with your will and to your glory. In the name of Jesus Christ our Lord, we pray. Amen.

Julia T. Gary
Decatur, Georgia

The Gift of a Lifetime

The Gift of a Lifetime program is the Presbyterian Church's response to the growing numbers of older adults among its members and in the communities where its congregations are located. This program gives older adults an opportunity to serve as fulltime volunteers, sharing with others the gift of growing faith, commitment, experience and skill.

The program has two specific goals: to help congregations develop new approaches to older adult ministry and to demonstrate the importance of older people's faith, experience, leadership and commitment. Volunteers are placed for two-year periods and begin their ministry assignments with a two-week orientation and training conference.

Presbyterian Office on Aging
Atlanta, Georgia

Editor's Note: Other denominations have similar programs for older adults. Contact your denominational office for information.

Appendix

CRAFT GROUPS

Self-Help Crafts Groups assist victims of poverty, famine, unemployment and injustice by providing markets for skilled craftspeople throughout the world. Gifts purchased from Self-Help organizations give twice: They make useful, lovely gifts for consumers and help provide employment and a fair income to economically deprived producers.

The following is a list of these groups arranged alphabetically by states. The asterisks indicate that mail orders are accepted.

Arkansas

ACORN Artisans
523 West 15th
Little Rock, AR 72202
(501)376-7151

Arizona

MCC Self-Help Program
The Oasis
3536 W. Glendale Ave.
Phoenix, AZ 85021
(602)841-1415

Third World Handarts
96 So. Carmichael
Sierra Vista, AZ 85635
(602)458-7639

Third World Handarts
c/o 415 S. 6th St.
Tucson, AZ 85701
(602)623-7094

California

MCC Self-Help Program
Et Cetera Shop
1298 North Wishon
Fresno, CA 93728
(209)233-3459

MCC Self-Help Program
Gift 'N' Nearly New
1012 G Street
Reedley, CA 93654
(209)638-3560

*International Gift Shop
  (SERRV)
122 West "G" St.
Oakdale, CA 95361
(209)847-4637

MCC Self-Help Program
Serendipity
116 N. Second Ave.
Upland, CA 91785
(714)981-4633

Third World Handarts
465 N. Anaheim Blvd.
Orange, CA 92668
(714)634-1685

Colorado

MCC Self-Help Program
Crossroads
203 Colorado Ave.
La Junta, CO 81050
(303)384-6620

MCC Self-Help Program
More For Less
6001 West Mississippi Ave.
Lakewood, CO 80226
(303)934-9967

Florida

*Mountain Maid
U.S. Forwarding Address:
Box 1560
West Palm Beach, FL 33416

MCC Self-Help Program
World's Attic
3344 Bahia Vista St.
Sarasota, FL 33582
(813)366-3573

Idaho

MCC Self-Help Program
More For Less
1211 A 1st St., S.
Nampa, ID 83651
(208)467-5980

Illinois

MCC Self-Help Program
Et Cetera Shop
107 S. Main St.
Eureka, IL 61530
(309)467-4211

MCC Self-Help Program
Plowshares
1216 W. Diversey
Chicago, IL 60614
(312)281-9040

MCC Self-Help Program
SELFHELP Village Crafts
41 E. University
Champaign, IL 61820
(217)352-8200

*SERRV Handcraft Gifts
   International
995 S. Dundee Ave.
Dundee, IL 60118
(312)741-7766

MCC Self-Help Program
Spare & Share
311 Woodford St.
Gridley, IL 61744
(309)747-2693

Indiana

MCC Self-Help Program
Dove's Nest Gift 'n Thrift
Georgetown Square
6746 East State Blvd.
Ft. Wayne, IN 46815
(219)493-4774

MCC Self-Help Program
Et Cetera Ecke
152 West Main St.
Berne, IN 40711
(219)589-2831

Friends of the Third World, Inc.
611 W. Wayne St.
Fort Wayne, IN 46802
(219)422-1650

Rio San Juan Sister State
   Project
c/o 524 Buckingham Dr.
Indianapolis, IN 46208
(317)283-3057

MCC Self-Help Program
SELFHELP Gift and Thrift
Peddler's Village
21656 CR 28
Goshen, IN 46526
(219)534-1828

Third World Shoppe
611 W. Wayne St.
Fort Wayne, IN 46802
(219)422-6821

Iowa

MCC Self-Help Program
Crowded Closet
1121 Gilbert Court
Iowa City, IA 52240
(319)337-5924

MCC Self-Help Program
Our Way
Main Street
Pulaski, IA 52584
(515)675-3493

MCC Self-Help Program
SELFHELP Gifts
111 South 13th St.
Ft. Dodge, IA 50501
(515)955-6734

MCC Self-Help Program
World's Window
805 East 18th St.
Cedar Falls, IA 50613
(319)268-1584

Kansas

MCC Self-Help Program
Common Ground
3950 Rainbow Blvd.
Kansas City, KS 66103
(913)432-4826

MCC Self-Help Program
Et Cetera Shop
119 North Main St.
Hillsboro, KS 67063
(316)947-3817

MCC Self-Help Program
Et Cetera Shop
18 North Main St.
Hutchinson, KS 67501
(316)669-8932

MCC Self-Help Program
Et Cetera Shop
748 South Kansas
Liberal, KS 67901
(316)624-8740

MCC Self-Help Program
Et Cetera Shop
712 Main St.
Newton, KS 67114
(316)283-9461

MCC Self-Help Program
The Olive Branch
119 S.W. 6th St.
Topeka, KS 66603
(913)233-4811

Kentucky

David Appalachian Crafts
Highway 404
David, KY 41616
(606)886-2377

MCC Self-Help Program
The Gathering
Covenant Crafts, Inc.
2722 Frankfort Ave.
Louisville, KY 40206

Grass Roots Craftsmen
Box 637
Jackson, KY 41339
(606)666-7371

Middle Kentucky River
   Area Development Council
Breathitt County Courthouse
Jackson, KY 41339
(606)666-2452

Maryland

*International Gift Shop
   (SERRV)
500 Main St.
New Windsor, MD 21776
(301)635-2111

MCC Self-Help Program
World Treasures
22 West Franklin St.
Hagerstown, MD 21740
(301)797-8624

Minnesota

MCC Self-Help Program
Care and Share Thrift Shop
208 10th St.
Mountain Lake, MN 56159
(507)427-3468

MCC Self-Help Program
Jubilee Shop
2001 Riverside Ave.
Minneapolis, MN 55454
(612)339-5133

Missouri

MCC Self-Help Program
Plowsharing Crafts
7360 Manchester Ave.
St. Louis, MO 63143
(314)644-4310

Nebraska

MCC Self-Help Program
Brass and Jute Works
5 East 24th St.
Kearney, NE 68847
(308)234-1418

MCC Self-Help Program
Et Cetera Shop
648 Seward St.
Seward, NE 68434
(402)643-4767

MCC Self-Help Program
Marion Friesen
Route 1, Box 148
Henderson, NE 68371
(402)723-4378

MCC Self-Help Program
Helping Hands
237 S. 70th; Suite 205
Lincoln, NE 68510
(402)466-1914

New York

MCC Self-Help Program
Global Village Crafts
Redeemer Community Church
42-54 149 Place
Flushing, NY 11355
(212)296-5600

MCC Self-Help Program
Agape Shoppe
95 Main St.
Akron, NY 14001
(716)937-3399

MCC Self-Help Program
Agape Shoppe
Globe Mini-Mall, Court St.
Watertown, NY 13601
(315)788-7470

MCC Self-Help Program
Common Ground Gift and Thrift
161 Main St.
Cold Spring Harbor, NY 11724
(516)367-4975

Simple Gifts
65 New Shaker Rd.
Albany, NY 12005
(518)456-3201

North Carolina

John C. Campbell Folk School
Brasstown, NC 28902
(704)837-2775

Madison County Crafts
P. O. Box 472
Marshall, NC 28753
(704)649-3231

Maco Crafts, Inc.
652 Georgia Highway
Franklin, NC 28734
(704)524-7878

North Dakota

MCC Self-Help Program
Gift and Thrift Shoppe
1809 S. Broadway Plaza
Minot, ND 58701
(701)852-3320

Ohio

MCC Self-Help Program
Care and Share Center
1309 S. Defiance St.
Archbold, OH 43502
(419)445-1926

MCC Self-Help Program
Columbiana SELFHELP
35 S. Main St.
Columbiana, OH 44408
(216)482-3667

*The Desert Homestead
3175 St. Rt. 3
Loudonville, OH 44842
(216)852-4527

MCC Self-Help Program
Et Cetera Shop
111 S. Main St.
Bluffton, OH 45817
(419)358-4201

MCC Self-Help Program
Global Crafts
Main St.
Sugarcreek, OH 44681
(216)897-5545

MCC Self-Help Program
Global Crafts
Walnut Creek, OH 44687
(216)852-2586

MCC Self-Help Program
Global Crafts
106 N. Detroit
W. Liberty, OH 43357
(513)465-3077

One World Shoppe
14549 Madison Ave.
Lakewood, OH 44107
(216)227-6475

MCC Self-Help Program
Orrville Thrift and Gift Shop
116 N. Main St.
Orrville, OH 44667
(216)683-6143

MCC Self-Help Program
The Thrift House
1295 Edison St., NE
Hartville, OH 44632
(216)877-2769

Oklahoma

MCC Self-Help Program
Et Cetera Shop
121 N. State St.
Weatherford, OK 73096
(405)772-7531

Oregon

MCC Self-Help Program
Et Cetera Shop
824 Main St.
Lebanon, OR 97355
(503)258-5614

MCC Self-Help Program
Portland Mennonite Church
1312 Southeast 35th Ave.
Portland, OR 97214
(503)234-0559

MCC Self-Help Program
SELFHELP Crafts
137 S.W. Court
Dallas, OR 97338
(503)623-3384

Pennsylvania

MCC Self-Help Program
Bird-In-Hand SELFHELP
2713 Old Philadelphia Pike
Bird-In-Hand, PA 17505
(717)392-7302

MCC Self-Help Program
Care and Share Thrift Shop
Souderton Shopping Center
Souderton, PA 18964
(215)723-0315

MCC Self-Help Program
Crossroads Thrift Shop
100 East Main St.
Norristown, PA 19401
(215)275-3772

MCC Self-Help Program
International Gift and Thrift
413 W. Main St.
Mt. Joy, PA 17552
(717)653-8318

*Jubilee Crafts
300 W. Apsley St.
Philadelphia, PA 19144
(215)849-0808

MCC Self-Help Program
Little Portion Peddler
P. O. Box 450, Main St.
Delaware Water Gap, PA 18327

MCC Self-Help Program
Oak Leaf Book Shoppe
Spruce Lake Retreat
R.D. #1, Box 605
Canadensis, PA 18325
(717)595-7505

MCC Self-Help Program
Re-Uzit Shop
228 W. Lincoln Highway
Coatesville, PA 19320
(215)383-5473

MCC Self-Help Program
Re-Uzit Shop
440 Locust St.
Columbia, PA 17512
(717)684-7621

MCC Self-Help Program
Re-Uzit Shop
20 E. Main St.
Ephrata, PA 17522
(717)733-4982

MCC Self-Help Program
Re-Uzit Shop
148 E. Main St.
New Holland, PA 17557
(717)354-8355

MCC Self-Help Program
SELFHELP Crafts
240 N. Reading Rd.
Ephrata, PA 17522
(717)738-1101

MCC Self-Help Program
Thrift and Gift Shop
12 N. Main St.
Belleville, PA 17004
(717)935-5233

MCC Self-Help Program
The World's Attic
109 E. Main St.
Somerset, PA 15501
(814)288-2338

South Dakota

MCC Self-Help Program
Et Cetera Shoppe
308 S. Main St.
Freeman, SD 57029
(605)925-7098

Tennessee

Dry Creek Co-op Trading
Rt. 2, Box 11A
Woodbury, TN 37190
(615)563-8207

Texas

*Pueblo to People
1616 Montrose Blvd. #5606
Houston, TX 77006
(713)523-1197

Visions
2019 Montana
El Paso, TX 79903
(915)532-4148

Virginia

MCC Self-Help Program
Gift and Thrift
227 N. Main St.
Harrisonburg, VA 22801
(703)433-8844

Holston Mountain Co-op Crafts
279 East Main
Abingdon, VA 24210
(703)628-7721

MCC Self-Help Program
People Place
Sherwood Mall, Suite 61 ½
Newport News, VA 23602
(804)877-0266

Washington

MCC Self-Help Program
Lynette Ratzlaff
6726 Sycamore Ave., NW
Seattle, WA 98117
(206)782-5608

St. Mary's Self-Help. Inc.
514-17 Ave. East
Seattle, WA 98112
(206)322-0946

Wisconsin

Direct Trade
c/o 437 W. Johnson
Madison, WI 53703
(608)251-0156

Meaningful Global Gifts
3721 N. 2nd St.
Milwaukee, WI 53212
(414)372-4186

CANADA

Ontario

*Family Pastimes
R. R. 4
Perth, Ontario, CANADA K7H 3C6
(613)267-4819

ADVERTISERS

The following is an alphabetical listing of organizations whose advertisements appear in this catalogue at the invitation of the Alternatives staff. The purpose of the ads is 1) to inform readers of the work of these important organizations; 2) to encourage people to divert money to these organizations as a part of their celebrations; 3) to offer further resources for alternative gifts; 4) to call attention to products and services that are consistent with our goals.

We are grateful for our advertisers' contributions to this catalogue of celebrations. We urge our readers to benefit from their resources.

Agricultural Missions, Inc., 114
Alternatives, 152
Baptist Peace Fellowship of North America, 130
Bread for the World, 154
Brethren Press, 131
Center for Global Service and Education, 129
Church World Service (CWS), 168
Committee on Religion in Appalachia (CORA), 163
Co-op America, 142
Cooperative Disaster Child Care Program, 132
Desert Homestead, 65
Discipleship Resources (UMC), 132, 129
Division of Overseas Ministries (NCCC), 152
Domestic Hunger and Poverty Working Group (NCCC), 86

Evangelical Lutheran Church in America, 153
Evergreen Society, 112
Faith and Life Press, 130
Federation of Southern Cooperatives, 141
Fellowship of Reconciliation, 140
Friends of the Third World, Inc., 66
General Board of Global Ministries, World Division (UMC), 164
Habitat for Humanity, 70
Heifer Project International, 68
Herald Press, 82
Hunger Action Fund (UCC), 83
Institute for Peace and Justice, 131
Interfaith Center on Corporate Responsibility, 166
Koinonia Farms, 66
Lutheran Human Relations, 131
Mountain Maid, 69
National Farm Worker Ministry, 111
National Sharecroppers Fund, 113
New Creation Institute, 113
New Windsor Service Center, 132
Oxfam America, 85
Paulist Press, 141
Pax World Foundation, 167
Peace Corps Partnership Program, 150
Phonefriend, 129
Potato Project (Society of St. Andrew), 85
Presbyterian Hunger Program, 151
Pueblo to People, 65
Red Bird Missionary Conference, 113
Reformed Church World Service (RCA), 165
Rural Advancement Fund, 113
St. Martin's Table, 130
SELFHELP Crafts (MCC), 69
SERRV (CWS), 64
Society of St. Andrew, 112, 85
Third World Handarts, 67
United Church of Christ Hunger Action Fund, 83
United Farm Workers, 114
UMC General Board of Global Ministries, World Division, 164
United Methodist Committee on Relief (UMCOR), 84

W9-BIQ-118

Call Me Magdalena

LATIN AMERICAN WOMEN WRITERS

Series Editors

Jean Franco, *Columbia University*

Francine Masiello, *University*
of California at Berkeley

Tununa Mercado

Mary Louise Pratt,

Stanford University

CALL ME

MAGDALENA

(Cuando digo Magdalena)

By Alicia Steimberg

Translated by Andrea G. Labinger

University of Nebraska Press

Lincoln and London

© 1992, Alicia Steimberg; © 1992,
Editorial Planeta Argentina
S.A.I.C.; © 1992, Grupo Editorial Planeta
Translation © 2001 by Andrea G. Labinger
All rights reserved
Manufactured in the United States of America
⊖

Library of Congress Cataloging-in-Publication Data
Steimberg, Alicia, 1933–
[Cuando digo Magdalena. English]
Call me Magdalena / by Alicia Steimberg;
translated by Andrea G. Labinger.
p.   cm. — (Latin American women writers)
ISBN 0-8032-4290-5 (cloth : alk. paper) —
ISBN 0-8032-9282-1 (pbk. : alk. paper)
I. Labinger, Andrea G. II. Title. III. Series.
PQ7798.29.T36 C8313 2001   863'.64 — dc21
00-066667

𝒩

Publication of this volume was assisted by
The Virginia Faulkner Fund,
established in memory of Virginia Faulkner,
editor-in-chief of the
University of Nebraska Press.

Call Me Magdalena

When you leave the main road you have to walk down a long dirt path to get to the entrance of Las Lilas. There's no gate: the wooden front door is tall and majestic, its topmost part safeguarded against furtive visitors by sharp little iron posts. On both sides of the door are walls whose uppermost portions are similarly protected. While the walls and door are almost impregnable, if you simply walk about fifty yards in either direction, you'll come upon a very thick, although not very tall, evergreen hedge. With the help of a machete, you can hack an opening in the hedge and pass through to the other side, or, by walking just a bit farther, the furtive visitor will discover that the evergreen hedge turns into a simple wire fence, not even barbed wire, that he can cross by placing one foot on the wire below and lifting up the wire on top with one hand. Once inside, the intruder will find himself in a cultivated field. He'll wend his way to the entry by sidling along close to the fence, and then next to the wall (since if he crosses the open field, his figure will be discernible from a distance). If the wheat is fully grown, he'll proceed waist-deep among the stalks. If he's not wearing boots, the thistles will prick him and he'll be exposed to snakebite, or he'll be covered by little red bugs that will torment him later on, because those red bugs get under your skin and you can get rid of them only by rubbing the affected part with soap, creating a layer of insulation that asphyxiates them.

We reached Las Lilas at nightfall, on a Thursday in November. Juan Antonio and Emi came out to meet us and offered to take us immediately to the rooms they had prepared for us during our stay at the *estancia*. I stopped for a moment in front of the house, at the foot of the front steps, next to a bed of purple flowers that smelled divine. Intoxicated by their fragrance, I looked around me. The flower bed on my left, on my right the swimming pool, and a little farther on, the wide, thatched roof of the gazebo. I climbed the marble staircase, admired the black-and-white mosaic tile (also marble), and leaned over the balustrade to contemplate the lovely scenery—the woods, the gently rolling, variegated countryside: greens, rusts, honey-hued fields. Far in the distance, a monstrously bright yellow piece of farm machinery destroyed my illusion of having traveled backward in time.

Instead of going to my room along with the others, I descended the staircase I had just climbed and walked along the gravel path. No one noticed me. I had gone about thirty yards among the shrubs and flower beds when someone called me from the doorway and I had to turn around and go back. I felt happy to be in the country and smiled at everyone who crossed my path: the occupants of the house, the servants, some geese unexpectedly traversing the road. I climbed the stairs again and entered a long hallway leading to the door of one of the rooms, where Enrique was waiting for me.

The room was spacious, furnished with a big bed, two night tables, and an unpolished oak dresser. On the dresser was an antique basin with a chipped rim. The latticed window faced the garden. The bathroom was enormous, with antique, yellowed furnishings. The bathtub had lion-claw feet.

Tastefully attired in a lime-green sundress and sandals, with a touch of Femme behind each earlobe, I sat down on the bed to read an old Ellery Queen novel I had found in one of the dresser drawers while I waited for Enrique to finish showering and dressing. I could feel the fresh evening breeze through the open window. I felt expansively happy at being in the country.

A half hour later, Enrique and I got together with the other guests and the owners of the house in the large parlor on the first floor. The parlor floor was also made of black-and-white mosaic tiles, rhomboid. There was a marble fireplace, where logs probably crackled in winter. Everyone was settled in chairs around a low table covered with glasses, bottles, and trays of hors d'oeuvres. In one corner of the parlor there was a baby grand piano, on which a child of Eusebio's—the man who had driven us there—practiced a silly tune, making mistakes with practically every note. Vexed, I looked at him, wondering how we would endure the next few days at the *estancia* with so many little kids, because in addition to Eusebio's two, there were Juan Antonio's and Emi's children, Gustavo's baby, and two other children who were friends of Juan Antonio's kids. I hadn't brought any along myself. My adolescents preferred to stay in Buenos Aires with their grandmother, devoting themselves to their noisy pursuits. I must confess I have no fondness for small children, especially if they aren't mine, and I had entertained fantasies of spending some peaceful days at Las Lilas, without squalling or spilled drinks or parents shouting at kids who had climbed up to some great height and threatened to fall into an abyss.

I was about to get away from the piano so the off-key tune wouldn't destroy my eardrums when I saw, on top of the instrument, a photo in a silver frame: Juan Antonio with his two sisters, all three in tennis outfits, racquets in hand. I didn't know why, but that photo attracted me like a magnet. On the shelves built into the wall behind the piano, there were other pictures of Juan Antonio's family, some of them quite old, depicting scenes on the *estancia*: men and women on horseback, with elegant riding clothes; young women in gauzy dresses sitting beneath an arbor in the garden.

"Just imagine! We haven't had breakfast yet, Enrique."

"What's your hurry to have breakfast? Last night's dinner was fantastic: twelve people around the table, uniformed attendants . . ."

"Did you say 'attendants'?"

"Yes, but I said it with some hesitation."

"Shouldn't you have said 'waiters'?"

"What for? Let's abandon any pretense of standard speech."

"No, but that's going too far. Let's stick with a more or less general sort of parlance, with a few inevitable regionalisms."

"Fine. The *attendants* finished serving dessert: homemade flan with *dulce de leche*. We adjourned to the first floor for coffee. Emi, wearing a huge straw hat and holding a riding crop in her hand, was stretched out on the divan like a queen."

"Is Emi a mulatto?"

"That's what she always aspired to be; Juan Antonio fell in love with her because he thought she was a mulatto. But she's just dark-skinned. She's of Spanish and Indian descent. Juan Antonio broke with his family back then and went to live with Emi in a one-room apartment that they cleaned and swept themselves. They were happy, though. Later Emi won over Juan Antonio's mother, and he got the *estancia* back and Emi helped him restore it."

"We were talking about Emi with her straw hat and whip, stretched out on the divan."

"Yes. We talked; we had coffee. Later we went to sit outside in the wicker chairs on the verandah, because it was a glorious evening, with crickets chirping, fireflies, the fragrance of flowers . . ."

"Sabina . . ?"

"Is my name Sabina?"

"Yes. Don't you like it?"

"No. There's something greasy about the name Sabina."

"What?"

"Greasy lips."

"Women named Sabina have greasy lips?"

"No. I meant that the *name* Sabina has greasy lips."

"All right. Gertrude."

"No. Women named Gertrude have thick lips and black ringlets."

"Curls. I think you're supposed to say 'black curls.' Magdalena?"

"All right. In spite of the fact that Magdalenas tend to be fat, with broad shoulders, and they run cattle farms with fifteen milk cows and a hundred barnyard fowl all by themselves."

"Magdalena. Nicknamed Maggie."

"What language are we speaking?"

"We already determined that. It's general parlance, the most universal modality possible, with a few regionalisms thrown in to reflect the speech of those middle-class Argentines who live in Buenos Aires and fancy themselves to be well educated."

"Then it wouldn't be Maggie, but rather Maggi. Now let's go have breakfast."

That night, our first night on the *estancia*, we had gone to our room and slept like logs until morning, when we were awakened by the birds singing, the children shouting, and a few hens cackling as they escaped from the henhouse. We also heard the shouts of the cook as she chased after them, followed by Emi's cries as she leaned out her bedroom window and shouted insults at the cook. A half hour later we met in the dining room for breakfast with the other guests. This room, like the rest of the house, was furnished simply: a tall, heavy table, covered with a red-and-white checkered tablecloth, a few equally heavy chairs with woven seats (the kind that leave marks on the back of your thighs), a sideboard, and two solid chests that reached waist-high on a person of average height. The children had to stand on tiptoe to see the tops of these pieces of furniture, which held trays or bottles that didn't fit on the table. At that time of day the sideboard held trays of toast and croissants and smaller trays with butter or *dulce de leche*, the *estancia*'s own famous *dulce de leche*, cooked in a copper kettle with vanilla beans. Someone always found a hard little piece of vanilla bean in the sauce and sucked it clean before tossing it out the window. Every so often I'm visited by the spirit of the countryside I knew when I was a girl: the birds singing, the *dulce de leche*.

"How strange! I thought you found the country boring."

"It never bores me to *talk* about the country, because I can talk about twilight, the breeze gently ruffling the stalks of wheat, the contentment of the farmer and the fragrance of the wisteria . . . Nothing about droughts or the va-a-a-st distances. In any case, we finally had our breakfast, together with some very badly behaved children."

"What were the children doing?"

"They were helping themselves from all the dishes and trays, and they left everything a mess. They were playing with a little rubber ball, and suddenly one of them missed the mark and the ball fell into Enrique's cup, and to top it all off he was dressed in a white shirt and blue tie at the time."

"My God."

"But nothing bothered us after the first bite of that crisp toast with butter and homemade *dulce de leche*. And right after that a good cup of excellent coffee."

"With milk?"

"Yes, it was already mixed with the milk, in an enormous coffee pot."

"Just like in those old-fashioned hotels."

"Everything was old-fashioned in that house. Even the kitchen helper, who was white and chubby, with a blue dress and apron and white slippers, with freckles on her arms and chest. She was the one who knew how to make a cocktail with port and a beaten egg."

"What's it like?"

"You have to go get the eggs from the henhouse and use them while they're still warm. You separate the whites from the yolks. You can reserve the whites to make meringue. You beat the yolks with sugar until they take on a whitish color, and you add the port drop by drop, beating all the while. That woman beats egg yolks with sugar and port all day long."

"Now let's have breakfast in Mar del Plata, as you suggested."

"This isn't the same place where we always go."

"But I like it, dear. It's sheltered from the wind and you can see the ocean. How many croissants do you want?"

"How many do you think? Three, of course. Don't they always bring three croissants with the café au lait?"

"No, dear, that was before. Now you have to ask for the number of croissants you're going to eat."

"Why did they change it, dear?"

"Because diets have become so popular: croissants are very fattening. By the way, shouldn't you be on a diet?"

"I'm not planning to diet in Mar del Plata, dear."

"But you weigh 125."

"And *you* weigh 150. Let's go to the casino."

"Later. I think I'm just going to order café au lait and nothing else. No croissants."

"I'll do the same, dear. Coffee with skim milk and artificial sweetener."

"Now you're talking."

"May I ask your name? We've called each other 'dear' so much I've forgotten your name."

"My name is Ignacio Ibargüengoitía."

"Basque?"

"Strange that you should ask after forty years of marriage. My grandparents were Basque, all four of them."

"Four Basque grandparents. It's Iñaki, then, not Ignacio. Does Basque use the same characters as Spanish? Or do they use a different alphabet?"

"No, that's Yiddish. I can't remember your name."

"Flora."

"Wasn't your name Sabina?"

"No, Flora."

"Flora Rosenfeld?"

"Rosenblatt."

"Rosenberg."

"Rosenblum."

"Rosenwasser."

"Rosenstein."

"I don't think so."

"But it is, though."

"Who said that, you or me?"

"I'm not sure."

"It doesn't matter. Flora, then."

"It sounds like you're saying my name for the first time."

"That's ridiculous."

"Yes."

"I'm referring to the name. You might as well be named Fauna. The name Flora sounds like it was invented by a Pole who didn't know much Spanish and thought all feminine nouns ended in *a*."

"Yes. Being called Flora has limited me quite a bit."

"I don't see why. Many great artists and scientists were named Flora."

"Nothing against the Poles, right?"

"Why are you asking me that now? You should have asked earlier."

"I was distracted. Got anything against the Jews?"

"You know I don't. My mother is Jewish."

"That's no guarantee of anything. The name Flora has limited me quite a bit in my life; it's a very rigid name. Like an artificial flower. It's hard to use the diminutive 'Florita.' And an abbreviation like 'Flo' sounds contrived."

"If I have a daughter, I'll name her Flor, or Florencia."

"You do have a daughter. Our daughter is thirty-nine years old, and her name isn't Flor or Florencia."

"That's true."

"Her name is Ana María."

"That's ridiculous."

"It was a fashionable name when she was born."

"Ana María, daughter of Flora and Iñaki."

"Rosenkrantz."

"Should we look in the telephone book?"

"No, it's useless to consult a book. The only thing that's useful is what's in your memory."

"Did you speak or did I?"

"I did."

"And my last name?"

"Ibargüengoitía."

"Iribarne."

"Uribelarrea."

"Altolaguirre."

"Carriquiriborde."

"That's impossible."

"No, it's not. It means 'house at the edge of the road.' "

"But I knew the Carriquiriborde girl. We went to school together."

"You've told me that a thousand times. Your little schoolmate Carriquiriborde. House at the edge of the road."

"Is it better to be Basque or Jewish?"

"It depends on where you are. I don't know what the Basques' situation is like in New York."

"How about we order just one croissant?"

" Just one for both of us?"

"One apiece. They're teeny."

"Teeny! I'm afraid that in general parlance you'd have to say 'tiny.' "

"Is it better to be Italian?"

"Descended from Italians? Named Bellagamba?"

"I don't know."

"Italian surnames sound nicer."

"The problem is language, then?"

"It's the main problem."

"The sun's getting too hot."

"Yes, let's go put on our bathing suits."

"And walk on the hard sand along the shore."

"Yes."

"What did you do after you had breakfast at the *estancia* ?"

"When we couldn't eat another bite, we went for a walk. Juan Antonio, good host that he is, immediately found something for all the guests to do, including the children, thank God. While those who remained on the balcony with Juan Antonio went off to visit the stables, I, who had been hiding behind a column, suddenly found myself alone in the house; that is, with only the servants, busy with their chores, for company. Now I could look around to my heart's content, gazing for as long as I wished at the silver-framed portraits of Juan Antonio and his family, and especially at the one of Juan Antonio flanked by his two sisters, all three of them in tennis clothes, racquets in hand. The three of them bathed in sunlight, barely smiling. Aristocratic smiles. A bit distant, disdainful. If you look closely, you can see that one of the sisters isn't smiling; it's an almost invisible, bad-tempered rictus. The other sister has the expression I already described; Juan Antonio is smiling more openly, and there's no scorn in his smile."

"Juan Antonio was a nice guy."

"*Is* a nice guy. He told me that when he was a boy he would jump in the swimming pool fully dressed to rescue the drowning butterflies that had fallen into the water."

"How strange that the butterflies fell into the water."

"That's what it was like in Juan Antonio's youth. He agreed to attend a regular school to keep his sickly brother company."

"Sickly?"

"A bit slower than ordinary children."

"Juan Antonio was a nice guy."

"*Is.* If he weren't, how could he stand to have all these people as guests on his *estancia*, when they don't seem to have anything in common with him or with each other?"

"How was it that Juan Antonio met all of you?"

"We were all classmates in a Mind Control course."

"In a way Juan Antonio is sort of déclassé, isn't he?"

"Yes, it started when he divorced his first wife for Emi."

"Was Emi a mulatto?"

"I already told you otherwise. But she had a splendid figure; she wore tight black dresses and an impressive golden metal belt. I'd say it was bronze if I didn't know how impossible that is, because bronze is too heavy. The two wide bracelets she wore on each arm *were* made of bronze, though, and each one had a piece of chain dangling down."

"Broken chains?"

"Of course, anyone who saw those pieces of dangling chain imagined them welded together. Emi with her hands chained, the links soldered together in the blacksmith's forge."

"But now she's a former slave."

"A haughty, gorgeous brunette, provocative, Latina, somewhere between Spanish and Indian."

"Yes."

"After breakfast, while everyone went out for a walk or horseback riding, I went to the parlor on the first floor. I stared and stared at the picture of Juan Antonio and his sisters. I stared at it until the tears flowed from the effort of imagining myself part of that family. Thinking I was the daughter, granddaughter, great-granddaughter, great-great-granddaughter of wealthy, refined people, and that I'd never done anything in my life except play tennis and smile scornfully."

"With several generations of Argentine ancestors?"

"Not necessarily. It wouldn't bother me to have played tennis in 1880 in a dacha near Yalta with my lazy, corrupt Russian cousins."

"Russian Jews?"

"Why not? They could be Jews, as long as they were never affected by poverty or persecutions. After looking at the picture for a while, I started to get bored and thought it wasn't so bad to have a history of pogroms in Russia, a tenement apartment in Buenos Aires, and an old Yiddish newspaper used for wrapping a jar of plum candy that my grandmother gave me as a gift."

"What was the plum candy like?"

"It was unique, just as it had been made in the kitchen of the dacha, by a barefoot, milky-skinned servant, with freckles on her arms and chest. A peasant who wasn't allowed into the parlor because she was so coarse."

"She was probably the one who deflowered the young men in the family."

"And later on they'd go to bordellos in Saint Petersburg."

"Is Yalta far from Saint Petersburg?"

"I don't know, and nothing in this world could make me want to find out. The servant would put the copper pot on the fire to boil the plums. You'd have to boil them every day. Let them cool off. Drain the water. Boil them again the next day. And so on for a whole week. On the eighth day, you'd weigh the plums on a scale and put equal amounts of plums and beet sugar in the pot, a sugar that was so hard that if you wanted to break off a piece, you'd have to use small scissors. Those were the scissors my ninety-five-year-old great-grandmother kept in a drawer in her room in Buenos Aires and took out only when she served tea in porcelain cups. On the eighth day, the servant would place the big copper pot on a slow flame. Equal amounts of plums and sugar, all covered with water. The water boiled gently, forming a purplish foam on the surface. My grandfather was my great-grandmother's oldest child."

"And he was fourteen years old at that time."

"Yes, he was fourteen, and he entered the dacha's big kitchen at siesta time to stick his hand down the servant's blouse."

"While the plums boiled slowly."

"You could tell when the candy was ready by putting a bit on a plate and cutting it with a knife. If the slit didn't close up right away, that meant the candy was ready."

"When it was ready, you took it off the flame and let it cool."

"The plums glistened like jewels in the syrup. You put a whole plum with syrup at the bottom of the porcelain cup, and you filled the cup with tea. You would admire the shadings and the clarity. It's strange that even at my age now, my heart beats faster and I get gooseflesh when I say I'm Jewish. It's odd that I have to think carefully before I say I'm Jewish and Argentine or Argentine and Jewish, so the word order won't upset anyone and in order to tell the truth. It's a common thing for two Jews to get together and make a few references to Jewish folklore, generally referring to their family histories — the inevitable immigration — or to tell some Jewish joke. After these preliminaries, which serve as a kind of safeguard, the topic of Judaism disappears from the conversation. When the meeting is between Jews and non-Jews, it's possible not to make the slightest reference to Judaism, but at times Jews will do so, if they need to affirm their identity, or rather if they need to anticipate a non-verbal reaction by the others. In a country like Argentina, with its huge waves of migration, people can detect your origin quickly from your surname. If I say my name is Rosenthal, Rosenblum, Rosenwasser . . ."

"Enough, enough!"

"All right. My cat is chronically ill."

"What's his problem?"

"He has arthritis of the spine and a dislocated kneecap on the right hind leg. Its cause is unknown, but it makes him limp. The dislocated kneecap could be fixed, but he can't have an operation because he has a heart murmur."

"Just therapeutic treatment, then?"

"A tonic that we mix with his milk, and a salt-free diet, because of his heart problem."

"And how's he doing?"

"Except for the limp and his reduced activity (he doesn't jump through the patio window onto the kitchen table any more, which always startled me and even cost me a teapot, although I must admit it was the only thing he ever broke in his countless leaps), he seems to have adapted to the situation, and at nine years old, he seems to have accepted a dignified old age."

With the passing of time, one surrounds oneself with more people one likes, people with whom one feels an affinity. People who read books and see films and who, if they have problems with their adolescent children, consult specialists so they won't become delinquents or drug addicts. Among these people there are Jews and non-Jews in varying degrees, with equally variable degrees of orthodoxy and religious practice. Certainly there are no fanatics. The families they come from are almost all Jewish or Apostolic Roman Catholic. Only occasionally does a child of Protestant parents appear, and never any Muslims or Shintoists.

One would have to travel to Japan to see a Shintoist up close; there must be millions of them there. How ridiculous it would be over there in Japan, among Shintoists, to worry about whether to proclaim oneself an Argentine or a Jew first. Surely there are Shintoists in the mountains who don't even know what it means to be an Argentine or a Jew. In any event, we're in Buenos Aires, at the beginning of the nineties.

What does it mean, then, to be a Jew? It's impossible to respond to this question by beginning with the usual "in the first place." No. In the first place, or the second, or in none at all, being a Jew means standing in the middle of the stage with a tormented expression and saying, "I'm a Jew." The audience bursts into applause, a real ovation. Without changing expression, the actor waits for the audience to quiet down while the stage grows darker until it's bathed in a gentle shadow. Then a screen to the left of the actor (that is, to the audience's right) lights up and scenes from the Second World War appear: long caravans in the fog; a train packed with people arriving at an empty station, also in the fog; columns of smoke from the crematoria; strings of skeletal corpses hanging like sides of beef; mountains of eyeglasses and dental bridgework snatched from the victims; a picture of the last Nazi war criminal extradited from Bolivia; a cabaret scene with a husky-voiced singer, marvelously sensual. The image on the screen disappears; the actor chats with a friend. The two of them are sitting in chairs, glasses in hand. As they speak, Zarah Leander's voice can be heard at low volume, singing cabaret songs from the thirties. "Is that all there is?" the friend asks. And the actor attempts a smile on his tormented face.

"Of course not. There's also the oval table in the grandparents' house, laden with good things to eat. It's Pesach. Pesach. Pesach. The Pesach holiday."

"Yes, I know."

"I'm repeating it so I can get used to it, to see if I can get over the effect."

"The word 'Pesach' affects you?"

"Yes. It disturbed me to hear Yiddish spoken when I was a child. I tried not to listen, not to learn it. And I didn't. But in spite of everything, I understand a little when I hear it spoken, and it makes me very happy. It's like an encounter with something very profound that I possessed after all, but which made me — and still makes me — ashamed, as if I suddenly found myself at a premiere at the Teatro Colón in my underwear."

"Is Pesach food good?"

"Fabulous. I always ate too much, partly because it was delicious and partly because I was bored. More than once mama had to call the doctor at dawn to cure me of a brutal bout of indigestion."

"Did you ever think what you would be like if you weren't Jewish?"

"Yes. I would be exactly the same."

"The same tormented face?"

"Yes."

"Tormented and proud, and very attractive to women?"

"Am I attractive to women?"

"Now you're going to tell me you didn't know, and you don't even know your name."

"I don't know what my name is or where I am."

"The stage lights grow dimmer and finally go out altogether. The screen lights up. You can see a cobblestone street, with houses on the sidewalks on either side and gardens in front. In the doorway of one of these houses is a six-year-old boy, skinny, looking intently at the opposite sidewalk."

"The *pavement*. The opposite *pavement*. There are no sidewalks in Buenos Aires. There are pavements. Only pavements appear in police reports."

"All right. Looking intently at the opposite pavement."

"How docile of you."

"How can I not be docile? I'm just a voice offstage. The camera pans to the opposite pavement to show what the boy is looking at: it's the front of a grocery store with cloudy windows, covered with dust. In the window you can see a row of cider bottles, also covered with dust, and in front of the bottles a piece of pastry wrapped in waxed paper . . ."

"Thank goodness. I thought the pastry would also be covered with dust."

" . . . a pastry wrapped in waxed paper on top of a nest of walnuts and hazelnuts. Everything's covered with dust. It's December; it's a Monday afternoon, at two o'clock . . ."

"How do the viewers know that it's Monday at two o'clock?"

"They don't know; that's why I'm telling you. At the door of the grocery stand a man and a woman, middle-aged. She's very fat and she's wearing a faded, shapeless cotton dress. She's wearing mules."

"How many people do you think know what mules are?"

"Do you happen to have a dictionary of general parlance handy?"

"No."

"Then take note of this: mules are shoes with rubber soles, and on top they have a kind of leather strap that crosses the instep, holding the foot precariously. It's hard to walk in mules; any little obstacle will make one fall off, and the wearer has to go back and look for it. We were saying that the woman is fat and shapeless; the man is fat, also, but not as much. He's wearing dark pants and an undershirt."

"Along the fence separating the garden from the street there's a tangle of freesia."

"I don't think so. If anything is tangled, it has to be musk roses."

"The boy sitting in the doorway looks like the actor with the tormented face."

"Yes, a skinny, serious little face."

"Does the boy know that the year is almost over?"

"Yes, he knows that the year is almost over, and that there will be two nights of festivities, the twenty-fourth and the thirty-first."

"Summer in Buenos Aires."

"Winter in Russia."

"Wasn't I supposed to talk only about what could be seen on the screen?"

"Where'd you get that idea? December twenty-fourth: cider, pastries, walnuts and almonds. And a little Christmas tree."

"What? The boy's family isn't Jewish?"

"Yes, but they live in Buenos Aires. They're not thinking about the Child who was born in Bethlehem; they're thinking that the year's about to end."

"Do they let the little boy drink cider and eat pastries and nougat candy? Later on they'll have to call the doctor, at dawn."

"On the screen it's two in the afternoon, and the sun is beating down like fire."

"The little boy could get sunstroke."

"Anything could happen."

"It's a holy time, siesta time."

"The hour when teenagers investigate sex."

"And those who aren't teenagers, too. No one ever learns enough about sex to give up investigating."

"People boast about how much they know."

"Yes, most people boast about it."

"But they secretly look at dirty books."

"The book of Tantric yoga."

"Nobody boasts in the book of Tantric yoga. Men and women with fishy expressions, sitting on a carpet, copulating in difficult positions, head up, head down, drinking tea all the while."

"Yes, there's always a teapot and some teacups in the picture."

"Is there any connection between sexual activity and tea?"

"Absolutely. If there's no tea served, sexual activity might be interrupted: erections would fall; lubrications would dry up; sensations would disappear. Of course, the best thing is not to subject the mind to any kind of discipline whatsoever, simply to let it concentrate happily on thoughts of pleasure."

"But, if it's necessary, don't you believe . . . ?"

"I don't believe anything."

All the students in the Mind Control class were — all of *us* were — between thirty and forty-five years old, which is to say we were at an age when one wonders what he is doing with his life and tries to follow a new path, to correct this or that, to find his true vocation. It's the time of life when one feels most anguished and when the certainty of one's own death is firmly entrenched, and one thinks, "Ah! If only I were twenty again, despite what Paul Nizan said!" A long time ago I was dazzled by that phrase, and I copied it on a piece of cardboard with Magic Marker and tacked it to a wall in the little house we rented in the Delta, on an island about a forty minutes' boat ride from the docks at Tigre. What Nizan said was:

AT THAT TIME I WAS TWENTY YEARS OLD, AND I WON'T LET ANYONE CONVINCE ME THAT IT'S THE MOST BEAUTIFUL TIME OF LIFE.

I used to like to tack up on the wall sentences from books that made an impression on me. There was also a reproduction of a Shurjin print, of some little kids who have only eyes but no nose or mouth, as well as a poster of a dove, by Picasso. I thought it was a good idea to force my friends and family to read the same sentences over and over again until it made them sick, although in truth that didn't happen: they got used to ignoring them and no one made any comments.

Nizan's sentence hung on that wall for at least two years. When our lease was up, and we went back to the little house to clean up those few belongings that were still there (some threadbare blankets; a couple of pots that had been blackened by the gas stove; some cups without handles; a set of green rubber froggy flippers belonging to one of my kids, the kind you put on your hands to propel a plastic boat downstream . . .), I found the quotation from Nizan on the wall, wrinkled and yellowed with dampness. I left it where it was, as a gift to future tenants. It wasn't until many years later that I realized that the phrase, which I had so ardently made my own, didn't coincide with my memories: my twenties were an enjoyable time for me, filled with parties, drinks at Pichín, brief, intense romances that never degenerated into tragedy. I had a clear head, an agile body, and a pleasant face. Other girls might have been tall, blonde, and slender, but I was fun to talk to (that's how it's always been, even now that all of us are old, or nearly old). ("Are you crazy? *You* old?" et cetera.)

There was no room for exchanging confidences in the Mind Control class, as we were all too busy learning various techniques to avoid becoming victims of modern life, as so many others had done. But after the class was over, we went to the corner bar, a pleasant, tranquil place, to have a drink and chat. I ordered a whiskey on the rocks, and then another, accompanied by a cheese sandwich on white bread. A cheese sandwich on white bread can be a bit dry and dull and stick in your throat, but the ones they made at that little bar were on very fresh English bread, smeared lightly with mayonnaise and delicate slivers of machine-sliced cheese. At that moment, and in that company, the effect of the whiskey was invariable: as I finished the first glass, I was filled with a strange happiness and confidence in humankind. All my friends from the Mind Control class seemed marvelous; our professor was a genius; the waiter who served us at the bar seemed very charming; the shimmer and transparency of the ice cubes in the whiskey were unsurpassable. With the second whiskey I became truly euphoric: I split my sides laughing with two or three of my classmates, and I would have accepted anything they proposed, even going along as galley cook on an Antarctic expedition. That's why it didn't surprise me when Juan Antonio, a rather quiet man who never socialized with us, invited all of us to his *estancia* for a few days, because the *estancia* was far away (at the southern end of the province, about four hours' drive) and, as Gustavo the TV actor said, you'd have to drag your wife or husband and the kids along in the car.

I think if we hadn't been drunk we wouldn't have accepted his rather awkward invitation just like that, especially since it didn't come from Juan Antonio himself. Instead it was Gustavo's suggestion, with that tendency of his to drag everyone along to do his bidding. I was just emerging from the depths of a wild spasm of laughter when I saw Juan Antonio drawing a map to get to the *estancia*. I loved the idea, since now that the kids were big and preferred to spend weekends on their own, we didn't go to Tigre anymore, and I complained about never getting out of Buenos Aires. It didn't even bother me that Enrique and I had to share the back seat of Eusebio's car with his two children. Eusebio was a painter who always went around talking about the Death of Art. The kids wriggled around like eels, and we were on the receiving end of their head-butting and kicking, while their parents did nothing at all to stop them. By the time I realized it, the car had stopped in front of a large gate and Enrique had gotten out to make sure the faded inscription on the metal plate said "Las Lilas."

Naturally, because those fragrant flowers in the flower bed next to the house were not violets or heliotropes, but lilacs.

"Has the film they were showing on the screen ended?"

"No, but now it's a still photo. The cobblestone street, the boy sitting in the doorway of the house, the fence covered with flowers, and the grocery store across the street . . ."

"But the scene isn't in darkness anymore. It's subtly lit, and the actor and his friend have disappeared."

"There's no more audience, either."

"Everyone's gone to pack their bags for a trip to Mar del Plata."

"To have coffee and croissants on the promenade at the Casino."

"Do you know exactly which bar that is, Madame?"

"Why are you being so formal with me?"

"Would you like me to call you Sabina, Madame?"

"Sabina is a brunette, with a strong, shapely body, medium height, olive skin, and very dark eyes. An almost aquiline nose; strong, very well-groomed nails. She always wears high heels and paints her lips vermilion red. She wears simple clothes: sweaters, shirts, and skirts in subdued tones: gray, brown, black, and white. She has a serious, melodious voice. She's always composed. Wherever Sabina goes, she leaves everything clean and sparkling. Even if I tried to imitate her movements one by one, I'd never be able to make a room seem so impeccable, or leave such a barely detectable fragrance in the bathroom, or have a shirt look so flawlessly washed and ironed. Any food Sabina prepares, no matter how simple, turns out first-rate: a tasty meat-and-potatoes stew in the winter, a fresh rice salad in summer. I've never seen her put on an apron or a chambermaid's uniform. ('Chambermaid' means 'a maid with her own chamber.' It's much more elegant and formal to say 'chambermaid' than to say 'cleaning girl.') Sabina is the finest of chambermaids, and yet she never refuses to do any chore. She uses lavender to remove the smell of cat piss, never splashing any on herself, nor does she ever put on rubber gloves to protect her lovely hands (soft, satiny skin that can withstand the harshest cleaning products) and perfect nails (sculpted, neatly filed, covered with vermilion red polish, with the little half-moons carefully exposed)."

"Did you know that Sabina's hands caress a man every night?"

"Yes. Sabina's life is simple. She cleans one house in the morning and another in the afternoon. She dispenses order, cleanliness, attention to detail, delicate, fresh fragrances. The employers who have been out all day long and return home at night feel that they've entered a haven of peace, a pleasant refuge where all kinds of relaxation are possible. And on a corner of the kitchen table, where they've left her pay, which she folds carefully and places in her brown leather change purse, they find a little slip of paper saying "detergent" or "furniture polish," or simply "salt."

"Sabina's a real firebrand."

"Yes, she's an ardent woman. While she cleans, she sings boleros in a quiet voice, as if she were singing them to herself: 'Stronger than pain, like the twining ivy . . ?'"

"Sabina has very clear ideas about what a man's body should look like for her to want to go to bed with him."

"About his body and about the man himself. She likes him to be hard and hairy."

"Not too muscular."

"She doesn't care for soccer players. She likes to caress a hairy chest, hairy thighs. She adores gentle stroking, fingers that visit her secret places for the first time as though they were entering a temple."

"As though they were entering a temple with a black-and-white mosaic floor in a checkerboard pattern, highly polished wooden prie-dieux, and rose windows through which light filters in a special way."

"She also likes rougher contact."

"She likes the shadows in a hotel room."

"The tenuous glow of the colored lights at the head of the bed."

"Does Sabina always meet the type of man she likes?"

"She never misses. There's something in a look that a woman exchanges with a man on the street, in a bar, that says so much. Sabina looks for a respectful glance that nonetheless seeks something serious. Where there's no room for deceit, or for disrespect, of course."

"A different man every day?"

"Yes."

"But isn't that just as though it were the same man every day? A serious, formal type, hairy, no soccer-player's legs . . ."

"Let's get rid of the name Sabina."

"Not before you explain to me why Sabina ended up becoming a Jehovah's Witness."

"It must have been to wipe away her sins."

"I don't know, I'm the one who's asking you."

"It must have been her age. Time passes quickly for everyone, and so it must have flown for Sabina. It doesn't matter if it happened at fifty or at sixty: at a given moment she must have noticed something about her body that she didn't want men to see, something by the tenuous light of a hotel room. Then she seized the first Bible she was offered."

"Couldn't it be that she just liked the guy who offered her the Bible?"

"What you just said is unbelievably vulgar, but it's possible."

"However, I don't believe Jehovah's Witnesses are allowed to have sex."

"But surely they can marry."

"It never occurred to me that Sabina might have gotten married."

"Why not? She was single, and so was the Jehovah's Witness who gave her the Bible. They probably got married in one of those communal ceremonies in the River football stadium."

"I don't understand why you agreed to be called Sabina, when we already decided your name was Magdalena."

"Okay, just call me Magdalena. To save time."

"We've got all the time in the world. Is December always this hot in Buenos Aires?"

"Almost always. Why are you asking me that question? Aren't you from Buenos Aires?"

"Yes, but for as long as I can remember I've spent the summer months in Mar del Plata."

"But not this year?"

"This is a special year. My children are grown and they spend the summers on their own, and my husband's on a trip, at a meeting in Vienna."

"So you're a married lady, pure and simple."

"Thanks a lot."

"Why don't you go to Mar del Plata this year too, to the English chalet in the middle of the garden, and watch the sea from your window?"

"So I can stay and talk to you, Magdalena."

"All right. Now you can say your own name."

"Flora, my name is Flora."

"How old are you?"

"Sixty-two."

"Weren't you having breakfast with your husband in Mar del Plata?"

"Yes, Magdalena, I was having breakfast with Iñaki."

"Is Iñaki a doctor?"

"Yes."

"It all fits together perfectly, then. You're my old friend Flora."

"Yes."

"We've known each other for thirty years."

"Yes."

"Winters in Buenos Aires, raising the kids, sending them to school. Summers in Mar del Plata, tanning ourselves carefully and using coral-colored rouge."

"Yes, and in the afternoons, going to the Torreón Café."

"Looking for adventure?"

"What a way to talk, Magdalena. Just like in the boleros. I went to the Torreón to dance when I was a teenager; as a married woman with children, I never went to dance at the Torreón. I read books in the afternoon. My children went in and out of the house, either alone or with a nanny when they were little, so I could keep reading."

"Let's go back to the time when you were a teenager, Flora."

"What for?"

"So we can talk about idle things. You're seventeen; you go dancing at the Torreón and there you meet Iñaki."

"Now Iñaki is sixty-eight. Then he was twenty-three and he squeezed me against him while we danced."

"Are we going to talk about sex, Flora?"

"As you wish, Magdalena."

"I like the fact that you still want to talk about sex at sixty-two."

"And you, at fifty-something . . . which side of fifty are you on?"

"Right on the nose."

"My Aunt Dora is eighty. She practices yoga and goes to Wagner concerts."

"My Uncle Pedrito is seventy-six and he plays basketball."

"My Aunt Clarita is eighty-five and her boyfriend's ninety-one."

"My mother-in-law is eighty-eight and she's a big fan of spy novels."

"Svetlana Stalin had a child at forty-six."

"My mother learned to ride a bicycle at seventy."

"My mother-in-law got it right: she said, 'When it comes, it comes. I just don't want to suffer.' And she didn't suffer. I mean, she didn't die, and she's not sick. She's eighty-nine."

"May God bless her."

"May God, in whom I don't believe, bless her."

"May God, in whom I sometimes believe and sometimes don't, bless her."

"May God grant her many years of peace and happiness."

"May God, if He exists, give us a rose garden to look at every morning."

"May He give us a garden with an old wall with creeping honeysuckle."

"May He grant us peace."

"And peace to the world."

"May there be times of well-being."

"May there be an end to war and poverty."

"May people die of old age, of natural causes, and without suffering."

"May there be another life after death."

"May we be reunited with our dead in this life."

"Especially with Uncle José."

"Who?"

"Uncle José, who at one time had a habit of showing up unannounced at lunchtime. Of course, those were different times; it wasn't essential to call ahead to announce that one was going to visit. At lunchtime only grandma and I were in the house. I was around nine or ten. It was summer, a very hot summer, like this one. Granny was preparing the meal: invariably some soup, steak, salad, and mashed potatoes. Grandma cooked, and I didn't do anything. There I was, lolling around with my head in the clouds, when Uncle José showed up on the patio with a little package. He entered without knocking, because the front door was standing open. All the houses used to be left unlocked, and people would go in and out as they pleased. Everyone did it: the little old man who delivered coal; the boy from the bakery who left the bread on the kitchen table; the man who came to clean out the sewers; the guy who came to card the wool from the mattresses, leaving them high and stiff for a while until they got soft again and sank in the middle; the medical student who stopped by to check grandma's blood pressure; the pale, fat woman with freckles on her arms and chest who brought freshly laid eggs from her henhouse to make a cocktail with sugar and port; the neighbor lady who brought over cookies with cream that she made herself, which they didn't let me eat because it might give me a stomachache. Among those who knocked and waited outside were the fisherman, who came with a basket covered with fig leaves and waited patiently while grandma stuck her nose in each one of his fish to see if they were fresh; the knife sharpener on his bicycle; the Arab with his basket of perfumed soap, ribbons, and lace. . . . These people would announce their arrival singing and shouting, and grandma and I would run to the door from the back room before they could get away. The only ones who actually rang the bell and waited outside were a few respectful beggars who asked for food. Grandma gave them a dish of stew meat and vegetables and a piece of yesterday's bread."

"Or from the day before."

"Yesterday's bread. Or from the day before. Grandma maintained that today's bread was bad, and yesterday's was good."

"And Uncle José?"

"He was old and jolly. He told jokes. He never worked in his life. One day he showed up, as usual, at lunchtime, with a little package. Grandma took the little package and set one more place at the table; she was resigned to feeding Uncle José every time he came. Then she opened the little package and wrinkled up her nose. 'Oh, no, José, I'm sorry, but I can't use this,' she said, sniffing the contents of the package conscientiously. My uncle said, 'Impossible, Clara, I bought it at the Mercado del Plata.' 'But it's spoiled, José,' grandma said, picking up a pale, limp mackerel and smelling it again as if she wanted to inhale it through her nostrils. And Uncle José repeated, 'But I bought it at the Mercado del Plata . . .?'"

"May there be life after death, and may Uncle José show up at lunchtime with a perfectly fresh fish."

"Amen."

"Were there any scandals at Las Lilas in those days?"

"There were no scandals, at least not as far as I know. It was more a question of gossip, of suspicion. There were two women who were noticeably interested in Juan Antonio: Inés, the psychologist, and Tabi, the architect. Inés put on riding clothes and boots and went out horseback riding. She wanted to show Juan Antonio that she was an outdoorswoman, too, and that she could imitate Emi perfectly. But as soon as she got away from the house, the horse took off on its own, galloping at full speed; Inés didn't seem frightened, and although she leaned forward a bit, she didn't manage to grab onto its mane. I didn't see the rest of the adventure, but the final version of the story had the horse running wildly toward the stables before the terrified eyes of some peasants who were working in the fields, and just before they reached a gate, Inés suddenly fell to the ground. The horse kept going, neatly clearing the gate and whizzing along like an arrow, finally disappearing among the planted fields. If I told you what the horse did after Inés fell off, how she was revived with cold water and a shot of gin by the peasants who witnessed the accident, and who, seeing that nothing was broken, carried her back to the house in a sulky, it's because what the horse did perhaps explains why Inés fell. The commonly accepted hypothesis was that when Inés saw the gate, she thought the horse was going to crash into it. Strange, isn't it? She didn't think it was going to *clear* the gate (which should have scared her anyway, since she had no experience jumping hurdles). No, she thought both she and the horse would be smashed to pieces against the gate. It didn't occur to her that this would have been a strange accident, since you hardly ever see horses smashed to bits after having crashed violently into something. That's what Inés thought, and so she fainted from fear and fell off the horse. When I finally saw her after the accident, she was sitting up in bed in the master bedroom with an ice pack on her head, and it was understood that there would always be someone with her to keep her awake, since fatigue might cause her to faint again and it was important to prevent any brain damage. All this happened the first day on the *estancia*, while I was alone in the house, looking at pictures of Juan Antonio's family."

"You couldn't really say it was a major scandal."

"No, but there was something to it, because Inés wanted to show off for Juan Antonio, just like Tabi. Only Tabi, who was more sensible, restricted herself to displaying her waist and her behind and her pretty blonde hair and her pretty, sunkissed face."

The terrible heat has let up. The sky is gray, and it's raining: we had to close doors we would have preferred to leave open to freshen up the rooms, but at least you can breathe. I put one more pillow under my head to reach a vertical position gradually. Blood is flowing; sap is flowing. My heart beats a little faster, but it's the excitement of a new beginning. Drops of water glisten on the leaves of the plants, and hot coffee streams into my blood, helping me maintain my vertical position.

"Maggi?"

"Oh, yes, Flora. It seems you're taking over Enrique's job, holding my arm just as I'm about to fall off the precipice."

"Precipice. Big word. How silly."

"There's a scent of newly blossomed jasmines mixed with the decadent fragrance of the yellowing jasmine . . ."

"Decadent. Words. Literature. Had anything sexual happened before the visit to the *estancia*?"

"Almost certainly. Sexual consummation is considered obligatory among consenting adults of our generation. But it has to be at least minimally effective in order to describe it in a book."

"In a book?"

"In a novel, one of those novels where the main plot has to do with detectives, or history, or politics, but where there are also some pages devoted to the sexual activities of the protagonists."

"It makes sense: crime and the struggle for power are too dry for the average reader. Besides, literature is useful for airing private matters that are usually kept secret because they frighten the middle class."

"We're middle class."

"And proud of it."

"Did I speak, or did you?"

"I did."

"Let's see, let's establish something: who spent countless summers in Mar del Plata in an English chalet in the middle of a garden?"

"I did, I did. And you were telling me that business about 'May God help you,' 'May God bless you.'"

"I was telling you that? When?"

"When we were sitting on a bench in the old garden, next to a vine-covered reproduction of the Venus de Milo, with the tip of her nose broken off; just when you could first detect the smell of damp earth, right before the storm."

"When Emi sat down at the piano? And as she struck the first chords, I was looking at the pictures of Juan Antonio and his sisters with their tennis racquets?"

"Yes, Maggi, I see you're beginning to remember. I was beginning to fear you were the one who had fallen off the horse. What was that business about 'May God bless you,' 'May God help you?'"

"They're things Catholics say."

"Jews must have their own equivalent."

"Sure, but without saying God's name. But I like to say it. Even better, I like to say these exact words: 'May God help you,' 'May God bless you.'"

"In a difficult, inexplicable world, it's nice to be able to tell your child, who's going off to school to take a test, 'May God help you,' 'May God illuminate you.' Or to be able to say 'May God bless you' when he's made some funny remark."

"There's also something I like to say in Yiddish."

"Say it."

"Shalom aleichem."

"That's the pseudonym of a great Russian Jewish, or Jewish Russian, writer, who was born in Poland in 1859 and died in New York in 1916."

"It's also a greeting. It means 'peace be with you.' The person who's arriving says 'shalom aleichem' and the other one answers 'aleichem shalom.'"

"Shalom aleichem."

"Aleichem shalom."

"Sholem Aleichem tells stories of poor Jews and rich Jews in his native country."

"May God bless Sholem Aleichem."

"What's going on? Are we crazy?"

"Yes, we're completely crazy."

"So I suppose there was a sexual consummation between Juan Antonio and Tabi before the visit to the *estancia*."

"Yes."

"But not between Juan Antonio and Inés."

"I don't think so. If there had been, Inés wouldn't have fallen off the horse."

"I don't know."

"In any case, after she fell, Inés spent an entire day sitting up in bed in the master bedroom with an ice bag on her head, and we took turns talking to her constantly and keeping her awake to prevent brain damage."

"Was Tabi there too?"

"No, she discreetly stayed on the fringes, sunning herself on the terrace."

"And Juan Antonio?"

"Juan Antonio's shift was between two and two-thirty in the afternoon. Emi accompanied him, wearing a riding outfit with a skirt that had belonged to Juan Antonio's grandmother, and a big straw hat, also the grandmother's."

"She rode in a skirt?"

"She rode in a skirt, English style, with a provocative smile."

"Did she look beautiful?"

"No, she was about twenty-five pounds heavier than she had been when Juan Antonio fell in love with her, thinking she was a mulatto. Needless to say, Inés wasn't worried about Emi, but about Tabi."

"Yes, of course. So they changed shifts every half hour?"

"Yes. Keeping Inés awake was a hard task; every minute she closed her eyes and slipped down into the pillows, and we had to shake her to be sure she didn't get brain damage."

"Poor Inés."

"Yes. At eight in the evening they let her fall asleep. She slept for twelve hours straight and woke up the next morning fully recovered, except for some pain from the fall."

"What day of the week was it?"

"Saturday. We had arrived on Thursday night; Friday was Inés's accident; and Saturday at noon they roasted a calf that Juan Antonio had ordered sacrificed."

"It doesn't sound like a very happy situation."

"It wasn't. Inés strolling around, rather bruised, everyone talking about the accident, the death of the calf . . ."

"Well, the beef we eat comes from animals that are killed mercifully. Any vegetarian scruples?"

"Not a bit, I'm Argentine. I like meat and eat a lot of it. The situation was unhappy because Juan Antonio started to show how annoyed he was by that invasion of people on his *estancia*, people who hardly even brought a bottle of wine as their contribution to living off his generosity for three days. The first dinner at the *estancia* was splendid, palatial. Juan Antonio opened up his wine cellar, and the guests behaved like revolutionaries at Versailles. When breakfast was served, with its abundance of butter and homemade *dulce de leche*, Juan Antonio and Emi were still asleep, but at noon, when everyone came back from their strolls and rides and we got together in the gazebo, telling jokes and making cocktails with Juan Antonio's liquor, garnished with mint leaves and marjoram from his own garden, he got into a very bad mood, and Emi, who's always been somewhat absentminded and doesn't notice anything, had to ask him what to order in the kitchen for lunch. Juan Antonio hesitated before answering. 'We could slaughter a calf,' he finally said, with great effort. Emi went to the kitchen, wiggling her behind under her riding skirt, and ordered them to prepare a salad and some dessert."

"Well, they could have picked the vegetables right from the garden."

"Yes, but a calf costs a lot."

"How much?"

"I've no idea."

"Would it have been a lot of money for Juan Antonio?"

"Probably not, but he surely felt obliged to be generous, to fulfill his role as *estancia* owner and host, entertaining his poor slob friends."

"Bourgeois pigs, oink, oink!"

"Are *estancia* owners bourgeois?"

"Who said that?"

"It would be easy to find out. Meanwhile, Gustavo, the TV actor, rode his horse up and down in front of the gazebo, so erect he looked like a stick."

"Waiting for the barbecue?"

"Yes. He had offered to make it himself, because, like all actors, he thought he could do anything even if he'd never done it before, just by imitation."

"Well, who hasn't made a barbecue at one time or another. And?"

"It was barbecued on crossed wooden stakes, not so easy to do."

"Delicious. Pit-roasted meat is also excellent, conveniently wrapped in aluminum foil and buried beneath coals . . . Why didn't they let Gustavo make the barbecue?"

"Because a half-breed boy was going to do it."

"You're completely crazy, Maggi. Here no one, not even the worst racist . . . We're not in South Africa! Here we just say 'a boy,' and nothing else."

"Or a *negro*. But he wasn't really black. He was brown. Do you want me to say a brown boy was going to do it?"

"Why do we have to identify people by the color of their skin?"

"All right, all right. The barbecue was to be made by a peasant who was born with skin the same brown color yours gets after a few months of careful sunbathing in Mar del Plata. That's why Gustavo was riding back and forth, inscrutable and a bit annoyed. If you talked to him he wouldn't even bother turning his head to answer. He looked straight ahead; he held the reins like an English lord promenading through his property, saying, 'Let the half-breed do it. Go on, let the half-breed do it.'"

The furtive visitor who manages to enter Las Lilas must first traverse the long road to the house sheltered by the shadows of the ancient trees whose entangled foliage forms a veritable canopy of leaves. On this path, as in the middle of the woods, it gets dark earlier than it does in the rolling fields on both sides of the road. It's very frightening to arrive at Las Lilas at night; if there's no moon, a beam of light from the most powerful lantern scarcely projects a weak, yellowish ray amid all that blackness.

The ideal time to enter Las Lilas furtively is at dusk, when the visitor can take refuge in the shadows cast by the trees. The path is five hundred yards long, although it seems longer because of the uniformity of the trees. The visitor must advance with caution, trying to camouflage himself among his surroundings — not a difficult task at all, because he's wearing a leaf-green shirt and brown pants, aided besides by his average height and chestnut-brown hair and eyes, with no distinguishing characteristics. He realizes he mustn't run, because the distance between the entry gate and the house is long, and running would tire him out. Therefore, he walks at a good pace, taking advantage of the scant light that filters between the tree branches, looking alternately to the left, right, and straight ahead. Nothing disturbs the peace of the fields on either side of the seemingly endless path. Suddenly the furtive visitor stops in his tracks, hiding behind a tree trunk, to observe some extensive, monotonous structures that look like sheds, and after that a series of little houses, equally extensive and monotonous: the homes of the *estancia* employees. Some dark-skinned men, together with other blond, blue-eyed ones, shamble by the houses, lugging equipment and putting away their tools. Several women meander here and there, surrounded by their broods, almost all of them carrying babies in their arms. The scene takes place in an atmosphere of the greatest fastidiousness and calm, because Juan Antonio runs a model *estancia*.

Satisfied with his inspection and confident he hasn't been spotted, the furtive visitor continues on his way. He knows it's not too much farther to the house. Now he hides behind a thick eucalyptus trunk, only thirty yards from the house. From his vantage point he manages to see the front of the house, noticing that there are people gathered on the verandah. The eucalyptus is completely in shadows; there's still a bit of daylight left in the garden, but the lights in the house and the lanterns in the garden have already been turned on.

"Tell me your oldest memories of the country."

"My memories are of a different countryside, not Las Lilas. When I was four or five, I spent a few days on an *estancia* with mama and papa. I don't know where it was, although . . . yes, yes, I do remember: it was out west, in Morón."

"An *estancia* in Morón?"

"Well, either in Morón or near it. I'm not even sure it was an *estancia*. Maybe it was just a farm."

"A farm can be very pretty."

"And very interesting, too, to show the kids the horses, the cows, the barnyard fowl . . ."

"And all the country chores: to let them see how to plant, irrigate, harvest . . ."

"To have them drink milk straight from the cow and eat freshly laid eggs . . ."

"City kids are fascinated by all these things, aren't they?"

"Not one bit! They find them terribly boring. All they want to do is read the comic books they've brought along and then get some more. They complain that they're bored all the time, and they become a real torture for their parents. And they don't like wholesome country food, either. Boredom makes them eat too much and then they get indigestion and allergic reactions, and you can't get a doctor at three in the morning. The local kids make fun of them because they don't know how to ride horses and they're afraid of snakes . . ."

"Why do parents insist on taking them to the country?"

"To improve their health and complete their education. A parent can't find peace until he's managed to drag his kid off to show him how a little calf suckles the cow's teat, while the kid bawls and tries to look away."

"What were those four days in Morón like?"

"We walked along a road edged with trees. On one side of the road, fields. On the other side, fields. And for lunch, borscht."

"Borscht?"

"Do you remember how Borges said he spoke one way with one of his grandmothers while with the other he spoke a different way? And only after a long time did he realize that those two ways of talking were called the Spanish language and the English language? Well, something like that happened to me, only one way of talking was Spanish and the other was Yiddish. Since Yiddish sounded harsh and unpleasant to me, I systematically refused to learn it. It was a language filled with mysteries that might reveal what I really was. From a very early age I was told to hide or disguise what I 'really' was, to pretend to be something else that, strangely enough, I also was. Yiddish concealed who knows what shameful secrets; I didn't like the way it sounded, and if, in spite of all my efforts to prevent this, I somehow managed to understand the meaning of a word, I tried not to show that I understood. I would rather have died than betray with a smile or an affirmative gesture the fact that I understood."

"What about the borscht?"

"Oh, yes, the borscht. Sometimes I get carried away . . ."

"It's understandable."

"As I was telling you, lunch hour rolls around and I find out we're having borscht. Borscht is a kind of beet soup that Russians eat — that Russian Jewish immigrants in Argentina ate."

"It's very tasty."

"You're only saying that because you've tried a cold, sweet-and-sour soup made of beets, lemon juice, pepper, and cream, with little squares of toasted bread . . . Very tasty, for sure. But that borscht was a kind of meat stew with potatoes, vegetables . . . and beets. As you can imagine, the beets took over the whole thing; everything took on the color and flavor of the beets. But that surely wasn't what made me so mad, because kids will eat anything . . . The terrible thing was that I found out there was borscht for lunch by overhearing a conversation my father had with the farm owner, in Yiddish. And I understood. You didn't have to know a whole lot. It was nearly lunch hour, and they repeated the word 'borscht' so many times there wasn't much room for doubt. I can still hear papa's enthusiastic voice, exclaiming: 'Borscht!'"

"And you really didn't like it?"

"I don't have the faintest memory of even having seen that borscht. I would have thrown such a fit that they probably didn't even show it to me. They must have given me French fries instead."

"Yes, I'll bet anything they gave you French fries. What else do you remember about those childhood days in the country?"

"I remember the room we had, where we all slept together: mama, papa, my little brother, and I. I remember that mama was taking a shower in the bathroom, which connected to the room, and papa went in there. I knew that you had to be naked to take a shower, and I was surprised that papa went into the bathroom when she was naked. I didn't know they were intimate . . ."

"Of course. An interesting memory. But I was referring to those memories that were strictly about the country. For example, the birds singing early in the morning, watching a cow being milked . . ."

"I don't have the slightest recollection of that kind."

"Then how do you explain your love of the country in your later years?"

"If I answer that question, will you promise to answer one for me?"

"Promise."

"I don't really know when I began to love the country; I think it was when I was old enough to dream, to become intoxicated by the smell of damp earth before a storm. Now it's my turn. Why are you asking me all this?"

"Do you really want to know?"

"I don't even know why you're here."

"Here? Where? Do you know where we are?"

"What are you doing here?"

"I'm listening to what you're telling me. What other memories do you have of those days in the Morón countryside?"

"Nothing else. All the trees were a single tree; all the cows were one and the same cow. They were all the same to me. May I ask you another question?"

"Go ahead."

"Are you Jewish?"

"No."

"You're Catholic then."

"My maternal grandparents were Catholic, practicing. My paternal grandfather was a rabid freethinker, the kind who would never set foot in a church even to go to his son's wedding. My grandmother was Catholic in her own way, although she didn't go to Mass in order not to go against my grandfather. My parents weren't religious, and I went to an English public school . . ."

"Yes, you're Catholic just as I'm Jewish. According to practicing Catholics, you aren't Catholic, and according to you, you're not Catholic, but for those who aren't Catholic, you're Catholic. You're Catholic because you're not Jewish or Muslim or Shintoist or Seventh Day Adventist. Silly, isn't it? Trivial. Does it bother you to be Catholic?"

"It doesn't exactly bother me. It's just that I'm not."

"On the other hand it often bothers me to be Jewish, and I can never say I'm not. You know how pathetic it is when Jews claim not to be Jews: *First and last names? Samuel Goldenstein. Oh, yes, Goldenstein. Are you Jewish?* I come from a German Jewish family, yes, but I don't practice the religion. Or: *First and last names? Samuel Goldenstein. Goldenstein . . . Goldenstein. . . . What kind of name is that?* It's a German name . . . German Jewish. *Oh, then you're Jewish?* No, my grandparents were Jewish, but my parents didn't practice it, and I'm even less . . . A pity, isn't it? And those responses are full of ill will. Everyone knows that in this business of being Jewish it matters very little whether or not you practice the religion. Being Jewish is a blend of many things: childhood memories, a special way of crying and complaining, a language that can't be understood, a need to go around reminding people all the time that Einstein and Freud and Marx and Chaplin were all Jews, the sensation that one is very ancient, more ancient than the Catholics. Being Jewish is a swastika, a star of David, a story by Sholem Aleichem, a page from *Die Presse* used for wrapping tomatoes, a caravan of shadowy beings on their way to the crematorium, the need to say 'I'm Jewish' even when it's not necessary . . . It's no surprise that those poor things prefer to say they're from a Jewish family, or of Jewish descent, and that they're nothing, they're simply Argentines and they don't practice any religion."

December in Buenos Aires. What have we accomplished this year? Was there anything to be accomplished? Why does one struggle, day after day? It's better not to know. It frightens me.

I'm as fearful as a mouse, and even mice frighten me. I'm not heroic. Rather than going out and protesting and risking being shot, I hide under the table. I've spent entire eras hidden under the table. I've never had a weapon in my hand. Whom would I fight against? Against someone with a machine gun? That's not fighting. That's committing suicide. How was the cat this morning? Not even a smile. Serious and worried like everyone else. Cats never smile. Except for the Cheshire Cat, the one who disappears, leaving his smile behind. A while ago I dreamed about a sick cat who was lying in bed, face up, like a person. It was a black cat, very big; standing on his hind legs he was probably almost six feet tall, with a skinny body and paws, like a rag doll shaped like a cat. He was a unique cat, but I couldn't say I've never seen one like him, because I have: Felix the Cat, from the comic strip. Felix the Cat was able to do things like go into the kitchen, open the refrigerator, take out a bottle of milk and pour some into a dish for himself. But how is it possible, I thought in my dream, that the owners of this exceptional cat would allow him to die? Why is it they don't lift a finger to save him, when he's Felix the Cat?

December 15. Hot. Dreary. Can someone without a weapon fight against an armed person? If only I were brave, even a little bit!

"What would you do?"

"I'd preach bravery. And as far as those people who go around threatening others with weapons are concerned, the ones who are so sure the unarmed people will surrender right away, I'd tell them to spend a few minutes every day observing their cat."

"Not everyone has a cat, Magdalena. When did you start to love the country?"

"It wasn't the country, exactly. It was the mountains. We spent many summers during my childhood in Córdoba, at Embalse de Río Tercero. When papa was alive, and even after he died. What I loved most was the mystery of nighttime in the mountains, when we returned home after dinner and you could smell the fragrance of herbs. . . . We used to spend the summer in a colony of government workers. Even then, although I was very little, it made me kind of proud that mama and papa were government workers. I still didn't know that it meant being—let's not say 'poor' (the word 'poor' always frightened everyone in my family), but certainly humble. In those days (the late thirties or early forties), the situation of government workers could be described as one of 'respectable poverty.' Papa and mama both worked; we were able to pay the rent and satisfy the needs of a simple life, without luxuries and with few diversions, and we could spend two or three weeks every summer in the colony."

"You were speaking of the fragrance of the herbs."

"Yes, when we returned home at night. 'Home' in Embalse was a small chalet in the mountains, among others like it, where families spent their summer vacations. At the foot of the mountains there was a dining room where we all met at mealtime. A siren would go off at noon and at night, and the families would come down to the dining room from their cottages. If I'm not mistaken (I have a miserable sense of geography), the dining room was located on a kind of mesa; the slope descended (if you can say that slopes descend) past the edge of the mesa, which was carefully protected by posts joined together by chains. Am I making myself clear? I'd like to make you a drawing to show you what those chains were like, between one post and another; they weren't stretched taut, but rather they curved downward of their own weight. You surely must have seen them surrounding some monument. It's really just a symbolic way of blocking something off, because anyone could slip one foot and then the other into the lowest rungs of the chain, and in a twinkling of an eye he'd be on the other side. If one of those kids who get bored in the country—and in the mountains, too—got the idea of placing his foot on one of the chains at the edge of the mesa, he'd receive a horrible hair-pulling or a blow on the head or a shaking from his parents, and usually he wouldn't do it again. Although you couldn't say that the thing on the other side of the mesa was a precipice, a child could fall from a great enough height to split his head open against the rocks."

"Did you go down to the valley from there?"

"Oh, no, no. I don't remember exactly how we went down to the valley, because I only recall how all of a sudden we were there. We used to walk. We walked all the time on those darned vacations in Embalse, and as you probably know, children don't enjoy walking very much. They tire quickly; they're not interested in looking around. The only thing they want is for the grown-ups to forget about their obsession with stretching their legs once and for all. So, on that day we were walking, just like every other day of vacation; I went along patiently, bending down to pick up a little flower or a stone flecked with mica. In the mountains, walking can mean only two things: going up or going down. This time we were going down, down; on either side of the road the vegetation grew thicker and thicker. I think I forgot to mention that the people walking were papa and I. We walked silently; I didn't know where we were going, and I didn't ask. Papa hadn't told me. Suddenly the path ended in a little thicket of shrubs. Papa took my hand and led me through the shrubs, and I saw the valley.

"In the first place, I was surprised that the valley was still in shadow, because it must have been early in the morning, and high in the mountains it dawned earlier than down there. I was at the age when, if you found yourself on a mountain slope, you didn't know, and you didn't think to ask, how far down the slope extended and what there was at the foot of the mountain. If they had told me the slope went on and on to the center of the earth, I would've believed it. If they had explained to me that the earth was supported by four elephants who held up four columns on which it rested, I would have believed that, too. And besides, I didn't give a damn.

"So there I am, in a field surrounded by mountains. That's the valley, and a stream runs through the valley, and next to the stream there's a farmhouse, and in front of the door of the farmhouse, there's a family: father, mother, several children — one of them very small, in his mother's arms. And even more important than the family, in front of the house there's a cow, and the man is milking the cow. Without noticing my astonishment, my father takes me firmly by the hand and makes me approach the cow; he assures me it won't kick me, cows don't kick like mules, and he makes me watch how the man pulls on the cow's long teat, and a vertical stream of milk pours out, falling into a jug where there's already an abundance of foamy milk. Pull. Squirt. Pull. Squirt. No one's laughing. On the contrary, they're all deadly serious, even papa. I'd rather not be so close. I'd like to back up a little so I won't smell that intense milky smell. Besides, I've seen the sad expression on a muzzled calf's face. I'd rather not be so close, not see the cow up close, the shadows in the valley that are dissipating now, giving way to a milky clarity, milky; the man is dark-skinned, his bronze-colored hand contrasts with the pure white color of the milk he's extracting. God, my God, you might say daylight has already broken. The sun has already reached the valley. Now it seems like everything is in motion: birds are singing; the woman gets up from the low chair where she's been nursing her baby and takes another child by the hand, leading him inside the house. They give me a chipped crockery mug filled to the brim with fresh, warm milk. Oh no, don't tell me I have to drink *this*.

How can you make me drink milk fresh from the cow when I've *never* drunk milk fresh from the cow? It seems there's no way out. It's strange: the milk attracts and repels me at the same time. It's awfully warm. Just pulled from the cow's teats. To the last drop, papa says. Manna from heaven, divine nectar — I don't know how I did it, but I've chugged it all down now. To the last drop. Confusing explanations by papa about the benefits of milk fresh from the cow. It builds strength, helps you grow. It gives you strong bones and blood. We want more milk. We want to climb back up the mountain with a pitcher of milk. I notice that papa's brought along a pitcher someone has loaned him, also white, made of chipped crockery. Now the sun is bathing the fields, the streams, the *estancia*, the cow. Now it bathes all of us and it's very hot. Now we've crossed over the little thicket of shrubs again and we're starting to climb the mountain, that horrible, tiresome chore that grown-ups inflict on themselves day after day as if they liked it. Finally we get home with the jug of milk and mama boils it in an electric heater so it won't spoil. What more can I say?"

To sum up: A few years ago (longer ago than I thought at first: I was counting back, and I've discovered that it's been quite a while), I was taking a course in Mind Control.

"Why did you take that course?"

"Because my ideas were all confused. Frankly, I was afraid of going crazy. Pressures of modern life, and all that. People who aren't familiar with these courses don't have any respect for them, as though they involve learning to make model airplanes through correspondence or becoming a Rosicrucian or something like that. But it's not. It's a matter of learning certain simple mental exercises. And I especially liked to get together with my classmates, go out for a drink with them after class. Are you falling asleep?"

"No, but I must admit that my eyes feel sort of heavy. Why are you so nervous?"

"I just split the cleaning lady's head open with the vacuum cleaner."

"Why?"

"She asked me if she should vacuum now or later. I was trying to think."

"Any loss of gray matter?"

"Yes, her skull split in half like a coconut that fell off a tree, and the floor is covered with her brains, all mixed with blood. At the bottom of the vacuum canister, which I used to split her head open, there are hairs mixed together with blood and brains."

"What are you doing, Magdalena?"

"Tanning myself."

"It's very hot."

"But it's comfortable here at the edge of the swimming pool. Every so often I stick my arms in the water and cool off. I can smell the fragrance of the lilacs in the planter."

"Are you happy to be back at the *estancia*?"

"Yes, especially now that everyone's gone away and I can imagine I belong to Juan Antonio's family and my past is full of fields and tennis games."

"Would you like to belong to Juan Antonio's family?"

"Never. I just like to imagine it for a while. It takes so long to come to terms with your own past! I'll stay with the dacha in Sebastopol."

"Are you sure?"

"There must be something in my past that makes me feel very comfortable here at Las Lilas, as if Juan Antonio's inheritance were also my own. Sometimes I really believe that I'm descended from nobility, as they taught us in school. I doubt that many children come from more than one generation of Argentines. Almost all of them had Spanish grandparents, or Italians, or Russians, or Poles. Those who were descended from many generations of Argentines usually had dark skin and were the poorest of all. But they made us think we were all descendants of Manuel Belgrano, José de San Martín, and Domingo Faustino Sarmiento. In actual fact, I descend from my class notebook, where I used to draw a little blue and white flag in the corner of each page every day in May. They taught us to love our fatherland. And our motherland, Spain. But my motherland was Russia. Or — who knows? — someplace in the Mediterranean . . ."

"Educational policies can be changed, Magdalena. They could include a question on 'Our Grandparents' on exams."

"Being careful not to hurt anyone. . . . There are children who never met their grandparents, or who don't know who they are."

"And there are some who don't know who their fathers are."

"Although they usually know who their mothers are. You haven't told me your name."

"My name is Ignacio Ibargüengoitía.

"Iribarne."

"Uribelarrea."

"Altolaguirre."

"Carriquiriborde."

"House at the edge of the road."

"Iñaki! So it's you!"

"How are you, Magdalena?"

"Much better. Weren't you in Mar del Plata with Flora?"

"No, I was at a meeting in Vienna."

"Did I interrupt you?"

"Oh, it doesn't matter. Those meetings are mostly social events. I'm glad to have an excuse to return to Buenos Aires."

"But did you come back just to talk to me?"

"Yes, Magdalena."

"Sometimes life is easy to understand."

"Yes."

"Everything goes click."

"Yes."

"Iñaki . . ."

"Yes?"

"Couldn't we go get a Campari on the rocks, with soda and a twist of lemon?"

"I'll go. You stay here and sunbathe."

"No, Iñaki, I'm afraid to stay here alone with the butterflies falling into the water, and then Juan Antonio will come back as a child and dive in fully dressed to save them."

"That shouldn't frighten you, Magdalena. Butterflies need to be saved."

It's hard to say how each one of the students of Mind Control felt when we decided all together to make the excursion to the *estancia*. Juan Antonio is a modest, polite person who never brags about his fortune, but everyone knows he's very rich. He doesn't own just one *estancia*, but three, and when his ancient mother dies, he'll become the sole owner of a small empire. All the other students in the class lived in a precarious middle-class world. Tabi, the architect, and Inés, the psychologist, suffered the vicissitudes common to their liberal arts professions. Gustavo, the TV actor, was unemployed more often than he was working, and he complained of feeling unfulfilled. Eusebio, a painter from the provinces, lived more or less comfortably from his salary as a graphic designer, but he didn't feel fulfilled, either, and whenever he had a bit too much to drink, he would involve you in interminable conversations about the Blank Canvas and the Death of Art.

I never figured out how much Juan Antonio's fortune was worth, but for me it seemed infinite. Juan Antonio could go out and buy himself whatever he wanted, and he'd always have some money left over to go hunting exotic goats in Smyrna, an activity that obliged him to climb such high mountains that, looking down from their summits, he could see the clouds. Excursions like these made him endure hardships: for example, camping on top of the mountain and suffering from cold and fatigue, waiting for those damned goats to show up, with nothing to eat but a little moldy bread. If you ask me why they didn't have more than just a little bit of moldy bread to eat, I'll answer with one of Enrique's typical expressions, something he learned from his father: "Ask me easier questions." Juan Antonio told me that, at a specific moment, when they were up there shivering with their shotguns at the ready, it occurred to him to look down, and he thought: "I'm nuts. I'm eating moldy bread and I can see clouds down below."

The fact is, at Las Lilas one would run up against Juan Antonio's money at every turn, and for one who has little money or rather for one who's in need, it was an annoyance. One might even think, although this wasn't the case with Juan Antonio, that someone who has a lot of money might scorn someone else for having very little. There are those who raise the flag and go around shouting that this type of injustice mustn't continue and that there should be a social revolution to correct the situation. I've already mentioned that I'm weak and cowardly and incapable of any kind of bellicosity. Even worse: in reality my dream isn't to take away what Juan Antonio has and appropriate it myself, but magically to get my hands on — let's not say *everything* Juan Antonio has, which I don't need, anyway, but just enough to be able to live as I wish, without worrying about money. I think I was more ambitious at other stages of my life, and for a while now I've resigned myself to poverty as long as I can indulge certain hobbies, certain obsessions.

Juan Antonio never snubbed anybody for not having money. Quite the contrary. As Gustavo, the TV actor, said, as he rode up and down, displaying his ramrod-straight form on horseback, Juan Antonio, in his miserable youth, when he drank a bottle of whiskey a day and slept in the car because he couldn't pay the rent for the apartment, befriended all the *lumpen* who gathered around him. After recovering with the help of Alcoholics Anonymous and meeting Emi, he spent a year working at Las Lilas alongside the peasants, living and eating with them, and in the Mind Control class he became friendly with everyone, without discriminating against anyone, no matter how humble.

December 19
One can always let one's thoughts wander:
a deserted beach at siesta time,
a Japanese girl with her kimono and parasol,
a celery plant flooded with water,
an ant that transports
a leaf bigger than herself,
frequent breaks to suck on a pill,
a house painter atop a ladder
with his folded-newspaper hat,
a newspaper boat
floating toward a drainage ditch,
somber mosaics in a church in Rome,
Hebrew letters
in the infinitely distant Torah,
the rounded belly of a gluttonous priest,
warm-hued amber oranges,
serious young men in woolen bathing suits
slipping down a slide
into a swimming pool,
crowds that intersect
and bump each other in the streets,
the great clock strikes four-thirty.

Grandmother has sliced the fish
into four equal parts,
the sun shone through the rain and the rainbow came out,
a woman dressed in a coarse white robe
walks around aimlessly
on a patio surrounded by high walls.
High walls, implacable moon,
the intruder advances through the thicket,
a young man
with no distinguishing marks.
It's nighttime, and he's going to peek
through the keyhole
to satisfy an old longing.
Under the roof of a little room
the madwoman has been locked up for forty years,
and when they take her out of there,
and she comes in contact with the air outside,
she turns into dust thou art and to dust wilt thou return.
Holy Mary, Mother of God,
conceived without sin.
Long live the Holy Federation.
Twelve o'clock and all's well.
I'm the little Indian girl who sells *empanadas*.

One must never think
about the same thing for very long
because the hinges of one's intelligence
might rust.
There are several kinds of clouds
that produce storms.
It's possible to find oneself suddenly
inside a men's barber shop
in nineteen thirty-three.
The old mother's hands,
slicing onions once again.
Everything shows up with regularity:
one thing after another

and now it's time to knock at the door
with the bronze knocker.
Almost certainly some chickens will appear
with their idiotic expression,
the doves will return to the dovecote
of the man who raises doves
and then roasts and eats them.
What a bitter mouthful,
years spent cooking them,
years spent chewing them,
only to find out that it's better
to eat other sorts of birds.

I grabbed the white napkin
that the waiter had draped over his arm,
I made him trip and fall
and when we were both on the floor
I apologized over and over.
I climbed onto a brightly lit stage,
I greeted the crowd,
it was raining flowers
and I suffocated to everyone's amusement.
They hoisted me up a flagpole like a flag,
they chopped me up on a wooden board
like parsley,
they shielded me from the sun with the little Japanese parasol,
they refreshed my memory
with sponges soaked in essence of orange blossoms,
they buried me in a meadow and
planted roses on my grave.
And the tombstone says:
One can always let one's thoughts wander.

There's Juan Antonio, quite content, sitting on the grass and leaning his back against the side wall of one of the houses, drinking *mate*

and chatting with the farmhands, who lead a decent life and love Juan Antonio because Las Lilas is a model establishment. There's no exploitation here: the workers live well; there's even a school on the *estancia* (just imagine how big the *estancia* is), and the women are taught to use birth control. It's not mandatory, of course, like in China, where each couple can have only one baby and the country has become so full of spoiled only children that they don't know what to do with them. No, on Juan Antonio's *estancia* the farmhands' wives all have several children, and there are no romantic scandals. But I'd be lying to you if I said I know what these people think and feel; at twilight on my first day at Las Lilas, I approached a cook who was shucking string beans on the back patio, and I said "How beautiful all this is." Astonished, the woman looked at me for a moment and burst out laughing. "It's marvelous," I insisted, and the woman guffawed. It was clear she wasn't laughing from pleasure, or because she loved the country. But I just repeated "How beautiful all this is," over and over like an idiot, and she laughed so hard her jaw flapped up and down, showing her missing teeth. In fact, she did have several missing. I tried to imagine her in my dentist's chair but it was impossible, like imagining a laying hen sticking a token in the turnstile in the subway station. I tried to imagine a Chinese woman — one of those who are allowed only one child — sitting in some Chinese dentist's office in China, and I saw him filling up the gaps in her mouth with false teeth, but they were made of cement.

"Why do they need cement teeth if all they have to chew is rice?" I asked.

"You're mocking the dictatorship of the proletariat," a guard spat at me in perfect Spanish.

"Nonsense," I replied, ready to crawl under the first available table. "I'm quite familiar with right-wing dictatorships. What do you expect? You think I'm about to unfurl an anti-Communist banner or something?"

The guard regarded me silently, as if he had never said a word.

"I don't want any kind of dictatorship," I shouted, running away. Nearly breathless, I reached the wire fence that separated the field from a eucalyptus grove. Only then did I stop running and try to breathe the perfumed air slowly. When I got to the edge of the woods with the large park before me, I was glad to see Enrique there, sitting on a marble bench, reading the paper next to a bronze reproduction of the Discus Thrower. Beside the Discus Thrower, four little toads, also made of bronze, spewed four streams of crystal-clear water from their mouths.

"Let's go have breakfast," Enrique said.

"Impossible," I replied. "It's twilight."

Enrique took my arm gently, as if to say, "This is a private joke between the two of us," and I stood on tiptoe to reach the coffee jar down from a high shelf.

"No, no, enough fooling around," Enrique said, growing a bit serious. "It's not true that it's twilight. But it *is* true that we're at Las Lilas."

Yes, we *are* at Las Lilas, but . . . what day is it? What I mean is, is this the second day, or rather the morning following the afternoon of our arrival? But that can't be, because we've had that breakfast already. Did I say "farmhouse?"

"When?"

"A while ago, when I was talking about Juan Antonio chatting with the farmhands."

"Yes, you said 'farmhouse.'"

"I want to clarify that it's one of those farmhouses made of concrete blocks, with a thatched roof. The houses at Las Lilas have every comfort, a large kitchen-dining room, three bedrooms, two baths . . ."

"An electric refrigerator?"

"Of course. What did you think? Everything's completely electrified here. In front of each farmhouse there's a little flower garden, and behind each farmhouse there's a small orchard for family use. And behind the orchard a chicken coop . . ."

"Don't tell me they have a cow, too."

"No. Meat and dairy products are distributed free of charge from the *estancia's* own production."

"And the thatched roof?"

"It's not a sign of poverty; it's the most interesting part of the house. The smell of that roof when it rains is one of the most enduring memories of my childhood."

"Yes, yes, I know all the stories about your vacations in the country."

"Iñaki?"

"Yes?"

"When do you return to Vienna?"

"There's no rush."

"In general parlance, wouldn't you say, 'There's no hurry?' "

"Maybe."

"One can't always be up to date on general parlance."

"I saw him yesterday."

"Who?"

"General Parlance."

"I don't believe you! Is he cute?"

"Well, I'm a man, Magdalena. I'm not about to tell you that General Parlance is *cute*. He's of average height, medium brown hair and eyes, regular features, white, even teeth, a frank smile. Now that it's summer, he goes around dressed in a cream-colored linen suit, with a red-and-white, narrow-striped shirt and a bordeaux-colored tie."

"Bordeaux?"

"Yes."

"Bird-do?"

"Bored, oh. Tan moccasins. Belt the same color as the moccasins."

"And is he young?"

"Around thirty-five."

"How strange. Young people usually wear less conventional clothing."

"He can't. He spends morning, noon, and night at the Richmond Café on Florida Street, clearing up any matter that may arise concerning language usage for anyone who might want to consult him."

"And doesn't he travel at all? Doesn't he go to Spain and throughout Latin America?"

"No, he's afraid his accent will be ruined."

"What's his accent like?"

"It's a neutral accent, with a slight differentiation between the *s* and the *z*, for example *gristle* and *grizzle*. Also between the *c* and the *z*, for example, *glacier* and *glazier*."

"That last bit strikes me as the height of preciousness. I imagine he'd never dream of saying 'y'all.'"

"Goes without saying."

"I have a horrible suspicion. Would his favorite topics of conversation be, perhaps, the shouts of street vendors in colonial Buenos Aires, or the germination of beans in glass jars, or the habits of the whooping crane?"

"Don't be afraid, Magdalena. He's not an elementary school teacher, although it's true he's the son of an elementary school teacher."

"Iñaki?"

"Yes?"

"I think I've been out in the sun too long. And you, squatting there at my side, patiently listening to me, all dressed up in your suit and tie. You probably want to change into a bathing suit to lie out a bit."

"I'm in no rush."

"Iñaki, Tomasa the cook's daughter is having an affair with Cirilo, the one who's in charge of taming the colts."

"'The one who's in charge of taming the colts'? Doesn't that sound strange? As if you had said, 'The one who's in charge of sending out invitations to the embassy reception.'"

"All right, whatever you like. Lately I can't figure out if I'm speaking or if you are."

"What were you saying about Tomasa's daughter?"

"That's she's having an affair with Cirilo, and it's going to turn out badly."

"Why?"

"Because Cirilo's married."

"What will you do while I change?"

"I'm not going to fall off any cliff, Iñaki. I feel fine."

December 21. How golden the wheat looks! In more civilized places it's snowing today and Santa Claus has somewhere to drive his sleigh. Here in Buenos Aires, it's suffocatingly hot and the streets are deserted, except for the boy sitting on the doorstep and the man and woman standing in the doorway of their grocery store on the opposite sidewalk. Buenos Aires is the center of the world. The City of Buenos Aires. Municipality of the City of Buenos Aires. The Bureau of Museums of the Municipality of the City of Buenos Aires. The Historical Division of the Bureau of Museums of the Municipality of the City of Buenos Aires. The Art Department of the Historical Division of the Bureau of Museums of the Municipality of the City of Buenos Aires. The Archival Section of the Art Department of the Historical Division of the Bureau of Museums of the Municipality of the City of Buenos Aires. The patient with a guarded prognosis can go on like this for hours, always finding new divisions of the divisions. If, as is customary, her treatment were to focus on determining the causes, one would have to mention a pockmarked ceiling; the noise produced by drops of water falling into a basin; the lack of an authority figure such as, say, an artillery captain or a scholar in a brown wig; famine in Asia, Africa, and some parts of Latin America; stern, continuous concentration on an illustration of citizens running in a downpour in London in 1922; a soldier in the War of Independence with his sword unsheathed, on the cover of a school notebook; a plum tree laden with ripe fruit in a remote field of the past; a few dead, beached fish lying next to the fisherman's basket; several dozen grosgrain ribbons in assorted colors, lying on a Lebanese merchant's counter; a large, pale banner partially covering some vulture heads; and way in back, way in back, a young girl dead at the age of twenty in the immensity of the pampa.

What's Tomasa's daughter's name? Her name is Candelaria. Candle. She has dark skin. Yes, brown skin. And Cirilo? He has brown skin, also. Do we know anything about them? Tomasa has been at

Las Lilas forever; no one remembers when she first arrived. Juan Antonio says she came from another place in the country. Do you think the business about the color of her skin has any importance?

"No, I don't think so. There's no racism in this country."

"But does any dark-skinned person hold an important government post?"

"I'm not exactly an expert in this area, but I don't think it has to do with racism. Here in Buenos Aires, for example, if a dark-skinned child shows up at school, they call him 'the Indian kid,' but it's not pejorative. In other places it might be considered an insult."

"Do you have any idea of the number of dark-skinned people in this country?"

"I don't have the faintest idea."

"What kind of personal contact do you have with them?"

"Through domestic service. I once had a maid we all loved very much, who helped me raise my youngest son . . . The bricklayer who came last month to do some repairs on the house has dark skin . . . The kid from the supermarket who delivers the groceries . . ."

"Does it bother you to talk about this subject?"

"I think so."

"Does it make you think of anything in particular?"

"Of those people who play the drums at demonstrations."

"Yes."

"Some are dark and some are white."

"Yes."

"I'm afraid of all of them. They make me very anxious. I prefer to listen to flutes or oboes."

"If you like, we can listen to flutes."

"No, no thanks."

"How would you deal with a campaign to bring together two such diverse strata of the population as the educated middle-class sector and the alluvial mass of dark-skinned people who have invaded the central city in order to escape from their poverty in the interior, looking for some means of subsistence in the capital?"

"Working with the literacy campaign."

"Is there a literacy campaign?"

"Yes . . . I don't know. I think the illiteracy rate isn't too high in Argentina."

"But is there or isn't there a literacy campaign going on?"

"I don't know. Stop harassing me."

"Is there any hunger?"

"I think so. It's not the same kind of hunger as in Asia or Africa. I don't think people are dying of hunger in the streets. I suppose there's malnutrition and some other problems . . ."

"You suppose? Don't you know?"

"Please! Stop harassing me. What do you want from me? To get rid of hunger in the world?"

"How would you envision a rapprochement between the educated middle class and the dark-skinned people in Argentina?"

"I think the only way would be to begin by talking about differences."

"Give me a concrete example."

"I'd take a dark-skinned person of any age or sex and I'd ask: 'Have you noticed a difference in color between your skin and mine?' In the worst-case scenario, the person would get angry and I'd have to keep talking quickly, explaining that *I* don't think it's better or worse to have lighter or darker skin, et cetera. But most likely he wouldn't get angry, although someone who comes from a country where there's racism might not believe me. For example: *Have you noticed a difference in color between your skin and mine?* Yes. My grandparents on mama's side were Indian. My father's mother also was Indian, but papa was Spanish. *And do you know why I have white skin, even though it isn't all that white?* It must be because you're Russian, right? *Don't get that wrong. That is: I'm not Russian, but all four of my grandparents were. Except you call all Jews "Russian."* Well, yes. The Israelites. *Do you like it when I call you Indian?* No, unless you mean it affectionately. My mama called me her little Indian. I don't like it when they call us 'those Indians' when they're talking about us, the people in the slums. *Well, I don't like to be called Israelite, either. You can call me a Jew, and if you want you can call me Russian, and I'll call you Indian. But don't call me an Israelite because it gives me gooseflesh.*"

"Allow me."

"Who's talking?"

"I am, sweetie. I must interrupt you to tell you that you started off pretty well, but you're losing sight of your objective. Do you want to lend the Indian a hand, or do you want the Indian to lend one to you?"

"Please, not that old folklore again. It gives me gooseflesh."

"You're very thin-skinned. Let's allow the Indian to take care of himself for a while. As far as the word 'Israelite' is concerned, I must confess I share your dislike for it. People say 'Israelite' in order to avoid saying 'Jew.' Because the word 'Jew' sticks in their throats, because they're afraid someone will notice they don't like Jews. Because 'Jew' sounds like an insult to them. Because maybe they've used it as an insult sometimes."

"Although this may be a bit out of line, do you think the Indians like the Jews?"

"I don't think they either like or dislike them. But wasn't I the one asking the questions?"

"How about you stop making jokes, at least for a while?"

"You haven't even asked me who I am."

"I'm not interested in finding out. You talk in that ugly, ugly way, like a reporter. So, let up."

"One final question: What are you going to listen to now?"

"The *Actus Tragicus* Cantata."

"*Heute, heute, wirdst du mit mir in Paradies sein?* "

"Yes, my friend."

"You finally came back, Iñaki."

"What happened?"

"Some guy was bothering me. Let's go back to the swimming pool."

"Mmm . . . how nice the water feels!"

"So, we already went back to the swimming pool, dived in, and swam two or three widths?"

"Don't you think General Parlance would say, 'So *we have al-*

ready gone back to the swimming pool, *we have dived in* and *we have swum . . ."*

"Possibly, but now let's continue talking just as if we were in Buenos Aires, so we won't digress from the main topic. I notice how quickly we covered the fifty yards between the front entrance and the pool. It all happened in less than an instant."

"One might say, at the least, that this is a very peculiar world."

"Is it raining?"

"No."

"The affair between Candelaria and Cirilo is going to turn out badly."

"How do you know?"

"Because Justa, Cirilo's wife, saw them riding at two in the morning by the light of the moon. Cirilo was riding the roan horse, and Candelaria was mounted behind him."

"The roan?"

"Yes, why?"

"It sounds strange to me. Candelaria was mounted behind him?"

"Why are you repeating it?"

"I like how it sounds. In Buenos Aires we'd hardly ever get the chance to say 'Candelaria was mounted behind him.'"

"Iñaki the gaucho."

"Magdalena the gaucho woman."

"Now I see it's a mistake for you to call me Magdalena."

"It's no mistake. Magdalena was a courtesan in Magdala, in Galilee, converted by Jesus Christ."

"She's the one washing his feet in the Veronese painting."

"Magdalena is also a river in Colombia; a city in Bolivia; a section of the Province of Buenos Aires; a place in the municipality of San Antonio de Cabezas in the province of Matanzas, Cuba; a town in Honduras; a village in Sonora, Mexico; a place in Peru; a sector of the municipality of Cartagena; a canton in El Salvador; and many other geographical locations."

"Why didn't you copy them all down?"

"Because in many of them the word 'municipality' is repeated.

There were also a princess, a queen, and a Carmelite nun named Magdalena."

"Then it's quite adequate. It's just that something gets stuck in my throat when I say Magdalena."

Who dragged me out of bed, still fast asleep, and stuck me in this car where I'm sitting on papa's lap? I don't know what time it is, nor do I care one bit. We're going down a gentle slope. The clean, slightly chilly scent of dawn filters through the window, gentler than the night air. My brother is sleeping in mama's arms. I see houses, trees, and thickets going by (of course I don't know the word 'thicket,' but I'm the one speaking for her). I don't know where we could be going so early in the morning, but I'm too sleepy to ask. Now, going uphill, the motor chugs. And now, going downhill a bit too steeply, I feel funny in my stomach. And up again along a wide, peaceful road bordered by pine trees, until we stop in front of a chalet that's larger than the others, with a red-tiled verandah on one side and in front a little porch just like the one all the cottages have in La Colonia. The driver, a fat guy wearing a gray cap, gets out first and opens the back doors so we can emerge. Legs numb, a funny feeling in my stomach, I watch the man open the trunk and take out our suitcases. Why, papa? Why? Because we have an extension. *Extension*. If you get an extension, you can stay in the mountains an extra week, going up and down, one more week smelling the fragrance of the wildflowers, walking interminably, playing with unfamiliar kids and drinking *mate* in the afternoon in big, chipped cups. This house is prettier than the other one. The funny feeling in my stomach is gone; now I'm just hungry. "These babies haven't had breakfast yet," mama says, taking clothing out of the suitcases and putting it away in a simple wooden dresser. I peek out of one of the two windows in the room. It faces the verandah. It's odd how little it matters to me whether we're here or there, in this house or in the other one. As long as they leave me alone and I can think. Mama calls me, and I can tell by her stern tone that it's not the first time.

I turn my head without answering and look at her. If only I could remember how furious this makes mama. Apparently what I'm supposed to do is say, "Yes, mama?" "Always with your head in the clouds!" she says. While she stuffs me into a wool sweater I don't need, I think: How strange. Maybe she doesn't realize it, but among the many, many places where my mind wanders, it's never once been in the clouds.

I go out to the verandah while they finish putting everything away before going down to the dining room. As I walk toward the porch, I hear my brother, who's just awakened, babbling. I step on the dew-covered grass and briefly regard the scenery. This scenery must be very pretty because the house is on top of a mountain, but if there's anything that doesn't interest children, it's scenery. I turn around to look at the front of the house, and I see, over the arch of the porch, an oval, white-painted metal plate with a number: 28. The last house was number 15. During this extension week, which extended our vacation to twenty-one days instead of the usual fourteen, we went for many car rides. The family who shared number 28 with us had a car, and although it was a tight squeeze, we all fit in well enough to go back and forth to and from the dining room and to visit places the grown-ups thought were beautiful. Whenever we passed by the house we lived in before, we shouted, "Bye, number 15!" And that always made me feel a slight rush of anguish.

But number 28 is better, dummy! Number 28 is bigger, dummy! Number 28 is in a prettier place. Anyway, we're going back to Buenos Aires soon, dummy! The last day, when we were carrying our suitcases and we weren't traveling in the neighbors' car anymore, but rather in a broken-down bus to get to the train at Almafuerte (how lucky that the station was called Almafuerte, strong soul!), we passed by our former house and we all shouted, "Bye, number 15!"

It's wonderful to watch the dawn every morning. Wrong. It's twenty to eight; you couldn't say it's exactly dawn. I didn't see the dawn; when I opened my eyes it was full daylight already. I meant to say that it's good to wake up every morning and verify that you're still alive.

"Are you about to die?"

"Not that I know of. But anyway, waking up alive is a miracle. Dreaming and wakefulness are miracles."

"The human body is a miracle. How each organ functions, each system . . ."

"The eye of God is in every drop of blood that circulates through the veins."

"Others might say that there's no eye of God. Everything happens by chance."

"And still others might say that it's impossible to know."

"I'm one of those, Magdalena. I think it's impossible to know."

"To tell the truth, I also think it's impossible to know. Or rather, I don't know. But someone knows, Iñaki. Or thinks he knows."

"How will we ever know?"

"Know what? If the soul separates from the body when it dies and flies like a dove toward its Creator?"

"Did you ever try to imagine a soul all by itself, without a body?"

"No, because the idea doesn't sound attractive, but I can imagine it right now. Or rather, I can't imagine it because it's invisible, but I can imagine what it does. It thinks, it reasons, it solves math problems, it penetrates the mysteries of the universe. It does everything it couldn't do before, because the body got in its way. It runs, it flies, it moves anywhere at all in a second, it goes through walls . . ."

"Then you think the souls of the dead don't leave this world?"

"I suppose some go to Heaven, to delight in God's presence, especially the souls of those who tried to behave themselves in order to earn that. I'd rather stay here a while longer, to see everything I couldn't see during my lifetime."

"I don't believe you, Magdalena. You must be dying of curiosity to see God."

"It's more than just curiosity, Iñaki. I'd almost say I'm fond of Him. He's been by my side, kindly and useless, my whole life long.

When I desperately want something, I ask Him for it; if I get it, I thank Him, because I think He's granted it to me. When I'm suffering I beg Him to stop my suffering, but I never think He's the one who caused it. If he frees me from suffering, I say 'Thank God.'"

"What are you suffering from now, Magdalena?"

"At this very moment, I'm not suffering. Thank God."

"Do you feel happy?"

"I feel happy to be here, at Las Lilas, sunbathing at the edge of the swimming pool and chatting with you. Every so often I dip my arm into the water and cool off. Only one thing worries me, and it's that you left your meeting in Vienna to come to see me."

"I'm your old family physician, Magdalena."

"Physician. How horrible that word sounds! I hear the word physician and I see everything all white. White smock. White hospital corridor. Big fat nurses in white uniforms and caps, with white, military-style shoes. The white, skeletal face of a terminally ill patient who turns toward the window . . . He's going to die. Tomorrow or the next day, any day now, his shoes will stop belonging to him."

"It's our common destiny, Magdalena. At some point we all lose our shoes."

"For ever and ever. Just like what happened to Freddy. Did I ever tell you about Freddy?"

"No."

"Freddy also took the Mind Control class with us."

"But he didn't come to Las Lilas."

"No, he didn't come to Las Lilas. He died three months before."

Freddy was a dyed-in-the-wool denizen of Buenos Aires. Tall and strong, quick to hurl an insult or throw a punch, son of a Hungarian Jewish father and a Romanian Jewish mother. He bore very little resemblance to the Jews who roam the Once District on Friday afternoons in their full beards and black suits and hats, hurrying to get home before the first star appears. Those pale Jews, with their prominent cheekbones and self-absorbed air, come from Arab countries.

Jews like Freddy have very little to do with them, and they believe that to be a Jew means to come from Warsaw, Odessa, Kiev, Budapest, or from long-vanished villages in Russia, Poland, or Ukraine, where everyone was a Jew and only Yiddish was spoken. They don't know much about the Sephardic Jews, those silent, ultra-religious beings, laden with children, who rarely smile, and they look on them with a certain disdain.

I said Freddy's father was a Hungarian Jew and not a Jewish Hungarian, since it was on account of his being Jewish, not Hungarian, that he decided to flee Europe before the Second World War and come to Buenos Aires. However, fed up with always putting his Jewishness first—and for such painful reasons—he never gave his children a Jewish education and never spoke to them in Yiddish, but rather in the Spanish of Río de la Plata, which he managed to learn thanks to the fact that he was a young man of seventeen with a good ear for languages when he immigrated. For that reason Freddy and his brother Danny could say they were Argentine Jews, more Argentine than Jewish. In fact, they simply said they were Argentine, period, because in Argentina there's a rule of etiquette that one doesn't mention one's religion or national origin unless one is expressly asked or if one chooses to announce it voluntarily. In Buenos Aires the Argentines who are considered totally Argentine are those with Italian surnames. In second place come those with Spanish surnames. And a special place is reserved for those who can flaunt one or two select surnames of the founding fathers.

It would be interesting to find out whether or not, when Freddy's father lived in Budapest, the other Hungarians thought he was a Hungarian Jew or a Jewish Hungarian, but at this stage of the game no one really cares. For its inhabitants, Buenos Aires is the center of the world, and all other places, for example, London, Paris, New York, even Madrid and Rome, are very far away; so why even mention anyplace as remote as Budapest? So the two male children of this naturalized Hungarian Jewish Argentine attended a rather expensive private English school and chose rugby as their sport.

You mustn't think Freddy's father was a renegade Jew. He had his two boys circumcised, although he never discussed the matter with them. He was a wealthy businessman who amassed a considerable fortune, at first by selling cardboard suitcases, later plastic suitcases, and finally leather suitcases. Anyone who's not familiar with cardboard suitcases doesn't understand what it meant to be poor in Argentina in the thirties. A poor man would travel with his cardboard suitcase tied up with twine; he would travel by coach, by sulky, by train. He was dying of poverty, sitting on a bench in a deserted station, his cardboard suitcase at his side.

The last time I saw Freddy was through the cloudy glass window of the door of the little bar where we used to meet after class. That is, I saw Freddy's outline, with his slightly hunched shoulders, leaning a bit forward to speak with someone, a position he often had to assume because of the difference in height between him and his conversational partner.

Now he's dead. Underground. Unless, knowing that he was going to die, he decided to be cremated.

Having oneself cremated is unpleasant. It means giving up all hope of an afterlife, as if one said, "I know that I'm dying for ever and ever." Who can assure you, after all, that after you're dead and cremated, with your ashes stored in a little box that someone will bury beneath a tree, or scattered on the waters of the Río de la Plata, that you won't end up in some acropolis for the souls of the cremated who, while they were alive, didn't think they had an immortal soul, but really did? It's horrible to imagine that yellowish place, surrounded by high, blank walls, where only portraits of Robespierre, Lenin, Bertrand Russell, Juan B. Justo, and Alfredo Palacios hang, assuring each other that there's no life after death.

Freddy wasn't a religious guy. He laughed at all the rituals, Jewish or any other kind. But when he found out he was dying, he went to a Catholic priest who promised him a kind of life after death that he could portray in images: a God with pretty dark eyes, a place in Heaven populated by musical angels. Maybe he looked at the reproductions of those paintings that show Heaven like the illustrations of a travel agency brochure.

He learned of the fatal diagnosis the year before our excursion to Las Lilas. I know they didn't conceal anything from him, neither the gravity of his illness nor the possible life expectancy, nothing. We used to talk to Freddy in the bar after class. We recalled hopeless cases of sick people who were miraculously cured with herbal infusions, or who escaped their illness by dedicating themselves to scaling Mount Everest. We tried to imagine the conversations between Freddy and the priest. Freddy, who was so cautious, who wanted guarantees for everything—wouldn't he have wanted to reserve a place for himself up there ahead of time? And why did he get cancer? Was it that he drank too much coffee, very strong? But that would have given him an ulcer, not cancer. He smoked liked a chimney, it's true, but that would have given him lung cancer, and he had cancer of the pancreas.

They told him:

"Freddy, you're going to die."

"Freddy, you have a tumor and you're going to die."

"No, Freddy, there's no hope."

"There's nothing to be done."

"It's better that you know, Freddy."

"So you can put your affairs in order."

"It seems only fair to tell you, Freddy. You've got to know."

"A few months, Freddy, it's impossible to say for sure."

Is it possible that Freddy ever appreciated the ineffable beauty of Christian music? Bach cantatas? Mozart motets? Would he have wanted to spend all eternity listening to those Hallelujahs? Why didn't he look for a Jewish Heaven, if in fact such a Heaven exists? (If it exists, it can't be represented in paintings and stickers, like the Christian Heaven with God the Father always alert, taking care of the business of Heaven and Earth, and the Holy Spirit in the form of a dove, Saint Peter with the keys of the kingdom, angels with their harps and melodies, millions and millions of good souls who got there over the course of centuries. If you could choose, who wouldn't choose that Heaven? We mustn't forget that Heaven isn't just Catholic. There are also Protestants there, from all denominations. What I don't know for sure is if good Jews and Muslims also go to Heaven. I don't think so.)

"What is it you're doing, then, Magdalena?"

"Telling this story? It's like making a very entangled skein of wool. But the skein exists beforehand. There are familiar things in it; the same things appear and reappear. For example, it seems I'm doomed to speak of the lagoon over and over again."

"The lagoon at Las Lilas?"

"Yes, there's a lagoon at Las Lilas. Juan Antonio usually goes duck-hunting there. It's a lagoon with transparent water; on the shores reeds grow and lilies bloom. There's no one there, not at the shore or for many miles around. A shot rings out. A duck that was flying over the lagoon falls into the water. The furtive hunter gets up from the spot where he was crouched among the reeds and walks away, down a path between cultivated fields toward a farmhouse in the distance."

"And that's all?"

"That's all. But there are still a few unresolved issues. Was duck hunting forbidden at that time of year? Did the hunter sneak into Las Lilas furtively? Is the farmhouse he's heading for his home, or is he going there in order to rob or kill someone? Considering that the duck he hit with his shot was going to fall into the water, why did he shoot? Was he just practicing his aim?"

"You have to go on, Magdalena."

"Doesn't it matter that it's December twenty-fourth?"

"We'll make a toast at midnight."

"With Flora and Enrique?"

"Yes, Flora's coming up from the south this afternoon, and Enrique's returning from Bolivia."

"Did you talk to them?"

"Yes, I talked to both of them."

"What did they tell you about me?"

"That you're much better, although I'd recommend a couple more weeks of rest. You can spend them here; Juan Antonio's off hunting goats in Smyrna, and Emi and the girls are at the beach."

"It's good to know that no one will bother us here. And your meeting?"

"It'll all get worked out."

"I'll stay at Las Lilas as long as necessary."

"You don't seem to be in a hurry at all."

"I'm not. Did you see my room here at the *estancia*? It's a square, spacious room, but not too spacious, and it's better like that: I don't like to sleep in a ballroom. A sofa, a desk and chair, walls covered with shelves filled with books. Nothing else. The balcony faces the back of the property; I can't see anybody coming or going. I choose peaceful reading material from the last century, where people move deliberately; no one thinks aloud or gets undressed in public. Everything happens in an orderly fashion, until some catastrophe takes place. If I'm sleepy, I sleep. Any time of day. When I want to talk to you, I look for you, and there you are. It's a shame this can't last forever. But, well, as long as it lasts . . .

"Thanks to the random things I read in my room, I've discovered something I suspected: the pages of the Old Testament don't prove that the soul is immortal, nor do they reveal any doctrine of future rewards and punishments. The rationalization that any reference to immortality is an argument in favor of the divine authority of Moses, who thought he was sent by the Lord and didn't need to resort to supernatural rewards and punishments (William Warburton, *The Divine Legation of Moses*, 1737) and other arguments like that don't interest me in the least. What matters is that a perfect Jew, or at least a very, very Jewish Jew, doesn't think about life after death; at least he doesn't think about it in concrete terms. But now I'm not speaking of perfect Jews, but rather of the imperfect Jews we know in Buenos Aires. No doubt they think, although they may not admit it, that perhaps there is a clean, well lighted place after all, with fluffy clouds and lyre and harp music (with the occasional intervention of a mysterious oboe), where they can spend the eternity that awaits us. Why are you smiling?"

"I was wondering if that's the peaceful material you're reading, with a catastrophe at the end. It's too hot here."

"It's suffocating."

"At this time of day there's a part of the swimming pool that's shaded by the trees. Let's keep on talking in the water."

"Yes, it's too hot to be outside. Have you started talking about Sholem Aleichem again?"

"Yes, because today I was reading Borges, and I remembered you could greet someone by saying 'Jorge Luis Borges' and the other person would answer . . ."

"Aleichem shalom."

The boy is sitting in the doorway of the house, with his back leaning against the black wrought-iron door with its chipped paint. Next to the door, to the boy's right, there's a low wall, topped by a black wrought-iron fence, also chipped, separating the garden from the street. In the garden are rose bushes, their blossoms quite open, supported by red-tipped white posts. At the back of the garden one can see the front of the house, a square, humble building, with closed shutters on the front door. At the side of the house, beyond the black-and-white tiled hallway, there's a large door, also made of wrought iron, that faces the side patio. It's Christmas.

The boy sitting in the doorway is motionless and has an expressionless face, as though he's not thinking about anything. The street is deserted; the doors and windows of the house are closed. Some empty cider bottles in the gutter bear witness to a street celebration the night before. There are also some burnt vestiges of firecrackers and bottle rockets. The metal grating on the grocery across the street has been pulled shut. It's brutally hot, a heat that didn't even let up during the night, but the boy doesn't feel it. Not only because he seems less a boy than the memory of himself as a boy, but because children don't usually feel the heat: it doesn't bother them, and, like flies, they even seem to find it exciting. But there's not the slightest danger this child will get excited about anything. It's also unlikely he'll ever move from that spot or utter a word. He'll watch the seasons go by, changing clothing if necessary; he'll watch the metal grating go up in the morning, and he'll watch it come down at night; he'll watch the grocer and his wife come outside and remain standing in the doorway when there are no customers; he'll watch them follow an old woman with a shopping bag and a gray kerchief over her shoulders into the store. He'll watch the humble people of the neighborhood go by, here and there, a man in a suit, tie, and stiff collar in the December heat; a woman carrying a baby in her arms; a widow with a black veiled hat and a big bouquet of calla lilies wrapped in newspaper. His eyes will pass through these shapes without seeing them. He won't notice whether or not the leaves have fallen from the trees, or if a pigeon has left its droppings on the sidewalk, if the water is flowing quickly in the gutter, falling through the grating down into unknown depths, if the sky has filled with black clouds and windstorms are furiously shaking the clothing hanging on the roof across the street. He won't be aware of how long he's been sitting in the doorway of the house or how much longer he'll remain there.

"Where are we?"

"I don't know, Iñaki, in a swampy region."

"It wouldn't be hard to sink in the mud up to our knees, and besides, we don't know when the bottom might cave in."

"Even so, there's no danger. No one drowns in a swamp in a split second; these things take time. If the bottom caves in, we'll head toward dry land over there, to the right."

"Couldn't we just walk on dry land from the outset?"

"I knew you were going to ask me that, Iñaki. I knew it just as surely as I know my name is Magdalena. Look over there, in the distance."

"A village."

"And in the village there's a tavern, or an inn, or a hostelry."

"But, look, we're already there."

"Yes, we're already entering the tavern."

"We got here in less time than it takes to think about it."

"And ever since we left the swamp and started walking on dry land and then over the cobblestone streets of the village, the wind has dried the mud on our feet and legs."

"The mud's falling off in pieces now, leaving our shoes and clothing perfectly clean."

"Ah! How nice it feels to be in here after being so cold outside."

"Yes, the scenery was desolate, with naked trees and not even a single bird. Do you know how to use this samovar?"

"I think you have to open up this little spigot."

"Look at this glass with a metal holder around it. There's a little plum jam at the bottom."

"There's a samovar on every table."

"And a bottle of vodka."

"Gustavo, the TV actor, and his wife, Helga the German, didn't get along."

"I knew that."

"How did you know?"

"You told me."

"Helga was the daughter of a former Nazi officer stationed in Córdoba. Her life hadn't exactly been easy, with an authoritarian, brutal father who lived in constant fear that they'd come to arrest him and take him back to Germany to judge him for his crimes in the Second World War."

"Did that ever happen?"

"No, he died first, of some illness. Helga, like her brothers, went to boarding school at a German academy in Buenos Aires, where, despite the strictness, her life was better than at home. The summer after her father's death, Helga returned to her house in Córdoba, a lovely European-style chalet in the mountains, near Alta Gracia. She was seventeen. Gustavo, who was thirty, was on tour in the provinces with a small theatrical company. They met at a civic center dance. Gustavo had that actor's vice that made him think he was capable of doing anything just by imitating gestures and movements and changing his tone of voice. He was quite good looking, although his stiffness detracted from his charm. Helga seemed quite stiff, too, with straight, golden hair down to her waist, green eyes, and an inscrutably serious face. She was a tall, athletic girl, carrying a few extra pounds she had acquired at school, where they made the students eat everything on their plates. She was very German, a real Valkyrie. She hardly spoke. Gustavo danced with her at the civic center and then tried to take her virginity in his hotel room. Even though he was quite drunk, Gustavo realized there was no virginity to take, and that made him angry. It made him so angry that he never stopped throwing it in Helga's face for the entire duration of their marriage.

"After the civic center dance, Gustavo and Helga began a formal courtship, plainly disapproved of by Helga's mother, who saw Gustavo as no more than a calculating lowlife who wanted to live off the family's fortune. Gustavo never saw a cent of that fortune. Helga's mother accepted the marriage when Helga became pregnant the summer after their courtship began. She bought the baby's layette and paid the cost of the delivery. But after the wedding, Gustavo and Helga went to Buenos Aires, to the same apartment where he had been living precariously for years from his sporadic earnings as an actor. Helga didn't know how to do anything, not even cook. More than once, disheartened and drunk, Gustavo shattered a dish against the wall. Without saying a word, Helga cleaned up what was left of dinner with a rag, but the stains never were completely erased and they made the already sordid apartment even more so.

"When Helga's baby was born, she cheered up quite a bit: she was enthusiastic about being a mother and she cared for the baby well. She had never paid too much attention to Gustavo before, but now she ignored him completely and left for her parents' household every once in a while on the pretext that the mountain air would do the baby good. When Helga was away from Buenos Aires, Gustavo nearly forgot about her. When she came back, he beat her, and she found herself trapped, because if she had returned from Córdoba it was precisely because she had fought with her mother. It was then that Gustavo enrolled in the Mind Control class. 'Let's see if this guy can fix up my head,' he said after the first class, as we had a drink at the little bar. 'If not, one of these days I'm gonna pulverize that German bitch.' Once Tabi asked him, 'Tell me, Gustavo, why did it matter so much to you that she wasn't a virgin?' Come to think of it, Iñaki, all of this is horribly unpleasant. I don't know why I'm telling it."

"You're telling it so we can get back to that excursion to Las Lilas with the people from the Mind Control class."

"I remember Helga, sitting on the rug in the parlor on the ground floor, holding the baby in one hand and a box of cereal to mix with the formula in the other, listening to Emi very attentively. Reclining on the divan, with her straw hat and a riding crop in her hand, Emi was talking about her superstitions as an actress."

"Was she an actress?"

"Didn't I tell you before? She was a cabaret singer in musical comedies. Pour me a little more tea, Iñaki."

"I'm afraid the samovar isn't here any more, Magdalena."

"What day is it?"

"December twenty-fifth."

"Shouldn't your wife and my husband have arrived at Las Lilas yesterday?"

"They did arrive, Magdalena."

"Was I with them?"

"Of course you were, and then you and Enrique went to sleep."

"Did you give me anything to take before falling asleep?"

"You know I don't give you any medication."

"I don't remember anything that happened before falling asleep. So last night was Christmas Eve?"

"Of course it was."

"I always like to make a toast at midnight on Christmas Eve. Even better if there are presents. It's what I call Jewish Christmas in Saint Petersburg."

"I've spent many of them at your house, Maggi."

"Even though no one thinks about the One who was born in Bethlehem."

"Well, even for those of us from Catholic families, it's hard to imagine a baby God."

"Yes, it isn't easy. Why do I get these little bouts of amnesia?"

"We'll talk about that later."

"Are you tired, Iñaki?"

"I'm perfectly fine."

"Sure, you're a doctor. Doctors never say they're tired. They always have to be ready to help, to serve, to get up at any time of the night and ride across the countryside on horseback to a farmhouse to close some old man's eyes, or bring a baby into the world, or hoist a sick person on their back and carry him to the town hospital to have his appendix operated on before it's too late . . ."

"I think you ought to rest, Magdalena."

Helga was only twenty at the time of the excursion to Las Lilas, and the baby was ten months old. Helga went around carrying him on her back all the time, but it didn't seem to bother her. Gustavo spent nearly the entire time mounted on a very tall horse, just as rigid as he was. He rode the horse back and forth, as stiffly as though he had a wooden spine. It was just the opposite of those plays where a person moves against a phony background: here the background was authentic, while Gustavo and the horse looked like props. Helga, who never spoke, talked quite a bit to Juan Antonio about his life in the country, there in the hills of Córdoba; the rest of the group, ignorant of anything concerning planting, harvesting, or raising animals, listened to her, their mouths agape. She seemed to have much more in common with Juan Antonio than with Gustavo. Even though Gustavo seemed to be concentrating on sitting upright on his horse, he was also listening, and he discovered a new person in Helga, a person who was somewhere between raw and refined, provincial and urban.

On our second day at Las Lilas, I offered to take care of the baby for a while so Helga could go horseback riding. Ten minutes later, as I pushed the little stroller among the eucalyptus trees, I saw her dashing across the countryside like an exhalation, riding bareback on a sorrel horse. Gustavo, who was still posing on top of his mount, saw her ride by also, and remained there with his mouth hanging open. Immediately he looked around, searching for the child, and he saw me with the stroller, coming out of the eucalyptus grove and heading for the wide expanse of lawn with planters filled with lilacs.

"Breakfast is served."

"Where are Iñaki and Enrique?"

"They had an early breakfast and went out walking."

"All four of us haven't been together since you arrived."

"Iñaki thinks it's better for you to be with only one person at a time."

"Aren't I better?"

"You're not sick, Maggi, just very tired."

"Am I having a breakdown from exhaustion?"

"Yes."

"That's what I thought. You're both so good to me, Flora."

"We love you very much, and besides, we have all the time in the world. Don't forget how old we are. My children can take care of themselves now. Iñaki goes to meetings mostly to amuse himself; he knows more than all those doctors put together. Now let's have breakfast."

"Café au lait with croissants, butter, and homemade *dulce de leche* from the *estancia*?"

"I'm afraid it's going to have to be non-fat yogurt, half a grape-fruit, and coffee."

"Shit. Tell me again how old you are, Flora."

"I'm sixty-two; Iñaki's sixty-eight."

"But you're as robust as a couple of apples."

"Thanks, Maggi."

"Today I feel a curious interest in everyone, including those who don't interest me. As I was telling the story of Gustavo and Helga, I was wondering why I told it in such detail. Could it be I'm fond of them?"

"Why not? But you said you'd talk about Inés today."

"I never said I'd talk about Inés, and you can't make me believe I did, no matter how much my little bouts of amnesia may prevent me from swearing I didn't. You want to make me think I said so in order to have me try to follow some logical order. I prefer chaos. I'd rather throw myself off the edge of a cliff headfirst into a raging river filled with crocodiles and kill them one by one with a knife held between my teeth. Inés is a psychologist."

"A child psychologist, right?"

"Yes. It's something she has a real passion for. Luckily there are some people who have the calling to devote themselves to children. Teaching them, healing them, dressing them, entertaining them. They use their imagination to serve children. Others do the same with old people. If someone ever tries to entertain me when I'm old, I'll kill him. I don't know much about Inés's family. When I met her, her father had died and her mother was a retired teacher, a very polite person who always wore a hat. Well-dressed. The same could be said of Inés, although she's constantly battling her weight. When we arrived at Las Lilas, she had just spent two weeks at a weight-loss clinic in Córdoba, and she looked pretty good. But she couldn't compete with Tabi. Inés was nicer than Tabi, and I think she was a better person, but Tabi was more attractive."

"Am I mistaken, or have we gotten to the topic of sex?"

"It's possible we're getting there. Tabi was Juan Antonio's lover."

"How do you know?"

"We're not trying to find out how I know things here, just what happened. If I tell you what happened between Juan Antonio and Tabi, it's so you'll understand what took place here at Las Lilas. I'm a little tired."

"Let's go for a sulky ride while it's still cool, and later we'll continue talking in the pool. Do you want more coffee?"

"Half coffee and half milk."

"How beautiful the countryside is."

"Over there, in the distance, look at Iñaki and Enrique walking along the road between the poplars."

"We'll all have lunch together at one. I've already spoken to the cook."

"I love how the only things that need to be planned here are the meals."

"We were talking about Inés."

"Inés was an enthusiastic, happy person, and it didn't matter if she drank a bit too much. I never saw alcohol have an unpleasant effect on her; it just made her a little happier, or it made her fall sound asleep. A short, failed marriage, with no children, had left her free and ready for adventure."

"Did she want to seduce Juan Antonio?"

"It was obvious."

"Didn't she know what was going on between him and Tabi?"

"I think so, but she didn't care. I don't believe Inés deliberately calculated anything or made plans. Rather, she followed her impulses at any given moment. It's likely, though, that on the *estancia* she may have noticed that the thing between Juan Antonio and Tabi was more serious than she had thought, and that's why she had that accident with the horse. But these are only conjectures."

"How was Inés after they kept her up for several hours to avoid brain damage?"

"I already said that when she woke up she was fine, just a bit sore from the fall."

"I was referring to her mood."

"She was happy, as always, glad she hadn't killed herself in the fall. She drank a little bit more than usual, and she kept up with the others during the excursions and other activities, although of course she didn't ride again."

"And Tabi?"

"She kept to herself, sunbathing, swimming in the pool, showing off her lovely figure. She had a room to herself and . . ."

"Don't tell me Juan Antonio went to her room at night."

"It seems so; we found out because there was a maid who said she'd seen Juan Antonio coming out of Tabi's room."

"Did that scandal have any consequences?"

"No. It was Juan Antonio's word against the maid's. The incident happened Friday night. By Saturday noon everyone's temper had calmed down, and people amused themselves in different ways, waiting for the barbecue to be ready. Juan Antonio had ordered another calf butchered."

7:00 A.M. Magdalena jumped out of bed, seized by sudden happiness. The night before she had gone to bed with the obsessive idea that she didn't want to be called "Magdalena." What if I call myself Marlene instead of Magdalena? She thought the name had been chosen too hurriedly, simply to satisfy a formality, as when they give a newborn the name of the saint on whose day he was born, or his father's name, or his dead grandfather's. "Magdalena" sounded harsh to her, ironed with starch, with a ridge down the middle. The biblical Magdalene, that crybaby, was someone she didn't — and didn't want to — resemble. She didn't like the nicknames, either: "Mag" and "Maggie" sounded foreign; "Magda" still had that ridge down the middle. "Maggi" was just plain stupid. A name change would prove annoying to those who had so generously devoted hours and hours of their time listening to her. But "Marlene" would be easy to remember because it started out just like "Magdalena," and also because of Dietrich. Dietrich was anything but a crybaby, and Magdalena wouldn't have minded resembling her a little. But in life there are destinies and destinies, and the destiny of someone named Magdalena was to be a nice, witty, solicitous woman, eager to be of service.

Naked as a jaybird, she put on her glasses to decipher the numbers on the scale: exactly 121 pounds. She smiled with relief. The day before she had indulged in certain excesses, but it was clear that a single day of excess didn't show up on the scale, and even though 121 wasn't her ideal weight (she really looked good at 105, when her love handles disappeared entirely), at that time of the year she was satisfied with simply not gaining. As she dressed (a black sundress with wide, embroidered straps — how many women my age dare go around without a bra?), Magdalena breathed the perfumed air that came in the window, filtering through the wooden slats of the shutters. It would be just as hot as yesterday. She glanced at Enrique, sleeping soundly on his left side, his back to her.

While Magdalena heated some coffee, the cat drank his milk with quick little laps. She poured it into a medium-sized cup, adding a splash of cold milk from the refrigerator, took four whole-wheat crackers from the tin, and went out the back door of the kitchen into the garden.

The garden was separated by a fence from the neighboring gardens and from the pine woods in back. The children had made an opening in the hedge, through which they passed directly into the woods. Magdalena sat down in a canvas chair, resting the little tray on the round marble table. Her heart was beating fast. What possible reason could she have for being nervous? The next two or three hours belonged to her; Enrique wouldn't get up before ten, and she could go for a walk and come back well after that. Why did she so appreciate these hours of solitude? So she could think. Think about what? About details, most of the time. The more one contemplates details, the more details are left uncontemplated, and it's as if something of unknown value has been lost. She thought she was like her grandmother, who had kept every swatch and scrap of cloth in a dresser drawer, in case she might find a use for them someday. She called them, unceremoniously, rags. Magdalena never saw her grandmother use those rags for anything, but as a girl, she had emptied the drawer many times onto the bedroom floor and had amused herself exploring different textures, thicknesses, and colors, and above all, smells. The smell of age and storage permeated everything else, but she knew how, by sniffing a piece of pale blue georgette crepe with sequins, she could evoke the tenuous fragrance of flowers (lilacs, perhaps? violets?), and she knew that someone had once put on a pale blue georgette crepe dress with sequins and had dabbed herself with perfume in order to find a boyfriend at the dance. There was also that flannel rag that smelled like mustard plaster. She wrinkled up her nose and drained her cup of coffee. Then she stood up a bit abruptly, went back into the kitchen, and left the cup in the sink.

She had the nagging idea that she had neglected to say, upon arising from her chair in the garden, that she had taken the cup, and the little dish and the teaspoon, too, and that if she didn't mention this someone might ask maliciously how it was that she left all that in the kitchen if she hadn't removed it from the little table in the garden beforehand. Annoyed, she looked at her feet. Did everyone know she was wearing white rustic cloth sandals? Rustic cloth, not exactly canvas, but something like sackcloth. She fixed her hair, mussing it a bit with her fingertips and massaging her scalp in the hope of improving the appearance of the outside of her head, and also in order to relieve the pressure on the inside.

What's going on? she asked herself. We'll soon find out, she replied to herself. She went running up the stairs to her room. I think I forgot to say earlier that I went downstairs, she thought, but anyone could figure that out. No, no, no! Mustn't let anyone figure out anything. After all was said and done, remembering and telling the story were like rummaging around in the rag box. She affectionately regarded Enrique's sleeping form, still lying on his left side. Twenty years. We've been together twenty years. Scenes from her life with Enrique during those twenty years rushed through her mind: good times, bad times, vacations, arguments, reconciliations, the time they went to Tigre with the kids, and the time when she tacked sayings from books that impressed her on the walls of the little house, in particular:

AT THAT TIME I WAS TWENTY YEARS OLD, AND I WON'T LET ANYONE CONVINCE ME THAT IT'S THE MOST BEAUTI- FUL TIME OF LIFE.

But she couldn't start reminiscing now. If she had run upstairs it was because she had something urgent to do. She quickly removed her clothing and put on a bathing suit. She slipped her sundress over it. She grabbed a little black coconut-fiber purse and slung it over her shoulder. She ran downstairs. In order to have done this, I must have left the room, she thought. It wasn't necessary to say that. Yes, it was necessary, because one should be coherent. All the details, or none at all. The living room was in shadow, with the blinds drawn. She opened the front door and ran out, letting the door slam shut. Still running, she crossed the small front garden, passed through the wooden gate in the painted white fence, and began running down the paved road to the corner, where she turned right in order to continue running down the side street toward the beach. How nice that we were able to spend this time at Iñaki and Flora's chalet in Mar del Plata, she thought.

Va-a-a-st. Especially now that the beach was deserted. The coastline vanished in the distance, interrupted only by the jetties. The sea was calm, perfectly blue. Interminable rows of tents dotted the sand in bright colors. She ran down the cement stairs; when she reached the sand, she turned right and entered the first in a row of yellow-and-green striped tents. She took off her sundress and slippers, tying them with the rope that hung at the back of the tent. Before going out to the sand she looked at her arms and legs. Quite firm, she said to herself. Still. And with a good suntan . . . She made sure she had her tube of suntan lotion in her little purse, slung it over her shoulder, and started walking toward the shore.

The dock ended at a pile of rocks against which the waves beat with heavy splashes of white foam. She chose a smooth rock to sit on, her legs hanging down. The foam beating against the rocks didn't quite get her wet, but it refreshed the air. Thank you, Dear God, for still allowing my body to enjoy the freshness of the sea.

"You're welcome, my child, you're welcome."

"Who said that?"

"It was I."

"The Big I?"

"Yes, my child."

"Well, since you've appeared to me, may I ask you a favor?"

"I haven't appeared; I've only spoken. Would you like to see my enormous Countenance outlined in the sky?"

"I'd be scared shitless, immense God. Oh! There You are. And I'm not afraid. Your Divine Countenance is outlined in the sky as transparently as a rainbow. It's Michelangelo's portrait of Moses."

"I'm not Moses. I'm the God of the Christians."

"Forgive me, Lord. Aren't you also Jewish?"

"Of course, my child. In my day, the Christians were Jewish."

"But You're not the God of the Jews."

"Oh no, my child, I don't even know that guy."

"Are you the God of all Christians?"

"I believe so."

"Also of the Jehovah's Witnesses?"

"I suppose so."

"Then you protect Sabina, the one who used to clean houses and who looked for a different man every afternoon, and who's now a Jehovah's Witness."

"I shall protect her."

"Will the Jews who behave themselves in this life go to Heaven after they die?"

"If they want to, my child. It's not mandatory."

"Are there many Jews in Your Heaven?"

"A handful."

"And there's no discrimination there?"

"None. We've all learned a little Yiddish."

"Let's not forget the Sephardic Jews, Lord. They don't speak Yiddish."

"We don't get too many of those. I think they go to Jewish Heaven."

"I thought Jews didn't have a Heaven to go to after death. When Freddy found out he was going to die, he went to see a Catholic priest in order to get an immortal soul and a place in Your Heaven."

"I think Freddy did some investigating and found out that there's some kind of Jewish Heaven, but this one has better lighting."

"It's logical Freddy would've considered that aspect of it. He was an architect. Lord! Your Divine Countenance is disappearing!"

"But my voice remains. I bless you, my child, and now I've got to go. I don't have all day to spend with you."

A wave higher than the rest splashed foam at a great height, erasing all the faint traces of the divine face that hadn't already disappeared.

She loped along the hard sand by the shore with an easy gait. How long had she been walking? She decided to impose a limit on herself: up to the next dock, and then she'd begin her return trip. The sun was already very hot. The waves had washed some little snails onto the beach, each one with its little opening. If I were a young girl, I'd make myself a snail necklace, she thought. But I'm not. Nonetheless she bent down and picked up two or three, storing them in her purse. She had reached the dock. She stuck her feet in the water. It wasn't cold. She tied her purse to a post on the dock and went in quickly, tolerating a cold shiver. After the first two or three waves broke on her, she began to enjoy the water. Soon she forgot about everything, submitting to the pure joy of the sea, her gaze on the horizon. She passed the surf line and began swimming parallel to the shore, letting herself be rocked by the gentle, uncrested waves, and returned to the dock. She rode a large wave back to shore. She untied her purse, slung it over her shoulder, and started back, her face to the sun.

December 28
Springtime laughs, and life's flight
opens lilies and dreams in the garden of the world.

Spring? How strange, I thought it was summer. Why strange? Everything is strange. It's a way to sidestep suffering, to survive. Why so much suffering? Did someone die? Many have died, but it's not about that; it's the suffering of having to tell the story. Why is it necessary to tell the story? Every day there are millions of stories that go without being told. But if you begin to tell a story, you have to finish telling it. And what if you don't? That would be a failure. A failure for the one telling it, or for the listener? A failure for the one telling it, and a cruel frustration for the listener. What would you like to do? Go back to bed; spend all day in bed reading, dreaming, and getting up only occasionally to go to the kitchen and make myself a cup of tea with milk and some Canale biscuits. Canale biscuits floating like sponges in the tea with milk? Yes, and the bedroom door open to the patio. It's spring; winter has hardly gone away, and a broad, diagonal band of sunlight dotted with dust motes shines in. If I open the middle door of the three-piece wardrobe and stand right opposite, with the edge of the door against my stomach, I can make a circular movement with my leg in front of the mirror, and it looks like I'm riding a bicycle in a special way, moving both legs in the same direction. And when I'm sure she's not there, I can open the forbidden drawer of the wardrobe and take out the purple lacquered box with a Japanese girl painted on the cover, open it, and look at the cufflinks and the tie pin, the ID photos where you can already notice how tense, how taut, my father's face looks, and the announcement cut out of the newspaper, and the note that describes the educator, the poet.

Later, the pressure in my chest relents, my tears dry up, and I walk in the park with its vast expanses of lawn, its little pine and poplar groves. Where am I going? Who knows. Is breakfast ready? Are we having breakfast again?

"I, for one, like to have breakfast every morning, Magdalena. A peach, some yogurt, cornflakes. Coffee with milk and whole-wheat crackers."

"Not so bad. Everything seems better after breakfast. *It's not just fire that burns between us.*"

"Shall we go down the path lined with ancient trees, at the edge of the canal?"

"Yes, and watch the barges go by carrying tree trunks."

"And the lunch boat."

"And another fast little boat, one that makes you realize how time has flown by."

"And also a narrow, gray boat, propelled with a single oar by a skinny man with sunken eyes."

"The man and the boat look black, outlined against the twilight sky, Iñaki."

"Yes."

"Where are we?"

"On that excursion to Las Lilas."

"Eusebio took Enrique and me in his car. Eusebio and Marina rode in the front, with us in back, along with his two annoying kids. Eusebio is from La Rioja; even though he's been here a long time, he still retains a bit of the Riojan accent and placid character. It helps him with publicity, and he earns good money, but he never stops complaining about how impossible it is to devote himself entirely to painting; I suppose that's why he talks so much about the Blank Canvas and the Death of Art. That's what we were discussing in our conversations in the little bar, because in the Mind Control class they don't deal with personal problems, just how to control the mind so it won't control us."

"So that's what the class is about?"

"What else? Delving into the investigation of causes, as they do in psychoanalysis, doesn't bring about quick results. In Freud's day a lady could allow herself the luxury of languishing on a divan for years while she extracted increasingly terrible things from her subconscious, but the closer we get to the year 2000, the more urgent the need becomes to search for quicker devices, before the hand that keeps us from falling off the cliff loses its grip."

"Are you holding on tight right now?"

"Yes, ever since Enrique yanked me up."

"Enrique's gone back to Bolivia."

"But we had a talk last night. He told me you recommended that I stay here a little longer, that it would be convenient for me to cling to you like a boulder . . ."

". . . at the edge of a cliff."

"Your head is on straighter than mine, Iñaki. Everything inside my head has come loose; my brains are dancing."

"It's stress."

"I suppose it's pointless to ask you how long we're going to stay on the island."

"As long as you like. From Tigre, we'll go to Las Lilas and Mar del Plata as many times as you want."

"Also to Córdoba and to Embalse de Río Tercero."

"Fine."

"In the Mind Control classes we never spoke about our problems, but after class we'd hang around the little bar. Whenever Eusebio had a few drinks, he would complain about his wife. It seems she didn't want to have sex with him."

"What's this business about 'having sex'?"

"That's how North Americans say it, and it seems quite adequate to me. 'Have' can mean many things in English: *have* a cigarette, *have* a cup of coffee, *have* sex. I'd never use a popular or slang equivalent even if you killed me; it would be like setting the table with a linen tablecloth and fine china, silverware, and crystal, and instead of napkins, throwing a dishcloth on the table."

"All right, then, let's say Marina didn't want to have sex with Eusebio."

"Really that's not as important as the way Eusebio described it. He said every night his wife went to bed early and slept like a log. And there he was, sitting in the living room with a hard-on. Let's make one thing clear: I'm not the one who says 'with a hard-on.' It was he who said it."

"Fine. Marina sleeping like a log and Eusebio in the living room, with a hard-on."

"The people listening to him suggested different things. There's nothing like revealing a problem to friends around a coffee table for getting everyone to express an opinion and give advice. One person told him to take his wife on vacation; another said he should try talking to her; a third person thought he should try to force her, and still another said he should look for another woman. I didn't say a word, but I sympathized with Eusebio. I thought she could have made a small effort and granted him that pleasure. On the other hand, I know quite well that sometimes a small effort isn't sufficient, and a huge effort is nonsensical; it doesn't do any good."

"Didn't Eusebio find any solution?"

"No. He went on to talk about the Blank Canvas and the Death of Art."

"Shall we sit down on this abandoned dock?"

"Yes. What lovely wisteria."

"You were saying that you and Enrique went to Las Lilas with Eusebio and his family."

"Yes. When we turned off the highway and onto the dirt path leading to the entrance of the *estancia*, I was filled with happiness. The treetops joined together in the middle, forming a canopy of leaves. The same thing happened after we passed through the door, along the path leading to the house."

"Let me remind you that we've already spoken about your arrival at the *estancia* and the dinner that night . . ."

"Yes, yes, I know. We're up to midday on Saturday. People are waiting for the barbecue to be ready. Meanwhile, they're eating sausages between two pieces of crusty bread, accompanied by a nice red wine that Eusebio drove into town to buy when he realized that Juan Antonio wasn't about to open his wine cellar again. Sausages and red wine are the local version of what the characters in postwar Italian novels eat when they stop alongside the road on their hikes in the woods and mountains. The translation said: 'We ate sausages and drank the harsh wine of the country.' "

"In the original it almost certainly said '*del paese*;' that is, not of the country, but rather of the village, the region."

"A bad translation, then. But it was lovely to imagine those two friends seated in the shade of a tree, on the mountainside, looking down on the valley below. The little red-roofed houses, some hay-stacks, a priest on a bicycle disappearing from view down a little road. And while they eat the sausages and drink the harsh wine of the region, the two friends discuss philosophical topics: life and death, the passage of time . . ."

"And somewhere far off, the commotion of the city continues: gray factories, leaden skies . . ."

"Yes. Iñaki, at some point, in spite of everything, I'd like to go back. The country is marvelous, and the island, and the mountains, and the sea. But I'd like to go back to Buenos Aires, even for just a week, take a bus to an unknown street corner, to an apartment building where I have to use the intercom to get up to the sixth floor, apartment B."

"What for?"

"It doesn't matter what for. Just to do it."

"Agreed. But not now. You have a job to do. You can't leave the story unfinished."

"How you've changed, Iñaki."

"I've changed?"

"Yes. Before, you were a sixty-eight-year-old gentleman who traveled with his wife to Mar del Plata to open up their summer house, and who asked for a recommendation of a good place for breakfast."

"It's true. But I'm still sixty-eight."

"Yes, and it appears you're in charge of my health."

"That's right. That's why I came back from the conference in Vienna."

"You shouldn't tell me things like that on the Day of the Holy Innocents, Iñaki."

I feel lazy; I don't know what I want. My eyes are closing, but I can't sleep. I lie down, stretch, turn face down, on my left side, on my right. I miss the city. The noise of the cars, the telephone calls. I can't return to Buenos Aires until I manage to remember certain things that happened during those days at Las Lilas. It's useless to say nothing else happened; they seem to think something serious happened, something only I know about. If it didn't concern three people who love me like Enrique, Iñaki, and Flora, I'd think they had gone crazy. However, I don't think that's what it is, because I was the one who agreed to come to Las Lilas years after that excursion. Iñaki is infinitely patient; he lets me talk about anything at all in the hopes that I'll return to the story. But now I don't want to talk; I'd rather have some tea with milk.

"Room service?"

"At your service, but — where do you think we are?"

"At the Majestic Hotel in Tandil."

"You're not mistaken. But remember that the Majestic Hotel hasn't been in existence for a while. I think that the building is occupied by a branch office of the University."

"You're not sure?"

"No."

"Can you bring me the tea anyway?"

"Yes, but remember that this is 1939, and you're only six years old."

"I'm six years old. If I weren't, I wouldn't be asking you for tea with milk and Canale biscuits."

"I don't know if I should be accepting a room service order from a child. Does your mommy know you ordered tea?"

"Yes, miss."

"A waiter will bring it to you in ten minutes."

(*Ten minutes later*).

"Here you are, miss. What do you plan to do this afternoon?"

"Climb up to the top of the mountain."

"Will you go all by yourself?"

"I always go with mama, papa, and my little brother, but it's just like they aren't there."

"What can you see from up there? I'm always down here, serving tea with milk in the hotel."

"Some cannons from I-don't-know-which war. And I think you can see the Moving Stone."

"Aren't you sure?"

"No. I think the stone fell down a long time ago and they want to put it back in its place."

"And then?"

"Then we'll climb down the mountain and come back to the hotel."

"Will you eat roast beef and mashed potatoes?"

"Like I always do."

"Aren't you a little bored with being a child?"

"Yeah. They drag me back and forth like a package."

"Excuse me, is the young lady Jewish?"

"Why do you want to know?"

"Sheer curiosity."

"Tell me why you want to know and I'll answer you."

"Out of curiosity."

"And if I tell you I'm Jewish, what else will you want to know?"

"Nothing else, miss."

"Then you're not curious. You're an idiot."

"Why do you say that, miss?"

"I tell you I'm Jewish and what do you do? You're thinking, 'She's Jewish and I'm not.'"

"No, miss, I'm not thinking anything."

"You're not just an idiot—you're a wacko. Aren't you interested in knowing what it means to be Jewish? Or not to be Jewish?"

"I think I know."

"No, you don't know. I don't even know. I'm just starting to find out. Being a Jew means having grandparents who speak broken Spanish; understanding and speaking Yiddish or not wanting to speak or understand it; not having First Communion and not going to Heaven after you die. Not being Jewish means saying your own first and last names calmly when someone asks you what your name is; making the sign of the cross when you pass by a church; and being able to enjoy the vision of God after you die; and above all else saving little pictures with prayers in between the pages of your reader."

"Do you want me to get you some of those little pictures?"

"Thanks, but I have good friends who gave me some."

"Did you memorize the prayers?"

"Yes."

"Do you say them?"

"You want to know if Jews pray?"

"Yes, miss, I'm very curious."

"They pray. There are also some Jews who don't pray. What else do you want to know?"

"Nothing else, miss."

"Even as a snoop you're a failure. Just take the tray away. I refuse to drink this tea with milk; the biscuits are floating around in the cup like rags."

"Have a nice walk, miss."

(The girl keeps walking around the room, muttering things under her breath. A female voice is heard offstage):

"Magdalena!"

MAGDALENA *(in a soft voice, as though talking to herself)*: Shit! They're still calling me Magdalena. *(shouting):* Yes, mama?

VOICE OFFSTAGE: Are you ready to climb to the top of the mountain?

MAGDALENA: Yes, mama!

VOICE OFFSTAGE: Come down to the dining room first. I'm going to give you a nice, freshly laid egg with sugar and port!

MAGDALENA *(to herself, in a soft voice):* I can't believe that here in Tandil they have chickens that lay nice little eggs so I can eat them with sugar and port that can fortify me in who-knows-what way. That cocktail is delicious, but it makes my legs feel weak. *(even more softly):* But if I say so, they surely won't give it to me any more. *(shouting):* Coming!

(Magdalena, Iñaki, and Flora, seated in lawn chairs around a small marble table, on a large patio surrounded by plants behind the house at Las Lilas. From here one can see a backdrop of waving fields, green, reddish, yellow. It's the hour just before twilight.)

IÑAKI: Well, Marlene — You see, we're calling you Marlene, in accordance with your wishes. Here we are, all three of us, just as you requested.

MARLENE: Thanks. It seems as though you live just to satisfy my wishes. But you won't let me go back to Buenos Aires. Besides, I have to use an unfamiliar form of the pronoun "you," and that makes me feel inauthentic.

IÑAKI: If you like, we can go back to normal usage.

MARLENE: Don't you see how ugly it sounds? It doesn't seem like serious theater.

FLORA: Is this theater?

MARLENE: Yes and no. It's easier to announce beforehand the name of the person who's about to speak than to have to add "so-and-so said" every few minutes.

IÑAKI: You suggested that all three of us have a conversation, Marlene.

MARLENE: Yes. Do you remember when we had those conversations in Mar del Plata, in that breakfast place I recommended?

FLORA: Yes, I remember quite well.

MARLENE: At that time you didn't even know your own names.

FLORA: It's true. But this is something that doesn't only happen to Central European Jews or to Basques. It happens to Italians, too. They told me about a young man who went to . . . I can't remember what the place was called, but it's the equivalent of the municipal hall of records in Rome, to complete the paperwork to get married. "Father's name?" the clerk asked. The young man told him. "Mother's name?" The young man scratched his head silently and finally answered: *"Be, non so." "Ma come non sai!"* the clerk exclaimed. *"Non so,"* the young man repeated, *"Io la chiamo mamma."*

MARLENE: It wouldn't be a big deal if each one didn't know the other's name. It's just that neither of you was sure of your own name.

IÑAKI: You, of all people, talking about name insecurity!

MARLENE: You frighten me, Iñaki.

IÑAKI: What is it that frightens you? That I let a bit of impatience slip out? I've been listening to you for days and days, in the hopes that you'll finish telling me the story of that excursion to Las Lilas once and for all. I left the conference in Vienna, where I so enjoy my hot chocolate and strudel with my colleagues, because Enrique summoned me, and . . .

MARLENE: What did he tell you?

Marlene opened her eyes and saw a milky brightness filtering through the slats of the blinds. She turned over so she could continue sleeping, but a stitch on the right side of her head stopped her halfway. If she went back to sleep and the stitch became a distinct pain, she'd wake up later feeling much worse. She groped for an aspirin in the night-table drawer, chewed it up so it would work quickly, and washed it down with a sip of water from the glass that was on the table. It was six o'clock. She stretched out under the sheet. Enrique was fast asleep, lying on his left side with his back to her. Marlene would have liked to hug him and go back to sleep, but she didn't do it, in order not to awaken him.

The stitch in her head was mild, but annoying enough to keep her from sleeping. She thought perhaps it would be a good idea to get up and declare the day officially begun; the cool breeze filtering through the openings in the blinds and the singing of the birds were inviting, but she still felt the heaviness of sleep in her arms and legs. She tried to loosen the tension in her shoulder and neck to get rid of the stitch. Those headaches were apparently produced by cervical tension. It wasn't clear exactly what produced the cervical tension, but it was sufficient to attribute it vaguely to the pressures of daily life.

That's why I'm here at Las Lilas, Marlene thought. To free myself of the pressures of daily life and to reconstruct the story, to tell Iñaki what happened right here with my Mind Control classmates. Marlene moved about in bed, enjoying the soft texture of the sheet. The stitch had almost disappeared. In order to tell Iñaki about it, I have to begin by remembering it myself, she said to herself.

She closed her eyes. She was completely awake, thinking about the people in the class, when the face of Alcides, the teacher, appeared before her. He was a man of about thirty-five, dark and thin, with regular features. The seriousness of his expression revealed that not only was he not laughing at that moment, but that he never laughed. His hazel, almost feverish eyes suggested a kind of fanaticism that made Marlene uneasy. If someone had asked her why she remained in the Mind Control class, in spite of everything, she would have replied that it was because Flora, a dear friend, was in it, and she was only following that Buenos Aires tradition of accompanying her friends to whatever classes they chose to take, as if she lacked an investigative spirit and didn't read the ads in the paper regularly enough to find classes for herself on her own.

The day she attended the first class, in an old building on Avenida de Mayo, she was surprised by the contrast between the ordinary appearance of the students and the ascetic demeanor of the teacher, who was dressed in a tan suit and worn-out but very shiny moccasins. When Marlene entered the room and silently occupied a place in the small semicircle of seats, the teacher was standing with his back to them, drawing a graph on the board, and she concentrated on his moccasins; she couldn't help imagining the teacher furiously polishing them. When he turned around, Marlene trembled. That dark, thin face, those feverish eyes, were exactly as she had imagined they would be while he was facing the other way.

If she had followed her instincts, that would have been her first and last class session. The teacher was demonstrating an exercise to enter the alpha state, or simply "to enter alpha," as they would say after they became used to it. The alpha state, as Marlene experienced it when they put it into practice, was a very pleasant state of deep physical and mental relaxation, which was reached by concentrating on a series of sequenced images. The series was easy to memorize; after a few practice sessions with the teacher, Marlene no longer needed to consult her notes.

The first step was to sit comfortably with one's feet together, knees separated and hands resting on the thighs, closer to the groin than to the knees, so that they wouldn't fall off if one fell asleep. But it was preferable not to fall asleep if at all possible, because to enter alpha one must keep one's mind very clear, concentrating on the prescribed images: total rest for mind and body.

Once one had assumed that position, one had to observe "the contents of the mind." Marlene imagined her mind like a space with a thousand doors and windows through which thousands of objects and beings went in and out in rapid transformation; that chaos made her feel panicky, and she quickly passed into the second state, which consisted of sighing or yawning and then mentally repeating the word "calm," *c-a-a-alm*, several times. After feeling a certain relief from tension, she began to visualize the sequenced images:

1. Imagine that one is in the middle of a beautiful landscape, sitting in a comfortable chair, which Marlene placed on a mountainside. At her feet, a little brook ran rapidly; a gentle breeze was blowing; there were trees and a vast blue sky.

2. A white cloud in the vast blue sky, and outlined against the white cloud, a red cask.

3. With all deliberate slowness, the red cask was replaced by an orange one, the orange one by a yellow one, and so on consecutively by green, blue, violet, lilac, sky blue, white, and gold.

End of the first series.

4. Imagine a pretty red door (it could be standing alone in the middle of a landscape, without any building around it, as in surrealist paintings); open the door and find a descending staircase (as in *Ali Baba*, as in *Alice in Wonderland*, as in *The Pink Panther*). The staircase has twenty-one steps. Slowly descend (Step twenty-one. Twenty. Lo-o-o-wer. Nineteen. De-e-e-per, the teacher said during group practice in class).

5. At the foot of the stairs looms the Golden Temple. I admire it. I am that temple; it is my Being, my intimate essence. Inside the temple, I admire the columns, the pulpits, the arcades, the stained-glass windows.

6. I walk twelve steps to the right. I stop and see a red flame, like a candle flame, but taller than an average-sized person. Then an orange flame. Then a yellow one, a green one . . . Toward the end of the series of flames, a human form begins to emerge in each one of them, and on reaching the last one, the golden one, it becomes three dimensional: it's alive; it smiles *and looks at me with its kind eyes*. It's a man (to tell the truth, the teacher didn't indicate if it should be a man or a woman, so Marlene chose whichever came to mind). I greet him with a slight nod, and I continue into my . . .

7. Mental Laboratory. There were no indications of what the laboratory should be like, only that one should imagine oneself sitting in a comfortable chair next to a blank screen. Then one had to pronounce this enigmatic phrase mentally: "I see the blank screen, *with the frame I made myself.*" Marlene never asked, that day or ever, what importance there was in the fact that one had made the frame oneself or why one had made it oneself, or anything else that might have clarified the matter. If there were doors rising in the middle of a field without any support, why couldn't it be possible for someone to make a frame for a screen, or rather that someone had already made one? Admitting her ineptitude at manual labor, Marlene imagined a simple tubular aluminum frame painted shiny white, and she couldn't help seeing herself standing in front of an enormous carpenter's bench, "making" it, although she didn't exactly know how.

But there she was, sitting in the comfortable chair with a red button on the right armrest for turning on the screen (of a television? It didn't matter; what mattered was seeing the screen). Then: I have a red tomato inside my head. I press the button. The screen lights up and the tomato appears. The tomato is cut in half all by itself: each half squeezes itself into a glass that fills to the brim with tomato juice. Then everything disappears and the screen goes blank. "I see the blank screen, *with the frame I made myself.*" Then: I have an orange inside my head. Same process as with the tomato, until you get to: "I see the blank screen . . ." Nothing else. One doesn't go through all the colors of the rainbow here. Instead, one sees a black screen. On the black screen an invisible hand writes my name: MARLENE. And underneath: WORLD.

8. Once the name and the word WORLD are erased, *from left to right*, the *programming* begins. One can program oneself to succeed in a job interview, to cure a loved one, rubbing him with gilt on the supposedly affected part (if he has a stomach ulcer, or if he's touched in the head . . .).

Marlene felt a noticeable sense of well-being in her motionless body; she didn't need to change position. Since the first part of the exercise, she had experienced an agreeable twinge in her hands, great relaxation in her entire body, regular breathing. Judging from the results, it was a good exercise. What did such inexplicable things — or things without explanation — matter? Does everything in life have an explanation?

At the other end of the semicircle sits Flora, dear Flora. A bit chubby, Flora didn't struggle with her excess pounds or her gray hair, which she kept very nicely groomed, because she thought the best way to stay young-looking at sixty-two was not to try to hide the signs of age, but rather to show them off to their greatest advantage. The wife of a respected physician, Flora epitomized, in Marlene's opinion, the ideal of peace and tranquility that she herself might never (*never!* what a dramatic word, Marlene said to herself, interrupting her own train of thought) achieve. But, do I really want that? she asked herself. And immediately she responded that if she allowed herself to digress she'd never finish recalling what had really happened at Las Lilas during that strange visit.

Next to Flora, at the opposite end of the semicircle of seats, was Gustavo, the TV actor; next to Gustavo was Tabi, the architect; then Freddy, who was also an architect and who, Marlene thought, unable to control herself, had left the class on account of death, his own. Ashamed of her frivolity, Marlene tried fruitlessly to think about Freddy's premature death more seriously, although no longer with grief, because she had genuinely felt grief and horror when she learned of the fatal prognosis, and after the cruel outcome, those feelings had faded over time. But she couldn't do it, and she chased Freddy's image from her mind by using a simple device: she thought about something else. Or about someone else: Helga, for example, sitting next to Freddy, with her straight blonde hair and her scrubbed German face, her big green eyes staring into the teacher's. Next to Helga, beside Marlene, was Juan Antonio, Flora's friend and, in fact, the person who had brought her to the Mind Control class, when Flora had to take care of three grandchildren because her daughter Ana María had come down with hepatitis. What Flora was looking for in the Mind Control class was obvious: to restore peace in her household, which had been destroyed by seven-year-old Nicolás, four-year-old Ana, and Cecilia, a six-month-old baby.

Marlene stretched her arms and legs contentedly. The stitch in her head had disappeared. She sighed out loud and enjoyed her feeling of well-being for a few seconds as she watched Enrique, who was still sleeping in the same position. Then she arose from the bed with flexible movements. (*Deliberately* flexible, she thought. But for how long? This question popped up frequently, although she tried not to think about it. After all, she was only fifty-eight. Hadn't there been ballerinas who danced till eighty? Wasn't Sandro Pertini president of Italy until he was eighty-eight? And Svetlana Stalin? Enough, enough, enough!) And Inés? Wasn't she among those attending class that day? Of course she was. She had arrived late, ostentatiously made up and bejeweled, in a cloud of Diorissimo. She had brought over a chair from the back of the room and placed herself in the second row, behind Juan Antonio. Marlene heard her rapid breathing; she surely had run up the stairs.

"Marlene . . ?"

"Yes, Iñaki?"

"I've been reading over these notes."

"Yes, Iñaki?"

"I think you've provided a brief profile of the group of Mind Control students who went to Las Lilas. Now it's time to head directly for the facts. We had gotten up to Saturday, the second day at the *estancia*."

"All the students from the class were there during those days, except Flora, who was with you in Vienna."

"Exactly. I was at a meeting, and Flora had gone along with me. In the ten days we were there, we each gained nine pounds thanks to a diet of hot chocolate and strudel."

"And then you lost it all by fasting."

"Yes, Marlene."

"I'm tired, Iñaki. Detailed stories wear me out. I think I should have said 'orderly' stories, or . . ."

"How did all of you find Alcides Ibáñez Regidor's address?"

"Oh, but that came after Las Lilas; it was when we returned to Buenos Aires. You're getting me confused, Iñaki."

"No, please. Let's go backward, then."

"Couldn't we continue this afternoon? I'm really tired."

"Are you beginning to remember?"

"Possibly. But I can't get ahead of myself; it's like a skein of yarn that's coming unwound. I can't see the innermost part."

"I'm not asking you to get ahead of yourself. If you're tired, we can continue in the afternoon."

"It's a splendid morning. Let's go down to the beach."

"We're at Las Lilas, Marlene."

"Let's go to the beach in Juan Antonio's plane."

"Would you mind going alone and leaving me here to read your notes?"

Marlene stretched a canvas mat out on the sand in front of the tent. She had hung her purse up in the back, tied with a piece of rope, and her black sundress was folded over the purse. It was a perfect morning, not too hot. Marlene placed the radio, which was playing frivolous but pleasant music, at one end of the mat; in another corner a book; in the third, her sackcloth sandals; and then she sat down to apply suntan lotion, afterward placing the plastic tube in the free corner, thus keeping the mat from being shifted by the wind. The fragrance of the suntan lotion was as stimulating as the smell of the sea; in fact, the combination was intoxicating (I'm crazy, I'm crazy; why did I think the towel was folded in quarters, but I didn't think about the color of the towel or the mat?). The mat was orange and the towel violet, she immediately thought, unparenthetically. What a pain, she thought, having to be here for who knows how long, face-down on a canvas mat with my head resting on a towel.

"You didn't know the others very well when you accepted the invitation to go to Las Lilas, did you?"

"Iñaki! You don't know how much I appreciate it that you came."

"I thought maybe you'd like to continue with the story now instead of waiting till afternoon."

"Luckily Juan Antonio has another plane."

"Luckily."

"Only now we have two planes here at the beach. What do we need two of them for?"

"I sent back the one that brought me, along with the pilot, in case Flora should want to go anywhere in a hurry."

"Flora Rauschenburg?"

"We said we weren't going to consult the telephone directory, Marlene."

"Are you really sixty-eight, Iñaki?"

"Yes."

"No one would guess."

"Please. Let's get back to our job. You didn't know the other people very well when you accepted the invitation to go to Las Lilas, right?"

"No. I knew Juan Antonio and Emi were friends of yours, and that they often invited you to the *estancia*."

"Yes, but not so much lately."

"*Alors*. Excuse me for interjecting a French word into another language, but here it seems perfect to say '*alors*.'"

"Marlene, why don't you tell me once and for all what you saw at the *estancia* that affected you so strongly."

"If you think I know and I don't want to say, oh how wrong you are! Whenever I talk, it's like pulling a thread, and the thread will bring out what we're waiting for."

"I wonder if you really don't know or if you don't remember."

"I'm impressed by your use of such informal address. I think it would have sounded better for you to say, 'I wonder if you really don't know, Miss Marlene, or if you don't remember.'"

"That's just one of your many strategies for changing the subject."

"Now that I think of it, I don't like the name Marlene, either."

"That's another one."

"I don't recognize you, Iñaki. You never were so rude before."

"I'm sorry. Let's go for a dip and then have lunch. It's after one already."

"Let's sit here, at the edge of the terrace. There's a lovely breeze under the canopy. What would you like to eat?"

"An avocado and crayfish salad, with strawberries and cream, and coffee."

"White wine?"

"Yes. Look at those sailboats, Iñaki."

"The sea looks like a mirror."

"When I offered to take care of the baby for Helga . . . I don't really know why I did it. We had been talking about how demanding babies are. I'm old enough to be Helga's mother. And the baby's grandmother."

"Yes."

"It's easy to say, but . . ."

"But hard to swallow."

"Yes, Iñaki."

"Did you want to be the same age as Helga?"

"At that time Helga was twenty years old, and I won't let anyone convince me . . ."

"Did you want to be the same age as Helga?"

"I think so. When I saw how anxious she was, and how pretty. Her anxiety made her look even prettier. When she passed in front of me, galloping with her blonde hair flying in the wind, and her anxious face so radiant . . . I was almost sure she was going to meet someone."

"But you didn't tell anybody."

"What was I supposed to say? That Helga's expression made me uneasy as I watched her ride away? Almost all the guests went out riding. I'm afraid, Iñaki."

"Now?"

"Yes, now. I'm very much afraid of finding out something that I might not want to know."

"You can't go on this way, either. Enrique and the children are waiting for you in Buenos Aires so you can resume your life with them and go on a real vacation, to a real place. For how long did you watch Helga's baby?"

"A few minutes. Gustavo came right away and said, 'Gotta feed the kid's face.' I offered to help him, because I had noticed that he never participated in taking care of the baby, and he accepted. We both went to the dining room, where we had eaten breakfast. There were several mothers trying to shove puréed squash and mashed bananas into their kids' mouths, accompanied by crying, pleading, stories, and threats; it's common knowledge that when children are taken out of their usual environment they become unbearable. Helga and Gustavo's was pretty calm, or else he was really hungry, I don't know. But anyway he swallowed his baby food right down, and Gustavo went back to the room with him."

"And then what happened?"

"Nearly everyone went to take a siesta. I stuck around, waiting for Helga to come back. I told myself it was none of my business, that I had no reason to be worried. But I never take a siesta. I simply can't fall asleep during the day. So I waited around, sitting in a wicker chair on the verandah at the back of the house, looking out toward where I had watched Helga disappear."

"And nothing?"

"Nothing. Five o'clock rolled around, and everyone went out to the garden for tea. I noticed Juan Antonio was missing, although he had always been there for meals. Tea was served with great fanfare, on cloth tablecloths spread out on the lawn. Such refinement was quite remarkable, compared to how primitive the barbecue had been, with people getting drunk on red wine and gnawing all the little bones to the last morsel. A pity for the sacrificial calf."

"A pity? Didn't they do it honor?"

"I was thinking about the calf. Or didn't she have an immortal soul?"

"That kind of irony sounds like something your grandfather, the freethinker, would have said."

"My grandfather would be completely old-fashioned today. Today it's in to believe in something."

"To believe in something, to go on a diet, to return to nature."

"May God bless us all, Iñaki."

"And Helga? When did she return?"

"I'd be tempted to tell you, dear Iñaki, that Helga never returned. And that the child was raised by nuns, and that Gustavo lost his powers of speech and never got off the horse again, that he went riding into the sunset of the screen to film soap operas. But Helga did return, Iñaki; she returned, and how!"

By Saturday afternoon we were all very tired of being there, especially those who had brought their children along. The very idea of pulling little kids out of their homes to take them on vacation is a big deal in and of itself; to take them away for two or three days to a place where they're going to be uncomfortable is a kind of insanity.

The kids miss their houses; they refuse to eat the food; they want mama or papa to carry them in their arms all the time; or else you have to go around watching where they're climbing or what poisonous fruit they might be ingesting; or else they simply disappear, and you have to organize posses with powerful flashlights to go looking for them, because they usually get lost at nightfall. Now I have a kind of respite from them until the grandchildren start to arrive, and I think I have the right to take advantage of it without having some little angel — who isn't even a relative of mine — spit the contents of his spoon in my eye, or scare me to death by climbing out on a fragile limb.

Helga's baby was delightful, however. He emptied his bottles like a suction pump; it didn't matter to him if someone other than his mommy changed his diapers; and in general, he seemed happy to be sitting on a canvas mat on the lawn, fingering his plastic toys endlessly. But that afternoon, until twilight fell and the guests who had remained in the garden after tea saw Helga's figure outlined on the sorrel horse in the distance, I was afraid that baby had been left motherless.

When Helga and the horse were close enough (the animal advanced, at a trot), those of us who were gathered in the garden could appreciate the state in which she was returning, with her blouse torn and her pants covered with mud, just like her boots. But there was something in her face, all scratched and dirty, there was something proud and furious in her face, that stifled the questions we all would have liked to ask her. It was a pure stroke of luck that the moment Helga dismounted in front of all of us and climbed the porch stairs to enter the house, Gustavo was busy giving the baby his bottle, with the help of one of the women in the kitchen. Helga disappeared into the house without saying a word, and we saw her again only when she appeared in the parlor on the first floor before dinner.

As usual, Emi was seated on a divan with her straw hat and a riding crop in her hand, talking endlessly. The guests, seated on pillows and on the carpet, formed a semicircle around the divan like a small entourage that seemed to drink up her words. Tabi, who had acquired a nice tan with her careful sunbathing, looked toward the entryway with poorly feigned indifference, perhaps because Juan Antonio hadn't been seen all afternoon. Inés laughed too loud at whatever Emi was saying, but she was really as uneasy as Tabi. Eusebio and Marina were sitting next to each other, very serious and bored, without ever taking their eyes off Emi's face, as if they expected it to break out in a sudden rash. Gustavo was standing, leaning against a marble column, unable to hide a certain deep anger. He didn't move a muscle, but his eyes shifted every so often to the marble staircase that Helga was supposed to descend. When she finally appeared at the top of the stairs, Emi was the only one who didn't look at her. Helga radiated all the beauty of her twenty years, her flexible body wrapped in a pale blue dress that had belonged to her mother, her straight blonde hair freshly washed, her green eyes in that Nordic face. I think Emi preferred not to look at her, because inevitably she would have had to compare that svelte figure with her own somewhat shapeless form lying on the divan.

"Shall we go back to the beach?"

"No, Iñaki, let's go to the chalet. It's a real stroke of luck that you and Flora have that chalet in Mar del Plata, so we can go visit whenever I feel like it."

"Yes, everything's turned out just right."

"Let's walk down the avenue a little."

"The sun's so hot you could fry eggs on the pavement."

"What a way to talk! I wonder if General Parlance would understand you. Whatever could have happened to him?"

"He's still at the Richmond, eating cheese sandwiches on white bread and drinking soda. In the afternoon he has a whiskey, but just one."

"Sometimes I wonder if the Richmond still exists. If Buenos Aires still exists."

"Oh?"

"Well, here we are at the chalet. We could go up to the top floor and sit on the balcony facing the sea. It would be a great idea if you got us some coffee, and I'll continue. Helga sat down on the carpet, a little bit apart from the rest of the guests, and then I saw the fury in her eyes. Sitting there, pretending to listen to Emi, she seemed to possess an unbreakable will. Will to do what? None of those who made up Emi's little audience were watching Emi anymore. All eyes were on Helga."

"A kitchen attendant peeked in to announce that dinner was served. Everyone marched silently toward the dining room, except Emi, who kept on talking endlessly. We had all taken our seats when the double doors between the dining room and the parlor opened, and in walked Juan Antonio."

"I forgot to mention that at eight in the evening it was still quite light out. The intruder, who had covered the long stretch from the front gate of the *estancia* to the middle of the park at a good pace, stopped for a moment to wipe his sweaty forehead. He detected a certain movement on the porch, although he couldn't quite make out the people there. On his left was the eucalyptus grove; he decided to stay there until after nightfall. He sat down on the grass beneath one of the trees and took a flat canteen out of his pocket to sip some water. He watched several of the guests descend the marble staircase and sit beneath an arbor to drink the apéritifs they held in their hands. Everyone was dressed for dinner."

"My dear . . ."

"Yes, Iñaki?"

"Could you please clarify which night we're talking about? We were up to Saturday at dinner time."

"We're talking about that dinner. We've gone backward in time, but just a little. Soon the guests will get together in the parlor with Emi."

"Before, we had gotten to the moment when Juan Antonio entered the dining room."

"All of this is happening while the intruder waits in the eucalyptus grove. But, Iñaki . . ."

"Yes?"

"I'd like a day off, even if it's only one. For weeks I've been living at vacation resorts—very beautiful, it's true—but I miss my own place."

January 1 in Buenos Aires. It's beastly hot. A gust of fire enters through the open doors of the balcony. I've taken the cover off the divan in order to lie down on the sheets when I feel like it. I'm listening to Rossini's *Missa Solemnis Brevis*. I'm taking a vacation from my vacation. Silence: January 1 at two in the afternoon. Only occasionally can you hear a car go by on Viamonte. The city's sleeping off a drunk. I'm worried about this practically undetectable bomb that blew up a Lufthansa plane yesterday in midair. Will they figure out how to detect it? I ask Enrique, who always finds a way to calm me down.

"Of course they will."

"Will they figure it out before the next time you or I have to travel by plane?"

"I don't know."

"We'll have to put ourselves in God's hands."

Enrique smiles.

Twenty to four. I've been lying on the divan, reading a book in which Borges discusses books and writers. Every so often I find a phrase I like; then I close the book and rest it on my chest, with one finger stuck between the pages to mark my place. "These stories belong to the oldest literary genre: nightmares. It's strange that our minds emerge every day from the senseless world of dreams and recover their relative sanity." I'm glad to be here; I don't want to be anywhere else. The house is in disarray; I'll have to vacuum. The air's on fire. January in Buenos Aires. No man's land.

It's important to drink plenty of water. A tall glass on the table, filled with prune juice. I drink, and the liquid refreshes my whole body. My body absorbs it as the desert sand absorbs a brief, occasional rain. I come to my senses, as though I had fainted. Where am I? Who am I?

The year doesn't really begin today. One must wait until March or April, with their leaden skies and their belated heat waves and sudden cold spells. And that bubbling of young blood on the way to school, which is something like saying on the way to prison and freedom. The real year, the year made of contracts and Telexes and urgent business, begins only after Holy Week, when wealthy industrialists and businessmen return from vacation with their families (flights are always all booked up in spite of the crisis, and those who are annoyed about it always say it's because the population is growing faster than the number of airplane seats). Then comes that feverish period that lasts until July, when it's interrupted by winter vacation, and it begins again less energetically in August, because the situation is bad, even worse in September. In October it's so bad that people start thinking about other things, but then we're already in the middle of a confusing spring that offers up days of incredible beauty, especially in San Telmo, with its old houses outlined against an impeccable sky, or in Recoleta, in front of the Church of the Virgin of Pilar; or driving south on 9 de Julio, from Viamonte and Cerrito, leaving Teatro Colón behind. Ah, Buenos Aires! Foreigners adore her; country folk regard her with an ardent blend of love and hatred; her inhabitants love her as one loves one's own skin, although at times we're ashamed to admit it.

The city. My city. The names of the central streets memorized, just as mama taught me: Esmeralda, Maipú, Florida, San Martín, Reconquista, 25 de Mayo, Leandro Alem, the port, the river as wide as an ocean, the Uruguayan coast, the rest of the world, money, freedom, life as a voyage, the ever-elusive future full of plane reservations purchased almost haphazardly, comfortable rooms reserved in foreign hotels, like the ones Freddy is enjoying right now up there in Catholic Heaven.

Let's allow granny to fix us a cold drink on this sultry morning: water from a bottle that's been resting between two blocks of ice, lemon juice, sugar, and a pinch of bicarbonate of soda. It's effervescent, refreshing, and horrible. Let's allow granny to drag her varicose-veined legs across the patio, with a damp towel on the back of her neck, little dark circles under her eyes, and her mouth half-open with her jaw flapping down. What? Am I painting an ugly portrait of my grandmother? Isn't my name Magdalena? Or Marlene? Aren't I tall, blonde, and svelte? Aren't I twenty years old? Thirty? Have I lost any vital organs? Negative. What am I complaining about? Who's complaining? Where would I like to be at this moment? At the beach, in the country, on the island, in the mountains. And why have I returned to Buenos Aires? Because, when a loved one has died, someone has to take care of going to his house and getting rid of his things: his clothing, his papers, his fountain pen that leaks and stains your fingers. The deceased died without finding out for sure if the problem was with the pen or the cartridges. Look, I think it was like this: they sold you some old cartridges, because who uses that kind of fountain pen these days (when will the teacher learn?). Why didn't you ever buy yourself a normal pen, papa? Don't you see that now you're dead forever and ever? Walking into the bathroom and smelling that Ambrée-scented soap, which is like saying the dead man's fragrance, because that was something you *did* like, fine soap, I don't know where he picked up such refined tastes, that son of immigrants, but, what the hell were you thinking, huh? That because he was the son of immigrants he had to bathe with laundry soap? And not even white soap, but rather that common, earthy soap that strips your skin off? Or the soap the Nazis made from human fat? What the hell do you want an immigrant's son to do? Are you going to show him what kind of soap he has to use, you, offshoot of several generations of Argentines, the great-great-great-great fucking grandson of Juan Díaz de Solís? Get over it. You make me want to puke with all that lineage and tradition. Go off to your tenement and learn how to talk like normal people, learn the painful pronunciation of those who speak broken Spanish.

"Magdalena?"

"Yes, Iñaki."

"It's unbearably hot in here."

"Yes. The rooms have no windows. Seven to a room, and the door closed in the middle of summer and dying of cold in the winter, and standing in line in front of the only bathroom . . . It's in all the comic operas, of course. And right now, practically in the year 2000 — Can you imagine, Iñaki, soon we're going to begin our letters by writing 'January 2, 2000'? It's terrible — just looking at it makes me sick to my stomach. And come to think of it, will I ever write that at the beginning of a letter signed by me?"

" Hey, of course you will; you're still a spring chicken."

"Careful, Iñaki, you're getting away from General Parlance."

"Let's go have a brandy Alexander at the Richmond."

"I'm afraid of that interminable room, all dark in back."

"In any case, let's get out of here. How about a hamburger at McDonald's?"

"How cruel you are, Iñaki."

"Well, let's go get a banana milkshake at a little café outside the Flores subway station."

"Never again . . ."

"Tea and cookies at the Copper Kettle? A cherry liqueur at . . . ?"

"They don't exist any more, Iñaki. They don't exist."

The week we returned from Las Lilas, some of us students from the class met in front of the closed classroom door where Alcides had taught. Normally the door would have been open; when we arrived, the students from the previous course would usually be leaving. There was no note on the door, no sign of anything. We all rode down in the beat-up elevator to look for the super. It was hard for us to get him to come out of his apartment, the last one at the end of a gloomy corridor with a glass ceiling. Grudgingly, he told us he didn't know anything about it, and grudgingly he jotted down an address for Flora on a piece of paper. As Flora was thanking him, he slammed the door in her face. I returned home quite calmly, almost celebrating the fact that the teacher had disappeared on his own, saving me the trouble of finding an excuse not to return to the Mind Control class, which I found completely useless. And I never would have thought about Alcides Ibáñez Regidor again if you weren't demanding now that I recall everything, for reasons that don't seem entirely clear to me. Therapy? Police work? Anyway, it doesn't matter all that much. I suppose at this point I can't, we can't, turn back anymore.

"Supposedly Inés knew a little more about the teacher's fate."

"Sure, but we couldn't ask her directly."

"Then we have no recourse but to carry out the investigation ourselves."

"I'd rather do it alone, Iñaki. And that's enough for today. Let's meet right here tomorrow at the same time and I'll tell you. Are you sorry? How many people would pay for the privilege of entering one of those guest houses and talking to the owner, a mistrustful woman, the mother of two young girls whom she sends to a school run by nuns so they won't get mixed up with what she considers the lowlifes who live at the guest house? Of course, we mustn't forget you're a doctor and you're sixty-eight years old, even though you look as fresh as a daisy. But in stories like these everyone tries to play detective."

"All right, Marlene, if that's what you want."

At 8:00 A.M. all the residents of the guest house were having breakfast. The room they used as a dining room was the same one that surely had been used as such by the very first inhabitants of the house. It was quite spacious, with a very high ceiling stained by dampness and a floor made of strips of moth-eaten wood. The double doors opened into a closed side hallway with stained-glass windows that looked discolored, but which certainly had always been that way since it's unlikely glass would have discolored. From that

hallway, and through the double doors, there entered a dirty light that bathed people and objects with an indeterminate sadness. The residents — pathological exhibitionists of the sort who display their genitals half-hidden behind a newspaper to little girls traveling at the back of a streetcar; couples comprising retired pimps and their most loyal prostitutes, who have by now acquired the dignity of wives and who dye their sparse, syphilitically diminished white hair bright orange; numbers runners in the last throes of depression ever since the legalization of gambling took away the aura of illicitness and adventure they had enjoyed for so long, who by now have lost all their teeth so they have to dip their buttered bread into their coffee in order to swallow it; former crooks; former purse-snatchers; former specialists in con artist stories; former demonstrators of a device called a mandolin that cut cheese, tomatoes, and hard-boiled eggs into thin slices, who used to set up on the most down-at-the-heels end of once-proud Florida Street; former ladies' washroom attendants from the third-rate movie houses on Lavalle Street, who eat lentil stew at night in dark, cheap restaurants, next to professional fake blind men; and the well-organized, voluble bag lady who sleeps right at Córdoba and Riobamba, usually on the sidewalk in front of Normal School Number One, and who has never been picked up by the officers of the rehabilitation center for the homeless, or maybe she was picked up, housed, bathed, dressed in clean clothing, well fed, and interrogated, but seeing that she didn't answer their questions and instead went on talking ceaselessly with her invisible companion, and that in the institution she began to wither away like a lily plucked from the shores of a lagoon, she was returned to her spot on the corner of Córdoba and Riobamba with her entire set of belongings — a bag of rags, blankets, and a smaller bundle no one dared scrutinize, which contained the keys to a previous existence that hadn't been clouded by insanity. The residents, as I was saying, consumed a breakfast that consisted of coffee, the kind of coffee that wasn't just the dregs of coffee but rather the dregs of human existence, a black, bitter liquid with an odor that would have been intolerable had it not been neutralized by the dominant stench of insecticide; an aborted loaf of bread, half uncooked and shapeless; a spiral of bright yellow, rancid butter, half melted from the relentless heat all night long that clung to the walls of the building without any noisy storm to shake it off; and a tiny pot of plum jelly that looked more like a glob of coagulated blood. As for the sugar, anyone who wanted some had to ask Segunda, the servant from Santiago who scrubbed the tables with the same mangy rag she used for scrubbing the floors and endlessly washing the dishes, and who in turn had to ask Miss Matilde, the owner of the guest house, the one whose two daughters studied with the nuns. The lady herself would then come into the dining room to determine that the sugar was for a guest and not for the maid from Santiago to stick in her pocket, and then she would open the pantry with her key and take out a little tin, which she would place on the table in front of the person who had asked for it, watch him serve himself two teaspoonsful (two was the limit), and return the little tin to the pantry, lock it up with a key, and then . . .

"Marlene?"

"Was that a question?"

"No, but I said it like a question. It was a wake-up call."

"Yes, Iñaki."

"What was the result of your investigation at the boarding house?"

"When I asked for Alcides Ibáñez Regidor, the owner of the guest house told me he had left on the day immediately before our trip to Las Lilas. Then I asked her if the teacher had left a forwarding address. She told me no."

"And then?"

"I proceeded as indicated in detective novels: I offered her money. At first she pretended to be offended, but she immediately began to tell me the story of her daughters and how much it cost her to have them study with the nuns. And how she, a poor widow, sacrificed, et cetera, and how hard it had been for her, a real lady, to be forced to rent rooms to that rabble, et cetera. I doubled my offer and suggested that it might be convenient for her to cooperate with me, because the police were looking for Ibáñez Regidor. The woman hurriedly assured me that the teacher was a very decent person who paid his rent religiously. I don't see how he had any choice, since that woman is the kind who collects up front, and who, if the rent is even one day late, puts all the deadbeat's belongings out in the hall and locks the door to the room."

"What kind of information did she give you?"

"When I came back with the cash, because she wouldn't accept any other form of payment, she wrapped it up like a magpie, and with a repulsive smile that was supposed to be friendly, she returned with something copied on a piece of paper. It wasn't an address; it was a map, a city map. She had copied it on the back of a receipt book. A map to get to Las Lilas. But not to the central part of the *estancia*; it was to a far-off house deep in the country.

January 4

Underneath the lantern, by the barrack gate,
Darling, I remember the way you used to wait,
'Twas there that you whispered tenderly
That you loved me, you'd always be
My Lili of the lamplight,
My own Lili Marlene.

"No, I refuse."

"I'm begging you, please, Iñaki."

"No. These changes are too frequent, and they cause confusion."

"It'll be the last time, Iñaki, you have my solemn promise."

"I might consider it, but only because it's a simple addition and not a complete substitution, if we always use the whole name. But Lili alone, never."

"I won't ask you for anything more, Iñaki. Lili Marlene forever."

"Are we going for a sulky ride around Las Lilas?"

"We're already flying like an arrow down the path between the fields."

"Isn't there a house over there?"

"Yes, an old mansion."

"Yes. It looks abandoned."

"The garden's been overrun by weeds."

"We'll be in danger of being attacked by red bugs."

"Patience. We're getting there."

"Even the porch has been overrun by weeds. Hand me the machete."

"Here it is."

"Whack, whack."

"Is that the noise a machete makes when it rends the air before it cuts down weeds?"

"Yes."

"But the onomatopoeia is in another language."

"I don't know what it's like in Spanish. We're at the main entrance."

"It's unlikely that anyone lives here, because they'd never be able to leave the house. Let's knock with this knocker that looks like a little bronze hand."

"I can see a long hallway with a mosaic floor through the broken glass behind the grating."

"Do you mean the door has a grating?"

"Yes."

"No one's coming."

"Could there be another entrance?"

"Yes. Considering that it's surrounded by a garden, there must be a door in back, the kitchen door."

"It's impossible to get in. There's a veritable mountain next to the house."

"Give me the hatchet."

"Here it is."

"Whack, whack."

"Periwinkle is growing between the wildflowers and the dry branches."

"We're getting to the back door."

"I think it's all useless. Let's get out of here."

"It would be impossible. The opening I had so much trouble making has already closed up behind us. The weeds grow very quickly and tangle up with other ones."

"If you're tired, I could use the hatchet."

"We're approaching the door. I'm going to knock."

"Iñaki . . ."

"Yes, Lili Marlene. Were you speaking in a whisper?"

"Yes. I just saw a shadow pass by a window on the top floor."

"Why don't they answer our knocking?"

"It must be the crazy cousin they always keep locked up there."

"No, Lili Marlene. It's Alcides Ibáñez Regidor."

"I think I'm going to throw up."

"Not too much longer. It's just that the plane is rocking so much."

"Are you all right, Iñaki?"

"Yes, I'm a doctor."

"The feeling is passing."

"That's the way! They're bringing lunch now."

"What's for lunch?"

"Airplane food: mashed stuff, all different colors."

"My lumbar vertebrae hurt a little. Are we coming or going?"

"Going."

"Where to?"

"To Copenhagen, with a stopover at the Richmond Café."

"It's not worth the trouble to go to the Richmond. General Parlance is attending to the Jewish actor."

"Was he a Jewish actor, or an actor who played the part of a Jew?"

"We'll never know. The actor is consulting him about the use of the word 'Peisach' in Spanish."

"What does he want to know? He doesn't know if he should say 'Peisach,' or 'Pesach,' or how should I know?"

"Does it really matter?"

"I'd almost say it's the heart of the matter: how do you introduce foreign words into a language."

"I don't know. I don't worry about those things."

"But someone has to worry about them, Iñaki. Someone has to bury the dead . . ."

"It's cloudy."

"Just as well."

"It wouldn't be so good for a storm to break loose now that we're halfway there."

"Is it necessary to point out that we're landing at the hangar?"

"At the *hangar*. I must remember that word. It's not necessary to point it out."

"A storm has broken, just like that."

"The large trees lining the path are shaking like lilies on the shore of the lagoon."

"But the downpour is as refreshing as a blessing from God."

"God sends us overwhelming heat and then a refreshing downpour. And sometimes vice-versa."

"Those are the ironic thoughts of a dyed-in-the-wool freethinker."

"The sea is fierce."

"But is it raining?"

"What a pretty song:

I sing it without peer,
The same way, it appears,
What a pretty song.

"We're landing now."

"But this isn't Copenhagen."

"Of course not. It's the hangar near the property at Las Lilas. We're in the area where the employees live. In that house, the first one on the left, they're holding a wake for the horse trainer."

"Las Lilas is a model establishment. You know something, Iñaki?"

"What?"

"This story could be told a different way. But I only know how to tell it the way I'm telling it."

"They're holding a wake for Cirilo here."

"Are there any professional mourners?"

"There are. There are big candles. There are waxy drippings on the candles."

"Is there any rum?"

"There's rum. There's gin."

"Gin rummy?"

"I'll deal."

"It's a deal."

"It's still very early."

"Yes, it's still very early."

"Today is going to be a very hot day again. I can't stand on my feet any more. I'm going to lie down on the divan in my room."

"The house is quiet: everyone's gone to the horse trainer's wake."

"Have them lower the blinds for me so the room will be darkened. Is there a little ice bucket with ice cubes on the night table, and a bottle of mineral water, and a glass?"

"What's the matter with the lady, doctor?"

"Nothing serious, Mercedes, just a touch of sunstroke."

"I see a ship sailing at dawn, near the sun."

"What's the lady saying?"

"Nothing important, Mercedes, she's delirious."

"Is it seasickness, doctor?"

"Yes, Mercedes."

"Do you need anything else?"

"No, thanks, I have everything I need. You can leave now."

"Call me when you need me, doctor. I'll be in the kitchen."

Living through the month of January in Buenos Aires is like climbing a high dune of shifting sand, without a single tree, devoid of a view of the sea. It's something like the way Christian Purgatory is described: without hellfire, but deprived of the vision of God. Of course in the definition of Purgatory is the Heaven You have promised me, I don't know if You've promised it to me, Lord, since I'm Jewish, but at least to them, to those who embrace Your faith, or even if they don't embrace it, they're just lucky to consider it their own, from the moment they're born into a Christian home.

Children who are born into a Christian home already have the future innately assured, from the moment they emerge from their mothers' wombs: they'll cross this vale of tears with a certain degree of luck, but merely by accepting the beliefs of their ancestors, they'll secure a place for themselves up there and they'll enjoy your presence (I'm omitting the capital letters, because I never know exactly where to put them, and because you and I have such a good relationship, Lord, so intimate, ever since the time we spoke through those prayers I learned secretly in Catechism class and through my school-mates' holy pictures, between the isotherms and the isobars, the discovery of America, the germination cycle of beans, the industry of bees, and the calculation of the point where two trains traveling at different speeds and from different directions — one from Tandil and the other from Trenque Lauquen — will meet).

The caravan advances slowly through the desert, climbing up the dune; the sea cannot be seen from any direction . . . what do I mean, the sea? Not even a stream, just dry, burning sand, and in this desert there aren't even those vast thermal spaces the books talk about; at night one sleeps in beds pushed up against the window, fruitlessly seeking a breath of fresh air. The water we drink is warm. Could you please throw an ice cube in this glass? The mattress is on fire. What if I tried to sleep immersed in water in the bathtub? When is the storm supposed to start?

"I don't know, Lili Marlene. The sky is perfectly blue."

"Flora! Where's Iñaki?"

"He's resting."

"What about your job?"

"I found a substitute."

"Why did you go to the Mind Control class?"

"I was going through some confusing times. Problems with the family, at work, everywhere. I didn't even know my name anymore."

"Yes, yes, I'm familiar with that part. But, why did you go to the Mind Control class with Alcides Ibáñez Regidor?"

"Ah, now I see what you're getting at! When Alcides was a child of three or four, Juan Antonio's mother, who had always lived at Las Lilas, decided to move to Buenos Aires, taking her personal maid, Ursula, and her son, Alcides, along with her. The child grew up in Buenos Aires, silent and introverted. By the end of elementary school, he was already interested in everything that had to do with the mind. Juan Antonio, who was then living with his mother, al-ways took care of Alcides. He enrolled him in high school, trying not to encourage the child's strong attraction to magic too much. In truth it relieved him that young Alcides, at the age of seventeen, decided to abandon his telekinesis studies and take a Mind Control class that was advertised in the paper."

"Now I understand everything, Flora. It's twelve-thirty. Shall we have something to eat?"

"What are they eating at the *estancia* today?"

"Sunday dinner: chicken with potato salad, ravioli with tomato sauce, flan with *dulce de leche*, or cheese and candied fruit. Sangria made with red wine, lemon, and sugar, with irregularly shaped ice cubes."

"Bring on the sangria!"

"So, at the age of seventeen, Alcides Ibáñez Regidor began to study Mind Control."

"Yes. Later Juan Antonio had a falling out with his mother; he lived in different places, including Europe, the United States, and Mexico, and he lost track of Alcides. When they saw each other again, Juan Antonio had been divorced from his first wife and was living a Bohemian existence with Emi. They lived in a one-room apartment that they cleaned themselves, et cetera."

"When Juan Antonio and Alcides saw each other again, was Alcides already teaching Mind Control classes?"

"That's right. Juan Antonio's mother spent her summers at the *estancia*, and she always brought along her personal maid and Alcides. Alcides didn't like country life. He spent hours locked up in an attic with his books. Once he began to teach Mind Control in the old building on Avenida de Mayo, he didn't return to the *estancia*. In fact, Juan Antonio didn't know where Alcides lived; it was the concierge of the building where he taught the classes who gave us the address of the boarding house."

"Isn't it odd that Juan Antonio decided to take the class? After all, Alcides was the son of his mother's servant."

"Juan Antonio's not one to go digging in his own psyche or plumbing the depths of his feelings. I think he goes through life a bit absent-mindedly, as if he weren't really aware of anything. It's other people, or rather, women, who determine his actions: his mother, his first wife, and later Emi. I suppose asking Alcides to put his mind in order shouldn't have seemed very different to him from asking his secretary to put the papers on his desk in order."

"But Juan Antonio is a nice guy."

"Yes, he is. But he's quite indifferent to anything that doesn't have to do with managing his property. I mean, strange things can happen right under his nose without his noticing. This flan isn't homemade."

"No. It's from a mix."

"I hate flan from a mix. When Juan Antonio invited all the people from the class to Las Lilas, it was just an oversight that he forgot to invite Alcides. In a sense it wasn't really necessary for him to invite him, because Alcides belonged to Las Lilas: he had been born here and his mother was here, attending to doña Matilde's needs, as usual. But there was, shall we say, a certain conflict between Alcides's position as the instructor of the Mind Contol class, where Juan Antonio was a student, and Alcides as the son of a maid on the *estancia* whose owner was Juan Antonio. If Juan Antonio had invited him, whom would he have hung around with during those days? Whom would he have eaten with? Where would he have slept? The situation of someone who has been raised with a family is uncertain: he doesn't belong to the family, but he's not just one more servant. He really doesn't have a place of his own."

"Besides, there was his relationship with Inés."

"Ah, yes, but that was the least of it. He had a relationship with Inés, but the one he really liked, or rather, the person who aroused true passion in him, was Helga."

What I like about Catholic Heaven (I'd say Christian Heaven, but I'm afraid of making a mistake; I know very little about Evangelicals and Seventh Day Adventists) is that it has well-defined limits. If there's anything that scares me, it's trying to imagine eternity, the infinite. Catholic Heaven has well-defined limits; it occupies one space among other spaces, which are occupied by Hell, Purgatory, and Limbo, a place as boring as a steady diet of egg whites, where unbaptized babies go when they die. In addition, Catholic Heaven is separated from the heavens and hells of other religions, as well as from that dark space full of question marks that is Jewish Heaven. But in spite of the fact that Catholic Heaven is clearly delineated (it occupies a vague area between Earth and Mars, and it only admits Earthlings), that space is surely very ample, clean, and well-lighted (*Ideal for diplomat*, the classified ad would say). How it must simplify life to think about that Heaven! A Heaven anyone can touch with his hands from the time he's a little kid, either on the way to the baptismal font or to the confessional and the eucharist. To think that one gesture, a single gesture on my part, now, while I'm alive, would be enough to have them say to me when I die: "Let's go, Lili Marlene, let's go up there; it's delightfully cool and they're waiting for you . . ."

"And why don't you make that gesture, Lili Marlene, if you find the idea so seductive?"

"I'm afraid that after all is said and done there won't be any Jews Up There, Iñaki. And that there won't be any Catholics like my friends, only those who have a banner of the Marian Year hanging on their walls. What would I talk to them about? If I'm not among my friends from here, if there's nobody I can nudge with my elbow and say, 'Hey, look how fat that dark-haired angel's gotten, the one who insists on accompanying his singing on the guitar instead of the lyre!'"

"And who sings better every day."

"Ah, Iñaki . . ."

"Ah, Lili Marlene . . ."

"No matter how much I say I will, I can't manage to wake up as early as I'd like."

"What you need to know right now is that you're calmer and it's just a question of taking a little more time for you to recover altogether and return to your normal life."

"How much time, Iñaki?"

"I'm sorry I can't say exactly."

"But, am I better?"

"Well, . . . at least now you're sure I'm Iñaki, your old family doctor."

"Nonsense. My old family doctor was Dr. Silverstein. Silverstein? Silverbaum?"

"You just made that last one up."

"But I can see that doctor in my mind as clearly as the tomato, the orange, and the lemon in the Mind Control exercise. His own head, I mean the doctor's, was large and egg-shaped, with his sparse hair plastered down on his skull with brilliantine. He leaned that big head of his against my chest to listen to my breathing, and then my back; he pressed down on my tongue with a spoon to look at my throat and almost made me vomit."

"In any event . . ."

"In any event, don't go away, Iñaki."

I sleep well, and I hardly dream. I proceed slowly through these evocations of the past. There's no doubt I know more now than before. The intruder who arrived at the central part of the *estancia* that Saturday night, who spied on us from the eucalyptus grove, and whose face I managed to see through the dining room window, and the furtive hunter who hit a duck that was flying over the lagoon with a shotgun while you, Iñaki, and I were hiding among the reeds, were one and the same person: the Mind Control instructor, Alcides Ibáñez Regidor. Why didn't I tell anyone I had seen Alcides through the dining room window as we were eating dinner? I don't know, Iñaki, something in that face must have frightened me.

Saturday night, after dinner, we all went out to sit on the verandah. It was very hot; I remember the children stayed up very late and were busy trapping fireflies, which they put into glass jars. The children's presence was useful in concealing the tension among us. Ever since Helga's return, neither she nor Gustavo had exchanged a word, at least not in front of the others. It was two in the morning when we were startled by the sound of furious galloping hooves approaching, and we saw the son of the foreman stop in front of the stairway by the portico. Juan Antonio sprang up from his chair and ran down the stairs. As soon as he heard the boy's news, he spoke briefly with Emi, who had also gone downstairs to find out what was going on, and he went alone to the garage to get his car. The foreman's son began his return trip, at a gallop, toward the section where the farmhands lived. Right away we found out that they had discovered Cirilo, the horse trainer, drowned at the bottom of the well.

This is the part of the story everyone knows. The horse trainer was killed when he fell to the bottom of the well, and his lover, Candelaria, the cook's daughter, disappeared that same night. It was hard to imagine that someone could have lifted a man with Cirilo's powerful physique up in the air and thrown him to the bottom of the well without anyone's having heard anything. Of course, someone might have killed him first and thrown him, already dead, into the well, but the autopsy showed that the bruises on the body were caused by hitting the side of the well, and that Cirilo died when his head collided with the bottom.

Also, everyone knows all about what happened after that rather macabre discovery. Juan Antonio and the overseer drove into town in Juan Antonio's car to notify the police; the incident was provisionally classified as a suicide; the wake was held for the deceased at the *estancia* and they buried him in the town cemetery; his widow and children collected a pension; and there was a pact of silence made about the disappearance of the cook's daughter. Juan Antonio didn't even mention the girl's existence when the police made a kind of census of all the people living on the *estancia*. It's just that Emi would have died—she really would have died—if she had been forced to give up her cook on account of some ill-fated investigation.

Cirilo's wake lasted from Sunday dawn until 10 Monday morning. On Sunday night, as the few remaining guests at Las Lilas hurried to depart (others had left at different times on Sunday, because the atmosphere wasn't festive anymore, or to tell the truth, it never really had been), people kept arriving from neighboring farms and from town to attend the horse trainer's funeral.

Let's get back to Ibáñez Regidor. I saw his face through the window as we were having dinner. All three nights at the *estancia*, we started dinner at nine o'clock sharp and left the dining room between ten and ten-thirty. I only saw him again the next day when you, Iñaki, and I were swimming in the lagoon and he fired at the duck. You saw him, Iñaki, but you couldn't have guessed who he was: you didn't know him, and I didn't say anything to you.

Why, I now wonder, didn't I say anything to you? If I try to remember what I felt at that moment, the first thing that occurs to me is that I had the sensation I should hide something. As if, in some mysterious way, I had something to do with Alcides's presence there. His mother had returned to Las Lilas after her employer's death, and she was in charge of the house; thanks to her, there were always fresh flowers in the vases, and guests always found their rooms in perfect order at night: beds turned down, with the comforter folded at the foot of the bed, sheets fragrant with lavender, all the towels changed and carefully folded in the bathroom.

But I had the strong impression that, if Alcides was at Las Lilas, if he had entered furtively, if the night before he had had something to do with the horse trainer's death, it was because *I* had done something to make all that happen, and I decided it was better, for my own safety and his, to keep quiet.

In time, we found out what Ibáñez Regidor's role had been in the Saturday night drama at the *estancia*. What I'm about to tell you is Candelaria's version, the cook's daughter, who was picked up by the police months after the tragedy at a mansion on the outskirts of Buenos Aires where she had gotten a job as a maid. Candelaria was a thin, very pretty brunette. She confessed that, the night of the tragedy, she was in the eucalyptus grove, waiting for the horse trainer with her flashlight turned off, in complete darkness, because she and Cirilo had a set place for their rendezvous: behind the thick trunk of the first eucalyptus on the left, facing the woods. That is, it was the most distant from the house of all the trees in the first row. Candelaria would arrive from the other side, so she couldn't be seen from the house or the garden, and she would wait patiently for Cirilo for as long as necessary.

When Alcides Ibáñez Regidor withdrew from the dining room window, he went to hide again in the eucalyptus grove. As fate would have it, he arrived at the same tree behind whose trunk Candelaria was standing. When she sensed someone approaching, she turned off the flashlight and, realizing that the new arrival was not Cirilo, she was about to scream, but Alcides quickly covered her mouth so she wouldn't reveal his presence. As he tried to calm her, Cirilo, who was coming from the other side of the grove, appeared, and misinterpreted the scene.

Many people say that, even though none of this might really have happened, Cirilo would have killed himself anyhow some day, because of his melancholy character.

"Lili Marlene!"

"Don't frighten me, Iñaki!"

"It's just that . . . to be blunt, Lili Marlene, couldn't we just get to the facts?"

"I'll do what I can, Iñaki."

We three, we're all alone
Living in a memory:
My echo, my shadow, and me.

We three, we're not a crowd,
We're not even company,
My echo, my shadow, and me.

What good is the moonlight,
The silvery moonlight that shines above?
I walk with my shadow,
I talk with my echo,
But where is the one I love?

We three, we'll wait for you
Even till eternity,
My echo, my shadow, and me.

"Does it sound very different in English?"

"No, Iñaki, it sounds the same, but in English. The Ink Spots sang it in who knows which decade. Enrique had the seventy-eight record, and I took it to have Freddy listen to it. I lent it to him, and then he died and took it with him to Heaven, along with his echo and his shadow.

"*Requiescat in pace.*"

"Who? Freddy?"

"No, the record."

"Why do we have to suffer like this?"

"Who's making you suffer?"

"All this effort to remember. I think I know why Ibáñez Regidor entered Las Lilas like an intruder, when he could have entered very calmly through the main door. He wanted to look at Helga one more time, even from afar. And when Cirilo discovered him in the eucalyptus grove with Candelaria, he used Mind Control to stop him and then to push him backward, toward the well, and make him fall in head first. Otherwise the dead man would've been Ibáñez Regidor."

"Lili Marlene . . ."

"I'm tired, Iñaki. It's almost autumn. The birches will be losing their leaves soon."

"Then, just as I thought, there were scandals at Las Lilas?"

"Did you think so?"

"Wasn't I the one who thought so?"

"I don't know; everything happened so long ago . . ."

"Would it be correct to say that someone, besides you and Enrique, remained unaffected by these scandals?"

"Nothing happened to Eusebio and his wife, Marina. I mean, they weren't splashed with mud and lava or touched by tongues of fire. Why did you think Enrique and I were unaffected?"

"How old are the two of you?"

"Ah, that's why."

"What was Helga like?"

"Helga was beautiful, young, blonde, tall, and slender, and she aroused a blind passion in Professor Ibáñez Regidor, just as she did in Juan Antonio. After her accidental encounter with Juan Antonio in the secret house and her return to the main house on the *estancia*, she didn't exchange a word with anyone, and the next day, she, Gustavo, and the baby returned to Buenos Aires. Later I found out that Helga and Gustavo had separated. I'd like to be able to say that

Helga and Alcides went off to Bariloche, where they've been living happily ever since, he directing a Mind Control institute and she selling regional candies to tourists. But in truth Helga never even found out about the passion she awoke in Alcides."

"Where did Alcides get the surnames Ibáñez Regidor, if he was the son of a servant of Juan Antonio's mother and of an unknown father?"

"As a youngster he was adopted by a bachelor cousin of Juan Antonio's, who gave him his surname and died a few years later after getting in the way of a shotgun bullet that was heading for a wild boar."

"Do they hunt wild boar with shotguns?"

"Oh, please, Iñaki, go find out for yourself and make the necessary corrections."

"Is there anything else known about Alcides?"

"No, he disappeared. I suppose he uses his own magic to disappear when it suits him."

"Are you afraid of him?"

"Sometimes I am. I think he might show up at this very moment, invisible as he is right now, lift up the surface of Las Lilas, fold it in quarters like a handkerchief and make it go up in a puff of air."

"Pay attention to the instructions I'm going to give you now, Lili Marlene."

"Yes, Iñaki."

"Go to your room and lie down with the blinds closed. You can order a light snack, for example, tea with milk and some wheat crackers and Petit Suisse."

"May I add a teaspoonful of raspberry jelly?"

"Even two. Rest until just before dinner. Then you'll get up, shower with Ambrée soap, and go down to the parlor to have a vermouth and watch the sunset. Will Flora dine with you tonight?"

"Yes, Iñaki."

"Don't stay and chat too long after dinner. You're very tired. You'll go to bed early, and if you need to read before falling asleep, let it be a children's story."

"Any children's story?"

"No, it should be about a childhood protected from all physical suffering. If the child suffers for other reasons, let it pass; but if, for example, there's a death, everything should take place in rooms with austere furniture and floors made of strips of polished wood."

"Yes, Iñaki."

"No harsh surfaces or drafts."

"No, Iñaki."

"And finally, Lili Marlene, so you'll sleep well, a glass of milk and a sweet biscuit."

"Yes, Iñaki. But how quickly the seasons go by here at Las Lilas. I'm all tucked into this enormous bed, but I'm only seven years old."

"The logs are crackling in the fireplace."

"What luck that the bed is beside the window. This way I don't have to get up to look outside."

"It's strange, this bed."

"It's an old Scandinavian bed with a headboard and a footboard. The headboard and footboard have . . . how can I describe it? . . . a very shiny little carved wood column at each end, where a child can hang up his hat when he gets undressed for bed."

"First the child takes off his cap, then his turtleneck sweater (my God! those turtleneck sweaters!), and then the suspenders that hold up his wool pants. The pants come to his knees. I think those pants are called breeches (Yes! My God, breeches!). The child walks around all day long in his turtleneck sweater and breeches, Scotch plaid knee-length socks, and highly polished shoes.

"He had a dog named Batuque."

"And he had a grandmother with a slack jaw and little glasses on the tip of her nose."

"Who's always angry."

"Here are the issues of *Billiken* you asked me for, from 1939."

"Do we know anything about the child's parents?"

"They never appear. The child is always with his grandmother."

"The child looks foreign."

"Not to me. The cartoon is in Spanish."

"But his clothes, the bed . . ."

"It doesn't matter. It lights up my seven years because I can see whatever he sees through the window, frosty fields, spruces without leaves, and then torrents of melted snow, cherry trees in blossom, golden stalks of wheat in summer . . ."

"Surely the child climbs trees in summertime, with his chest in the air, his suspenders hanging down over his breeches."

"To look for ripe cherries."

"What could we do to find out who just spoke?"

"We'll have to go back to the beginning of this dialogue, or to the place where we mention each other's names. And then we count: Lili Marlene, Iñaki, Lili Marlene, Iñaki . . ."

"I'd never go to all that trouble, but I think I'm Lili Marlene. Iñaki, am I crazy?"

"You *are* crazy, but I mean it affectionately."

There's a psychological test that consists of showing the subject a series of slides with drawings that are more or less fuzzy and undifferentiated, and asking him to say what he sees in each slide. The vagueness and lack of differentiation of the drawings increase as the slides parade before the subject's eyes. In the first ones there are elements that are more or less clear. If the test is given to several people at the same time, they'd all agree that they see a house, a tree, a sky with clouds, two people, a staircase. But in these drawings there are ambiguities that stimulate discussion. Are the windows of the house open or closed? Are the people in the slide facing the house, or do they have their backs to it? Are they going toward the house or away from it? Little by little, at first very timidly, questions arise among those who are looking at the slides, questions whose answers are not in the drawings themselves. Is the house a home? A school? A hospital? Is it in this country or in Europe? Are the two people young or old? Are they two men, two women, or a man and a woman? Are they dressed in modern style, or are they from another time? Are they happy because they're returning home? Or sad because they're leaving it? Or are they happy because they *can* leave it? Or are they feeling sad about returning? Suggestions begin to arise about the situation: those two people, who appear like a pair of

Siamese twins in the ambiguity of the drawing, are talking about something related to the house: going to the house, leaving the house, something that's happened in the house, what? A death, perhaps? That's not the same house where they live now; it's their childhood home. Those two people are *talking* about their memories; they're talking about a death, a death that happened inside that dark, melancholy house, with austere furniture, with a floor made of strips of polished wood. Those two people (husband and wife? brother and sister? father and son? two friends?) are evoking a sad memory. No! No! Someone suddenly shouts. Those people in the slide are two thieves planning a robbery. No, no! They're not *planning* the robbery; they've already entered the house! Don't you see that bundle on the floor, beside the woman? The woman? But they're two men!

And meanwhile, the psychologist jots down in his notebook that the subjects are unable to tolerate a melancholy situation, and many other things that I can't even think of, because I'm no psychologist or psychiatrist or psychoanalyst. As Enrique would say, I'm just crazy.

I feel better. It's as if many things that were jammed up in my head for years are finally finding their way out. Last night I dreamed about a room in my old house. I dreamed about the living room, with its big window facing the street, papa's desk and chair in the middle of the room. If I sat in the chair, which was a revolving chair, and turned 180 degrees, I found myself facing the library with its glass doors; if I turned another 90 degrees, I would see the shelves containing the twenty-eight large volumes of the 1912 edition of the *Hispano-American Encyclopedic Dictionary*. And if I turned another 90 degrees and faced the desk again, I'd see some hard wicker chairs against the opposite wall, and on that wall, a big, framed painting of anemones, covered with glass. It was an austere room, without carpeting or cushions, without softness, suitable for concentrating, I suppose, on equally austere thoughts, like those of monks in their cells, although in those austere cells one can also let one's thoughts wander, and that's why monks whip themselves with disciplines and put on hair shirts to fight off lascivious, concupiscent, voluptuous thoughts. Voluptuousness. Sensuality. Nymphomania. Satyriasis. Erection. Emissions. Masturbation. Coitus = copulation: within marriage it's legitimate, and outside marriage it's always illicit and bad. Whore: describes a woman who engages in commerce with her body. Illustrative aphorism: Whore of a bitch/whore of a pup/Whore of a blanket/That covers 'em up. From the most remote antiquity: hetaeras and geishas . . . How many words! How many definitions discovered at age twelve in the 1912 edition of the *Hispano-American Encyclopedic Dictionary*! I turn another 90 degrees and find myself before a large window facing the street, and I see paradise: the big tree that filled up with lilac-colored flowers in springtime. At that time I was twenty years old, and I won't let anyone convince me.

In order to leave the central part of Las Lilas and reach the entry gate and the road, all one has to do is to advance in a straight line along the path, leaving behind the expanses of lawn, the planter filled with lilacs, the cheerful garden chairs, and all the amenities surrounding the house that make one forget one is in the middle of the immensity of the pampas. Practically no one walks along the poplar-flanked path, except a furtive visitor. The man hiding in the eucalyptus grove waited for darkest night before passing from the woods to a planted field, and only later did he return to the path. He went away without even once turning his head back, and without anyone noticing his presence, and after slipping between two barbed wire guideposts, he disappeared down the road as inexplicably as he had arrived.

The test slides keep coming, each time blurrier and more ambiguous; it's impossible to maintain the same flow of conversation as at the beginning. One can't tell whether those shadows are cliffs, or women holding their children—in the final throes of hunger and desperation—in their arms, or a leper colony, or a cemetery with little piles of earth marking the places where the victims of some absurd war are buried. One can't tell whether those wavy lines are torrential waters, or a river of lava flowing out of a volcano that will bury cities, or a cloudy, threatening sky that will split in half to reveal the presence of a vengeful god, or some writing, a chain of words that convey the diagnosis of a fatal illness.

Nothing can be sadder, more definitive. It's the empire of grayness. Those who look at the slides feel united by a melancholy destiny; behind them lie the golden fields, the frolicking in love's bed, the age of happiness (although deep down it might be unhappiness), the wonder that is the rebirth of light every dawn. Then, when one no longer hopes for anything and it seems as though everyone's about to let themselves die right there where they are, the slide is changed for the last time, and the one now appearing before the incredulous eyes of the beholders is a blank page:

AT THAT TIME WE WERE NO LONGER TWENTY YEARS OLD,
AND WHOEVER WANTS TO CAN SAY IT WAS THE MOST
BEAUTIFUL TIME OF OUR LIVES.

"Enrique and I were going to have lunch at La Churrasquita. We chose a table against the wall, and Enrique asked for the menu and a pitcher of the house wine."

"Before, you used to look at the animals displayed in the refrigerated glass case facing the street. A whole suckling pig, with its head and tail and a lettuce leaf stuck in its ear. A Gran Paraná fish and a pink lobster. Rolls of *matambre*. Ribs of beef."

"We held hands as we looked over the menu."

"Your hands sought each other, blindly."

"Enrique ordered grilled salmon with tartar sauce, and I had chicken provençal."

"Only that table existed, and you talked about who knows what, and you laughed like crazy at whatever you were saying."

"Suddenly I saw those identical twins, sitting at their usual table."

"Two fiftyish types, tall and thin."

"Dressed identically."

"We haven't mentioned their faces: there are just two blue suits on top of two white shirts with blue ties, sitting in the chairs."

"The twins were extremely pale and bald."

"And they always ate the same thing: big boiled potatoes with oil and salt."

"Then the twins and the boiled potatoes and the other tables and the other customers in the restaurant disappeared."

"And the faces of the living and the dead appeared, little stories that took place thirty years ago."

"Enrique told me his Russian grandfather never learned to speak Spanish."

"And that, when he wanted to tell the streetcar guard he had to get of at Federico Lacroze Street, the closest thing he could find to Federico Lacroze was 'Ivan the Terrible,' in Russian."

"I always thought he lived on a street in Buenos Aires called Ivan the Terrible."

"After eating, we held hands again and continued telling stories."

"You talked about the future and everything was possible."

"We talked and talked, and we laughed."

"Enrique called the waiter over and paid the bill."

"And when we got up from the table, we clasped hands very tightly to keep our balance."

"It wasn't just the wine."

"No. It wasn't just the wine. When we stepped out into Corrientes Street it was the month of October and it was sunny. We walked with our arms around each other's waists and I rested my head on Enrique's shoulder."

"It wasn't just the wine."

"No. No. I only want to know one thing, Iñaki."

"Yes, Lili Marlene?"

"Am I better?"

"Better?"

In the Latin American Women Writers series

*Underground River and
Other Stories*
By Inés Arredondo
Translated by Cynthia Steele
With a foreword by
Elena Poniatowska

*Dreams of the Abandoned
Seducer: Vaudeville Novel*
By Alicia Borinsky
Translated by Cola Franzen in
collaboration with the author
With an interview by
Julio Ortega

Mean Woman
By Alicia Borinsky
Translated and with an intro-
duction by Cola Franzen

The Fourth World
By Diamela Eltit
Translated and with a
foreword by Dick Gerdes

The Women of Tijucopapo
By Marilene Felinto
Translated and with an
afterword by Irene Matthews

The Youngest Doll
By Rosario Ferré

*Industrial Park:
A Proletarian Novel*
By Patrícia Galvão (Pagu)
Translated by Elizabeth
Jackson and K. David Jackson

In a State of Memory
By Tununa Mercado
Translated by Peter Kahn
With an introduction by
Jean Franco

Call Me Magdalena
By Alicia Steimberg
Translated by
Andrea G. Labinger

3 9082 09025 4452

DRAG☆N BALL

story and art by Akira Toriyama

The journey begins when Bulma, teenage genius, meets Goku, a naive young monkey-tailed boy who has never left his mountain home. But Bulma needs Goku's help...and his super-strength...on her quest to find the seven magic Dragon Balls which, when gathered, will grant any wish! Along the road, they meet strange friends and stranger foes in this weird, wild, funny adventure.

CALL OR GO ONLINE FOR DRAGON BALL MONTHLY COMICS!

Order by phone at
(800) 394-3042
Fax **(415) 348-8936**
Online **www.vizkids.com**

GRAPHIC NOVELS
192 pages
$14.95 each

Vol.	Catalog No.
1	C-T-DB001
2	C-T-DB002

...OMICS.™
...ds.com

AUBURN HILLS PUBLIC LIBRARY
3400 E. Seyburn Drive
Auburn Hills, MI 48326

Dragon Ball ©
All rights reser
First published
SHUEISHA, In

50

Q. The caricature that you draw of yourself in the comics looks like a dirty old man, so I thought that you probably looked like a dirty old man yourself. But I saw your photograph in **Shōnen Jump** and you looked very handsome.

Yasuhiro Ando
Aichi Prefecture

A. Ha ha ha! You think so? You're right! I *do* look good! You're a great guy! Unfortunately, I just can't get too excited about a *guy* complimenting me like this…

Q. What are those six marks on Kuririn's face? Is it a scar? Please tell me.

Yasuto Tamagawa
Osaka Prefecture

A. Ah! You noticed it! The marks on Kuririn's forehead are incense burns. Sometimes you see these scars on Chinese monks in the movies. I thought I should add them because Kuririn's face is so plain.

Q. Often in the last page of your comic in **Shōnen Jump** [the "free talk" page, where the artist answers letters from readers and talks about upcoming projects], you write about how you have pet birds. I would like to become a manga artist, and I also love animals. I would love to draw manga and have a lot of pets.

Koki Yasuda
Osaka Prefecture

A. I think it's a great thing to be an animal lover, although if you are going to have pets you should be responsible for them. In my household we have a bird, a cat, and a dog. Actually, if I could, I would love to also have a goat and a chicken.